# Policy Games
## for
## Strategic Management

# Policy Games
## for
## Strategic Management

Richard D. Duke
Jac L.A. Geurts

**Dutch University Press**

ISBN: 90 3619 341 9
NUR: 740

Cover design: Puntspatie, Amsterdam
Cover Painting: "Terra Incognita" by Ria Lap, 2001
Lay-out: HAVEKA BV | *de grafische partner*, Alblasserdam
Graphics: Andrea Frank, Cardiff University, U.K.

Dutch University Press, Rozengracht 176A,
1016 NK Amsterdam, The Netherlands.
Tel.: + 31 (o) 20  625 54 29
Fax:  + 31 (o) 20 620 33 95

E-mail: info@dup.nl
www.dup.nl

*Dutch University Press in association with Purdue University Press, West Lafayette, Ind. U.S.A & Rozenberg Publishers, The Netherlands.*

To those

who will see the secrets

of the future:

Our children and grandchildren

# Contents

# Section V - Conclusions                                              307

# Appendix

# List of Figures

# *Preface*

### STRATEGY GAMES WITHOUT THE GENERALS

Imagine that it is 1702 and one of history's more successful entrepreneurs, the young Prince Peter of Russia, later to be remembered as Peter the Great, is playing a war game near his castle. The spectacle is impressive; it looks like a mass scene in a Dino de Laurentiis or Spielberg war movie. The smell of gunpowder fills the air, platoons charge under the cover of smoke and young drummer boys run for cover. The "generals" are having a great time – this is top entertainment for the extremely wealthy. The prince owns a specially created and well-trained mock army that he can activate any time he wants. It is his toy for doing what he likes best: testing his strategic talents and living out his war fantasies. War games are the thing to do in these days. The full-time members of his prestigious "fun" army come from the best families and top army schools. Peter and his young noble friends do not hesitate to blow up farms and woods (and now and then one another) during their favorite pastime (see Massie, 1991).

Two hundred and thirty years later, in 1932, in the very city that Czar Peter founded and named after himself, a related development occurred. Maria Birhstein, a young Russian professor at the Institute of Engineering and Economics, had a remarkable idea: she developed, as far as we know, the first industrial application of gaming. In retrospect, Birhrstein's creation marks an important date in the history of gaming. The technique was brought out of the military to become a tool for non-military training and decision making in schools, corporations, hospitals, city councils, etc. Our colleagues John Gagnon (1987) and Joe Wolfe (1993) recorded the history of this breakthrough in the *Simulation & Gaming* journal. (This journal, published by Sage, is an excellent source of information on the discipline.)

By 1932, St. Petersburg had become Leningrad (having adopted the name of yet another Czar). The Soviet Union needed managers for its factories, and Birhstein created a game that dealt with managing the assembly line of the Ligovo Typewriter Factory. The aim was to develop skilled workers, plentiful in this industry, into managers, which they desperately needed. The initiative was followed by many more gaming projects; in eight years' time, over 40 games were produced.

After World War II, the story of gaming-without-the-generals developed with increasing speed. An important catalyst was the invention of the computer. Large multinational companies discovered the technique and created war rooms for their senior management in which they used specially developed and up-to-date games to prepare and test their strategies.

In the late 1960s, Richard D. Duke, working with a team at the University of Michigan, used an 8k (!) computer – which filled a large room – to run a game and simulate urban planning problems for the city of Lansing, Michigan. The initial game, Metropolis, was used by the City Council for developing the long-range Capital Improvements Budget. The descendant of this game was called Metro-Apex; it kept 100 people very busy and lasted for days (Duke, 1966). Almost a half century later, it is still in use. Of course, modern personal computers and many software innovations have revolutionized the format of the exercise.

Near Vienna in Austria, there is an institute for systems analytical studies where, even during the heyday of the Cold War, Eastern and Western scientists carried out ecological studies: the International Institute for Applied Systems Analysis (IIASA). IIASA held "war gaming" sessions with the aid of sophisticated computer models and scenarios about difficult problems concerning international environmental policy in which top researchers and policy makers from diverse political systems participated (Toth, 1988). To characterize these events, IIASA introduced them as "policy exercises" (see also Gary Brewer, 1986), a label which we will also use in this book when we refer to non-military strategy games. These are primarily made to support a policy process rather than for teaching or training purposes.

However, the computer did not dominate all non-military policy games that emerged in this multimedia area. Chapter 3 of this book relates the story of some young professionals in London who formed a company to run policy games in the public sector. One of their breakthrough projects concerned Margaret Thatcher and her pro-market policies. In the middle of her "reign," she presented drastic proposals to bring market mechanisms into the national health system. In the city of Cambridge, some 40 managers, clinical staff and policy makers who were actually involved in adopting the changes were worried. As prominent, well-informed people, familiar with the regional healthcare system, they foresaw potential problems.

For three days in a row, they engaged in a non-computer simulation that dealt with healthcare in two districts. They negotiated and concluded contracts, all under the proposed new system. The results were catastrophic. The market collapsed, and efficiency and effectiveness suffered. Participants and commentators were convinced of the realism of the simulation: they believed that what happened in this session could also occur in real life. The results of this project received considerable attention both regionally and nationally. While the game was still under development, some voices in politics and the media referred to it cynically as "those war games in Cambridgeshire." But once completed, the results of the simulation were urgently sought by the Prime Minister, and questions were put forward in the British parliament.

This book is about these adventure stories and the methodology behind them. Gaming/simulation has become established as a mature professional discipline; it is effective in helping organizations solve serious strategic policy problems. Several good references to the gaming discipline are present in the international professional literature. There are also well-documented books on the many uses of gaming in training and education. However, as far as we have been able to determine, the uses of gaming as a decision aid for strategic policy making have not been systematically addressed to date; this book is the result of our efforts to fill this void.

## LEGO® BLOCKS, GLOBAL PROBLEMS AND MARKET GARDEN

This book is the product of an American - Dutch academic friendship. It started 25 years ago at a location where, a few decades earlier, American paratroopers had landed to fight in the infamous Battle of Arnhem, also known as Operation Market Garden.

Jan Klabbers founded the Social Systems Research Group (SSRG) in the Netherlands. Its main focus of enquiry was the development and use of "methods of interactive simulation" in various projects at the science/policy interface. Klabbers, working with the international project team of the second Club of Rome, arranged a workshop in Berg en Dal, a small town near Nijmegen. The workshop proceedings were covered in the report: Klabbers, Geurts, van der Hijden, 1977.

Richard D. Duke, who had written his book *Gaming: The Future's Language* in 1974, was invited to present a technique that he called gaming/simulation. The games Duke introduced at the conference did not use computers, but rather, cardboard, LEGO® blocks and dice. To Jac Geurts, a computer-trained researcher on Klabbers' team, Duke's games looked frivolous and alarmingly low-tech. But Jan Klabbers had the professional insight and courage to put modelers and gamers in one hotel and make them explore each other's work. Reluctantly, Jac Geurts participated in Duke's Hexagon game and was immediately sold. "I have played a game today," he told his wife that evening, "and I must admit, it probably has 500 percent more effect on a person than any of our computer models."

Duke and Geurts started to talk at that meeting, and together they toured the area. They discovered that, in 1940, Jac's father's platoon had been overrun by German invaders in the village of Overasselt, exactly the same place where, in 1944, Dick's older brother J. Paul was shot as he came from the air to liberate the Low Countries. He died there and is still remembered in the Memorial Chapel at the Groesbeek War Museum.

We know that an account such as this is somewhat out of place in an academic monograph. But for us, it remains a positive, symbolic story of synchronicity.

There are 4000 miles between Ann Arbor and Nijmegen – what are the odds of this connection between two families?

In 1983, Geurts, armed with a Fullbright grant, joined Duke at the University of Michigan. As a result, we ended up working together on a daily basis for an entire year. From that point on, although both of us have continued our work on opposite sides of the Atlantic, we have met up almost every year to share in each other's projects, classes and executive training sessions. We have coached students together and, whenever possible, stimulated the intercontinental networking of maturing colleagues. We have had a ball!

But, for some reason, we somehow forgot to write together, or perhaps we should say that we never found the time. Gamers always have more urgent things to do than writing, mainly because there are tantalizing prospects for yet another gaming adventure. But now our work is finally finished, and this book is complete. We hold it in our hands and there is nothing more to do than to offer it to the reader. We feel like most professionals who have set themselves to writing: proud and insecure at the same time. We have done the best we could, it is now up to the reader to judge the result.

### SIMULATIONS AND THE NEW GREAT GAME
This book was being developed during the fall of 2001. September 11, 2001 is a date that few of us will ever forget. The terror in New York and Washington D.C. and the fighting that followed brought personal loss and suffering to many. It also created a mental shock wave of vulnerability and uncertainty about the future. And we, two professionals who have made a rewarding career out of helping others prepare for the future, felt for quite a while that the optimistic tone we were using to write about our past experiences would be out of place. The huge progress in the futuring disciplines had not protected us from this evil. On the contrary, was it not sorrowfully ironic that the terrorists used the very kinds of tools we are writing about here to prepare for the attacks? If the media reports are correct, the attacks could only have been prepared and executed because advanced pilot training simulators were available to the attackers.

In the aftermath, yet another war in Afghanistan was launched. To our surprise, we saw the name of our profession also mentioned in this context. Some historians and journalists started to refer to the allied actions as the "New Great Game." Like most people, we did not see any gaming element in this or any other war. To provide some historical perspective on the use of this phrase, the original "Great Game" was the struggle between England and Russia for dominance in Central Asia, which lasted for a good part of the 19th century (see Hopkirk, 1990). Notwithstanding its gentlemanly, sports-like label, this conflict was cruel and there were no winners.

It took us some time and discussion to comprehend that these awful events should serve to motivate instead of intimidate those involved in the positive side of the gaming/simulation discipline. The roots of our discipline lie in the age-old human drama of war. As described in more detail in Chapter 1, Asian strategists probably developed the first war games. That was more than a thousand years ago, and, geographically speaking, not too far from the playing field of the current Great Game.

And then, the next war was launched in Iraq. Once again, gaming played a remarkable role, both in the preparations preceding this war and during its aftermath. In this context, the largest war game ever held was in the summer of 2002. Known as the Millennium Challenge, its scenario pitted a blue party against a red party, the latter looking quite similar to Iraq under Saddam Hussein. Lieutenant-General Paul van Riper (a Vietnam veteran) played the role of Saddam and was declared the winner (see the Guardian, September 6, 2002, article by Julian Borger). We know now that the actual campaign in Iraq ended differently, and that the Allied Forces had to take on a new, unanticipated and very difficult role, i.e. that of bringing order and safety to Iraqi cities and villages. An age-old game was called upon to capture the key members of the old regime. A classic deck of cards, featuring the faces of the wanted members of the former Iraqi administration, was distributed in great quantities throughout the country. This game was apparently successful, as most of these suspects have been apprehended.

Military war gaming is like any other military activity: if it proves necessary, you better do it right and with as little public exposure as possible. As a consequence, we know more about the past history of war gaming than about its present use. However, we do know enough to appreciate that these games can be used as a tool to prevent ineffective action and thus save lives. It all depends on how the tool is used: just like a hammer can be a weapon of aggression, it can also be used by a carpenter or sculptor to create works of art. In this vein, a simulation can prepare and train people either for good or evil ends. In this book, we will show how processes that often appear very similar to war games help companies, governments and nonprofit organizations to improve performance and continue their positive roles in society. When done right, these types of games do, in fact, have winners.

## TOO MANY NOTES, MR. MOZART
In the famous Hollywood movie *Amadeus*, we observe the Austrian Kaiser, much to the delight of the wicked Mr. Salieri, unwittingly yawning during one of Mozart's operas. The young master's music was too delicate and too detailed for the poor Kaiser's ears. "Too many notes, Mr. Mozart," was his honest yet painful remark to the disappointed rising star.

Both authors have tried to suppress the seductive tendency of filling each page of this book with endless notes and references to supporting sources. The two of us have worked in the same academic field for many years. We have been lucky to receive the stimulating support of many other professionals. After eagerly reading the work written by our past students and other young colleagues, it would not be difficult to make this book into a "who wrote what, when and where" about gaming. However, we have set out to write a convincing monograph, not a historical bibliographical review.

There is a downside to this approach. Over the years, many colleagues from all over the world have contributed to our thinking about gaming and strategic management; for example, through their presentations at the annual ISAGA, SAGSET and ABSEL conferences, as well as through their articles in the journal *Simulation & Gaming*. There is no way to reconstruct all these influences, nor is it possible for us to honor every insight from each colleague by referring to their work. As a result, many important and well-written pieces on gaming and policy making will not be referenced. We apologize to each individual whose ideas we have gratefully absorbed but whom we do not credit in this book. It is with regret that we acknowledge that the human brain is subject to certain limitations, and that it may play the trick of unnoticed knowledge conversion on all of us.

We acknowledge a debt to all the hard workers in our discipline who love their gaming so much that they regularly attend international meetings to share their experiences with others in the field. Gaming is, first of all, a form of communication, a claim we substantiate in this book. We have always enjoyed the fact that gamers are so enthusiastic about communicating with other gamers. Without this, our discipline would be far less open to newcomers. We hope that our book will prove to be an informative and stimulating link in the chain of communication within our discipline. At the same time, as we state elsewhere, we hope this monograph strengthens a potentially valuable, but currently weak communication link: that which exists between policy and strategy disciplines and the gamers themselves.

# *Acknowledgements*

As the authors, it is our honor and pleasure to thank the colleagues and students with whom we have worked side by side on the projects presented in this book. Given geographic realities, there are two networks to be mentioned here, one in the U.S. and the other in the Netherlands. Below, we will thank quite a list of colleagues, without spelling out why we have appreciated the opportunity to work with each individual. Otherwise, the Kaiser might fall into a deep sleep.

## THE ORANGE TEAM

On the Dutch side, we want to make one exception to the above rule by singling out our dear friend and colleague Dr. Cisca Joldersma. Her enormous energy and enthusiasm has served as constant motivation for us to continue our work on policy and gaming. In addition, we will never forget her friendly, merciless, but always accurate remarks—nor will the Tilburg students she has coached to become experienced gamers. Cisca Joldersma's esteemed reputation in policy and games will now benefit the country, in addition to our discipline, in her new role as a member of the Dutch House of Representatives.

Other Dutch gaming friends we want to thank are: Frank Bongers, Piet Biemans, Leon de Caluwé, Janneke Ewals, Gerton Heyne, Robert Hooyberg, Peter de Klerk, Hans van Kuppevelt, Igor Mayer, Vincent Peters, Rob Pranger, Ellie Roelofs, Pieter van der Hijden, Juliette Vermaas, Geert Vissers, and Pieter van Wierst.

With the risk of insulting his nationalistic (soccer) feelings, we want to include Dr. Laurie McMahon as part of the Dutch team. As Director for Practice Development and one of the founders of the Office for Public Management in London, he provided us with the case study on the Rubber Windmill. He was also a team member of the University Hospital project (see Chapter 3).

The Tilburg Institute for Applied Social Research (IVA) and the Department of Social Science (FSW) of Tilburg University must be thanked for financially supporting the writing of this book.

The Trappist monastery Our Lady of Koningshoeve at Berkel Enschot (the Netherlands) and the Fundacion Cultural Knecht/Drenth in Callosa d'en Sarría (Spain) opened their doors and allowed us to write this book on their beautiful and inspiring premises.

## THE MAIZE AND BLUE TEAM

On the American side, we will again make an exception to our rule by singling out Steve Underwood for his contribution to several of the cases presented in this book (Pharmaceutical Decision Exercise, Office of the Secretary of Defense, and the IJC Great Lakes Exercise.) The Corporate Culture Exercise was developed by Simulation Solutions under the leadership of Steve Underwood; this group included Mark LeBay, Andrea Frank, and Tom Reed.

It is also appropriate to mention the other central team members for each case. The members of the Pharmaceutical Decision Exercise were Hemalata Dandekar and Nancy Frost. The Conrail Policy Exercise team was Gery Williams and Kathryn Rickard. The staff for the Office of the Secretary of Defense was Lorraine Atoui and Tom Gerschick. The IJC Great Lakes Policy Exercise was headed by Steve Underwood and included Mark LeBay, Andrea Frank, Jim Nicita and Tom Reed.

The teams for each of the case studies presented in this book always included students. It is not possible to mention their specific contributions, but a few of the American students that we wish to thank are: Rob Cary, Chris Davis, Lynda Duke, Charles Hall, Pat Sweet and Ivo Wenzler.

We would like to thank Prof. Moji Navvab for his long-time support of the Certificate Program in Gaming/Simulation at the University of Michigan; this program supplied many of the students who worked with the design teams on several of these projects.

Special thanks are due to Prof. Mieko Nakamura and Prof. Arata Ichikawa for their work in translating *Gaming: The Future's Language* into Japanese. Discussions concerning that project are reflected in Chapter 5.

A debt is also owed to Prof. Nakamura for her contributions during her visit to Ann Arbor during the 2001-2002 school year (she reviewed this manuscript with painstaking care and provided many excellent suggestions). Richard D. Duke, Jr. also reviewed the entire manuscript in detail.

Our special thanks go to Andrea Frank for her meticulous preparation of the artwork; we would also like to thank Bea van Wijk for her assistance. Prof. Shigehisa Tsuchiya was kind enough to contribute the City Budget Schematic located in the appendix. Tina Sergi provided the final edit for the manuscript; she worked patiently with us through this process. We are especially grateful to Ria Lap for providing the original artwork that is used on the cover.

And last, but by no means least, we would like to thank Marie Alice Duke, who edited the complete text, and whose basement was the real center of this writing conspiracy. Her excellent food kept us going and kept our cholesterol level low; her smile cannot be found anywhere else in the world, least of all in a Trappist monastery.

## *The Primary Goals of this Book*

THE PRIMARY GOALS OF THIS BOOK ARE TO:
- Contribute to the further dissemination and development of the discipline of gaming/simulation as a method to solve strategic problems; and
- Improve communication between this discipline and related policy fields.

These goals imply that we are aiming at a diverse set of readers: but primarily professionals, academics and students. More specifically, we believe that this book contains relevant theories, ideas, tips and methods for the following categories of readers:

- Policy makers and supporting staff as well as consultants who advise and/or decide on the strategic processes for critical "bet the organization" decisions;
- Academics who study the processes of policy analysis and strategic management within and between organizations;
- Professionals who design and facilitate policy processes;
- Specialists in the gaming discipline who want to broaden their understanding of the uses of gaming in policy settings;
- Advanced students in the academic disciplines dealing with management, decision making, strategy and policy, and organizational change;
- Professionals who want to apply this methodology.

## The Structure of this Book

This book brings together theory on strategic processes and policy analysis, the theory and methodology of gaming/simulation, and detailed descriptions and analyses of several policy games. The book has the following structure:

### Section I - Setting the Stage

Chapter 1, *About this Monograph*, describes our assumptions, goals and key concepts; it presents a short history of serious gaming, and positions policy games among related management techniques.

Chapter 2, *Entering Uncharted Territory*, looks at the nature of macro-problems and gives a historical overview of the policy and strategy literature on how to handle macro-problems.

### Section II - Practice: Description and Analysis

Chapter 3, *Eight Case Studies*, describes *intra-* and *inter-organizational* policy exercises. In the intra-organizational cases, the client is a large organization and the participants came from within that organization. The examples are taken from public and private organizations. The inter-organizational cases are mostly situated at the public/private interface. Both types involve cases from Europe and the U.S.

Chapter 4, *Five Key Criteria*, is analytical and evaluative: it looks at the application of the process criteria defined by the five Cs (Complexity, Communication, Creativity, Consensus, and Commitment to Action). We review each of the five Cs and establish what it is in the nature of policy games that enables this technique to help organizations realize these criteria, and consequently how one should design a game to enter terra incognita in a successful way.

### Section III - Theory and Research

Chapter 5, *Multilogue – a Language for Complexity*, looks at the underlying communication patterns that are unique to gaming/simulation; it describes "multilogue" as a language for moving into the future.

Chapter 6, *Empirical Research and the Policy Exercise*, explores three important links between empirical research and policy games, i.e. research to prepare for gaming, research to evaluate gaming, and research that uses policy games as an environment to study individual and group behavior.

## Section IV - Designing Games for Strategy

Chapter 7, *Understanding the Policy Exercise Construct*, identifies and defines the elements that constitute a policy game. An understanding of these building blocks is essential for the productive use of this discipline.

Chapter 8, *Designing the Policy Exercise*, is technical in nature. It describes the design process for the policy exercise as applied in the majority of the cases presented. This chapter is not a complete "how to" guide for designing your own policy exercise – that is beyond the scope of this book. However, we do present the main design ideas and provide some technical details (these are also supplemented in the Appendix).

## Section V - Conclusions

Chapter 9, *The Potential of the Policy Exercise*, looks back at our initial concerns and definitions. What is the strategic role of the phenomenon we have been calling policy games? What future do we envision for policy games? The main components of our answers to these questions should already be clear to the reader. We see a promising future for policy games and summarize why this is so in Chapter 9.

## Appendix

The Appendix includes Supplemental Hints, Glossary, Bibliography and an Index (see pg. 5).

## Four Functional Reading Paths

Different audiences will have different objectives when reading this book; the following suggestions might be useful in selecting a relevant reading path:

- To focus on the *practical contributions* of gaming/simulation for policy and strategy, read Chapter 1, Section 2.5, a selection of cases in Chapter 3 and, in particular, Sections 4.7 and Chapter 9.
- To understand the *link* we have established between gaming/simulation and *policy and organization theory and research*, read Chapters 1 and 2, a selection of cases in Chapter 3, and Chapters 4, 5, 6 and 9.
- To review the *basic concepts and theory of gaming as a discipline*, read Chapter 1, a selection of cases in Chapter 3, and Chapters 5, 6 and 9.
- To understand what it takes to *design a policy exercise*, read Chapter 1, a selection of cases in Chapter 3, Chapter 7, Chapter 8 and the Detailed Design Tips located in the Appendix.

# Section I

## *Setting the Stage*

**INTRODUCTION TO SECTION I**
This section includes Chapter 1 – About this Monograph, and Chapter 2 – Entering Uncharted Territory.

Chapter 1 makes a start by linking gaming/simulation to the world of strategy and policy. In a sense, it re-establishes this link, because it describes the military roots of gaming as a tool for strategy development and the teaching of strategic skills. Chapter 1 also introduces the reader to the special class of strategic problems for which we think gaming/simulation is the proper decision aid. We define these as "macro-problems" or "strategic volcanoes," and explain what they are.

The conceptual link between this information on macro-problems and the technique of gaming/simulation is established and summarized by the idea of the five Cs. Only a process that will *simultaneously* master *complexity*, optimize *communication*, stimulate *creativity*, lead to *consensus* and develop *commitment to action* can hold the promise of leading organizations through the unknown and helping them deal with strategic volcanoes.

Chapter 2 deepens the reader's understanding of these macro-problems. It gives many examples of macro-problems and analyzes their common features. In addition, this chapter reviews the literature on policy and strategy and sets out insights from the past and present on how to deal with macro-problems.

Section I as a whole provides the reader with the proper conceptual framework to study the case studies described and analyzed in Chapter 3.

# Chapter 1

## About this Monograph

### 1.1 INTRODUCTION

This chapter describes our assumptions, goals, and key concepts; it presents a short history of serious gaming, and positions policy games among related management techniques.

### 1.2 ASSUMPTIONS AND GOALS

This section addresses four concerns: the phenomena of urgent organizational crises that we label "strategic volcanoes"; the challenges that leadership faces when entering uncharted territory or "terra incognita"; the creation of "safe environments" that assist organizations in preparing for the unknown; and a statement of the primary goals of this book.

#### 1.2.1 About Strategic Volcanoes

In the life of each organization, situations arise that are completely new to the history of the organization. These situations are complex, surprising, urgent, inspiring, threatening and sometimes enduring. Leadership is forced to bring the organization into uncharted territory. Facing these situations, and often after a period of muddling through in a business-as-usual way, leadership has to recognize that a breakthrough response will only emerge from a previously unexplored (and, for this organization, a revolutionary) strategy process. Think about the bewilderment in a high-tech company when an emerging technology from a competitor threatens the whole existence of their organization. The California energy crisis in 2002 is another example: by initially oversimplifying the problem and failing to identify and evaluate major alternatives, the state found itself in a crisis of its own making. If there had been proper communication about this complex system among all interested parties (e.g. suppliers, regulatory agencies, distributors, and consumers), it is unlikely that the decisions made would have proven so unsatisfactory. Yet another instance is the dilemma faced by a nationalized railway or postal service – is deregulation an opportunity or a threat? Should they lobby against adoption of a new deregulation law, or pursue it as a great opportunity?

According to William Halal, who assessed the state-of-the-art of strategic planning in his study of 25 major corporations:

"Issues can be thought of as stress points resulting from the clash between the organization and its continually changing environment. The magnitude of change is so great now that the social order has become a discontinuity with the past, creating a deep division between most firms and their surroundings that allows the environment to bear against the organization like a drifting continental plate. Issues comprise the societal hot spots that are generated at this stressful interface, forming social volcanoes that often erupt unexpectedly to shower the corporation with operational brush fires" (Halal, 1984, p. 252).

Several examples of such change are cited in the following chapters. Suffice it to say that there is a class of macro-problems in uncharted territory which lead to "bet the organization" decisions.

### 1.2.2 How to Enter an Unknown Land?

Much has been written for leaders of organizations about the need to improve the quality of strategic decision making when one is faced with conditions of turbulence and revolution. Decisions have to be taken faster, they have to be more creative, they must draw on the wisdom of many, and they also need the commitment of several internal and external stakeholders. Academic and popular writers on strategy and policy mention the growing complexity and turbulence of the environment, the growing interconnectedness of organizations, and the growing importance of stakeholder participation and organizational responsibility. Management must become aware of the need to flatten the organizational structure because of increasing knowledge intensity and the escalating professionalism of work.

This is just a short list of the underlying causes for the need to dramatically change the style and process of strategic management. When entering terra incognita, leadership has to ensure that those involved in policy development create consistent, doable, relevant and creative strategies. These must be based on a shared understanding of context and totality, an inspiring image of the future, clear value tradeoffs and well-tested and explored alternatives for action. How is it best to realize all these demands? How can all of this be brought to life in a typical conference room? That is the question this book addresses. We want to show how a discipline called gaming/simulation can help organizations to realize these objectives.

There are reasons enough to become somewhat cynical when one reads the above summary. Many limiting factors in the capabilities of even the wisest individuals and the best-run organizations make it very difficult to even begin to live up to the standards of decision making now required. There are always time and resource constraints, and there is the basic human tendency to simplify complexity. Because of differing (and often conflicting) perspectives pertinent to the many disciplines and functions present in every large social structure, organizations frequently face severe communication problems. Within and between organizations, many opportunities for cooperation are never explored because of real or perceived differences in values and interests. There is often a lack of talent, imagination and/or patience to examine a strategic issue thoroughly instead of adopting the most obvious alternatives, which are easiest to implement given the existing balance of power.

### 1.2.3 Policy Exercises: Preparing for the Unknown

In this book, we analyze the structure of strategic problems in uncharted territory and explore what it takes to handle these problems. We show in detail how certain organizations have successfully dealt with them, using the policy exercise methodology based on the discipline of gaming/simulation. Experienced and responsible clients and observers of this methodology have evaluated this approach as very effective and practical. To stay in line with common practice, and also for stylistic reasons, we use the terms "policy exercise" and "policy game" synonymously.

The policy games presented in this book were created as "safe environments" where people who have a key role in confronting major problems can bring their knowledge and skills to the forefront of the strategic debate. They provide the opportunity for "as real as possible" experiential learning to mobilize core competencies and test the skills that may be needed in the future. They help to develop confidence and ownership and reduce the fear of the unknown. Games have an important role in making sure that strategies are doable in the eyes of the doers. The basic assumption and thus the message of this book is that gaming/simulation is a powerful strategic tool for organizations which are required to enter uncharted territory.

A gap exists between the gaming discipline and the literature on strategic management. In professional and academic journals on policy, strategy, and organizational change, one finds little about successful gaming applications. This is unfortunate, because a properly devised gaming/simulation rapidly enhances the sophistication of the participants. The technique is particularly well suited for circumstances where the objectives are to provide an integrative experience, illustrate management techniques in an experiential manner, develop esprit de corps among a group, convey an overview or systems "gestalt" (the big picture), and provide an environment for experimenting with improving group process. Gaming/simulations offer a fruitful potential for melding many skills.

### 1.2.4 The Goals of this Book

Two goals motivated the authors to write this book. These aims are inseparably intertwined but require independent logic to be properly addressed:

- We want to contribute to the further development of the discipline of gaming/simulation as a method to solve strategic problems; and
- We want to improve communication between our discipline and the related policy disciplines.

The current state of the gaming/simulation discipline is represented by a wide array of formats in projects where this technique has been employed worldwide. To the uninitiated, this great variety (scope, purpose, subject matter, technique, nature of the product, etc.) implies that gaming/simulation is all things to all people. The image conveyed does not contribute to the credibility of the discipline.

The irony, of course, is that the allied fields of policy, strategy, and organizational change are each well-established users of gaming/simulation. The difference is that each of these fields tends to select gaming applications as specifically appropriate to their need. As a consequence, colleagues from these fields are often unfamiliar with the broader spectrum, the history and the methodology of the discipline of gaming/simulation.

Policy issues must increasingly be resolved under conditions of complexity and there are few effective techniques for dealing with these situations. With this book, we want to show that a well-understood, clear, replicable and practical method to create policy games exists for the unique decision situations that organizations sometimes face.

### 1.3 KEY CONCEPTS

The more conceptual parts of this book analyze the gaming/simulation approach. This approach is relevant for strategic problem solving because – in a well-structured, transparent and effective way – it can put into operation a large number of the lessons that have emerged from the literature that deals with resolving macro-problems. To capture these lessons in a tangible format, we define five key process criteria for handling macro-problems or "bet the organization" decisions. We have labeled these criteria the "five Cs": *complexity, communication, creativity, consensus,* and *commitment to action*. We give a short introduction to these key concepts below. Chapter 4 contains a more detailed analysis of each of the criteria.

#### 1.3.1 Complexity

Macro-problems are complex from a cognitive point of view. Framing such problems correctly is difficult. There are many variables involved, but no one knows what and how many the important variables are. The same is true for the relationships between the variables. The causes of the problem are often obscure, and so are the future trends. There is no overview or solid past knowledge of how to act vis-à-vis this problem. Usually, many potentially relevant sources of knowledge are available, but the existing knowledge household might prove to be scattered and incomplete, and its elements are often of unequal quality. It is not available in a format useful for decision making, nor is it shared by the relevant people.

In the case of the IJC Great Lakes Policy Exercise, the policy exercise designers had to identify and cope with close to a thousand variables. The exercise was intended to help the assembled group arrive at a holistic understanding of a complex problem. This could only happen if the "shared images of reality" were viewed as authentic by a clear majority of the hundred (or so) policy makers as they debated the best course of action to pursue (this story is told in Chapter 3).

The first criterion for entering the terra incognita of macro-problems is that one must apply a method for handling the complexity of such a problem. As we will demonstrate, gaming/simulation can produce policy exercises in which many different sources and types of data, insights and tacit knowledge can be integrated in a problem-specific knowledge household. Furthermore, these policy exercises provide an environment that allows the exploration of possible strategies for entering uncharted territory. These games offer a safe environment to test strategies in advance. They help decision makers to create a possible future and allow them to "look back" from that future. We call this capability of gaming "reminiscing about the future" (Duke, 1974).

### 1.3.2 Communication
Communication is essential when important decisions are to be made. There are not many organizations in which one individual has the authority to make strategic decisions alone. Even when a final decision will be taken by a single individual or a limited number, these top decision makers have to rely on and collect the wisdom of many people within and beyond the borders of their organization. In complex situations where a group must resolve a perplexing issue, traditional modes of communication have proven not to work very well. New methods are needed which provide an overview and stimulate gestalt communication. This book will show that policy games, if applied properly, are a hybrid form of communication. They are hybrid in the sense that they allow many people with different perspectives to be in communication with each other using different forms of communication in parallel. We label this the multilogue characteristic of policy games (Duke, 1974); this phenomenon is presented in detail in Chapter 5.

### 1.3.3 Creativity
In many cases, problems can be approached with new combinations of proven and well-tested lines of action. But this can only be done if the analysis of the problem leads to the "aha" effect of recognizing the analogy between the new situation and familiar examples. Discovering analogies is basically a process of creativity: it needs the playful exchange of perspectives and the retrieval of intuitive or tacit knowledge. Accumulation of experience in a person, a team or an organization leads to the development of a repertoire of responses to many different challenges. As Mintzberg (1994) points out, finding the appropriate response to a challenging issue is not a science, but a craft. It is about combining experience

with creativity to find a new, original, inspiring and adequate pathway into the unknown. To the extent that science does *not* have a complete answer, the policy exercise can provide a disciplined approach that requires confronting the known and the unknown.

> '[S]cience is an endeavor in which one gets such wholesome returns of conjecture out of such a trifling investment of fact" (Mark Twain)

The Dutch philosopher Johan Huizinga (1955) has made a major contribution to the understanding of the fundamental link between play and creativity. In his famous study on man as a player (*Homo Ludens*), Huizinga puts forward the thesis that innovation can only be achieved by play. In the free and safe activity of play, and consequently in the free spirit of a playful mind, the individual can go beyond the borders of the limiting forces of everyday life. Only through play can new combinations be developed which, according to Schumpeter (1934), is precisely what innovation means. Policy exercises combine the realistic element of simulation with the playful stimulus of gaming. People in roles explore the dynamic consequences of the available knowledge base in a free and stimulus-rich environment. They test each other's responses to trigger novel alternatives and to challenge and play with any idea that seems to have potential.

### 1.3.4 Consensus
New challenges often bring out old, and sometimes unsuspected, conflicts of values. Organizations in a steady-state situation have often developed a balance in "frozen" conflicts. In most organizations, conflicts of values and interests have been brought to rest. They have resulted in workable arrangements: compromises that reflect the existing power balance. In short, there is a workable degree of consensus. But in turbulent times, in periods of transition, and under the strong pressures of major challenges, this consensus will be tested.

The power balance might shift because the owners of new and suddenly relevant resources (skills, knowledge, networks, capital, etc.) want a stake in the issue. Newly affected parties appear in the arena and the old supporting stakeholders may become marginal or even hostile. As a consequence, "new rules of the game" have to be defined. There is a need for a new consensus, which, preferably, should not be the result of a long and costly battle in the period after a strategy has been chosen. The concerted action and support of many stakeholders is needed to deal with major problems. Gaining understanding (with regard to complexity), finding a novel course of action (with regard to creativity), and the negotiation of consensus should all be part of the process of communication which precedes the adoption and implementation of a strategy. A painful and conflict-ridden collective thought experiment is much more desirable that a conflict-ridden and stalled implementation process.

The simulation character of policy games helps to avoid a major threat involved in other forms of finding a consensus. When a group of people reaches consensus without proper analysis or without looking beyond the borders of traditional perspectives, there is a real danger that only politically feasible and easy-to-implement strategies will be discussed. In the literature, this is called "group-think" – and the history of organizational decision making is full of fateful examples of this phenomenon.

Policy games are "social simulations" (Van der Meer, 1983) in the sense that they model the social organization around an issue. They put real people in roles as caretakers of certain interests and positions and distribute resources as in real life. They allow players to explore the consequences of the issue at hand within the existing structures and rules. In a game, one is often surprised to discover that the gains and benefits of a certain strategy affect parties in a completely different way than expected. Win-win options might be discovered, and the "early warning" nature of the game might signal potential win-lose situations at a stage when policy adoptions can still be discussed.

### 1.3.5 Commitment to Action

People are action-oriented beings. This is especially true for individuals who have a long career of "making things happen." Of course, strategy without action is not strategy at all. Initiatives lacking the entrepreneurial drive to succeed will soon end up on the pile of good intentions. That is why a good process for entering into the unknown must create a commitment to action for those people whose energy and endurance is vital to the success of the strategy. Charismatic and dedicated leadership is important, but, increasingly, this is not enough. In the de-layered, more knowledge-intensive, more professional and faster-moving organizations of our time, strategy is realized in the day-to-day decisions of many individuals and teams in the work force at the points of interaction with clients and other stakeholders. More and more people are active in realizing a strategy as relatively autonomous decision makers. It is essential that all members of a group move into uncharted territory at the same time. This presupposes that all the individual actors understand the problem, see the relevance of the new course of action, understand their roles in the master plan, and feel confident that old skills or skills to be acquired in due time will help them to conquer the obstacles and seize the opportunities ahead.

### 1.4 A Short History of Policy Gaming

Space permits only cursory attention to this topic. Suffice it to say that there is a rich history of gaming activity and much of it relates to policy concerns. The purpose of this section is to describe the origins and evolution of the policy exercise as a relatively new phenomenon that emerged out of a very old tradition. Games are as old as humankind, and have always had a culture-based learning function.

Tribal rituals, games of the young knights in the Middle Ages, the childhood games of our youth; these are all examples of games to internalize rules and master important skills.

### 1.4.1 Games for Learning

Gaming has been used for centuries as an exercise in military strategy; the technique has also been widely used for other serious learning purposes. Since World War II, gaming has expanded its scope to include theoretical and practical endeavors in every imaginable discipline. Beginning with the advent of training games for business, the field has broadened to embrace the social sciences and educational needs of modern society. Information and communication technology has fundamentally changed (and will keep on changing) the gamer's toolbox. The new technologies have given the gaming discipline an enormous boost. Improved computational, graphic and communication methods have resulted in games with more dynamic realism, a much shorter production time, and simpler facilitation procedures.

The element of simulation can also be found in games from the past. In their extensive study of the history of games and play, Gyzicki and Gorni (1979) found that backgammon is the oldest known board game in the world, dating from 2450 B.C. Backgammon, of which many varieties exist all over the world, simulates a match on a track court.

### 1.4.2 Early War Games

The origin of war games is unclear; however, it is likely that chess was one of the earliest versions of this activity. The game of chess, originating in the army of India around the fifth century, simulates a war between kingdoms. Not only the shapes of the figures, but also the hierarchy and the mobility of the pieces represent the structure of an army from that period. Shubik (1975) found concepts of gaming and elements of a theory of strategic gaming in the writings of a great Chinese military genius, the general Sun Tzu (original about 500 B.C., republished 1963), whose book on the "art of war" is still widely read.

Certainly there is a great similarity between chess and many of the later versions of war games played on a board as the symbolic equivalents to warfare. They represented abstractions of military confrontations, and by the turn of the 18th century, they were formalized to ensure consistency of play governed by rules and standardized penalties. Significant changes were introduced into the "new" German war games in that actual maps (instead of a grid game board) were used, and a greater complexity was introduced into the decision structure. By the 19th century, because of the different requirements for "realistic" as opposed to "playable" games, their construction split along the lines of "rigid" and "free" games. Both versions tended toward a higher level of sophistication, but whereas the former version relied heavily on formalized procedures to govern play (maps, charts, dice, extensive calculations), the free games substituted the judgment of experienced umpires to expedite the play. Both have been employed as techniques for analyzing and evaluating military tactics, equipment, and procedures.

Casimir (1995) studied two 19th century German textbooks on war gaming in the library of the University of Göttingen. In Von Aretin (1830), Casimir found a discussion on the development of war games between 1664 and 1825. Von Aretin sees a development of constant decrease in the level of abstraction and a growing complexity of the games. Casimir quotes Von Aretin's very modern-sounding opinion on the value of the war game as a tool for training: "that playing a game is better than listening to long, tiring, half-understood and quickly forgotten lectures or paging for hours through books" (Casimir, 1995). In Meckel (1873), Casimir found a summary of the many advantages of war games compared to other forms of learning, such as practice in giving and receiving orders. This, as Casimir rightly points out, is quite comparable to modern experiences with the use of games to train for teamwork (Geurts, et al., 2000).

The two major forms of war games, free play and rigid play, still exist. Both are used as techniques for analyzing and evaluating military tactics, equipment, procedures, etc. The free-play game has received support because of its versatility in dealing with complex tactical and strategic problems and because of the ease with which it can be adapted to various training, planning, and evaluation ends. The rigid-play game has received support because of the consistency and detail of its rule structure and its computational rigor. In addition, the development of large-capacity computers has made it possible to carry out detailed computations with great speed, and thus enabled the same game to be played many different times. These developments have allowed for an increase in the number and types of war games.

Concurrent with these developments, there has been an increased popularity of war gaming, and the technique has spread to other countries. Initially, West Point copied various British versions, and war gaming developments have continued in the armed forces to the present. Prior to World War II, Admiral Isoroku Yamamoto convinced the Naval General Staff to stage a theoretical attack on Pearl Harbor during the annual naval war games. During the early days of the Gulf War, some 50 years after the attack on Pearl Harbor, newspapers reported that Norman Schwartzkopf had been given operational responsibility for this mission in Kuwait and Iraq. Schwartzkopf was selected because he had prepared a new and surprising strategy for this mission in a war-gaming exercise. These are just two of many instances where military leaders have utilized games for both training and problem-solving purposes. One thing is clear: war gaming is a very important predecessor of the form of policy gaming described in this book.

### 1.4.3 Modern War Games

Over a 3000-year period, the prime use of war games has been for instruction. However, they have also been used for analysis (as in the Pearl Harbor incident), particularly with respect to testing alternative war plans. The Axis powers made more extensive use of war games during the period leading up to World War II than did the Allies.

In addition to the Japanese Naval War games previously mentioned, the Japanese Total War Research Institute conducted extensive games. Here, military services and the government joined in gaming Japan's future actions: internal and external, military and diplomatic. In August 1941, a game was written up in which the two-year period from mid-August 1941 through the middle of 1943 was gamed and lived through in advance at an accelerated pace. Players represented the German-Italian Axis, Russia, the U.S., England, Thailand, the Netherlands, the East Indies, China, Korea, Manchuria, and French Indochina. Japan was not played as a single force, but instead as an uneasy coalition of the Army, the Navy, and the Cabinet, with the military and the government disagreeing constantly on the decision to go to war, X-day, civilian demands versus those of heavy industry, etc. Disagreements arose and were settled in the course of an afternoon with the more aggressive military group winning most arguments. Measures to be taken within Japan were gamed in detail and included economic, educational, financial, and psychological factors. The game even included plans for the control of consumer goods, which, incidentally, were identical to those actually put into effect on December 8, 1945. Postwar military gaming efforts have reached high levels of sophistication, approaching the ingenuity displayed by science-fiction writers.

There have been other extensive war gaming developments since the advent of the computer. For reference purposes, see Shubik (1975), Brewer & Shubik (1979), Osvalt (1993) and Boer & Soeters (1998). On a happier note, gaming efforts are now being directed towards the pursuit of non-military purposes as evidenced by the examples put forth in Chapter 3.

## 1.5 POSITIONING POLICY GAMES

The above section has made clear that gaming/simulation has a long tradition and that games can have many forms and functions. Although we explain our view on the policy exercise in more detail in later chapters, this introductory chapter provides an initial definition and positioning of policy games. Section 1.5.1 addresses the central characteristics of play, and Section 1.5.2 compares simulation vs. gaming. In Section 1.5.3, we give a first definition of what we mean by policy exercises, and in Section 1.5.4, we position this form of gaming among many other gaming applications. We suggest that policy exercises are one manifestation of the discipline of gaming/simulation.

### 1.5.1 Meaning of Play – Central Characteristics

Play is a central human characteristic; a basic counterpoint to life itself. The Dutch philosopher Johan Huizinga has probably contributed the most to the systematic analysis and philosophical interpretation of the concept of play. Huizinga (1955, p. 1) views man as a game-playing animal: "play is to be understood ... not as a biological phenomenon but as a cultural phenomenon. It is [to be] approached historically, not scientifically." Huizinga notes that animals play, therefore playing is not solely a human activity. Games have been a fundamental aspect of our lives from infancy. There is both playful play and serious play (e.g. Russian Roulette as a pastime by soldiers on the front line). Huizinga claims that play is the basis of culture from which myth and ritual derive. In his book *Homo Ludens*, he finds several elements that define a game (see also Geurts, et. al, 2000). In this context, he states that play:

- Is a voluntary, superfluous activity (one enters into it out of free will);
- Is stepping out of real life into a temporary sphere of activity;
- Means being limited in terms of time and place;
- Has fixed rules and follows an orderly process;
- Promotes the formation of new and different social groupings;
- Is itself the goal; and
- Is accompanied by a sense of tension and joy and the awareness that the activity is different from normal life.

There seems to be a contradiction here: is a game only a game if the activity itself is the goal? For Huizinga, game and play are the main forces for cultural change and innovation: only by stepping out of the ordinary routine of everyday life will individuals discover new routes and perspectives. "Culture arises in the form of play," says Huizinga (1955, p. 46). There is only a hazy border between play and seriousness. Just as humankind is able to develop more and more games for joy and entertainment, in the same way, there seems to be no limit to the fantasy of people when creating games in which creative and learning effects are directed towards a consciously chosen "outside-the-game" goal.

### 1.5.2 Comparison of Simulation vs. Gaming

Gaming is valuable in part because it responds to a human need – people crave information: they enjoy exploring, discovering and learning. They do not like just to be told about something; they learn most readily from concrete instances and information strong in imagery. A simulation generally involves a detailed representation of reality in a computer whereas, in a game, the players are the central part of the model construct. Gaming has some valuable features:

- It is an explicit statement that provides a framework that incorporates player strategies in an integrative structure;
- It permits players to employ these strategies in a group process;

- It provides the opportunity to break through old interpretative frameworks; and
- It brings many ideas to bear on the problem at hand.

What is simulation? The Latin verb "simulare" means "to imitate" or "to act as if." Duke (1980) defined simulation as "a conscious endeavor to reproduce the central characteristics of a system in order to understand, experiment with and/or predict the behavior of that system." To be able to simulate the behavior of a system, one creates or uses a model of that system. Leo Apostel (1960, p. 160) defines a model as follows: "Any person using a system 'A' that is neither directly nor indirectly interacting with a system 'B,' in order to obtain information about system 'B,' is using 'A' as a model for 'B.'" Simulation models are specifically made to help clients understand the systems in which they are embedded.

A model can have many different forms: a road map, a three-dimensional representation of a building, a mathematical algorithm or a complex computer program possibly accompanied by graphical representation. A gaming/simulation is a special type of model that uses gaming techniques to model and simulate a system. A gaming/simulation is an operating model of a real-life system in which actors in roles partially recreate the behavior of the system. The word "partially" refers to the fact that a game can contain many other elements that play a part in simulating the system, such as maps, game pieces (e.g. poker chips) and computer software (see Chapter 7).

The game invites the players to jointly create a future from a starting position. Step by step, they make decisions, alter cooperative or competitive relations, and act within the rules of the game on the basis of their joint or individual insights and preferences. The policy exercise can be thought of as a small group problem-solving technique that offers a means of experimenting with the management of complex environments (these are often called "wicked problems"). The approach clarifies these problems and demonstrates to managers the need to be proactive in exploring a variety of solutions before a decision is taken.

A simulation is an operating model of the central features of a system; that is, it shows functional as well as structural relations (Greenblat, Duke, 1975). Some simulations are operated within computers, other types are performed by human players. This eliminates the need to build in psychological assumptions. The actions of players within the game consist of a set of activities aimed at achieving goals in a limiting context with many constraints.

At this point, a clarification of terminology is important since this definition of gaming/simulation encompasses a wide range of exercises. Business games, war games, operational gaming, management games and other exercises with a great variety of prefixes fall into this category. The function of these gaming/simulations will vary. There are exercises to motivate a group, ice-breaking activities, games for education and training in schools or organizations, and games for policy making. Our focus is on the latter and we will start to explore them in the next section. Figure 1.1 helps to illustrate the nature of these different approaches. The figure shows that the level of abstraction appropriate for policy exercises can be placed between very abstract games and very detailed large-scale simulations that prove useful for operational planning in well-understood areas.

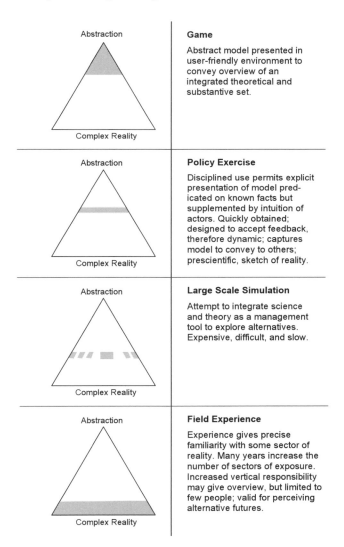

**Game**

Abstract model presented in user-friendly environment to convey overview of an integrated theoretical and substantive set.

**Policy Exercise**

Disciplined use permits explicit presentation of model predicated on known facts but supplemented by intuition of actors. Quickly obtained; designed to accept feedback, therefore dynamic; captures model to convey to others; prescientific, sketch of reality.

**Large Scale Simulation**

Attempt to integrate science and theory as a management tool to explore alternatives. Expensive, difficult, and slow.

**Field Experience**

Experience gives precise familiarity with some sector of reality. Many years increase the number of sectors of exposure. Increased vertical responsibility may give overview, but limited to few people; valid for perceiving alternative futures.

Figure 1.1 | Communicating Complexity: Positioning Policy Exercises

### 1.5.3 Policy Games: One Form of Gaming/Simulation

A policy exercise is a gaming/simulation that is explicitly created to aid policy makers with a specific issue of strategic management. A policy exercise will function as a managerial support process that uses gaming/simulation to assist a group in policy exploration and execution. A large and growing number of professionals devote a substantial part of their energies to the effective use of gaming/simulation tools. In each new situation, the professional has to complete essentially the same sequence of activities:

- Validate the decision to use this approach;
- Clarify the client's needs;
- Structure the problem effectively;
- Develop a prototype exercise;
- Test and modify the prototype;
- Deliver the exercise to the client; and
- Evaluate the final product.

A major characteristic of the policy exercise approach is that it allows players to experience the complexity of strategic problems and their environments. It allows the players to understand the interaction of social, economic, technological, environmental and political forces that exist in planning and decision making problems. The objective of a policy game is to create an operating model of the problem environment that is general and structural. The use of a game employs a process that lets the participants debate the model; it also makes the model vivid so that it will be retained. As a consequence, facts and particulars will be better understood (bits and pieces now have a logical place to be stored). It is best to think of the policy game as falling along a continuum of related phenomena ranging from sports and pastimes, educational games, policy games, man-machine simulations, and pure simulation to the mathematical theory of games (Figure 1.2).

| Educational Game | Business Game | Policy Game | Man-Machine Simulation | Game Theory |

**FIGURE 1.2 | CONTINUUM OF RELATED PHENOMENA**

Meier (1962) described gaming/simulation as "invention in reverse"; it transforms a macro-phenomenon into a workable exercise. The degree of compression in time and scale must achieve a reduction or magnification of several "orders of magnitude" as it combines experience with technology, frequently using trial-and-error methods.

There is the challenge of retaining verisimilitude while selecting one part per million. The challenge of designing an exercise is well stated by Meier & Duke (1966, p.12):

> "... the real challenge is to reproduce the essential features of a (complex system) in a tiny comprehensible package. A set of maps is not enough. Years must be compressed into hours or even minutes, the number of actors must be reduced to the handful that can be accommodated in a laboratory ..., the physical structure must be reproduced on a table top, the historical background and law must be synopsized so that it can become familiar within days or weeks, and the interaction must remain simple enough so that it can be comprehended by a single brain. This last feature is the most difficult challenge to all."

The policy exercise method uses a variety of design features to ensure a seamless integration of the final product. Both Richard E. Meier (1962) and Harold Guetzkow (1963) have emphasized simulation as an "operating representation of the central features of reality." The list of techniques from which to draw is long; however, these are central:

- The selection of critical variables
- Contrived face-to-face groups
- Role playing
- Time compression
- Scale reduction of the phenomena
- Substitution of symbolic for alpha-numeric data and vice versa
- Simplification
- The use of analogies
- Replication

A policy exercise typically involves extensive preparation and analysis of the system being addressed, setting the stage for a workshop where expert participants work through scenarios from various stakeholder perspectives. The game is made to represent the current situation in an organization; very often the policy exercise is used only once. That means that great care has to be given to the aspects of validity, reliability and credibility. The policy exercise is designed to provide a shared image of the complex system under investigation. This enables participants to communicate about the issues, appropriate strategies, and the probable impacts of policy decisions.

To be able to deliver these services to a client, the game designer has to use a well-structured design process. Given the nature of policy games, this design process must include:

- Techniques from model building (to represent the system);
- Concepts from strategy theory (how to model the strategic "space");
- Design techniques for ad hoc work environments (ergonomics; e.g. players have to be able to handle the materials and master the rules and steps of play); and
- Techniques involving arts and crafts (e.g. creating visual representations).

Armstrong and Hobson (1973) have developed a useful diagram (Figure 1.3). If simulation (Quadrant I) can be described as the reasoned reaction to complexity, gaming (Quadrant IV) can be described as the intuitive reaction to complexity.

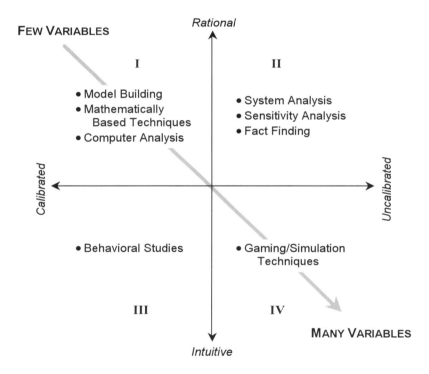

**FIGURE 1.3 | DECISION HELPING TECHNIQUES: A TYPOLOGY**

Simulation (pure Quadrant I mathematical simulation) cannot be used as a foundation for the synthesis of complex systems to invent new patterns. Simulations only allow you to repeat history – they do not permit a group to "play" with new ideas, whereas games allow a group to "invent" the future. Simulation must be exclusive in the variables it incorporates; a game is inclusive and forces players to confront these factors even though they are vague. Simulation is useful in purely scientific environments (e.g. sending humans to the moon) where the environment is data-rich and the solution must be mathematically correct.

However, in dealing with problems that have Quadrant IV characteristics, there is a risk of over-reducing complexity and oversimplifying the problem. If a Quadrant I technique is used in a Quadrant IV environment, things must be rationalized, measured, logically structured, quantified, and carried through a logical process that gives logical results. Incorrectly employed Quadrant I techniques can produce a self-fulfilling prophecy; on the other hand, a properly used policy exercise can, and often does, produce profound counterintuitive results.

### 1.5.4 Towards a Professional Gaming Paradigm

The gaming/simulation approach to strategic problem solving described in this book is a multidisciplinary and eclectic modeling methodology. It is nurtured by and uses theorems and techniques from a wide variety of professional and academic fields. Humankind has created many areas of expertise, each with its own knowledge, tools, recipes and specialized skills that are potentially relevant when designing a strategic game to analyze a perplexing strategic problem.

Figure 1.3 positions policy exercises on a continuum of modeling techniques that are reflected in the main disciplinary and professional areas the reader will encounter in this book. The book will hopefully convince the reader of the added value of the risky but stimulating adventure of crossing the borders of the many mature and fast-moving disciplines that appear in Figure 1.4.

Multidisciplinary oriented academics, like the authors, are motivated by strong ideals of enlightenment, relevance and the unification of science. However, they run the risk of falling into the trap of academic hubris or even worse, of propagating and using half-understood or obsolete knowledge from fields that are not their own disciplines. There is only one good preventive line of conduct to avoid these fallacies: dialogue with specialized colleagues: in our case, with the disciplines of organization and strategy. As we said in the introduction, we sincerely hope that this will be one of the functions of this book.

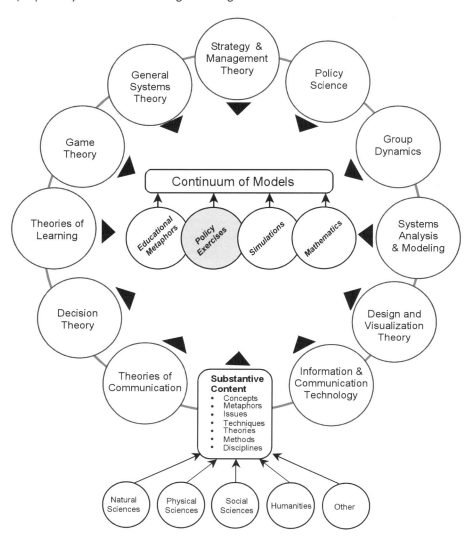

**FIGURE 1.4 | THE POLICY GAMING PARADIGM**

# Chapter 2

## Entering Uncharted Territory

### 2.1 INTRODUCTION

In this chapter, we explore the nature of macro-problems and the current literature that describes why these problems are so difficult to handle. We then try to understand what the organizational and policy literature has to offer as positive suggestions for dealing with these problems. We show that there are many relevant ideas that offer a pathway out of the struggle with the ill-structured problems which organizations sometimes cannot avoid facing. In order to bring some structure to the many ideas on how to improve the quality of decision processes, we have derived from the literature five central design criteria, albeit difficult to realize and sometimes conflicting. As explained in Section 1.3, we have labeled these criteria the five Cs for approaching macro-problems: *complexity, communication, creativity, consensus* and *commitment to action*. These criteria are further discussed and defined in Chapter 4.

In addition to this introductory section, Chapter 2 has four parts: examples of macro-problems, the nature of macro-problems, a review of the strategic process literature for dealing with macro-problems, and a summary of this chapter.

### 2.2 EXAMPLES OF MACRO-PROBLEMS

The best way to illustrate the concept of the macro-problem is to cite some examples. These illustrate that macro-problems can be quite diverse—the underlying structure can differ considerably from one situation to the next. To varying degrees, the characteristics of a complex environment are evident in each case. Perhaps of even greater significance, the examples share these additional characteristics:

- Management viewed the cited problem as being of central importance to the organization;
- Traditional methods had been tried and exhausted;
- There was an urgency to the resolution of the problem; and
- Management elected to use a policy exercise in an attempt to resolve the problem.

Chapter 3 explains eight case studies in more detail—including the exact role, structure and results of the exercises. To protect the interests of the clients, some of the case studies have been made anonymous and taken out of their precise historical context. The cases are presented in brief summary form below:

Exploring New National Healthcare Systems (see Sections 3.2 and 3.9) – Several countries in Western Europe launched new policies to dramatically change the way healthcare is delivered and financed. For example, two decades ago, proposals in the British government report "Working for Patients" described a radical change in the organization of the National Health System. The proposals mainly concerned the creation of a regional market for healthcare where agencies providing and receiving care would negotiate with one another. Regional organizations were expected to emerge in response to the new situation; they would outline the internal market. The consequences of the new market relations for care providers, consumers, competitors and local welfare were unclear. There was a danger that arrangements would be made in the regions without clearly understanding what problems might be created. In the Netherlands, the government modified the legal base and promulgated new regulations governing healthcare. This created a situation for which there was no precedent, and as a consequence, the stakeholders recognized they would be required to put aside old ways of conducting business and to negotiate manageable arrangements under the new system. Both the United Kingdom and the Netherlands faced the reality of solving these problems in real time when the new laws came into effect. In each country, the responsible agencies elected to have policy exercises created that would serve as a forum for stakeholders to gain a better understanding of how the system might work. As these exercises were used with a variety of stakeholders, it became clear that certain elements of the new regulations were unworkable. Evidence emerged that resulted in further modification of the law. Similar health management problems have been addressed in the United States using the policy exercise format.

Research and Development in a Global Company (see Section 3.3) – In response to changing international market conditions, a large U.S.-based pharmaceutical company developed a series of alternatives that would potentially be employed to protect and strengthen its competitive position. A new and profound element in its strategy was a proposal to start an R&D facility in Europe. R&D management had the task of putting the strategy into operation. There were many important considerations (whether to expand, and if so where; evaluating what new skills should be acquired; etc.) Many issues complicated the decision making: the future of healthcare in Europe, differences among the potential host countries, emerging technologies, the consequences of decentralizing R&D, and many others. The issues were controversial, and whatever option was chosen, the strategy would be expensive and risky. Yet a decision had to be taken in such a way that the senior R&D staff and the Board of Directors would accept the decision as realistic and legitimate. The company opted to use a policy exercise that would require top management to explore the issues and options in a simulated environment.

Deregulating Railroads (see Section 3.4) – This case deals with the issue of deregulation: does it pose a threat or an opportunity to a rail company? After the major
Eastern railroads failed, the U.S. Congress created a new organization, Conrail,
to consolidate the remnants and create a viable rail system in their stead. Conrail
was successful, but only due to the continuing infusion of massive amounts of
public funds. During the Reagan administration, deregulation became a central
policy, and the railroads came under scrutiny. Conrail management, faced with
this threat, employed a policy exercise with several objectives. First of all, they
needed to better understand the implications of deregulation. They then had to
formulate a policy in response to the pending changes. Finally, the company
needed to influence various stakeholders with regard to the type of legislation
that would be passed. Participating in the exercise allowed them to envision new
opportunities under modified deregulation legislation. The exercise was used to
lobby members of Congress and enlist the support of the management of competing transport systems (trucking and air).

The Reorganization of a Federal Ministry (see Section 3.5) – In the mid-1980s,
the U.S. Department of Defense (DOD) was facing budget cuts and reorganization. The Office of the Secretary of Defense (OSD), which resides within the
DOD, was required to undergo a review of its structure and organization. This
review process addressed the appropriateness of the functions of the OSD; it also
considered alternative forms of organizational structure. The three major
branches of service (Army, Navy, and Air Force) produced and submitted plans
reflecting their own vision as to how the reorganization should be undertaken,
but there was little overlap among them. These plans were thick documents
reflecting the primary need to protect old positions rather than to envision any
significantly new organizational scheme. A policy exercise was commissioned
that would allow for a comparison of the three proposals. Each branch of service
had an opportunity to present its plan through the policy exercise; after further
discussion, the exercise was again used to negotiate a single compromise plan.

Cultural Change within the Technical Components Industry (see Section 3.6) –
A large Technical Components firm elected to spin off a major division as a new
entity. The belief was that the division, as embedded historically in the parent
company, was inefficient and a drain on scarce resources. It was believed that,
once established as a free-standing firm, the division would be able to compete
directly with the other major suppliers. An independent company with a new
organizational structure was formed. This was a major undertaking requiring
top-to-bottom restructuring of management style, the acquisition of new facilities, and the sorting of employees into those who stayed behind and those who
would be part of the new company. There was no experience with creating and
conveying the vision of the new management style. This client commissioned a
policy game to assist in this effort.

Managing Information for a Governmental Social Program (see Section 3.7) – Within the Dutch Ministry of Social Affairs and Employment (1986), the Directorate for Complementary Social Provisions (CSV) was entrusted with the Social Employment Program. This program incorporated more than 200 social workplaces in which approximately 70,000 disabled people worked. The program regulated the money flow and had to adapt the program to changes in overall national policy priorities. Management made proposals for improvement in the efficiency and effectiveness of the execution of the program and attempted to relate program activities to the other programs in the social security field. The CSV maintained an information system that would support the introduction of a radically different system of budget financing; the quality of this system had always been a heavily debated subject. The client was convinced that a new and usable information system would only be created if central government started an open dialogue with representatives in the field, something he believed had not been done enough in the past. A policy exercise was selected to achieve this objective.

Science Policy for the Great Lakes Ecosystem (see Section 3.8) – The Great Lakes, located between Canada and the United States, represent the largest body of fresh water in the world. These lakes, in combination with the St. Lawrence Seaway and other connecting bodies of water, are of global significance. The client for this project was the International Joint Commission on the Great Lakes (IJC); a cooperative institution of the Canadian and U.S. governments, which is responsible for recommending research policy. The IJC adopted an ecosystems approach to establishing research priorities. This required a framework for discussing and evaluating priorities, an interdisciplinary science-policy dialogue that included both human and natural systems. The IJC held a series of meetings in an effort to determine how best to respond to these concerns. As a result, the IJC decided to commission a policy exercise that included two elements: an ecosystem game/simulation and a policy seminar. In combination, the two instruments aimed to improve communication among groups in the policy and research communities about the needs within the Great Lakes ecosystem. The objective was to ensure that the establishment of research policy was communicated as a palatable and effective process to the appropriate stakeholders.

## 2.3 ON THE NATURE OF MACRO-PROBLEMS

### 2.3.1 What is a Policy Problem?
The title of this subsection seems to ask a trivial question, but that is not the case. This book is about policy and strategy and therefore deals with a very distinct type of problem that managers and policy makers are sometimes forced to address. Not every problem is a policy problem, and a cynic might observe that not every policy concern deserves the label "problem."

What then is the distinction between problems and policy problems? A problem refers to an undesired state of affairs or expected future development. A problem may or may not become a policy problem; it reaches this status when the leadership of an organization sees the problem as a serious threat. Those who see a problem as a policy problem assume that one can or should do something about the undesired state of affairs or prevent and/or react against the unattractive development. So, the assumption behind a policy problem is that it can be influenced. Apart from this characteristic, Dunn (1981) points at five other important characteristics of (policy) problems:

- Problems are artificial, they are man-made, and they only exist after a process of recognition;
- Problems are subjective and pluriform: defining something as a problem depends strongly on and thus varies with human values, norms and perceptions;
- Problems are changeable or unstable; this is true both because the societies or organizations in which the problems are discovered change, and because the values and norms that drove the problem definition evolve. One should keep in mind that the initial solution to a problem may not be valid indefinitely; furthermore, a solution to the problem may come so long after the problem formulation that the problem itself may have already changed;
- Problems are often interdependent: problems in one functional area or policy field often have strong connections with problems in other sectors and functions (e.g. R&D and manufacturing or ecology and economy); and
- Policy problems are often a selective redefinition of problems in terms of the options available as seen by the person defining them. Managers and public policy makers have the tendency to define a problem in such a way that it can be attacked with instruments that are readily available (e.g. an environmental problem becomes a taxation and/or public education problem).

### 2.3.2 Characteristics of a Macro-Problem

Macro-problems have all the characteristics listed above; it is important to keep them in mind when reading the other sections in this chapter. Although it is difficult to define a macro-problem with precision, they are frequently associated with certain characteristics. The following list is typical and it represents many of the factors that made the problems described in Section 2.2 perplexing and difficult to deal with. Of course, a given problem will have only a sub-set of these characteristics:

The environment of the problem:
Accelerating technological innovation
Complex, turbulent and intrusive institutional environment
Continuing concern for the quality of performance
Increasing economic and resource dependencies

Shifting population dynamics
Changing the socio-political context of decision making

The definition or understanding of the problem:
Complexity and interconnectedness
Concepts cannot be easily defined or mathematically represented
Multi-dimensionality
No satisfactory model exists (either conceptual or pragmatic)
Qualitative nature of the variables encountered
Quantifiable data not available and expensive to collect
Relationships among the variables are ambiguous and unknown
Subjectivity (e.g. people are not neutral information processors or cognitive machines)

The actors involved:
A great variety of players and interactions
Need to convey image to outside group
Conflicts among groups of people should be expected

The goals and objectives:
Ambiguous, lack of clarity of goals
Value dilemmas
Conflicting objectives

Necessary or potential actions:
Future orientation
High risk - high reward
No clear paradigm for action
No single correct answer
Precedent and the lessons of the past are of limited value
Unknown sequence of actions
Need for learning a problem-solving style

The outcome:
Unpredictability or low ability to predict
Uncertainty about the outcome of decisions

### 2.3.3 Positioning Macro-Problems

A macro-problem typically will combine several of these characteristics. In trying to define what a macro-problem is, many authors have discovered that the most productive approach to understanding these kinds of problems is to make clear how they differ from other problems. This has resulted in several categorizations or typologies of policy problems.

The term macro-problem, as used throughout this book, is derived from the work of Cartwright (1987). He addresses this concept by differentiating problems into four categories. In his article, Cartwright presents four categories: simple, compound, complex, and macro-problems; defining each of the categories as follows:

Simple Problems are "fully closed in scope and detail; all variables identified and response to intervention is predictable."

Compound Problems are "a collection of simple problems, loosely connected." The individual parts of the problem are well understood but the relationships among them cannot be anticipated.

Complex Problems are "inherently subjective in nature ... plagued by imprecision." Their solution requires "a procedure that puts less emphasis on analyzing and evaluating the problem and more emphasis on securing consensus among the interests involved." Usually the full scope of these problems is reasonably well understood, but the details are not subject to full investigation nor is anyone able to predict the response to intervention. These problems need a procedure that puts less emphasis on analyzing and more on securing consensus.

Cartwright gives an excellent characterization of the fourth category, macro-problems, by the following statements (Cartwright, 1987, p. 95):
- "neither their full scope nor details are understood
- ...connections exist among the various factors
- ...useful to focus on them collectively
- ...defined by a focus rather than a boundary
- ...flexibility and adaptiveness are essential for dealing with macro-problems
- ...require a heuristic approach..."
- "Macro-problems tend to have unintended consequences, side effects, unexpected spin-offs," etc. The dilemma is that we have to simplify it, but we worry how far we can "afford to simplify a problem ... in order to make it manageable."

Many other authors have recognized and addressed the phenomenon of the macro-problem. A frequently quoted typology was created by Mitroff and Sagasti, (1973). In this typology, the concept of a macro-problem is defined as "ill-structured."

Figure 2.1 shows that macro-problems are ill-structured in several ways. Many decision makers are involved, there is conflict on values and objectives, and the number of alternative strategies or actions considered potentially relevant is unlimited. In addition, the possible outcome of these alternatives is unknown and there is little insight into the occurrence probability of certain outcomes. Figure 2.1 also makes clear that the distinctions are a matter of degree: a problem can be more or less ill-structured.

| ELEMENT | STRUCTURE OF PROBLEM | | |
|---|---|---|---|
| | Well-Structured | Moderately-Structured | Ill-Structured |
| Decision Maker(s) | one or few | limited | many |
| Alternatives | limited | limited | unlimited |
| Utilities (Values) | consensus | consensus | conflict |
| Outcomes | certainty or risk | uncertainty | unknown |
| Probability | calculable | incalculable | incalculable |

**FIGURE 2.1 | MACRO-PROBLEMS ARE ILL-STRUCTURED PROBLEMS**
*(source: Dunn, 1981)*

Rittel and Webber (1972 pp. 236-37) describe the principal properties of wicked problems in contrast to tame problems. Wicked problems have distinguishing characteristics and we quote them:

- "[T]here is no definitive formulation of a wicked problem" ... Therefore "... you cannot understand the problem without solving it, and solving the problem is the same as understanding it."
- "Wicked problems have no stopping rule ...the process of solving the problem is identical with the process of understanding it..."
- "Solutions to wicked problems are not true-or-false, but good-or-bad." ... "many parties ... are entitled to judge the solutions ..."
- There is no ... "ultimate test of a solution..." "... any solution ... will generate waves of consequences over an extended ... period of time."
- "Every solution to a wicked problem is a 'one-shot operation.'"... "But, normally, ... a host of potential solutions arise..."
- Wicked problems do have "an innumerable ... set of possible solutions ..."
- "Every wicked problem is essentially unique."
- "...every wicked problem can be considered a symptom of another problem..."
- "[D]iscrepancies... can be explained in numerous ways."
- [Whereas] "... the scientific community does not blame its members for postulating hypotheses that are later refuted..." ... "the planner has no right to be wrong" ...
- "...members of an organization tend to see the problems on a level below their own level." [but] "If ... the problem is attacked on too low a level ... [it may make] ... things worse, because it may become more difficult to deal with higher problems."
- "[D]iscrepancies... can be explained in numerous ways. As a consequence, ... the analyst's 'world view' is the strongest determining factor in ... resolving a wicked problem."

Several authors emphasize *the need for a proper overview* when addressing a macro-problem. They warn that failure in this regard results in decisions that will ultimately make matters worse.

### 2.3.4 The Challenge Raised by Macro-Problems

Macro-problems are increasingly important as our world grows more complex. Traditional methods of investigation have resulted in piecemeal observations, premature conclusions and advice that proves inadequate for the resolution of macro-problems. In response to these circumstances, recent decades have seen an evolution of new approaches to address the intricacies of these complex environments. These methodologies seek both to improve the scope of vision of the investigators as well as their ability to communicate in both scientific and policy environments.

Herbert Simon (1969) wrote an early but still inspiring pamphlet (*The Sciences of the Artificial*) on the need to broaden the scope of traditional policy-oriented research (i.e. Operations Research) in order to help managers handle the wicked or ill-structured problems they face. Simon's book contains definitions and a history for Artificial Intelligence (AI) and Operations Research (OR). Simon suggests an incorporation of AI tools into the OR method applied in Management Science (MS) especially for "ill-structured, knowledge-rich, non-quantitative decision domains that characterize the work of top management and that characterize the great policy decisions that face our society" (p. 8). Simon addresses the "non-quantitative equal qualitative" decisions which correlate to the characteristics of macro-problems. Operations Research is defined as the application of optimization techniques to the solution of complex problems that can be expressed in real numbers (a numerical analytical approach).

Artificial Intelligence is defined as:

> "... the application of methods of heuristic search to the solution of complex problems that defy the mathematics of optimization, contain non-quantifiable components, involve large knowledge bases including knowledge expressed in natural language, incorporate the discovery and design of alternatives of choice, and admit ill-specified goals and constraints" (Simon, 1969, pp.10,11).

For some kinds of complex problems, both analytical and descriptive methods are necessary to achieve progress towards a solution. That means that the methods used to solve a problem have to be chosen according the problem type and not vice versa.

> "We ... should aspire to increase the ... kit of tools that can be applied to the kinds of ill-structured, knowledge-rich, non-quantitative decision domains

that characterize the work of top management and that characterize the great policy decisions on peace, energy, and environment that face our society" (Simon, 1969, p. 15).

Ultimately, any successful problem-solving methodology must serve to integrate all characteristics of macro or wicked problems. Certain problems exist in today's world that cannot be resolved using traditional methods. These macro-problems demand a fresh understanding and require a new approach for their intelligent resolution.

Rhyne (1975, p. 16) made the point that "the arenas within which partial solutions are illusory have grown remarkably in subject, scope, spatial extent, and time." In many cases, there is evidence that these macro-problems have come about because the original conception of the problem was framed improperly (e.g. conflict among warring nations has deep roots; a long string of interactions precede various current crises). To cite Rhyne: "Continents are just as apt to be the stage as countries are. Knowing the present and the ... past no longer will suffice, since change demands equivalent concern for the future ..." Rhyne's purpose was "to stimulate exploration of the means whereby appreciation of complex wholes may be more quickly and more reliably told to others" (op. cit. pp. 16, 17).

Macro-problems are by nature ill-defined and fuzzy. Typically, they "grow like Topsy," there are seldom sharp lines of distinction which indicate when an organization has progressed from routine complexity into this more troublesome type of problem. As a consequence, it is common for various traditional techniques to be employed; these may repeatedly reveal piecemeal "solutions" before the true nature of the macro-problem is understood. This results in sequential actions being taken which serve to aggravate the management situation. Because the problem is not clearly understood, these actions have the effect of forcing the organization to "back into a corner."

Donald Schon (1986) has important things to say about what a discipline can learn from the decision making styles of experienced professionals. The "artistic processes [of practitioners] ... do not meet the prevailing criteria of rigorous practice." ... When "competent practitioners recognize the pattern in a maze of symptoms ... they do something for which they cannot give a complete or even a reasonably accurate description. By defining rigor only in terms of technical rationality, we exclude ... much of what competent practitioners do" (Schon, p. 231). There are "signs of a growing crisis of confidence in the professions" because of "the complexity of phenomena" that professionals are called upon to address (p. 232): "action under uncertainty of conditions..., irreducible residue of art in professional practice," and "problem solving [vs.] ... problem finding" (p. 233).

"The doctrine of technical rationality promulgated in the universities infects the young professional with a hunger for technique. Yet professionals who confine their practice to the rigorous applications of research based technique would find ... [they could not] work on the most important problems ... [nor] practice in the real-world...." They will have to gain experience through trial and error, muddling through and burdened by a nagging sense of inferiority (Schon, p. 238).

## 2.4 Towards Quality Strategy Processes

A dedicated scientific approach is required for addressing macro-problems. Simon (1969) suggested a form of problem solving that allows for the use of heuristics instead of optimization, because macro-problems defy the assumptions of classical operations research. Rhyne addresses two ideas. In the tradition of General Systems Theory, he asks for problem structuring methods that can help us understand the gestalt or the "wholeness" of macro-problems. At the same time, he brings forward the need for new forms of communications (a new "language") which allow groups of individuals to share and jointly explore their gestalt conceptions of macro-problems. Schon helps us to think about the kind of attitude and skill one needs – more that of the mature practitioner than of the purely analytically trained.

In this section, we look for related ideas which can help us find the proper characteristics of a methodology for dealing with macro-problems. First, we try to collect the main insights from the evolution of a body of knowledge which can best be labeled "strategic planning theory" (Subsection 2.4.1). In the conceptual parts of this book, we underscore the differences between planning/policy development in private organizations and public organizations. There are different styles and strategies between organizations working in public or private environments; however, the case studies in Chapters 3 illustrate that there are also a host of similarities between the public and the private sectors when they struggle with macro-problems. The type of strategic problem solving that we witness around macro-problems is always "multiparty collaboration," even when a policy issue can be dealt with primarily by actors from a single organization. We call on the network theory of organizations to lay a conceptual foundation for the proper process approach to macro-problems whether they are within or between organizations. In Subsections 2.4.2 and 2.4.3, we concentrate on publications which try to understand the causes and dynamics of "great policy disasters and decision failures." The purpose is to find suggestions on how these disasters could have been avoided.

### 2.4.1 Learning from Strategic Planning

There are many lessons on strategic planning documented in the literature; some traditional, some more recent. It is not our purpose here to summarize the entire relevant literature; such would be a major research effort in itself. It would bring us to fields like corporate strategy theory, planning theory, organizational change, decision theory, operations research and the forecasting and futuring disciplines. Instead, we limit ourselves to describing those trends in the literature that we think are most relevant for the types of problems addressed in this book.

We start with a notion that has been in the literature for a long time: the concept of complexity. Most intensively developed in the schools that see strategy making as rational problem solving, the complexity of macro-problems was first approached as an analytically complex puzzle. Operations research, decision analysis, systems analysis, econometrics and many other applied disciplines have built up a vast experience and created many tools to help unravel the analytical complexity of macro-problems. On the other hand, a rational approach alone is not sufficient and sometimes even harmful when dealing with macro-problems. The quotations from Simon, Rhyne and Schon in Section 2.3.4 illustrate part of this debate.

The most difficult characteristic when analyzing the complexity of macro-problems is undoubtedly uncertainty. Explanations on the causes of problems, extrapolation of trends, assessments of impacts, statements about long-term consequences of policy decisions; in fact, all the cognitive statements concerning macro-problems can only be produced with a varying, but usually high degree of uncertainty. For any statement about a macro-problem by an expert, another expert can be found to doubt his colleague's position or contradict it. Uncertainty and controversy go hand in hand, when the scientific debate is accompanied by conflicts about norms, values and objectives.

Rip (1991) points out that there is relatively little difference between internal scientific controversies and science-induced organizational or societal controversies. The difference between uncertainty and risk illustrates this interconnection. Uncertainty refers to lack of knowledge, while risk adds an element of valuation to uncertainty. Risk is a function of uncertainty and the degree to which the uncertain events are desirable or undesirable. Achieving closure of a societal or intra-organizational controversy by consensus or compromise and closure of debates on scientific uncertainty are not independent processes. They influence each other and are often inseparable.

The more controversy on knowledge and values, the more energy it takes to organize a robust knowledge household around a policy issue (Rip, 1991). The term "knowledge household" refers to the system of arguments, claims, interests and values on which policy options are based. In the scientific literature on policy, this same concept is defined with several terms, e.g. cognitive map, mental map, theory of practice, policy theory and mental model. Following Vennix & Geurts (1987) and Vennix (1990), we consider these concepts synonyms.

It is possible to consider a policy theory both a characteristic of individuals and of a collective. For example, we speak of a policy theory of a manager and the policy theory of an interest group. It is hard to formulate general rules about the relationship between individual and collective policy theories. Hoogerwerf puts forward the hypothesis that an actor's policy theory will have a bigger influence on the collective policy theory and on the resulting policy decision, if the actor, when compared to other actors, is more goal oriented, informed and powerful with respect to the prevailing issue (Hoogerwerf, 1992). One way or another, a process of integration and exchange of the actors' policy theories takes place. The outcome is a collective policy theory that feeds partial decisions in the various stages of the policy design process.

This line of thinking about complexity has a strong element of futuring in it. Quite often, as a reaction to relatively uninspiring rational analyses, there have been schools in strategy theory that stress imagination and creativity. "All great things in our society first happened in somebody's imagination" (Astrid Lindgren). "The best way to predict the future is to invent it" (J. Scully). The "rediscovery" of this need for creative thinking received a very strong push in many markets when innovation became a key competitive factor. New techniques such as brainstorming, lateral thinking, synectics and many others are now widely used in organizations all over the world.

The creativity element is dominant in Henry Mintzberg's famous article "Crafting Strategy" (Mintzberg, 1987). Mintzberg's analysis of "the rise and fall of strategic planning" argues that rational planning is not a correct empirical description of how strategists make decisions. There is ample empirical evidence that strategy making is a craft rather than a science, and that the decision maker's tacit knowledge and intuition are as important explanatory factors for the outcome of a decision as the planner's rational strategy.

Many authors on strategy and planning have interpreted some of the obvious weaknesses of rational planning by stressing the need for step-by-step learning. In 1973, Don Michael published his impressive critique on the dominant rational planning tradition under the title *On Planning to Learn and Learning to Plan*. This book contained a message that came too early, but it is certainly a remarkable indicator of a new wave of thinking that Michael's book received a second edition in 1998, 25 years after it was published! Another authoritative spokesman of the learning view of the planning and strategy process is former Shell strategist Arie de Geus. His 1988 article "Planning as Learning" makes clear that policy analysis of complex problems should allow step-by-step learning.

A new view on a complex and uncertain problem is not created in a short span of time. Therefore, the methods should be flexible to the extent that they approach a problem in several learning cycles, allowing participants to adapt the problem definition, the search process, and/or the planned implementation process. This means that the analytical policy process should be participatory: the relevant stakeholders in a policy process should be emphatically engaged in all phases of a long-range policy study. As De Geus rightly puts it: "The only relevant learning in an organization is the learning done by those people who have the power to act" (De Geus, 1988, p. 70). According to De Geus, planning and learning are synonyms and this means that decision-oriented study of macro-problems should be participatory.

There are several other trains of thought that result in the conclusion that planning should involve communication and participation. One is the emergence of the concept of the network organization. Simply speaking, there are intra- and inter-organizational implications of this theory. The de-layering of organizations, the professionalization of work, the virtual organization, and the need to draw on, develop and concentrate on core competencies: this all leads to the idea that strategy processes should draw on the wisdom of many in the organization. In a flat professional organization, every worker is a strategist because the center has to rely on the judgment of the independent professional (alone or in a small team) to realize the collective ambition. In a professional organization, the strategic information comes in via the professional and has to be pieced together in a bottom-up process.

In his extensive review of the literature on strategic processes, Hart (1992) shows how the literature about imagination and creativity has become linked with the need for involvement and commitment. Hart has determined that, as a reaction to the limited possibilities of rational planning, a new thinking has emerged about the task and function of top management in strategic management. He states: "thus, rather than seeking to be comprehensive – the ideal of rationality – top managers work to create a general sense of purpose and direction that will guide the actions taken by organizational members..." He continues: "As part of the vision, top managers must capture the imagination of organizational members... Accordingly, commitment through involvement has emerged as an important ingredient in the strategy-making literature of the past decade" (Hart, 1992, pp. 350-51).

The *intra-organizational* change literature states that the more professional an organization becomes, the more important it is to involve many members of the organization as early as possible in the strategy process, because without this, no successful implementation of new strategic ideas will occur (Weggeman, 1995).

The *inter-organizational* literature stresses that, to an increasing extent, the borders between companies disappear because of revolutionary changes in technol-

ogy and new demands on the flexibility of purchasing/manufacturing/distribu-
tion chains. The popularity of the concept of "corporate governance" indicates
that traditional relations between private organizations and a wide variety of
stakeholders are quickly changing and that corporations must develop many new
forms of stakeholder participation.

The borderlines between public and private organizations are modified as a consequence of fundamental changes in the way the societal function of "governance" is perceived. Inter-organization or network theory has explained that, in
modern society, policy programs are the product of complex interaction among
organizations, each seeking to influence the collectively binding decisions that
impact their interests. "Policy networks" have thus become a central concept in
modern policy science (Boons, 1992). Key elements in this theory are:

- Actors in networks are organizations, not individuals;
- Actors pursue different strategies based on different interests and power
  resources; networks produce policy programs: a series of binding decisions for
  all network actors;
- No single actor can control the formulation and implementation of the resulting program; and
- The distribution of power, the ownership of strategic information and sources
  of knowledge and the formal and informal rules of the network are decisive
  for the outcome.

The more both public and private strategy making has become recognized to be
a form of multiparty collaboration, the more attention has appeared in the literature addressing the fact that strategy making involves value trade-off and consensus building. With each strategic decision, the power balance between the
negotiating parties is at stake.

To what conclusions on the nature of strategic problem solving do the insights in
this section lead us? A useful and valid way of summarizing this section is to
refer to the insights collected during a very extensive empirical study at the
University of Bradford in the U.K. The study is described in Hickson et al., 1986.
Hickson's team followed and compared strategic decision making processes in
private, public and not-for-profit organizations. They concluded that the rational
problem-solving model of strategy making is not an adequate predictive theory of
what goes on in the organizations studied. They conclude that the traditional
problem-solving rationality of a decision is only one of the factors required to
explain decision making. Many decisions that are rationally correct are not taken.
Also, managers are "rational" in more than one way. Their decisions also have to
find enough political support to be implemented. Hickson et al. call this the
interest-accommodating rationality of strategic decision making.

But there is more. Many decisions that are rational from a problem-solving perspective and for which "political clout" can be achieved are not taken for very "rational" reasons. Governing and managing is about keeping an organization or a network intact. Managing means that you may not always use your power freely to push an individual decision through, because soon you may again have to work with the victims of that decision. The culture that governs according to the "way we handle things in our company" limits the degrees of freedom at the top. Hickson et al. call this the "rationality of control": the decision should be taken in such a way that the social fabric is not damaged more than necessary, or preferably, that the decision makes the network of relations stronger.

In a limited sense of the concept, strategic decisions are irrational, for they are the product of three simultaneous rationalities: each strategic decision is a result of weighing the problem solving and interest-accommodating rationalities with the rationality of control. However, the problem-solving rationality is certainly an important variable, as Hickson et al. have found. The search for this side of good decision making explains many of the steps taken in a strategic process. Hickson et al. use the label "aspiration": the aspiration to be rational from a problem-solving perspective is a strong explanatory factor in the cases the University of Bradford team has studied.

For any form of strategic analysis or planning support to be successful, it has to support the mental processes of policy makers who play this "three-dimensional optimizing game." They must assimilate new knowledge in the form of scenarios or trends, the careful ex ante analysis of alternatives, and the use of models to support logical reasoning. All these rational instruments on the analysis/policy interface should help to enable this three-dimensional optimizing process, this internalization of knowledge that Caplan (1983) calls "knowledge conversion." From the point of view of problem-solving rationality, strategic decision making will always concern limited rationality.

### 2.4.2 Learning From Decision and Planning Disasters

There is a large literature, both empirical and conceptual, that tries to understand complex decision making by studying situations of failure and disaster. For our further understanding on what it takes to handle macro-problems, we have selected a few publications on failure and disaster, which we considered inspiring and complementary.

An excellent contribution is the work of Dietrich Dörner (1996). As a cognitive psychologist, he explores in his book, *The Logic of Failure*, the problems of error in complex decision situations from the perspective of the individual decision maker. His book has a dual significance for our work. First, Dörner contributes to the understanding of why we so often fail in complex situations. Second, he uses computer-based games as his main research tool.

Dörner has conducted many experiments in which he invited a wide variety of subjects (both experts and novices) to manage, both individually and in small teams, simulated cities and regions. His subjects had to focus their policies, set goals and define objectives, and make appropriate decisions. They were offered many sources of information (to the point that they could drown themselves in data). Dörner recorded their behavior and results. At the same time, he taped and analyzed the deliberations of the decision makers (he asked all subjects to think aloud). In this way, he built up an enormous database. By comparing relatively successful subjects with the styles and behavior of those who created disaster and crisis, Dörner was able to make many interesting observations about what causes failure and how to prevent it.

The simulated systems into which Dörner put his subjects all have much in common with the problem areas we study:

- Their complexity is derived from the presence of many interrelated variables;
- The systems are only partially transparent: the subjects cannot observe everything they would like to see;
- All development is independent of external control: they follow their own internal dynamic; and
- The systems are so complex that the people who have to govern them do not fully understand the systems, and even make false assumptions about them.

Dörner (1996, p. 37) sees these four characteristics—complexity, lack of transparence, internal dynamics and incomplete or incorrect understanding of the system—as basic to all "intricate situations in which individuals are called upon to plan and act carefully." In a separate case study, he shows the strong comparisons of his "gamed problems" and the "logic of failure" he finds in them, with the well-documented characteristics and decision failures that resulted in the Chernobyl nuclear disaster.

People have difficulty in all aspects of making decisions concerning these "intricate problems": setting goals, handling information, developing models, dealing with time sequences and planning for action. Dörner sees four basic causes or human limitations that explain this "logic of failure":

- Human thinking is slow. This is not to say that our unconscious information processing is slow, because it is not. But: "our conscious thought, the very 'tool' we need to deal with unknown realities, functions rather slowly and is not capable of processing many different pieces of information at the same time" (Dörner, 1996, p. 186). So, we have to economize. We have to leave out certain steps in the process of thinking. We use known situations as analogies for unknown ones; in short, we simplify as much as possible.

- It is very human to try and preserve a positive view of our own competencies. "Without some expectation of success, we are unlikely to act at all and will rather resign ourselves to letting fate take its course" (op. cit. p. 188). This need for "self protection" is at the root of many decision failures, e.g. the tendency to solve only the problems we know we can solve and avoid those we cannot.

- "Not only is our conscious thinking slow, but the speed with which the storage system of the human memory can absorb new material is also relatively slow. Human memory may have a very large capacity, but its 'inflow capacity' is rather small" (op. cit. p. 189). We can use very little of the information that we see in a temporal configuration unless we can form a picture of that configuration. For Dörner, this explains in part the ad hoc behavior of some of his subjects and other subjects' obsession with the status quo.

- "We don't think about problems we don't have. Why, indeed, should we?" (op. cit. p. 189). However, the complicated systems Dörner's subjects are dealing with demand attention for possible side effects. We are, as Dörner puts it, "captives of the moment," focusing only on immediately pressing problems.

Is there a way out of this "logic of failure?" What are the possibilities for improvement? As a true experimental psychologist, Dörner looks for experimental answers to this question. He compares the simulation results of students (laymen) with experienced practitioners who held management positions in business and industry (practitioners). None of these people had experience in the content matter of the game (managing a Sahel region). In terms of almost all the criteria Dörner applied, the practitioners created better results. Dörner finds his observations corroborated by other studies; older participants with more experience in planning and decision making performed better.

Dörner can find only one explanation for this. He calls it operative intelligence: "the knowledge that individuals have about the use of their intellectual skills." Practitioners not only know the rules about how to behave in complex situations, they also know when to apply the right rules at the right time. Dörner refers here to two concepts that are very relevant for this book. One is the concept of the reflective practitioner, which was so eloquently introduced by Donald Schon (1986): practitioners reflect on a situation and build up a repertoire of appropriate responses. The second important concept that Dörner refers to here is "contingency." There is no one best way of handling a complex situation. There "is no universally applicable rule, no magic wand, that we can apply to every situation and all the structures we find in the real world. Our job is to think of, and then do, the right things at the right time and in the right way. There may be rules for accomplishing this, but these rules are local – they are to a large extent dictated by specific circumstances. And that means in turn that there are a great many rules" (op. cit. p. 192).

In the following chapters of this book, we show how much we support Dörner's ideas. What he observes for decision making in general is of course also true for one aspect of strategic decision making, that is, the design of processes to assist decision makers. We argue that each policy exercise will have to be created in a way that does justice to the specific system and policy issues at hand. We provide many rules (such as the ones connected with our five Cs), but Dörner's message is that one needs experience to select the right rules at the right time. That is why this book pays so much attention to practical case studies as one way of stimulating the operative intelligence of the reader in designing effective policy games.

We would do injustice to Dörner and the discipline of gaming if we did not conclude this discussion of Dörner's work with his views on gaming as a tool for decision makers.

> "We must learn to think in systems. We must learn that in complex systems we cannot do only one thing. Whether we want it or not, any step we take will affect many other things. We must learn to cope with side effects. We must understand that the effects of our decisions may turn up in places we never expected to see them surface."

> "Can we possibly learn all this? We can't in the real world, where expanses of time and space hide our mistakes from us. Hence my plea for simulations. Time passes quickly in a computer, and distance does not exist. A simulation can make apparent the consequences of our decisions and plans; in this way we can develop a greater sensitivity to reality."

> "[S]imulations ... can place people in the same kind of crisis again and again to hone their sensibilities to specific features of such situations."

> "We have the opportunity today to undertake this kind of learning and teaching. Make-believe has always been an important way to prepare ourselves for the real thing. We should use this method in a focused manner. We now have far better tools for this purpose than we had ever before. We should take advantage of them. Is that a frivolous idea? Playing games in dead earnest? Anyone who thinks play is nothing but play and dead earnest nothing but dead earnest hasn't understood either one" (all quotations: op. cit. p. 199).

Dörner's contribution to the study of macro-problems is strongly influenced by his discipline: cognitive psychology. His focus is on the limitations of the individual decision maker in understanding and governing policy issues in complex systems.

The approach to understanding policy fiascoes as found in the policy science literature differs strongly from Dörner's, and it has other interesting insights to offer in the development of our thinking on the role of policy games. In an extensive review of the literature, the Dutch policy scientists Bovens and 't Hart (1996) show that policy theory on fiascoes is, if anything, very pluralistic. Even the definition of a policy outcome as a fiasco (bad management) or a misfortune (just bad luck) is often a matter of controversy and perspective.

From the literature, Bovens and 't Hart develop four ways to order popular explanations of fiascoes. Figure 2.2 shows four different policy situations that follow from the combination of the variables "foreseeability" and "controllability" of relevant contingencies. In Type I situations, mismanagement and policy failure are the clear causes of the disappointing results. In the other cells of the typology, several arguments of misfortune may be heard and may also be valid.

| Type I | Type II |
|---|---|
| foreseeable/controllable contingencies | foreseeable/uncontrollable contingencies |
| Type III | Type IV |
| unforeseeable contingencies | unforeseeable/uncontrollable contingencies |

**FIGURE 2.2 | A TYPOLOGY OF MISFORTUNES IN GOVERNANCE**
*(Source: Bovens and 't Hart, 1996)*

Bovens and 't Hart (op. cit. p. 87) use a game-related expression to characterize the nature of policy making in the Type II, III and IV situations: under these conditions, policy making resembles "fuzzy gambling." The authors quote Dror when he says that, in these cases, policy making is nothing but a "choice between bundles of ill-defined and ill-definable uncertainties and ignorance, with the aim of influencing the probability of alternative possible futures" (Dror, 1986, pp. 167-168, quoted in Bovens & 't Hart, 1996, p. 87).

The Dutch policy scientists' study seems to result in a relativistic and rather pessimistic view on the role of policy making in society and the limitations of policy analysis in assisting policy making on wicked problems. However, that is only part of the truth. The authors cannot avoid using the sobering lessons from the past to take some distance from "the new apostles of success and excellencies." They do not want to be presumptuous and write an "operational guide on how to avoid policy fiascoes." That is why what these careful authors say about the position of policy analysts in the debates on wicked problems is so interesting. Following Majone (1989) and more specifically Schon and Rein (1994), Bovens and 't Hart argue for a more "comprehensive logic of discursive or communicative policy design." Let us quote their argument:

> "There is a case to be made that many policy fiascoes are a form of post-hoc 'policy back talk' by stakeholders and communities who found that policies inimical to some of their deep-rooted myths, beliefs and values had been imposed on them. In this view, policies that solicit opposition and controversy that is left unarticulated or ignored during policy design will eventually come to haunt their makers during implementation. Policy fiascoes are nothing more and nothing less than a manifestation of the 'rhetoric of reaction.' Fiascoes of this kind might be prevented when the design process is opened up to become more iterative, evolving around continuous dialogue about what the problems to be solved look like and what strategies for resolution solicit the necessary agreement" (Bovens & 't Hart, 1996, p. 156).

### 2.4.3 Why Decisions Fail

There is probably no one in empirical organization research who has studied strategic decisions longer than Paul C. Nutt. In 2002, he published his account on *Why decisions fail*. The recommendations in his book are based on a database of 400 systematic case studies (which took him 20 years to complete). These case studies focus on important decisions of top managers in private, public and nonprofit organizations in the U.S., Canada and Europe. In this particular book, Nutt has taken fifteen descriptions of decision debacles from his database. Reading this material is a constant "aha" experience, because all the dramatic stories became public and were widely discussed in the media. And for some, history seems to keep repeating itself. The reader comes across stories like Shell's Brent Spar disposal, the Waco siege, the collapse of Barings Bank and the North East U.S. blackout of 2003.

*Why decisions fail* will be a discouraging reading experience for some. The conclusions seem so easily recognizable, but decision makers keep on making the same mistakes. Nutt finds three types of blunders in his cases: "Half of the decisions in organizations fail, making failure far more prevalent than previously thought. Blunders that lead to failure stem from using failure-prone practices, making premature commitments, and spending time and money on the wrong things. Failure can be directly linked to the actions of the decision makers" (Nutt, 2002, p. 22). And also: "Debacles follow a chain of events that unfold as blunders create traps and traps bring about failure" (op. cit. p. 23).

Nutt finds that, by making the above-mentioned blunders, managers get caught in one or more of seven traps, and this provokes more blunders and this creates disaster. The seven traps are:

- The failure to reconcile conflicting claims;
- The failure to manage the forces stirred up by a decision;
- Providing ambiguous direction;
- Pushing for the quick fix: limited search and no innovation;
- The misuse of evaluation for defense and justification;
- Ignoring the win-lose ethical dilemmas; and
- Failing to reflect and learn from the past.

Within the context of our book, two of Nutt's analysis points on how to avoid decision traps stand out:

- His description of decision processes that prove to prevent failure; and
- The intriguing concept of "perverse incentives."

Regarding the first point, Nutt sharply contrasts two processes, one failure prone and the other successful. All failures prove to follow an "idea imposition process": "A claim suggested by a powerful claimant is adopted. The arena of action implied by the claim is never questioned, and the idea called for by the claim or offered by a powerful claimant is identified, evaluated and installed" (op. cit. p. 59). The best practices discovered by Nutt, follow a "think first" or "discovery" process that has five stages; both the order and the activities in each stage prove to be important. These stages are: "collect information to understand the claims calling for action, establish a direction that indicates the desired result, mount a specific search for ideas; evaluate these with the direction in mind; and manage the social and political barriers that can block the preferred course of action during implementation" (op. cit. pp. 41-42).

Nutt comes close to the participatory, open and playful style of processes we believe in, when he makes the link to the constructionists' process-idea called "appreciative inquiry" (see for example: Cooperrider, Barrett and Srivastva, 1995). Nutt (2002, p. 257) states that his observation of the stages in the discovery process are related to the stages in appreciative inquiry, i.e. discovery, dreaming, design, and destiny. We expect to be able to show in the rest of this book, that the gaming process has the right order and the right stages to realize, in operational form, this flow of activity that Nutt calls a "discovery process."

"A good process proves to matter" is the conclusion that clearly follows from Nutt's empirical data. However, the ability to call on the right process is also a cultural and structural competence of an organization (see also Hart, 1992, discussed later on in Section 4.7.3). Nutt explains how some organizations prevent or block good processes by pushing "perverse incentives" on their employees and stakeholders: "Perverse incentives coax subordinates to do things management insist they do not want. A perverse incentive can be implicit or explicit. The explicit perverse incentive rewards the wrong things. The implicit perverse incentive lurks in the climate in which decisions are made" (op. cit. 2002, p. 228).

An explicit perverse incentive was clearly at work in our case of the sheltered employment program for handicapped workers described in Chapter 3. Very strict financial demands from the government forced the employing agencies to hang on to their most productive workers. But, at the same time, those workers were the ones that an agency could deliver to the regular labor market, and one of the first goals of the program was to prepare handicapped people to return to normal jobs. In fact, less than one percent of the workers flowed back into the regular labor market. The financial stimulus acted as a perverse incentive and it made a good program very costly – and it almost lost its political support. A policy exercise of the kind we describe is an important platform for subordinates to clarify to their top managers what the "wicked" dynamic consequences of such perverse incentives are.

The culture of an organization can contain all kinds of implicit perverse incentives (op. cit. pp. 228-244). The climate can be so focused on creating winners, not tolerating any mistakes and blaming the bearers of bad news, that decision weaknesses get "buried." To put it simply: people start to hide information and activities and end up lying to each other. Since they are part and parcel of it, leadership usually does not observe the defensive and negative character of a culture, so it tends to persist and grow. There is a clear learning trap at work here that is only avoided when a new way of inquiry and inference making is adopted. This "ladder of inference" calls for one to:

- "provide directly observable data for evaluation
- ... explore these data jointly
- ... look for unintended consequences
- ... develop shared conclusion" (op. cit. p. 240).

For Nutt, the most important point is the first one: to agree on the data and make it directly observable. In our cases in Chapter 3, two aspects of the gaming approach proved very helpful:

- The interactive preparatory systems analysis to agree on the database for game design; and
- The use of multimedia and many physical tools, plus the role playing, made initial conditions and decision consequences extremely observable: there was no way not to see them.

From Nutt we learn that it is essential that decision processes help to: "drive out perverse incentives... [and] encourage people to find best practices and share them" (op cit. p. 240).

Social psychologist Karl Weick is fascinated by organizations that cannot afford to make mistakes and he tries to understand what one can learn from them about managing the unexpected. A nuclear power plant, an aircraft carrier and a hospital emergency ward: all are High Reliability Organizations (HRO); see Weick and Sutcliffe (2001). Any time there is activity in these organizations, there is a potential of disaster. These organizations, though constantly bombarded with unexpected events, prove to be able to avoid accidents and do their work professionally and with stunning reliability. And still, sometimes even these specialists in unexpectedness experience a "collapse of sense making" and disaster is the result.

For example, Weick (1993) has analyzed a fire disaster that happened in 1949 in the Mann Gulch area in Montana. It cost the lives of 13 firefighters. The story is dramatically described in Norman McLean's (1992) book *Young Men and Fire*. Weick also analyzed the Tenerife air disaster where a KLM plane took off without clearance and collided with another 747 on the runway (Weick, 1990). These are, of course, examples of failing operations, not of misdirected or mismanaged strategy. But, in a sense, when a strategic challenge knocks on the door of an enterprise, that organization also has to become an HRO and handle the "bet the corporation" situation with professional resilience and reliability.

For our purpose of laying out a conceptual foundation for the role of gaming in strategic management, Weick's insights are extremely relevant. And since Karl Weick is a master in creating a new and intriguing jargon for expressing his ideas, we will quote a few of his most striking observations. According to Weick, the Mann Gulch Disaster was created by a combination of events and conditions that put the fire fighters in a "cosmology episode." Such an episode occurs: "... when people suddenly and deeply feel that the universe is no longer a rational, orderly system. What makes such an episode so shattering is that both the sense of what is occurring and the means to rebuild that sense collapse together. Stated more informally, a cosmology episode feels like vu jàdé - the opposite of déjà vu: I've never been here before, I have no idea where I am and I have no idea who can help me" (Weick, 2001, p. 105).

What can organizations do to prevent their workers falling into such an episode? Weick has identified several remedies. In Weick (2001, p. 110) he gives four means to become less vulnerable and we claim they are all relevant for (and can be learned from) the disciplined use of tailor-made policy games. As four "sources of resilience" he identifies:

- *Improvisation and bricolage* – i.e. the ability "to create order out of whatever materials were at hand" ... "Bricoleurs remain creative under pressure, precisely because they act in chaotic conditions and pull order out of them" (op. cit. p. 110-111).

- *Virtual role systems* – a role system, if internalized well, can stay intact in the minds of the individuals even when it collapses in practical situations. And if all roles can be taken by all people, each person can reconstitute, coordinate and facilitate the group.
- *A culture and attitude of wisdom* – to know and accept that one cannot fully understand what is happening right now, because one has never seen such an event before. A wise person will react with curiosity, openness and complex sensing; such a person will neither be extremely confident nor super cautious.
- *Respectful interaction*: – the respectful and honest "merged subjectivity" of each individual in a crew will be needed to overcome a cosmology episode. There should be enough trust in a group to free itself from the limitations that a formal role system might prove to have in a crisis.

In *Managing the Unexpected*, Weick and Sutcliffe (2001) explore the concept of mindfulness, which is the collective and enhanced ability to discover and correct errors before they escalate into crisis. In an HRO, management is extremely focused on operations and on discovering weak signals of unexpectedness. HRO managers refuse to simplify reality and they acknowledge that reality can sometimes be very "messy." Weick shows again how he supports the idea of multiple realities. In an interview with Diane Coutu, he says: "If an organization finds itself unsure of where it is going, or even where it's been, then it ought to be wide open to a lot of different interpretations, all of which can lead to possible action. The action and its consequence then begin to edit the list of interpretations down to a more manageable size" (Weick, quoted in Coutu, 2003, p. 88).

In this interview, Weick proves to strongly support Dietrich Dörner as both authors stress the need for the Homo Ludens. Weick does this by explaining his personal use of the verb "to galumph": "... I use the term to mean a kind of purposeful playfulness. It is not frivolous or aimless play but a kind of improvisation whereby organizations try out different possibilities" (op. cit. p. 90). He refers back to the firefighters and their modern training exercises, in which, in one activity, they practice the counterintuitive act of throwing away their equipment: "If they understand that survival literally depends on the ability to see things differently, they will learn to be more mindful. It's the same for executives: Galumphing helps them enlarge their repertoires and gain confidence in alternative ways of acting" (op. cit. p. 90). In the remainder of this book, we hope to make clear that one way of collecting relevant action experiences and transforming them into "intelligible worldviews" is by having more and more executives "galumph" in well-designed policy games.

### 2.5 SUMMARY: NEW APPROACHES FOR UNCHARTED TERRITORY
Section 2.5 is a stepping stone for the next chapter. We define the methodological and epistemological principles that underlie a current trend in policy analysis

and policy support. We see the policy exercise as an important realization of the ideas behind this current quest for participatory policy analysis. This section owes a great deal to the excellent Ph.D. work of Igor Mayer (1997) at Tilburg University.

The work we describe fits into the current thinking on the nature of strategic management and the literature on policy and planning fiascoes. In both of these realms of literature, one can witness a trend away from rational and expert-oriented problem solving and a move towards participation and communication, thus towards the facilitation of debate. In this section, we integrate the main ideas and observations from the sections above by positioning policy exercises in the rapidly evolving field of participatory policy analysis.

Dunn (1981, p. 35) defines policy analysis as "an applied social science discipline which uses multiple methods of inquiry and argument to produce and transform policy relevant information that may be utilized in political settings to resolve policy problems." Let us note that the term "political" does not limit this policy analysis tradition to the area of public policy. There is nothing apolitical about the complicated decision making around the examples of macro-problems given above which were taken from private organizations. Politics has to do with solving value dilemmas; there are many dilemmas involved in the examples given above.

We have adopted the terminology from policy analysis to formulate our views on what we think is the core of the methodological principles underlying this book. It may be clear from Section 2.4.1 that some labels may be different from the strategic management literature; however, the basic ideas are the same.

Practitioners in the policy field have started to experiment with new methods to involve a pluriform set of stakeholders in preparatory activities for policy development. This development has led to a plethora of new methods, which have come to the market under many different names and mnemonics. As we shall document, we believe that policy exercises are one very strong example of this set of techniques. Policy scientists use different names (e.g. communicative, interactive or participatory policy analysis) to describe the current innovations in policy analysis practice. In this book, we use the term participatory policy analysis (PPA) following De Leon (1988) and Durning (1993).

The emergence of participatory policy analysis can be interpreted as an evolution of different schools in policy analysis. These different schools have motivated the need for participation for different reasons. Consequently, the evolution of alternative proposals for a "best practice" of policy analysis can be explained by studying the different schools which have formulated the critique on the traditional rational-synoptic-comprehensive approach to policy analysis (Hawkesworth, 1987). These alternative proposals to what Lindblom & Cohen (1979) have called the straw man of policy analysis (and what Mintzberg would call the "planning school" in strategic management), have different answers to dimensions such as the nature of social reality, epistemology, rationality and policy problems. Although there are many internal differences, several general models of policy analysis can be distinguished in which a participatory approach to policy analysis is a consistent element.

The *pluralist model* of policy analysis (Wildavski, 1979; Lindblom & Woodhouse, 1968) combines a view of bounded rationality and incremental problem solving with a political perspective on policy analysis. Pluralist policy analysis is partisan analysis accepting the reality of political bargaining and compromise when an analyst has to assist in solving macro-problems in and between organizations. The pluralist mode of policy analysis separates the synoptic-scientific rationality on the one hand from the political rationality or "rationality-in-practice" on the other hand. Consequently, advocates of this type of policy analysis, such as Wildavski, emphasize the importance of the political skills of the analyst. However, empirical research can lead to "inter-subjective" knowledge about reality and expert advice based on this knowledge can make a difference. The analytical problem is further complicated by human cognitive limitations, as illustrated by Dörner's experiments described above. Multiple advocacy procedures and methodological diversity can both cope with the political nature and bounded rationality of the analysis of policy problems.

It is clear that a pluralist model of policy analysis will support the inclusion of participants in multiple advocacy procedures both on political and analytical grounds.

There are other models of policy analysis that support participation and multiple interaction. The *critical model* of policy analysis is most relevant for the debate on macro-problems in public policy. It attacks the disguised ideological character of the rational and the conservative character of the pluralist model. According to the critical analyst, both models promote (neo) positivist methods without escaping scientism and technocracy; this has an important negative effect on democratic societal decision making. The main objectives of policy analysis, the critical analyst argues, should be the design of a discourse on values, replacing instrumental rationality with preferences and ends, and a genuine challenge to the status quo. The pluralist model relies for methodological answers on a diversity of techniques and bargaining by influential political actors. In contrast to this, the critical model of policy analysis seeks participation for empowerment and support of the less-represented groups in society. Participatory procedures of the critical model are communicative (Habermas, 1981), adversarial and critical.

The *constructivist model* of policy analysis supports participation not so much for pluralistic or empowerment reasons but for epistemological and ontological reasons. Reality is socially constructed and knowledge can only be acquired through an ongoing process of the construction of meaning. Multiple frames of reference interact and communicate in an ongoing process to give meaning to problems, solutions and actions. Policy analysis, in the constructivist's view, is a hermeneutic debate among different perspectives, worldviews or cognitive maps. Rationality is produced through interaction. Tacit knowledge has equal status to other forms of knowledge. According to Kelly and Maynard-Moody (1993, p. 138) the proposal for the constructivist or interpretative model of policy analysis is "... to conduct policy analysis within interpretative forums ... by engaging in practical reasoning. ... The policy analyst is not an expert but a facilitator, who lends his or her own subjective but outsider perspective to the evaluation process."

Finally, the *strategic model* of policy analysis has a relativist or pragmatic position towards social reality. Definitions of reality and actions are real as long as they are functional for the realization of strategic objectives of the key actor in a policy network. The key actor (the client of the policy analyst) is entangled in a web of interdependencies with other actors within policy processes and policy systems (networks). Most frequently, the strategic model defines a network being constituted by persons, institutions, problems and strategies (Heclo, 1978; Kingdon, 1984). Strategic planning is non-rational, i.e. the result of a combination of different rationalities, which makes the final outcome of planning processes highly unpredictable and uncontrollable (Hickson et al., 1986; Marsh and Olson, 1976). Therefore the function of policy analysis is to be persuasive (Whyte, 1994) or rhetorical for the network as a whole. Policy analysis is strategic intervention to make sure that opportunities can be seized at the right moment, and that the effectiveness of the interaction between strategies can be estimated and tested. When necessary, strategies between actors can be coordinated and legitimated. Participation therefore is interpreted with reference to interdependency and strategic games within a policy network.

The network concept and the related concept of policy programs support the pluralistic and interactive views on the role of policy analysis. They can accept the role of policy analysts to facilitate the development of rationality-of-interaction. What should be clarified further is how participatory policy analysis can and should support the cognitive elements in policy debates. Empirical research has shown that the critique on the synoptic/rationalistic model in policy sciences is justified. It does not accurately describe the process of decision making on complex strategic problems. That does not mean that this problem-solving rationality is not a relevant element in decision making. As we explained above, Hickson et al. (1986) (and others) have shown in their elaborate comparative studies that problem-solving rationality is an aspiration that guides the seeking of information, the completion of reports and the deliberation on alternatives. Many of the steps taken by the parties in a complex decision making process are guided and explained by the desire to optimize the problem-solving rationality. Even if the resulting decision is a product of simultaneous rationalities, one can observe a tendency in the preparation of strategic decisions to optimize the knowledge household around the policy issue.

As we stated in Section 2.4.1, a process of integration and exchange of the policy theories of various actors takes place. The outcome is a collective policy theory that feeds partial decisions in the various stages of the policy design process. The question is what policy analysis can contribute to collective policy theories if one is realistic about what research and analysis can do, given the nature of decision making in policy networks. In many debates on the role of policy analysis, there seems to be an expectation of instrumental impact of policy analysis. This requires that new knowledge be immediately useful for a policy issue and that scientific research directly provides practical consequences for policy. As Caplan (1983) shows, many social science statements about the future do not provide this kind of contribution; but this does not mean that they do not have any contribution.

On the contrary, Caplan and his fellow researchers of the "utilization of knowledge" school show that research on ill-structured problems often has a conceptual impact on policy; the cognitive complexity is increased. To a certain extent, decisions are irrational, for they are the product of three "simultaneous rationalities": a balancing (or weighing) emerges of problem-solving and interest-accommodating rationalities and the rationality of control (Hickson et al. 1986). This means that new knowledge has to be incorporated in the mental models of policy makers who play this "three-dimensional optimizing game" in their heads. Instruments on this analysis/policy interface should help to enable this process of what Caplan (1983) calls knowledge conversion.

The agenda for participatory policy analysis is to be pluralistic, interactive and informative at the same time. That is the challenge of modern policy analysis: to preserve the relevant values of "old" policy analysis (i.e. high-quality inquiry and argument) while, at the same time, using interactive tools to help the multitude of different stakeholders to interact productively in a policy process.

To conclude this section, we adopt from Geurts and Mayer (1996) the following working definition of participatory policy analysis:

"Participatory policy analysis is an applied social science discipline that uses multiple methods of inquiry, argument and process facilitation to assist a pluriform set of stakeholders in a policy network to explore and exchange in a direct interaction with each other their different mental maps regarding values, definitions, causes and solutions of problems and to develop and test ... a shared and robust policy theory on an issue. The ultimate goal is to improve the problem-solving capacity of the individual stakeholders and the policy network as a whole" (Geurts & Mayer, 1996, p. 17).

In the next section, using several detailed case studies, we want to illustrate how these ideas can be realized in actual gaming projects. The methodology of gaming/simulation provides us with a practical approach to realize the summarized ideas and ideals of participatory policy analysis. The first author of this book formulated this aspiration as follows:

"In response to the increasing complexity of many human problems, new cross-disciplinary techniques to assist decision makers are rapidly emerging worldwide. Scientists around the globe have been experimenting with new methods of perceiving, understanding and communicating complexity. Many techniques and technologies have been used with varying results. The more successful have attempted to capture problems in a systematic way, to facilitate group participation in the articulation of alternatives for action, and to enable a group to evaluate various alternatives. Inevitably, these efforts employ a method for communication that is less sequential than written language and more "right brain" in encouraging spontaneity, but nonetheless disciplined in use to ensure reasonable results" (Duke, 1987, pg. 5).

# Section II

## *Practice: Description and Analysis*

### INTRODUCTION TO SECTION II

There are two chapters in this section. Chapter 3 presents eight selected case studies that illustrate the central themes of this book. Chapter 4 reviews the five key criteria (complexity, communication, creativity, consensus, and commitment to action) as they relate to the eight cases.

In each of the cases, the client was in a rapidly changing, dynamic environment where data and information did not equate with knowledge and the wisdom required for action. In each of the cases, a study of the problem context revealed hundreds of variables (many of which were difficult to quantify). For each of these clients, a decision was not the prerogative of a single individual, but rather the result of an interactive process in which multiple players each had different interests to protect. The policy exercise approach permitted the group to assemble in a "safe environment" to establish richer communication about the underlying problem. This creative approach, in turn, permitted the participants to open up their thinking and to mutually explore alternatives that might not otherwise have surfaced. These new options revealed a basis for consensus that did not previously exist; most importantly, the process resulted in a commitment to action by the organization that was more than a "decision" in that the underlying rationale was understood and supported by appropriate levels of the organization.

The policy exercises in Chapter 3 are comparable in that they are designed for organizations facing a serious strategic problem; however, the examples are also different in many respects. In all the cases, many different perspectives and many different actors were brought together. Some of the examples are best described as intra-organizational processes, others are interaction processes in which representatives of different organizations meet. The policy exercises presented differ in strategic scope. Some play a role in the early phases of strategic management, e.g. problem awareness, futuring, and scanning the environment. Others are intended to support strategic choice or implementation, and there are examples where the exercise and its preparatory process cover integrally all the important steps of strategic analysis and choice. Both business and governmental organizations are represented in the examples.

The term "strategic management" is usually intended to include strategic analysis, choice and implementation. Our cases illustrate all three of these phases. However, in this book, we want to emphasize the policy development function of gaming/simulation. As a consequence, our selected cases do not emphasize the function of this method for strategic cultural change. There are many cases where games are designed as tools to be used especially for company-wide implementation of behavioral changes. Only two, albeit quite spectacular examples, are described in this book. One is addressed in this chapter and it deals with an industrial components manufacturing firm (see Section 3.6). Further on, in Section 6.5.4, the work of de Caluwé at Delta Lloyd Insurance company is summarized. However, there are many more intriguing and convincing case studies scattered throughout the literature. For a deeper understanding of this type of application we refer you to *Changing Organizations with Gaming/Simulation* by Geurts, de Caluwé & Stoppelenburg (2000).

All examples reconstruct the whole process of designing and using the policy game and there are interesting differences to note. Although all projects have been conducted in a participatory manner, the intensity of client participation varies by project. Projects of particular interest are those in which the game is more or less the culmination and end stage of a long process of strategic communication that is organized along the steps of game design. The game design process becomes a participatory process of strategic orientation and group modeling (often including the final participants). The game itself is the finale of such a process. There are examples of games constructed by a staff team that is independent of future participants; there are also examples in which these two modes have been mixed.

Chapter 3 describes the cases with as much relevant detail as possible to bring these projects alive for the reader. We have ordered the cases starting with the intra-organizational applications, which are followed by the inter-organizational examples. We begin with the examples that have a narrower strategic scope and gradually add examples that are more complex in this respect. One important reminder: these cases have been abstracted and, where possible, made anonymous to protect the interests of the clients. We have tried to avoid being too specific about the calendar dates of the events that we describe. Observations on all these cases belong to history. Much has changed in and around the organizations with whom we have dealt, and we ask the reader to keep this in mind when reading the case studies.

Chapter 4 analyses the criteria (complexity, communication, creativity, consensus, and commitment to action) in some detail as they emerged in the cases. This chapter shows how the problem statement for each project suggested a different emphasis on one or more of the criteria; we explain the techniques and provisions with which we tried to do justice to the relevant criteria.

Please note: *In order to avoid duplication, certain text is not repeated for each case* (e.g. the logic of the development of the schematic – see Section 3.2.6). As a consequence, the reader will gain a fuller understanding by reading the cases in sequence.

# Chapter 3

## Eight Case Studies

### 3.1 INTRODUCTION

The first five cases (Sections 3.2, 3.3, 3.4, 3.5 and 3.6) introduce the application of the policy exercise in intra-organizational settings. In each case, the client is a large organization and the participants came from within that organization. The examples are taken from public and private organizations both from Europe and the U.S.

The final three cases (Sections 3.7, 3.8, and 3.9) describe the use of the policy exercise in inter-organizational settings. One organization invites members of its own organization as well as many other stakeholder representatives to jointly explore the future. The examples are mostly situated at the public/private interface and involve two cases from Europe and one from the U.S.

All of these cases were developed using a standardized process of design; this process is described in detail in Section IV – Designing Games for Strategy (Chapter 8).

### 3.2 STRATEGY MAKING IN A UNIVERSITY HOSPITAL

#### 3.2.1 The Client
As far as the strategic agenda for the University Hospital was concerned, there were several issues that needed hospital-wide thinking and concerted action. For example, the future patient flow was expected to change radically, from inpatient care to outpatient care. One of the forces behind this was the need to reduce healthcare costs. The case is a good example of some of the core functions of gaming. It is about collective futuring in a safe environment in order to experience the problems of current strategic patterns and to explore new and more productive lines of behavior. It is also an interesting example of strategy making in a large professional organization. The intended outcome was not so much a strategic plan of action but rather to improve the strategic capabilities of all the relevant professionals who actually create the future of the hospital in their day-to-day actions.

The University Hospital is part of a large Dutch university, and is also one of the most highly regarded medical institutions in the Netherlands. The organization has three primary processes: patient care, research, and education. In the Netherlands, all academic hospitals fulfill these three functions, and the non-academic hospitals usually restrict themselves to patient care. The client hospital was a very large and diverse institution. The many different functional departments all exerted constant pressure internally to search for the optimal contribution to the three primary processes. However, this does not mean that the hospital was not affected by pressures from its environment. On the contrary, one of the more pressing issues at the time of the project was how to respond to an emerging trend in healthcare policy. Increasingly, organizations like the hospital had to work more closely with local peripheral health institutions.

The hospital's initial structure was strongly dependent on the concept of the matrix organization. This proved to be incapable of dealing with the complexity facing the organization. Due to internal and external pressures, a new organization structure had been introduced some eight years earlier. The Board of Directors created a divisional structure that proved to be rather successful. This was based on the business unit structure adopted by many large corporations in the private sector. The model that the new structure followed was the concept of the functional division in which the three primary processes were fully integrated. Division management was given considerable autonomy to decide on resource and task allocation. In the divisions, medical professionals were "put in the lead." Cooperation with other divisions was accomplished via contracts, and coordinating structures were created for the training programs and the multidisciplinary research programs. The supervising board took on more of a coaching and facilitating function and formalized the agreement with the divisions in contracts and budget statements.

Within the 11 newly created divisions, the managers proved to be successful in managing their own operations and staying within their budgets. External assessments of the hospital research and training showed that the new structure was both efficient and effective: the assessments continued to be rated good to excellent. However, for some members of top management, the new structure created an awareness of a serious danger: perhaps the innovation had been too successful.

### 3.2.2 The Problem
The division structure had been operational for several years. Some members of the Hospital Board and some division leaders had observed a tendency by the division managers to focus primarily on issues of their own concern. The Board of Directors considered this to be a serious problem. When resources had to be divided over the 11 divisions, the division managers defended the interests of their own division as much as possible. The new division structure and the idea of the medical professionals being in the lead assumed that the division managers would agree on resource distribution while balancing divisional and general hospital interests. It was further assumed that they would be able to do so without strong interference from the Board of Directors; however, this proved to be

very difficult. Gradually, some members of the hospital administration began to worry that there was neither sufficient stimuli in the new structure nor a proper attitude to take care of the interests of the whole hospital both now and in the future. At the same time, there was no real interest in reinstalling the Board's former central powers. The challenge was to solve this danger of a "tragedy of the commons" within the existing structure.

As far as strategic and hospital-wide challenges were concerned, there were several issues that needed strategic thinking and concerted action. For example, in the future, the patient flow was expected to change radically from inpatient care to outpatient care. One of the forces behind this was the need to reduce the cost of healthcare. The Board of Directors, working with the senior managers, identified several problems:

- Within the hospital, there were internal and structural determinants that complicated decision making on organization-wide issues;
- Divisional managers had developed stereotypical behavior that complicated the search for an organization-wide strategy; and
- The hospital as a whole was confronted by a strategic challenge so important that the Board of Directors had to take the initiative to drastically improve joint decision making.

These convictions and insights were not yet shared by all the division executives and central services managers. In order to meet the expected future challenges, a shared awareness and definition of the problem was needed among both the members of the Board and all divisional management team members.

### 3.2.3 Goals, Purposes, and Objectives

The policy exercise had to fulfill two main goals within the hospital organization. On the one hand, the hospital management needed to become more aware of the problems mentioned above. In that sense, the game had to function as a mirror. On the other hand, the game needed to help the participants explore more productive ways of making decisions that were vital for collective future success. This was called the "window on the future" function of the game. These two goals can be divided into four objectives:

- Participants had to learn about known and unknown strategic challenges within their organization. There needed to be an increased awareness of the problems of the internal organization and in the rapidly changing external environment;

- Therefore, the participants needed to develop a joint problem definition. The game needed to help them to communicate about the general organizational obstacles;

- Participants had to learn to act more flexibly. This was unavoidable in the complex organization of the hospital environment; and

- The game needed to stimulate the participants to develop a more positive attitude towards change. It had to motivate employees to consider important conditions for change in the organization.

### 3.2.4 Why Did the Client Select the Policy Exercise Process?

The Board of Directors had tried to communicate their concerns about the problems through a report and several discussion meetings, but this effort had no serious effect on the behavior of the relevant managerial echelons. For this reason, they adopted a Board member's suggestion to apply the gaming technique. This member of the Board had heard about the potential experiential learning power of the gaming tool. He was convinced that top professionals working in the hospital would be more open to this involving and confrontational type of interactive learning than they had been to reports and non-committal discussions.

### 3.2.5 Specifications for Policy Exercise Design

The exercise was designed for use in an eight-hour framework that included the introduction, playing time, and a debriefing session. The game was designed for 36 people and was to be used only once.

The exercise was initially intended for the Board of Directors and Division Management. During the interviews in the systems analysis phase, it became clear how important the department heads were for the gamed problem (departments are units within the division usually chaired by a professor). Several of these senior professionals indicated that they did not want to be excluded. After careful reconsideration, the Board of Directors decided to involve the department heads. Finally, the following participants were selected:

- Hospital Board of Directors (4 people);
- Divisional Management Teams (11 times 3 people: a senior professor as chairman, a manager of patient care and a finance and operations manager); and
- Department heads (variable numbers).

### 3.2.6 The Schematic: A Model of Reality

A schematic of the problem was developed in an attempt to create a visual presentation of the internal and external characteristics of the hospital (see Figure 3.1). The initial description of the problem environment usually emerges in discrete, partially organized, and sometimes conflicting pieces. It is the task of the research team and the client to synthesize these elements of the system into an integrative and explicit model that can be easily described and discussed. The objective is to develop a graphic on a wall-size chart which contains the "Big Picture," or an overview of all the considerations that might be significant to the policy issue being addressed by this process. This schematic is an indispensable element of the game design process and its use brings about some surprising results. The schematic is discussed more fully in Chapters 7 and 8. *Please note that most of the schematics shown in this book are highly simplified and at greatly reduced scale.* See Section 8.2, Step 7 and the Appendix for more detailed examples.

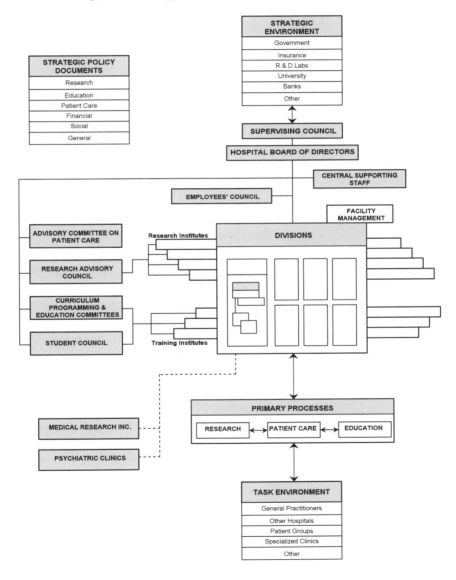

**FIGURE 3.1 | UNIVERSITY HOSPITAL SCHEMATIC (SIMPLIFIED)**

### 3.2.7 Description of the Policy Exercise

The design team followed a formal process (described in Chapter 8) to create, employ, and evaluate the policy exercise. Only a few steps central to the understanding of the significance of the exercise are described below. The design team consisted of four external gaming specialists and two members of the hospital organization. This team had several meetings with an ad hoc advisory group within the hospital. The design team studied a large number of documents and interviewed many representatives of the managerial echelons. A number of external experts were also interviewed. A period of 15 weeks elapsed between the initial agreement on the project contract and the final use of the game.

In cooperation with the client, the consultants decided to develop an open game format (Chapter 1). In this case, it was not important that the effects of decisions be simulated in a detailed way (the participants were expert enough to know what the results of certain actions would be). What was needed was a very flexible form of role play on the basis of one or two scenarios about the future. The game needed to start with steps of play that mimicked the normal routine of decision making. The game was to be observed by external experts. Both the experts and the players were able to ask for timeouts to discuss and possibly improve the style of collaboration and negotiation.

The scenario was as follows:

> It is now January 2003. The strategic plan for 1997 (the year in which this game was played) is valid. The organization has not changed much compared to 1997, but some relevant developments have taken place in the meantime. The emphasis has been put more and more on the transformation of care to permit patients to be increasingly cared for in their own environment. For this hospital and other large hospitals, this has led to a radical decrease in the number and duration of admissions, while the number of outpatient treatments has clearly risen. The Ministry of Health, with the support of the Association of Academic Hospitals, has approved the enlargement of the hospital's outpatient clinic to twice its current size; by the end of 2003, a plan of implementation has to be ready. The plan has to be neutral budget, which means that the resources have to be reallocated internally. In addition, the plan must be supported by the Board and the managers present at this meeting.

### 3.2.8 Major Sequence of Activities

*Pre-Exercise Activities* – The Hospital Board sent personal invitations to all participants announcing the date of the Hospital Strategy Simulation. To give the participants enough time to prepare, the organization took great care to provide clear information concerning the goals to be reached. The invitation to all participants asked that they contribute to the realization of the plan. In the plan, many decisions had to be made, including the distribution of the budgets for the divisions (for research, education, patient care and personnel). The participants had to decide how these decisions were to be made, by whom, and when. All participants played roles that corresponded with their real positions within the hospital organization. In the game, the hospital had six divisions with corresponding management teams. The board was fully represented and present during the exercise. Several department heads played the roles of the leadership of the coordinating research and education programs, positions they also held in real life.

*Policy Exercise Activities* – The participants started play in the morning with a role-specific brainstorm session about the consequences of the enlargement of the outpatient clinic. They had to take into account the consequences for budgets and personnel and the effects on research, education and patient care. The remarks were written on flipcharts and, after the brainstorm session, every team had to give an opening statement; this technique ensured that all the participants were informed about the others' points of view.

The next step consisted of deliberation and negotiation. The participants had the opportunity to meet other teams to talk about the proposed approach for doubling the size of the outpatient clinic. Important aspects of this part of the session were continuous consultation, lobbying, and informal decision making. After that, a meeting was held between the Hospital Board and division chairpersons. The other players were the audience; however, they were permitted to intervene with written questions.

In the afternoon, a new cycle started. Each original team had a new opportunity to offer a brief opinion about the outpatient clinic and the negotiations and meetings. The Board provided a response to these interim statements and some observations by the external experts were discussed. For the second time, the participants had the opportunity to meet other teams informally and talk about the plan. This was followed by another meeting between the Hospital Board and the division chairpersons. The other teams served as the audience and were permitted to intervene.

*Post-Exercise Activities* – Finally, an extensive and lively debriefing session was held with the players and the consultants. Summaries written on the overheads were used to extract interesting remarks, and to explore the ambitions of the participants. The objective of the last activity of the exercise was to evaluate and learn from the sessions. Questions addressed included: What have we achieved today? What have we done differently than usual? Did we do better than normally? What do we have to do differently from now on? Each team had to summarize its deliberations on an overhead sheet, and these were used in the critique. Questionnaires were completed before and after each cycle of play. The results were publicized in the final report.

### 3.2.9 The Results

During the game, attention was directed primarily towards the first goal (hospital members should become more aware of the problems) and, to a lesser degree, towards the second goal (exploring strategic challenges). Agreement about the problem was a necessary condition for the success of the concept of "medical professionals in the lead." The game assignment had required them to make a plan for the strategic challenge presented in the scenario; this was used primarily to obtain a joint problem definition and secondly to give some insight into possible solutions. With regard to the first goal, the game can be considered a success. This can be concluded from the debriefing and the questionnaires. In January 1998, a final report that contained conclusions by the participants and consultants was sent to the Board of Directors. Four important lessons can be distinguished:

- The Board of Directors should consult the division managers about strategic issues before establishing a policy framework;

- The division managers should consult each other more often about strategic issues;

- Ways need to be found to take advantage of the expertise of the nursing and financial managers for the formulation of the general hospital policy; and

- There is a need to pay attention to the essential role of the department heads and other executives in developing and implementing the general hospital policy.

The participants agreed about the overall value of the simulation, but when answering the question: "Did you learn anything?" they indicated that the upper hospital management had probably learned more than the participants themselves. This can be seen as a remarkable unanticipated result. During the game, top management paid little attention to the department heads (many of these players complained that they were bored and underused). In the evaluation, this led to the recommendation to involve them more intensively in the client's policy cycle.

### 3.3 Globalization and Pharmaceutical Research & Development

In this case, a large U.S.-based pharmaceutical company had developed the idea of starting an R&D facility in Europe. R&D management, whose task was to put this strategy into operation, had to address several important questions: Should we expand into Europe? If yes, what activities should we expand? Do we need to acquire new skills? Where should we locate these new activities? And, how should we best implement these plans?

They opted to use a policy exercise that required top management to explore the issues in a simulated environment as they thought through the implications. The result was unexpected, in that the leading option at the outset was *rejected in favor of an alternative that was not articulated until the exercise was played.* As a consequence, much smaller sums of money were put at risk and favorable results were achieved in a fraction of the time the initially favored option would have required.

This case is noteworthy because it was a good example of the game design process actually guiding the strategic debate. The project covered both the phases of strategic analysis and strategic choice. The participatory systems analysis proved vital for the proper framing of the problem. In this phase, it became clear that enormous sets of data had already been collected. The game design process helped the client to develop a format for analysis so that scattered data became real information. It proved essential to ensure that all the tacit knowledge of the relevant professional functions was used.

### 3.3.1 The Client

The client for this project was the pharmaceutical research and development division of a large international drug company. The company was faced with increasing problems in getting new products developed and to market. A multinational, publicly held corporation, the company had substantial existing foreign investments. In response to an expanding global awareness, they were concerned with remaining competitive in the rapidly changing pharmaceutical industry. To remain competitive, they had to adapt to a changing environment; it was essential for them to examine the corporate mission as it needed to change in the future. To achieve the goal of timely product introduction worldwide, thus increasing market share and profitability, it was felt within the company that its drug discovery and development effort had to be extended into new markets; the establishment of new foreign discovery capabilities was thought to be essential. A new R&D facility in Europe was believed to be their best option.

An earlier decision to expand in another country had not gone well. Analysis revealed that this was largely due to a failure to recognize the complexity of the decision environment and the importance of involving key personnel in the process. As a consequence of these difficulties, management resolved to use a process that would involve the appropriate people within the organization from the outset. Due to many uncertainties associated with this decision, they elected to use a policy exercise to help them decide on a specific location. The aim was to have a consensus-building activity that would draw upon the wisdom available within the organization.

The main decision under consideration concerned the expansion of pharmaceutical R&D facilities. Since the decision would impact on many facets of the corporation, the proposed European Discovery Facility (EDF) needed to be evaluated in terms of key endogenous and exogenous factors, with a future's perspective in mind, as the 5-year, 10-year, and 25-year implications of any decision were investigated. At an operational level, they were concerned with how to implement the EDF to enhance the company's long-run global posture.

The external considerations affecting their mission were:

- The state of the global economy;
- The public's growing concern over the burden of healthcare costs;
- A shift in the provision of healthcare services from the expert to the concept of self-help;
- The possibility of reduced rates of return in the pharmaceutical industry;
- The prospects for supporting research and development with diminishing resources; and
- The increased significance of new product introduction in the pharmaceutical industry.

In response to these changes in the industry, they had to address a number of strategic and operational issues. Strategic issues that were considered included:

- Research and development productivity;
- The company's foreign role;
- Internal standards and their application abroad;
- Enhancement of a global posture; and
- The strategic policy implications of a European Discovery Facility.

### 3.3.2 The Problem
In an effort to remain competitive in a rapidly changing international context, the company decided to seriously examine the pros and cons of locating a research facility in Europe. The problem was to identify all the significant variables, to delineate these variables in some clear format, and to analyze them to establish their relative priorities. All of this was accompanied by the need for participatory decision making and effective communication among the staff of the R&D Division, as well as with other divisions and upper management.

In this particular case, the problem that was initially presented by the client was: "In which country should we locate this facility?" After a period of time, the question changed to four broad questions that addressed both strategic (what?) and operational (how?) considerations: Should we expand? If so, how should our capability be changed? Where should we locate? And, how can we bring this transformation about?

The 16 tasks given to the participants during the exercise were designed to help the R&D staff formulate an accurate and innovative conceptualization of the EDF problem. Participants in the process were asked to make a decision on questions centered on the following areas:

- Discovery and development emphasis;
- Research activity proposed for the EDF;
- Therapeutic/technical mix;
- Geographic location of the EDF;
- Structure and implementation of the EDF;
- Internal organization;
- Degree of home office involvement; and
- Staffing the EDF.

### 3.3.3 Goals, Purposes, and Objectives
The exercise was developed to aid top management in formulating and assessing their strategy. The explicit objectives were:

- To assist R&D management in the development of the parameters for the proposed research facility (location, style, capacity, configuration, and primary mission);
- To provide for participatory and interdisciplinary problem formulation and effective communication among the management team facing the decision;
- To help management of the R&D Division reach consensus on the optimum siting of a new facility in Europe, thus aiding the Office of the Chairman in reaching a decision; and
- To encourage the advancement of alternative approaches to research, thus helping to formulate an innovative conceptualization of the problem; and
- To transmit to appropriate staff the decision process as well as the dimensions of the problem that had to be considered in reaching a decision.

### 3.3.4 Why Did the Client Select the Policy Exercise Process?
In their attempt to deal with the problem, management selected the policy exercise methodology as the most appropriate one because of its ability to:

- Investigate the complexities of important, non-reversible decisions under conditions of uncertainty by identifying all the variables under consideration, delineating them in a clear format; and analyzing them by establishing relative priorities;
- Provide explanatory, if not predictive, insights about the problem and its environment to participants in the process;
- Overcome disciplinary, language and cultural barriers; facilitate communication in a situation where varied jargon was used; induce and evoke a high level of participation; and, allow participants of widely varying perspectives to gain

a shared overview of the problem;
- Compress time, and when employed through several cycles representing defined time spans, enable the long-range outcomes of one or another course of action to become more comprehensible; and
- Augment the rational systems approach to problem solving by allowing infusion of subjective judgments into the process.

### 3.3.5 Specifications for Policy Exercise Design

The successful development of an exercise requires a careful delineation of responsibilities and lines of authority. These, and other appropriate administrative matters, must be fully resolved before the substantive material is addressed. In this case, it proved necessary to explain the approach to the central stakeholders. Although the technique is very old, its use in serious policy debates in large corporations is relatively new. Special attention on the part of the project team was required at this stage to legitimize the effort. The project team consisted of researchers from the University of Michigan, an internal (client) advisory committee and external consultants. The duration of the project was negotiated to be four months.

It was important at the outset to define the criteria that would later serve as the measure for the evaluation of the product. The objective of the specifications was to raise and address specific questions that pertained to and anticipated the final conditions that would govern the design and use of the exercise. This is a natural extension of the problem statement, in which the objectives and constraints for assessment of design, construction and use are made explicit. In this particular case, the specifications included a definition of the intended audience, primary goals, stylistic considerations (reflective, mutual problem-solving style), and practical constraints: duration (one day), number of participants (12-18), computer usage, room and material requirements, and the planned recording of the participants' responses.

The participants were drawn from the Research & Development, Control, International, Medical Affairs, Manufacturing, Regulatory Affairs, and Treasurer divisions. These participants were senior staff members who were asked to work from one of five "perspectives." The perspectives did not coincide exactly with the position these participants held in real life; rather, they were an amalgamation of several executive responsibility areas. The players were selected on the basis of their familiarity with the actual role that was subsumed under that perspective.

### 3.3.6 The Schematic: A Model of Reality

Several trial schematics preceded a final form for delivery to the client. This graphic had been reduced to those factors considered relevant within the constraints of the problem statement; this process of selection took place in the context of an ongoing dialogue with the client. The final document needed to retain enough detail to adequately represent the problem environment; however, it also needed to communicate the central aspects visually and quickly. It became an integral part of the exercise and provided the frame of reference for the policy exercise activity. A simplified version of the final schematic of the EDF problem environment is presented below in Figure 3.2 (for a more complete understanding of the schematic, see Section 8.2, Step 7 and the Appendix). The schematic places the following elements in relation to each other:

- The primary stages of the drug development and drug discovery process;
- The interaction of this process with related exogenous processes (competition, universities, etc.);
- The primary in-house (endogenous) perspectives (medical, marketing, regulatory, management, manufacturing and science);
- The relationship of the discovery and development process with the rest of the company, the market and the company owners;
- A wide range of endogenous and exogenous concerns placing the discussion about the discovery facility against a 25-year time horizon; and
- The four central questions that the gaming exercise addressed: What was the future of the drug development and discovery process? What type of facility was required? Where should it be built? And, how can the plan be placed into operation?

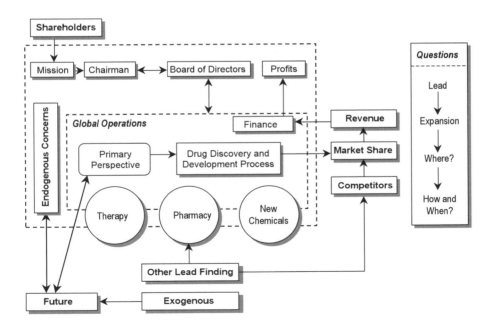

**Figure 3.2 | Schematic of the Pharmaceutical Case (Simplified)**

The interactive development of the schematic was an important part of the process for the client who viewed this document as extremely valuable. The schematic was significant for the following reasons:

- It showed the client that the consulting team had reached a mature understanding of the problem and its environment; as such, it was an early step in the legitimization of the project;
- It served as a discussion vehicle because it forced the respondents who held different views on how the organization functioned to resolve those differences among themselves. Conflicting views of the "big picture" had to be integrated into this compromise view;
- It forced all the different stakeholders to look beyond the boundaries of their normal work environment and, in doing so, it established a sharp image of the problem; and
- It was a solid basis for the selection of the main topics to be addressed by the exercise.

The problem set, as initially perceived, was too broad to be included in the exercise. The factors of primary concern were identified based on the original problem statement and the specifications. The schematic proved very useful in the process of selecting components for inclusion in the exercise. The process guaranteed that the exercise met the primary criteria: it was situation specific, relevant and parsimonious.

The evolution of this schematic experienced a dramatic moment! It had been reviewed and approved by all senior staff except the Vice President of Sales (the design team had not been allowed to present the draft to Sales because "We create products; they sell them!"). After the schematic was finalized, the design team prevailed in getting access to the Vice President of Sales. He immediately recognized that the drawing was invalid in capturing the primary research flow process – it failed to illustrate products that were licensed at the several decision points in the development of a product. The schematic was redrawn and an intense debate followed; it was approved as modified. During the play of the game, this information proved decisive in rejecting the leading pre-game strategy and in the development of an unexpected (and successful) final strategy.

### 3.3.7 Description of the Policy Exercise

The EDF format employed participants playing roles that represented diverse perspectives on the problem. The exercise consisted of 16 tasks designed to help the R&D staff formulate an accurate and innovative conceptualization of the problem. The focus of attention was on the parameters of the primary mission (location, style, capacity, and final operational configuration). The overall purpose was to identify the R&D activities that would increase their ability to remain competitive over the next 20 years.

The scenario focused on the question: What should their strategy be to be successful in the 21st century? The scenario outlined a brief history of the corporation, the company's mission, the pros and cons of a European Discovery Facility, and future considerations from a variety of perspectives (science, medicine, management, manufacturing, marketing, regulatory activities, international concerns, drug development, etc.). The scenario focused on the premise that the expansion of the research and discovery activities in Europe would:

- Contribute to their acceptance as an international pharmaceutical company;
- Increase scientific networking with the international academic community;
- Allow them to tap local and regional knowledge relevant to new drug discovery;
- Expand the pool of scientific talent that they could tap to fill critical staff positions;
- Improve their ability to develop drugs outside the U.S. regulatory climate;
- Accelerate the registration process in the region where the facilities were located;
- Allow for more effective capacity to respond to regional disease entities;
- Expand marketing potential outside the U.S.; and
- Inject fresh ideas and approaches into the thinking of the R&D organization.

During the course of the exercise, events were introduced to update the scenario; players were expected to evaluate the impact of these events on their decisions.

The roles in the EDF exercise represented the key perspectives that influence the R&D process. The participants were asked to assume and represent the issues and concerns that would be particularly important for each perspective. Following are short role descriptions for each role.

- The Management Advocate Role was responsible for administrative efficiency; management style; personnel and staff development; finance, including budgeting; and efficient utilization of resources; and exogenous concerns such as economic conditions in the marketplace and communications.

- The Manufacturing Advocate Role dealt with equipment and technology requirements, production scheduling, development, feasibility, and efficiency; its exogenous concerns were new process technology developments, governmental standards and controls; and consumer safety.

- The Marketing Advocate Role had to think through strategies on product promotion and recognition, pricing, corporate image, product line; and analysis of domestic and international markets and distribution, market share, competition, and cultural sensitivity to therapeutic needs.

- The Medical Advocate Role was responsible for thinking through strategies that related to lead finding, therapeutic needs, new indicators, product introduction, drug development and testing technologies. Exogenous concerns included access to and strength of academic/clinical contacts, clinical support, journal publication, data transfer, and cultural sensitivity to therapeutic needs.

- The Regulatory Advocate Role was to create the strategies about internal control standards, licensing, and corporate liability. Exogenous concerns included country-specific drug registration, patent requirements, governmental standards/controls, consumer safety, and political concerns.

- The Science Advocate Role focused on strategies that related to lead finding, pre-selection of new drugs, pharmaco-therapeutic concepts, new chemical entities, drug development, internal research environment and support, and research flexibility. Exogenous concerns were access to the scientific community, publication in journals, new drug development technologies, communication and data transfer networks, external lead finding, new chemical entities, pharmaco-therapeutic technologies and concepts.

The complex nature of the problem being addressed by the EDF exercise required that players have access to a wide variety of specific and factual information. As the exercise did not intend to make factual experts of the players, the majority of the information and data was presented as accessory material that was available for players to draw upon as the need arose. This information assisted players in realistically assuming and playing their roles. The data was made available through a number of formats including document files and abstracts, topic-specific notebooks, charts, and graphs.

The need for accessible information dictated a format that allowed for easy filing, storage, retrieval, and presentation of data essential to the decision-making process. The selected format made extensive use of graphic displays, indexed notebooks, and computerized database capabilities. The room layout and environment was similar to a war room model. Graphic displays were posted in ready view of all participants and additional information was easily accessed in the notebooks or from a computer. Trained staff was in the room to assist as required.

The document files provided a source of primary, uncondensed data for the players. Information contained in the document files was also abstracted. The abstract directory, abstracts and document files were available to the players throughout the exercise. The most important and pertinent information was condensed into topic-specific notebooks of the following types:

- Country-specific notebooks for each country being considered as a potential EDF site;

- Topic-specific notebooks pertaining to the subject areas of the advocate roles;
- Strategic question notebooks containing background information and evaluation criteria; and
- A notebook containing historical and current information on the corporate mission, goals and strategies, growth and profit, public image, public interest and other general types of information on the corporate operation.

These formats were used to simplify the presentation of data and encourage its use; they promoted the desired policy exercise format and playing environment. Following are some examples of the types of data presented through this form:

- Country/company-specific production over time;
- Country/company-specific market shares over time;
- Country/company-specific drug development activities;
- Competition and market share;
- Drug development costs;
- Regulatory criteria and timelines for U.S. and international registration; and
- Markets and market share.

### 3.3.8 Major Sequence of Activities
*Pre-Exercise Activities* – Participants were required to participate in a three-week pre-game set of activities. The first week, they were given a reference manual and access to reference staff. The next week, the participants received pre-game reading materials, which raised substantive and theoretical issues. Finally, one week before the exercise, the vice president of R&D made a presentation to all the prospective participants; at that time, he again emphasized the significance of the project. The project team then distributed pre-game manuals. These manuals had 17 steps; each step was a pre-structured decision exercise, related to one of the central questions of the exercise. Each participant, acting alone, was required to answer all the questions from the perspective of his or her role. The pre-game manuals were returned to the project team for evaluation and encoding onto wall charts. This process forced each participant to assume a posture on each question; during the game, these were modified after discussion.

Before the beginning of the exercise, the facilitator gave a brief introduction to orient the participants to the exercise. Next, the participants were given the player's handbook including the introductory information, problem background, problem schematic, scenario, sequence of activities, role descriptions, as well as the following questions:

- What is the industry-wide future of the pharmaceutical drug discovery and development process?
- What is the mission of the proposed EDF facility? How should this be defined?

- Where should the EDF be located? What key attributes should be used to rate individual countries?
- How should the EDF be placed in operation? This question addressed the physical plant, internal organization, the degree of home office involvement, and staffing as key components.

In addition, participants were given a suggested format for a response to the questions, an individual decision form, a group reconciliation decision form, abstracts drawn from the document files, as well as other appropriate data and/or information. After going through these materials, the participants filled in a matrix on future impacts on drug discovery. This concluded the pre-game activities.

*Policy Exercise Activities* – The actual play of the exercise consisted of three cycles. Each cycle addressed one of the strategic questions introduced during the pre-game activities. By addressing these questions in the order they were presented, the participants evaluated and made judgments on the essential variables in the EDF location decision. If, for some reason, an important variable was missing or was not accurately represented, the participants offered suggestions about possible new variables or representations.

Each cycle represented one progression through the steps of play. The progression of activities within each cycle was characterized by three general activities (phases): value clarification and strategy generation (advocate position phase); strategy evaluation and design of a hybrid strategy (reconciliation phase); and impact evaluation (impact evaluation phase).

In the first phase, the participants assumed the roles of advocates for various interests in the drug discovery and development process. These interests included the scientific, medical, management, marketing and regulatory perspectives in the drug discovery process. In the advocate roles, the participants formulated strategies from their role's perspective and identified the values and assumptions on which their strategies were based as a response to the strategic question presented at the beginning of the cycle.

The participants were asked to take a critical look at the question: Europe or not? Based on their previous detailed consideration of the proposed European Discovery Facility, they were now asked to use the insights they had gained to compare their chosen European location with other alternatives including expanding at home, further development of a facility in Japan or other possible locations.

In the second phase, the participants had to reconcile their differences and produce a group strategy. All the participants made judgments and acted in the corporate interest as defined by the corporate mission statement. In this phase, the players evaluated the recommendations from the previous phase, considered forces and events outside the corporation, formulated a hybrid strategy in response to the strategic question, and developed a mission statement.

In the third phase, which occurred after all the strategy questions had been addressed, the impact of the selected events and various strategies were examined. The impact assessment was based on 25-year forecasts generated by the exercise participants. This involved evaluating the decisions they had just made. Participants were asked to step out of their roles; they were required to summarize the decisions that had been completed. In reviewing their decisions, participants were asked to keep in mind the importance of getting the EDF on line as quickly as possible. The group was given the task of constructing a decision tree that helped to summarize their individual responses to the previous tasks.

*Post-Exercise Activities* – After the third cycle ended, the exercise director led a post-game discussion and evaluation. The first phase of this debriefing involved letting the players discuss the things that happened during the exercise. This allowed the players an opportunity to leave behind their feelings and emotions about the exercise. Following this catharsis, the model of the EDF problem that had been presented in the exercise was analyzed from the perspectives of the different roles. Finally, in the last stage of the debriefing, the players and the facilitator made an effort to assess the EDF problem as an actual decision. This was achieved by reviewing strategy statements from the three cycles, evaluating overall strategies with regard to corporate goals, introducing events, and reviewing the possible impacts of events on decisions to be made.

### 3.3.9 The Results

In this case, it was essential that the results of the exercise be transformed into a report that captured the main arguments, opinions, and any agreements or decisions that might have been reached. In the run of the exercise, all conversations of the players were tape-recorded (each of the five groups individually as well as the general group discussions). The process was self-documenting in the sense that all group and plenary votes were registered on the wall charts. Staff summarized all information in one document, a white paper that captured the discussions, points of consensus, and areas where there was still a difference of opinion. This "white paper" summarized the response and supporting rationale to the four primary questions raised about the Pharmaceutical Drug Discovery and Development process (in the context of an EDF).

In addition to presenting the results of the exercise to the company Board of Directors, a follow-up version of the exercise was used in the management development program of the company as a hands-on case study of in-house decision making.

The exercise was evaluated using a composite set of criteria based on the design specifications and our general objectives in designing a strategy formulation exercise. Although the exercise was not evaluated extensively, a systematic feedback component was built into the materials. Participant evaluations were elicited through post-game debriefings that included an informal discussion of the process and results of the exercise as well as a questionnaire that assessed the success of the exercise on several criteria.

The data from the questionnaire indicated that the participants perceived the policy exercise to be successful in accomplishing most of the stated objectives. They were particularly satisfied that the exercise created a positive atmosphere for open discussion of the sensitive issues. All the participants felt free to contribute their perspectives on these issues. Furthermore, it was their overwhelming opinion that the exercise was an enjoyable process for formulating company strategy. They felt that the policy exercise uncovered aspects of the problem that they had not been aware of before and that they themselves had come up with some new ideas that were given careful consideration.

The process of development of the exercise modified the perception of the problem, thus changing the definition of the problem itself! Because of the design process used, it was possible to use progressive insights into the problem. It was discovered that product development as seen by R&D was only part of the picture (it undervalued products that were licensed during the several stages of product development). This led to a re-framing of the problem and, in the play of the exercise, a new and innovative solution was conceived that involved not building a new center at all.

In this particular case, the client viewed consensus as a very important issue (a prior decision had *not* been based on consensus and significant problems had resulted). This exercise did not guarantee that the resulting consensus was the "best" one – there is no decision process that leads to "certain" results in highly uncertain environments. The purpose of the exercise was not to predict or reach a final decision, but instead to be sure that the actors were very carefully grounded in the data, rationale and literature of the problem and to ensure them an opportunity to be heard.

Before the start of this project, the client had assembled literally a room full of data. For several years staff had collected data and expert opinions, and many studies had been completed. One of the activities of the project was to develop a computerized system for storing this information. In designing the exercise materials, a careful effort was made to connect the data and the literature with the process. For each question the participants addressed, there were specific documents that dealt with that concern. In this way, a considerable amount of data was brought into the process. They were buried in data, some of which had been transformed into information; knowledge was largely segmented on a "need to know" basis; and they were in dire need of wisdom for making their decision. The process used for this game/simulation facilitated an effective data -> information -> knowledge -> wisdom sequence.

The EDF process resulted in the formulation of two options for the structure and organization of the proposed facility. The group came close to making a consensus decision. The first option was a centralized facility located in one of several (specific) countries, while the second option was a satellite concept that would identify and support the best available talent wherever this might be found. Both of the options would tap resources unique to the European scientific community and enhance their potential to discover new pharmaceutical agents for research and development.

The client readily acknowledged sharp changes in the players' views of the new facility resulting directly from the exercise experience. Interestingly, the decision ultimately taken by the company was unique, dramatic, and clearly emerged during the discussion of the exercise:

"... through your gaming technique you allowed us to come to closure on this problem and to present to ...[The Board of Directors]... a proposal which will have profound effects upon the future of the R&D program ... the concept was very enthusiastically received and final closure for action was achieved."
(Director of International Programs, June, 1985)

### 3.4 DEREGULATION AND A RAIL CORPORATION

#### 3.4.1 The Client
The client for this exercise was the Office of Governmental Affairs for the Consolidated Rail Corporation (Conrail) in the U.S. Note that this exercise describes a historical situation – recently, Conrail has confronted new challenges that are not addressed here.

This policy exercise dealt with questions pertaining to the survival of a major corporation with serious implications for national policy. The Conrail Company was formed from several defunct railroads; subsequently, it was subsidized at great expense by the federal government. The situation Conrail faced was little short of desperate. Fearing deregulation of the railroads, Conrail initially requested an exercise that could be used to influence policy makers to sustain the subsidy. The design team rejected this approach (for ethical reasons) and convinced Conrail to develop a policy exercise to deal with its larger problems. National energy concerns required that efficient transport be developed (competition and the free enterprise system were presumed to be part of the answer); inflation fears at the time were also of great concern (Would deregulation feed the flames?)

### 3.4.2 The Problem

Conrail, a private for-profit corporation was created by Congress to take over the Penn Central Railroad and five other northeastern rail lines that had gone bankrupt during the early 1970s. It was created as an alternative to liquidation of the bankrupt lines on the one hand, or their nationalization on the other. Conrail's mission, as set forth in the Regional Rail Reorganization Act, was to integrate the six lines into an economically viable system capable of providing adequate and efficient rail service at the lowest possible cost to the general taxpayer.

Initially, Conrail was given federal loans to underwrite a massive rehabilitation of the physical plant and to absorb operating deficits as the operations of the six predecessors were reorganized and integrated. Despite these loans, Conrail continued to experience costs substantially in excess of service-generated revenues. Profitability and financial self-sustainability had yet to be achieved. The federal government was eager to transition the railroad from dependence on federal loans to self-sufficiency. This was to evolve through achievement of vigorous management reforms undertaken by Conrail management and the continued restructuring of Conrail's services and operations. In addition, the development of a customer-generated revenue base was to finance the costs of those services and to create capital for continuing reinvestment.

Conrail management initiatives encompassed efficiencies through cost reductions, prudent capital investment (federal loans, private financing, etc), increased labor productivity, aggressive sales and marketing, and improved service. Conrail management was not convinced that deregulation of governmental controls over railroad economic activity would facilitate the drive towards self-sustainability. Therefore, deregulation was a public policy issue of utmost importance. It was a concept that was highly complex and difficult to comprehend in terms of the specific implications for the relationships between Conrail and its 60,000 customers. The prospect of economic deregulation raised fears among shippers, communities, and public officials as to the consequences of such public policy – the potential for economic dislocations was of special concern.

The problem was to develop a tool that would help in communicating the benefits and potential problems inherent in deregulation (within a Conrail context) to all actors involved in the northeast rail situation, and which would show how Conrail could operate without economic regulation in its relationships with customers.

### 3.4.3 Goals, Purposes, and Objectives

The management of Conrail wanted to develop a more complete understanding of deregulation (as it was shaping up in a particular legislative bill) to gain some perspective on the in-house options available if deregulation should come to pass. They wanted to convey their new understanding to Members of Congress, their competitors, the regulatory agencies, and the public. The management objective was to allow top management to evaluate the impact on Conrail of the pending deregulation of the rail industry. The subject of this exercise was railroad deregulation; this was complex, technical and dry; nonetheless, the main actors had a serious interest in the subject. If any insight was to be gained, they would have to be pulled far enough away from their day-to-day interests so that they might distinguish the "forest from the trees."

The primary objectives of the Railroad Deregulation Game were the following:

- To sensitize the players to rail economics within the transportation industry (especially focused on the Conrail profit/loss situation);
- To provide the players with a cognitive map with which they could learn the dynamics of the critical issues facing Conrail and the transportation industry in the northeastern U.S.;
- To communicate that the economic regulation of railroads impedes market responsiveness and corporate economic vitality and to show the social and economic benefits, as well as potential problems associated with reduced economic regulation of the railroad industry; and
- To elicit and promote discussion by the participants about the comparative costs and benefits of different restructuring scenarios and to provide a vehicle for making in-depth proposals for deregulation.

### 3.4.4 Why Did the Client Select the Policy Exercise Process?

The desire for a policy exercise tool originated within the ranks of Conrail's middle management. Acting as the client, they articulated several purposes, each catering to a different audience which they hoped the exercise would serve.

The first and most important audience for the policy exercise would be Conrail's top level managers, the Board of Directors and the vice presidents. The client believed that, while top management was extremely competent in matters strictly related to the management of a railroad, it was less than fully cognizant and/or appreciative of the political context within which Conrail was forced to operate. The client was concerned that these people would base their management plans on a configuration of the system (i.e. regulatory environment and service level) that would be ideal from the management perspective but, in view of political exigencies, impossible to achieve. The client was interested in creating a simulation that would reveal to those top-level managers what the political reactions to various systems alternatives could be. The managers would then be able to form a consensus on an alternative that, though perhaps less than perfect from a management point of view, would be politically feasible.

The second audience was to be Members of Congress and their staff. The client assumed that, once Conrail management had decided on a policy direction, the exercise could be used to explain to various politicians why the proposed changes made sense. The client was interested in altering decision makers' beliefs about what the legitimate functions of a railroad ought to be. They were interested in communicating the notion that the decision to drop particular branch lines was not proposed as an end in itself, but was a by-product of the decision to drop particular commodities or services.

A less subjective purpose was also expressed. Management believed that the exercise should be used to represent to political actors the various options that were available for Conrail's configuration and operation and the extent of the existing regulations. Associated with each option would be, of course, various costs and benefits. Underlying the entire process would be the trade-off between the level of service desired and the willingness to spend public money. It would be up to the politicians themselves to choose the most attractive alternative. The purpose of the exercise would be merely to present the alternatives in such a fashion that this trade-off would be emphatic, helping the decision makers to discern how the system really worked, to be aware of the policy options, and to comprehend the political consequences of each option.

The client believed that the exercise could be beneficial in educating congressional staff, mid-level managers and state rail officials about how the Conrail system operated and why deregulation would be necessary for Conrail to move toward self-sufficiency. In addition, the exercise could be used to demonstrate why particular lines of business would be dropped if regulations were removed.

Finally, top management had a very short time between the time they resolved to look at the deregulation question and the time that they expected Congress to act. There was simply not sufficient time to justify more elaborate or rigorous scientific methods. Further, it was assumed that the problem was understood and the real question was to communicate the character of the problem to someone outside the railroad industry. Therefore, one of the primary functions of gaming, namely to transmit knowledge to some new group, appeared to validate the decision.

### 3.4.5 Specifications for Policy Exercise Design
The exercise was designed to be used in a four-hour session that included the introduction, play, and debriefing session. The intended audience for the exercise was to be representatives of government, shippers, labor, trucking, railroads, and

Conrail managers. The completed exercise was run initially for the assembled senior vice presidents in a formal setting; after final approval, it was run for the Board of Directors. Subsequently, it was used extensively in two modes:

- Within the organization as a way of transmitting to middle management the concept of how the organization would deal with the new deregulated environment; and
- Externally as a way of showing Members of Congress, State Governors, and people in competing transportation modes what the new model for Conrail would be.

### 3.4.6 The Schematic: A Model of Reality

A problem environment schematic was developed in an attempt to create a visual presentation of the network depicting the cost/price mechanisms of the economic system within which Conrail operated. Once developed, the schematic was used as a basis for deciding which issues were important enough to be represented in the final exercise. A simplified version of the railroad deregulation problem schematic is presented in Figure 3.3 below (for a more complete understanding of the schematic, see Section 8.2, Step 7 and the Appendix).

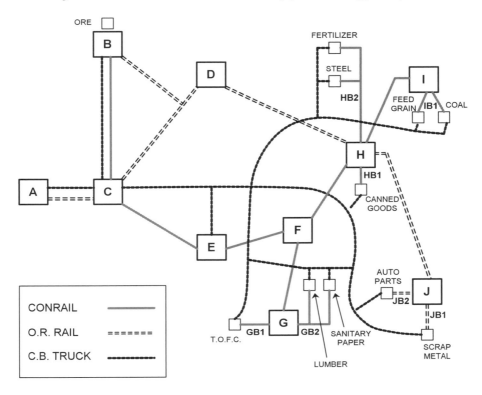

FIGURE 3.3 | CONRAIL SCHEMATIC (SIMPLIFIED)

### 3.4.7 Description of the Policy Exercise

In response to observations made while developing the schematic, the policy exercise design team selected a format that mimicked the Conrail war room located in Philadelphia. This took the form of a railroad route map that underwent a series of simplifications. The original 4,000+ terminals became 7; the 1,000+ competing transport lines became 3; the 10,000 shipment types became 11; and the 7 distinct car types evolved into 1. In turn, the process of rate setting became more central than these omitted details. The accounting system was relegated to a computer; and the final exercise became very much like a "live" case study, with the arguments and processes of rate setting being highlighted after the technical detail had been presented in the original exercise.

In the Railroad Deregulation Game, there were four main roles – Conrail, Customer, CB Trucking and OR Rail; the last two representing the competition. Real players performed these roles and made simulated decisions during the exercise. In Step 1, all participants played the role of customer; during Step 2, they were divided into the remaining roles. The objectives of these roles were as follows:

- Conrail – The primary objective of this role was to shift Conrail from deficit operations (costs in excess of revenues) to profitability. This could be achieved through rate and division increases; capturing additional, profitable traffic through competitive pricing; and/or reduction in costs by eliminating unprofitable services and their associated variable and fixed costs. The challenge to the participants was to optimize each customer and node, through various strategies, and to bring Conrail to aggregate profitability.

- Customer (Shipper) – The primary objective was to minimize transportation costs while preserving competitive service options and adequate service quality. During the run, Shippers individually or collectively negotiated rates and service with carriers for the lowest cost transport options. They were required to encourage carrier competition for their business, and if severely abused by rates (because no modal options were available), they could refuse to do business and relocate.

- CB Trucking (a competing industry) – The primary objective of this role was a continued record of profitability. They were expected to increase revenues through rate increase and/or through increased market share in profitable markets. During the exercise, the assumption was that all customers were accessible to trucks and that equipment was available to carry any and all the various commodities. The players were expected to look for opportunities to shift unprofitable rail service to inter-modal rail-truck options. If unable to increase market share directly through competitive pricing, the players were allowed to seek out opportunities with negotiated drayage charges.

- OR Rail (a competing rail company) – The primary objective of this role was to continue a record of profitability. They were expected to increase revenues through rate and division increases. An increase of revenues could be achieved through capturing additional profitable traffic through competitive pricing, and/or reduction in costs by eliminating unprofitable services and their associated fixed and variable costs.

### 3.4.8 Major Sequence of Activities

*Pre-Exercise Activities* – All participants had been given materials to read in advance as well as a workbook to complete. These materials briefly introduced the history of Conrail, and described the exercise including the objectives, the sequence of cycles, and the steps of play.

*Policy Exercise Activities* – Each completed play of the exercise required the completion of four cycles under three different sets of regulatory rules: Status quo (one cycle); Revised Regulation (one cycle); and, Deregulation (two cycles). Each cycle consisted of three steps: the Shipment Phase, the Management Phase, and the Policy Phase:

**Step 1** (Shipment Phase) – In this step, all players assumed the role of customers. They consulted rate tables and chose the cheapest transport company as well as the routing for their shipment. They drew the appropriate number of chips from the bank and paid shipment costs by distributing the payment directly on the map.

**Step 2** (Management Phase) – In this step, all players changed roles and became managers rather than customers. Each team went to the rate tables and determined this cycle's revenues and also calculated and prepared their profit and loss statements. Subsequently, the players determined the total transportation cost to the customers. At the end of this step, they determined the effects of changes in rates with the help of the facilitator.

**Step 3** (Policy Phase) – In this step, the facilitator announced and explained the rules for rate making, as well as the rules for service and line abandonment. Each team was then given a summary sheet encapsulating the situation of each customer, a table describing the costs of each shipment, and a table to record the new rates for the next cycle. After consulting traffic and cost sheets, the players set rates for each commodity according to the regulatory rules governing the round. The new rates were then posted and subjected to challenge by both competing transportation companies and shippers under the regulatory rules governing the round. At the end of this step, all players switched their roles back to customers and began the new cycle of play.

*Post-Exercise Activities* – The post-exercise stage focused on an extensive debriefing of the exercise. Debriefing was done in three phases. The first phase primarily involved discussions about the exercise and the experiences of the participants from the perspective of their roles. The second phase focused on the attempt to improve the transport companies' economics *under regulation*. The third phase focused on the attempt to improve the transport companies' economics *with deregulation*. In all phases, the issues discussed included a review of economic results and of transport company strategies. The style for presentation was a series of rate-setting problems using standard forms with a computer backup and wall graphics.

### 3.4.9 The Results

What made the Conrail exercise so challenging to create was that the development of the exercise itself modified the perception of the problem for which the exercise was intended. Thus, the definition of the problem changed substantially over time. The plasticity of the problem definition could have caused a lot of doubt. However, because of the manner in which design proceeded (see Chapter 8), it was possible for the client to gain progressive insights into the problem, and as a consequence, to develop increased confidence in the product.

The results were surprising. When the managers, as a group, were presented with the initial schematic that had been pieced together from the bits of information provided by each of them individually, it was not acceptable to any of them. At this point, it became clear that no progress could be made until the managers were able to agree about how Conrail actually operated and the mechanisms affecting the corporations' performance had been identified. Consequently, the first weeks of the design phase were devoted to working with the group of vice presidents to achieve this end. Information was solicited from each member of the group; this information was then processed and abstracted into a model (the schematic). The model was then presented to the group. The group, inevitably, would break into heated arguments over specific aspects of the model. Through several iterations of this process, the model was refined to a point where everyone could agree that the schematic was a fairly accurate representation of the Conrail system.

This process proved very valuable to Conrail's management. By forcing individuals to communicate with each other about specific elements of the system, a more elaborate, comprehensive and consistent model of the system was developed. The most significant fact about the model, however, was not its greater complexity, or its increased accuracy, but that all the managers now shared very similar concepts of the underlying system. As a result of the exercise, Conrail executives realized that rather than being a threat, deregulation could improve their position, and they used the exercise to help policy makers understand the issues involved.

The effect of this newly shared conceptual model was a quantum leap in communications. One result of this more efficient and effective discussion was the discovery that there were untapped opportunities within the system for improving profitability that could be pursued immediately and that were not dependent on regulatory reform for their success. Another result was that the managers' ideas of what type of deregulation legislation would be appropriate were substantially modified. The managers were quick to take advantage of their newfound insight. Before the exercise was ever played, policies had been initiated (as a consequence of the process used to develop it) that would eventually lead to significant improvements in Conrail's profitability.

In some respects, then, the policy exercise was a success before it had even been completed. The designers, by forcing the clients to refine their cognitive map of the problem, had room to maneuver as the perception of the problem began to shift. When the clients first approached the designers, they thought they knew two things: how the Conrail system operated, and what deregulation would mean (and they were not in favor of it!) It became evident very early on that these were untenable assumptions. The focus of the exercise design process had to shift gears rather dramatically and rapidly. It was very fortunate that this was possible, since the primary value of the professional design process employed was derived from the initial effort to develop the fundamental model of Conrail (the schematic) for the subsequent exercise.

Some evidence of success is evident in the following statement:

"[M]y experience with the benefits of gaming/simulation (for Conrail) have been profound. ..."

"As you know from your involvement, the Conrail deregulation game/simulation was an outstanding success, from a number of perspectives. The design process ... forced Conrail management to understand the nature of the problem we were attempting to solve, as well as the alternative solutions, in a manner that no other mechanism offered. Subsequent to the design of the game, we were able to use that vehicle to communicate to the body politic the benefits of economic deregulation of the railroad industry – including senior policy makers in the federal government and Congress. Many of these policy makers and federal legislators have reported to me that the game/simulation contributed significantly to the landmark legislation which, indeed, deregulated the railroad industry."

"[T]hese experiences ... have convinced me that applications of this technology offer boundless benefits in both education and industry."
(Vice President of Sales, Conrail)

## 3.5 RESTRUCTURING THE OFFICE OF THE SECRETARY OF DEFENSE

This section tells the story of the reorganization of a federal ministry. This example shows how gaming can help force strategic decisions in a crisis. The project had very little time (less than a month from inception to completion), the game format was simple and effective, and it helped to focus on the most important issues and criteria (e.g. by bringing in the outsider's perspectives via role play).

### 3.5.1 The Client

In the mid-1980s, the U. S. Department of Defense (DOD) was facing budget cuts and reorganization. The Office of the Secretary of Defense (OSD), which resides within the DOD, was required to undergo a review of its structure and organization. This review process addressed the appropriateness of the functions of the OSD; it also considered alternative forms of organizational structure. The client for this project was the OSD.

Colin Powell, on assuming his job as Chair of the Joint Chiefs of Staff, elected to review the organization of the OSD. In response to Powell's directive, the three major branches of service (Army, Navy, and Air Force) produced and submitted plans reflecting their own vision as to how the reorganization should be undertaken, but as can be imagined, there was little overlap among them. As can be expected, these plans were very thick documents reflecting the primary need to protect old positions rather than to envision any significantly new organizational scheme. A policy exercise was commissioned that would allow for a comparison of the three proposals. Colin Powell was an observer of these runs. Each service had an opportunity to present their plan through the policy exercise; after further discussion, the exercise was again used to negotiate a single compromise plan.

### 3.5.2 The Problem

A number of activities were undertaken in conjunction with this review of the OSD. Various studies were completed and a significant amount of data was assembled. In addition, a number of interviews were completed. The documentation was substantial, running to many hundreds of pages. Through a group process, these materials had to be transformed into a single brief final report with which the three services could agree. The problem addressed by this policy exercise was to create, among the group to be assembled, an environment that would permit an efficient dialogue about the impact, effectiveness, and possible unintended consequences of the proposed changes.

### 3.5.3 Goals, Purposes, and Objectives

The primary objectives of the OSD Policy Evaluation Exercise were:

- To help the review group visualize the big picture of the OSD over a medium to long-term horizon (5-15 years);
- To organize the central OSD study materials, and to present these to the review group in an efficient way;
- To evoke thoughtful discussion of the major recommendations to be presented by the study, and to capture from the discussion the agreements and disagreements and their underlying rationale; and
- To reach consensus, where possible, on recommendations to be included in the final report.

### 3.5.4 Why Did the Client Select the Policy Exercise Process?

The military has a long history of using war games (see Chapter 1); all senior officers were familiar with this approach. As a consequence, it was unnecessary to explain the technique to the central stakeholders. The OSD recognized that although this was not war, the stakes were nevertheless quite high. It was instinctive for them to turn to the policy exercise as a civilian version of war gaming. The client's belief was that most of the significant issues of concern in determining the impact, effectiveness, and unintended consequences of the proposed organizational change could be adequately introduced only through an exercise of this type.

### 3.5.5 Specifications for Policy Exercise Design

The project team consisted of researchers from the University of Michigan, an internal OSD advisory committee and external consultants. The project was negotiated to be of three weeks' duration.

The exercise was designed for use during several four-hour time periods; each included an introduction, playing time, and a critique. The game was designed for 30 players at each usage (15 senior participants and a support staff member for each). The participants were senior officers from each of the three services and several consultants who had conducted various studies pertaining to the review.

Evaluation criteria were defined at the outset. The objective of the specifications was to raise and address specific questions that anticipated the final conditions that would govern the design and use of the exercise. This is a natural extension of the problem statement, where the objectives and constraints for assessment of design, construction and use are made explicit. In this particular case, the specifications included the intended audience, the primary goals, stylistic considerations (reflective, mutual problem-solving style), and practical constraints like the duration, the number of participants, computer usage, room and material requirements and the planned recording of the participants' responses.

### 3.5.6 The Schematic: A Model of Reality

As part of the design process, a schematic was prepared which illustrated the position of this exercise relative to the activities of the OSD study group (see Figure 3.4). This schematic portrayed the big picture; it was supplemented by many graphics that had been developed to reflect the views of the individual services (for a more complete understanding of the schematic, see Section 8.2, Step 7 and the Appendix).

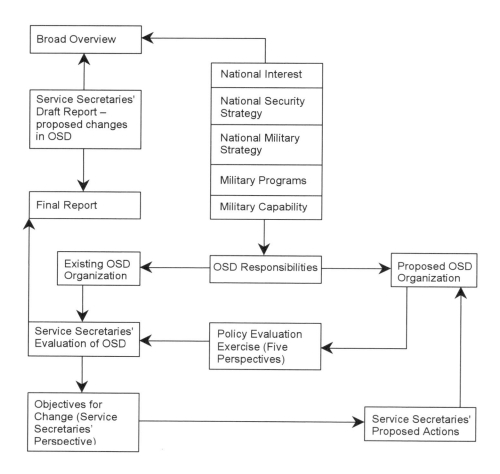

**FIGURE 3.4 | OSD SCHEMATIC (SIMPLIFIED)**

The setting for the schematic was the primary national interest in terms of national security strategy, military strategy, military programs, and their translation into military capability. Each of the service secretaries (Army, Navy, and Air Force) had developed a detailed draft report. These were in essential agreement concerning the existing organization of the OSD. The service secretaries each completed an evaluation of the existing OSD structure and effectiveness; this served as a basis for the changes recommended by each service. Several perspectives on the problem were represented (e.g. Assistant Secretaries of Defense, Service Secretaries, Congressmen, Secretary of Defense, etc.). The policy exercise was used to improve communication about the nature and implications of the proposed changes, to evaluate these changes, and to seek consensus on a proposal to reorganize the OSD.

### 3.5.7 Description of the Policy Exercise

The format of the OSD policy evaluation exercise was simple and straightforward, with little paraphernalia used. The setting was comparable to a highly organized seminar. The sequence of activity throughout the day was the same as the order of presentation of materials in the pre-work notebook (see below). The objective was to move towards consensus on as many issues as possible, to record agreements and disagreements, and to capture the essence of the arguments raised in all cases. The materials used during the exercise consisted of role-specific spiral binders. Participants were asked to address the issues by marking decision charts. These charts were developed as wall-sized materials by the OSD for display during the exercise. These materials facilitated the self-documentation of the process.

### 3.5.8 Major Sequence of Activities

The OSD policy evaluation exercise consisted of three distinct phases: pre-game, game, and post-game. During the pre-game phase, the roles were individual. During the exercise, three roles were combined into one team (five teams, 15 people). Staff were assigned tasks as required. Discussion was first within teams and then between teams. Participants were combined into groups of three and asked to join together as one "perspective" on the problem (Assistant Secretaries of Defense, Service Secretaries, CINC, Congressman, Secretary of Defense, etc.).

*Pre-Exercise Activities* – During the pre-exercise activities, the participants were given pre-work, which required that they review the materials and commit to a position on each major issue presented. They were to do this from the perspective of the role to which they had been assigned. Participants were required to do two types of pre-work:

- Reading assignments – Selected readings were sent to the participants before the exercise. These were essentially abstracts of significant documents that were intended to refresh the memories of the participants; and
- Pre-game workbooks – A decision book was completed by the participants and returned 24 hours before the run of the exercise. This consisted of a separate decision sheet for each proposed action under consideration by the study group.

*Policy Exercise Activities* – The game was designed to run for a full day, broken into two sessions. The morning session lasted three hours and the afternoon session lasted four hours. After the sponsor introduced workshop participants, stressed the importance of the exercise, and introduced the facilitator, the facilitator described the purpose of the OSD Policy Evaluation exercise, the teams were formed and the time horizon and inter-team competition were established. After these initial activities, the participants engaged in the evaluation of proposed actions from their role perspectives. The steps were as follows:

- Development of new ideas for actions;
- Discussion of the objective within teams;
- Recording of team decisions on worksheets;
- Transfer of decisions to wall charts;
- Team presentations;
- Inter-team discussion; and
- Final evaluation of actions from team perspectives.

The issues discussed were:

- National strategy linkages;
- Effective and efficient defense;
- Reduction of OSD micro-management;
- Effective defense planning;
- Consistent policy direction; and
- Clear lines of authority.

In this phase, the teams confronted the decisions of the individual members. To the extent that different positions had been taken, arguments were advanced within group discussions; the objective was to reach consensus. If consensus could not be reached, the rationale of the various positions was recorded for inclusion in the final report. As the exercise progressed through several iterations, each team was given a worksheet on which to record answers to the questions presented. These were then posted on the wall charts for the entire group to view and to guide subsequent discussions (See Figure 3.5).

*Post-Exercise Activities* – The post-game activities for participants included the debriefing of the exercise and out-of-role discussion and evaluations of proposed actions. Following the post-game activities, participants completed an evaluation. A white paper was also developed that captured arguments (pro/con and modifications to) the proposed actions.

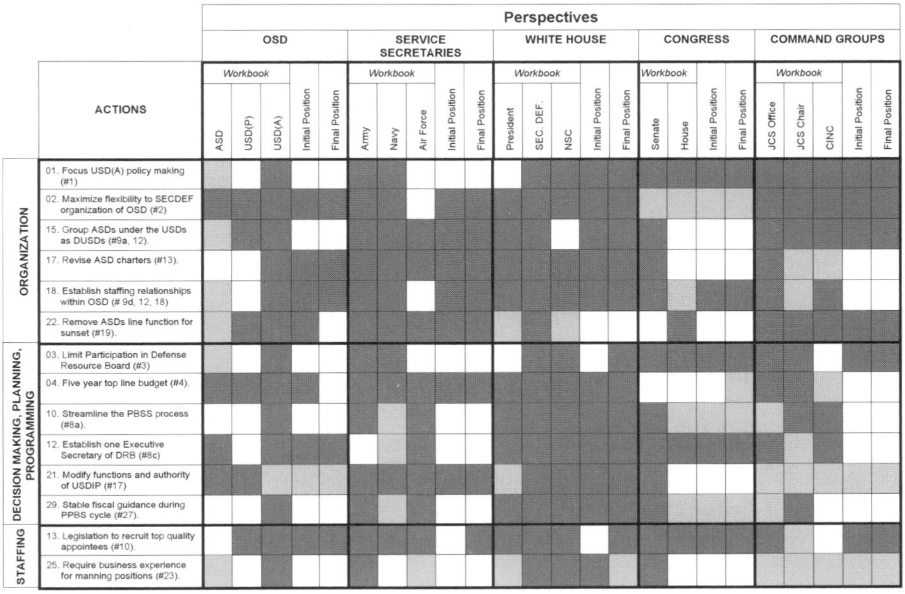

| ACTIONS | Perspectives | | | | | | | | | | | | | | | | | | | | | |
|---|---|---|---|---|---|---|---|---|---|---|---|---|---|---|---|---|---|---|---|---|---|---|
| | OSD | | | | | SERVICE SECRETARIES | | | | | WHITE HOUSE | | | | | CONGRESS | | | | COMMAND GROUPS | | | |
| | Workbook | | | Initial Position | Final Position | Workbook | | | Initial Position | Final Position | Workbook | | | Initial Position | Final Position | Workbook | | Initial Position | Final Position | Workbook | | | Initial Position | Final Position |
| | ASD | USD(P) | USD(A) | | | Army | Navy | Air Force | | | President | SEC. DEF. | NSC | | | Senate | House | | | JCS Office | JCS Chair | CINC | | |

**ORGANIZATION**
- 01. Focus USD(A) policy making (#1)
- 02. Maximize flexibility to SECDEF organization of OSD (#2)
- 15. Group ASDs under the USDs as DUSDs (#9a, 12).
- 17. Revise ASD charters (#13).
- 18. Establish staffing relationships within OSD (# 9d, 12, 18)
- 22. Remove ASDs line function for sunset (#19).

**DECISION MAKING, PLANNING, PROGRAMMING**
- 03. Limit Participation in Defense Resource Board (#3)
- 04. Five year top line budget (#4).
- 10. Streamline the PBSS process (#8a).
- 12. Establish one Executive Secretary of DRB (#8c)
- 21. Modify functions and authority of USDIP (#17)
- 29. Stable fiscal guidance during PPBS cycle (#27).

**STAFFING**
- 13. Legislation to recruit top quality appointees (#10).
- 25. Require business experience for manning positions (#23).

**FIGURE 3.5 | OSD WALL CHART: POSITIONS TAKEN ON ACTIONS**

### 3.5.9 The Results

Results of the run were outlined in a white paper, which presented the perspectives that were represented, advocated, and discussed at the run. The three services (Army, Navy, and Air Force) each recommended policy changes. For each recommendation, there was a presentation of each of the perspectives (i.e. Congress, White House, Service Secretaries, Office of the Secretary of Defense, and Command Groups). These recommendations were designed to achieve a number of objectives as designated by the study group. The eventual resolution was the development of a hybrid plan that involved parts of all three proposals. These recommendations were designed to achieve a number of objectives as designated by the study group:

- Provide for a clear linkage between National Strategy and Defense Programming;
- Provide for more effective and efficient acquisition of defense capability;
- Reduce micro-management by the OSD of the various Department of Defense components;
- Provide for more effective defense planning;
- Improve feedback of the program planning and budgeting process;
- Provide for more consistent policy direction by the OSD; and
- Improve the clarity of lines of authority.

The results of the exercise are best summed up as follows:

*"[T]his was a very 'short fuse' project, with requirements changing daily..."*

*"[T]he Policy Evaluation Exercise that was developed and run by [your team] has been very helpful in assisting our team in the development of the rationale supporting the recommendations to be included in the report. We were impressed not only with the value of the discussions evoked from the 'roles' employed, but also by the general utility of your process in helping the participants communicate. There is no question that your methodology helped us move to consensus more quickly than would have otherwise been possible. ..."*

(Study Director, Office of the Secretary of Defense, Department of the Army)

### 3.6 Cultural Change within the Technical Components Industry
(The consulting organization that developed this policy exercise was Simulation Solutions of Ann Arbor, Michigan. This case description uses materials provided to us by Steve Underwood, President, Simulation Solutions).

The client in this case is a very large company in the high tech and global components industry. This industry has become intensely competitive in recent years, as the result of a variety of factors in this complex market. In the U.S., domestic producers are putting an increasing (some might say bewildering) array of new products on the market each year. Foreign manufacturers have become highly competitive in several ways: many new products enter the market each year; the quality of some foreign producers is perceived as superior to American ones (as reflected in sales figures); and these other firms are competing effectively on price. As a consequence of these and several other trends, the situation facing the industry is critical.

#### 3.6.1 The Client
In response to these pressures, a large U.S. firm elected to spin off a major division as a new entity. The belief was that the division, as embedded historically in the parent company, was inefficient and a drain on scarce resources. Further, it was believed that, once established as a free-standing firm, the division would be able to compete directly with the other major competitors. An independent company with a new organizational structure was formed. This was a major undertaking requiring top-to-bottom restructuring, the acquisition of new facilities, and the sorting of employees into those who stayed behind and those who would be part of the new company.

The new company was formed to enhance and expand one of the most comprehensive product ranges among the world's comparable component suppliers. To succeed, the client had to accelerate growth, expand systems and module capabilities, create catalysts for growth and change, establish a clear brand identity, and assist in making its customers successful.

The new management team developed a corporate model reflecting their vision, mission, strategy and processes. There was an intense and expensive effort to abandon old ways and to "turn things upside down" in the search for an effective organization. After due process, the company was launched with considerable public fanfare.

### 3.6.2 The Problem

The new organization had two categories of employees: holdovers from the parent company and new hires. Management felt that it was essential to establish a completely new corporate culture and to imbue each employee (old and new) with a working knowledge of the new vision and mission. Management of the new firm was concerned that employees from the original firm would carry over loyalties, attitudes and procedures from the original company (e.g. we have always done it this way); they would say the correct things, but fail to take the appropriate actions. It was felt that the potential for conflict between the two groups was large. There was a strongly perceived need to address this problem forcefully.

After review, management felt that employees needed a tool to help them understand and adopt this new culture. Traditional methods were reviewed with care. A training division was established and it quickly created ten training modules designed to reflect the new corporate model, each requiring a half-day of classroom teaching. Testing these modules revealed two things: they were thoughtfully designed and well presented; however, they were not creating any sense of enthusiasm on the part of the trainees (they required four eight-hour days of sitting and listening).

The structure of the new company differed dramatically from the parent company. The parent company had a "silo" or "chimney" organizational structure; the new organization had a matrix organizational structure. To succeed, the client had to ingrain in its employees both an understanding of the matrix structure as well as a sense of how to use the new structure effectively. The problem was this: traditional methods (lectures, presentations, readings, etc.) were neither getting the message across nor building esprit de corps. The client wanted a dynamic tool that would induce participants to become fully engaged as a consequence of internalizing the lessons presented through the exercise.

### 3.6.3 Goals, Purposes, and Objectives

The primary goal of this exercise was to give managers and employees a new perspective on the business. There was a need to train all employees (old and new) about the new corporate culture. The exercise was to provide an awareness of the systemic relationships among business departments such as operations, finance, engineering, sales, and other functions. The objective was to create a highly interactive learning process that would permit the group, through self-discovery, to identify new opportunities to learn and to practice new skills. The substantive areas to be addressed included (among others):

- Creating an awareness of the organization's strengths and weaknesses;
- Fostering the need to communicate and express new ideas;
- Encouraging and reward teamwork;
- Creating a stressful "real world" environment where tasks and people are managed simultaneously; and
- Through the financial aspects of the simulation, allowing people who traditionally work independently to see the benefits of working together.

### 3.6.4 Why Did the Client Select the Policy Exercise Process?

One member of the training team had previous experience with gaming/simulation. She prevailed on management to consider proposals from outside consultants to design a week-long gaming exercise into which more compact versions of the original training modules would be injected between cycles of play. The truncated content of the modules would be incorporated into the game.

Management was wary. They perceived the situation as urgent and of central importance. They wanted to "hit the ground running" because survival depended on their ability to go it alone – support from the parent company would not be available to bail them out. A major investment was required to develop the exercise and train their staff in its use. Several intense meetings were held, calls were made to previous gaming clients, and a further analysis of the already finished teaching modules was completed. Management decided to take the risk of going ahead with a policy exercise.

### 3.6.5 Specifications for Policy Exercise Design
The intent of the interactive format was to increase participant learning and transferability to the work environment; it was also intended to make the learning experience more enjoyable and memorable. A detailed set of specifications was negotiated. This was an unusually complex task because the organization had no "history" of training (it was a new company) or previous experience with gaming. Some of the major agreements were:

- The simulation would require four or five days (a function of variable training constraints);
- The exercise had to work with as few as 18 participants or with as many as 50;
- The optimum number of participants was to be in the low 30s;

- Larger numbers (in the range of 40 to 60 participants) would require two exercises to be run simultaneously;
- The exercise would require a single well-trained facilitator (subsequent experience with the game revealed that it is best to use two facilitators;)
- The graphics for the exercise had to be readily portable;
- All pieces needed to be reusable;
- It should take no more than an hour to set the exercise up and about the same to dismantle it;
- Content modules were to be interspersed between the exercise cycles; and
- The combined training modules and play of the exercise required a week (more or less).

### 3.6.6 The Schematic: A Model of Reality

The model for the exercise was an integration of several theoretical models, including the prisoners' dilemma and the three-person coalition exercise. The payoff structure permitted the participants to benefit if they communicated well among divisions and discovered opportunities to integrate their own products. It also helped them to communicate among job functions that included marketing, engineering, and manufacturing. The structure also created dilemmas when two of the divisions could benefit most from cooperating. However, by adding a third division to the mix, someone had to take a loss (i.e. the coalition dilemma).

One of the special features of this exercise was that the simulated product (i.e. the components) was very abstract; it can be used to train with different "product" environments. The exercise provides opportunities for systems integration within divisions for product development, marketing, and manufacturing/operations (game pieces are abstract).

### 3.6.7 Description of the Policy Exercise

In this exercise, the participants designed, manufactured and marketed products while running their own company. This exposed new employees to dilemmas that they had to resolve by adopting strategies based upon the new company's management principles and philosophies. During this activity, the employees created their own spontaneous learning experience.

Because the company had a matrix structure, participants each carried two roles throughout the exercise. These included managerial roles (vice president of marketing, vice president of operations and vice president of support) and divisional roles (strategic business units, marketing and operations). The horizontal rows in Figure 3.6 illustrate the type of communication and coordination that had to occur to achieve a successful company (e.g. price, cost, shareholder value, etc.).

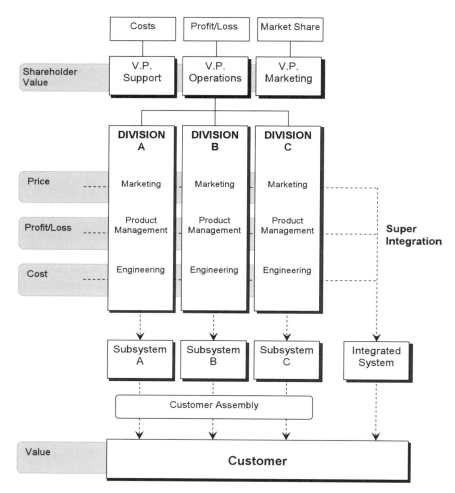

**FIGURE 3.6 | CORPORATE CULTURE SCHEMATIC (SIMPLIFIED)**

The managerial roles were responsible for company-wide activities. The vice president of marketing was responsible for marketing, sales and service; the vice president of operations for developing products consistent with the company's strategy; and the vice president of support for human resources, accounting, payroll, and information technology. The company had three divisions. Each of these strategic business units bore responsibility for a single product. Marketing was responsible for price, product, promotion, and physical distribution. Operations represented the physical plant where production occurs.

The exercise had a rich visual environment; players handled colored artifacts that represented production. These were placed on large wall charts to reflect the processes employed. As the sophistication of the group increased, these wall charts reflected the progress of each of the three divisions. This gave the participants an opportunity to see how each division was doing and provided clues as to how greater cooperation could be achieved. These wall charts also provided an excellent backdrop for the end-of-cycle critiques and the final debriefing. There were one or more facilitators present, depending on the size of the group (typically there were two).

### 3.6.8 MAJOR SEQUENCE OF ACTIVITIES

*Pre-Exercise Activities*

Appropriate materials were distributed beforehand; these included:
- A letter of invitation with the particulars of the exercise;
- A description of the purpose of the exercise;
- A description of the logistics;
- The activities associated with the experience;
- What was expected of the participants;
- A description of the roles to be played in the exercise;
- The scenario; and
- A summary form of the basic materials that the participants would encounter.

*Policy Exercise Activities* – The exercise was conducted over a period of four or five days. The exercise began with a morning welcoming and orientation session (See Figure 3.7). Each half day following, a new problem (training module) was introduced and a new cycle of play was completed. Between each cycle, the facilitators fed in players' decisions to a computer simulation and calculated the current status of the business. The results of these calculations were employed to introduce the next cycle of play.

| DAY 1 | DAY 2 | DAY 3 | DAY 4 |
|---|---|---|---|
| *Welcome* | *Check-In* | *Check-In* | *Check-In* |
| VALUES AND BEHAVIORS | TRANSFORMATION | OUR BRAND | DIVERSITY |
| Simulation Cycle 1 (Walk Through) | Cycle 3 (New Markets) | Cycle 5 (Expanding Markets) | Cycle 7 (Pulling it all together) |
| *Lunch* | *Lunch* | *Lunch* | *Lunch* |
| Cycle 2 (New Horizons) | Cycle 4 (Customer Relations) | Cycle 6 (Customer Demands) | Pulling it all Together |
| INDUSTRY AND COMPETITION | FEEDBACK | BUSINESS ACUMEN | *Evaluation and Check-out* |
| *Check-out* | *Check-out* | *Check-out* | |

FIGURE 3.7 | MAJOR SEQUENCE OF ACTIVITIES

Each cycle had five identical steps of play: planning, negotiation and design, production and testing, assessment (scoring) and the critique.

*Post-Exercise Activities* – A debriefing was conducted at the end of the exercise; this was carried through two distinct stages. The first was an initial "venting" session during which the participants were permitted to talk about things that happened during the exercise. This process promoted open discussion and led to the second stage of the debriefing: focusing the group's attention on the central purpose of the exercise. Participants were provided with material that summarized the events of the exercise; these notes served to reinforce the "message" from the experience. Finally, the participants completed a post-exercise evaluation form.

### 3.6.9 THE RESULTS

The policy exercise has been successfully employed as part of the business orientation program since the fall of 1999. To date, several thousand employees have been through the exercise; the intention is to provide all employees with the opportunity to participate.

Formal technical evaluation was undertaken at each of the major phases of development (see Section 8.2.4, Step 15); subsequent evaluation was continued during the use of the exercise. Participants scored early tests runs (while the exercise was under development) 3.6 on a scale of 5; each subsequent run was evaluated. The final three test runs scored 4.5 or better. Surveys document that the participants really enjoyed themselves. The exercise created an esprit de corps that was evidenced by the creation of an informal "club" of those who have played the exercise as well as by evidence of enthusiasm in the workplace attributed by the workers to their participation.

An unexpected benefit was the function served by the exercise as an ice-breaker for new employees. This was one of their first activities after being hired and it was an immediate and direct challenge of their capabilities. Because they were successful by the end of the week, they left with a sense of exhilaration that they shared with their colleagues (See Section 7.4.1 The Presentation of the Exercise).

Some evidence of the reaction of participants is reflected by these comments:

> "... [the] exercise ... is getting rave revues. The simulation, complex though it may be, is adding value." (Director, Employee & Organization Development)

Typical of the comments from the participants:

> "... the new employee orientation ... [was] ... a true learning experience. I now ... have a better understanding of ... where we, as a company, are heading. I do

have to admit that the first day was rough and not much fun. The simulation start-up took its toll on me, but I got over that the second day and things got better as the days progressed. Thank you for providing a very useful learning tool, instead of just another class that you sit in, listen to people and try not to fall asleep."

## 3.7 MANAGING INFORMATION FOR A GOVERNMENTAL SOCIAL PROGRAM

### 3.7.1 The Client

This section describes how gaming helped the Dutch National Social Employment Program (SEP) develop a strategic Management Information System (MIS) that would support the introduction of a radically different system of budget financing. There was significant time pressure; the game (SWIFT) was primarily structured to force strategic decision making through negotiated compromise. The SEP incorporated more than 200 social workplaces in which approximately 70,000 handicapped people worked. A special provision in the law required that the program had to be coordinated by the Ministry of Social Affairs; however, the executing organizations had almost complete operational freedom as long as they worked within the framework of the law that governed the SEP.

Unfortunately, there were no generic assessment methods available for this unique program. One reason was that the program had both social and economic objectives. Standard assessment procedures from the private business sector were only partly relevant. Operational assessment techniques for an organization like the SEP cannot be found in the literature. As a consequence, an assessment system had to be created using the wisdom of as many internal experts as possible.

The program was offered to people who were able to work, but because of their disability or other factors (e.g. mental problems), they were not yet able to hold a job under normal labor market conditions. The SEP's intention was to create work that was focused on the recovery, conservation and improvement of the working skills of the disabled individual. The program had 10,000 supporting staff that managed the individual workplaces and provided medical and other forms of service and coaching.

The central government was responsible for the formulation of the general SEP policy. It controlled the execution of the law and provided 80 percent of the funds. The local municipality contributed 20 percent of the financing. The day-to-day operation took place in local organizations with local management teams. A board represented local government and several local stakeholders on behalf of the sponsoring organizations. The central government was represented in the regional areas by a regional advisor. This senior employee of the central government fulfilled a communication function between local agencies and the central program administration. He was available for consultation and was responsible for part of the supervision.

Within the Ministry of Social Affairs and Employment (in 1986), the Directorate for Complementary Social Provisions (CSV) was entrusted with the Social Employment Program. CSV regulated the money flow and had to adapt the SEP to changes in overall national policy priorities. It also made proposals for improvement of the efficiency and effectiveness of the execution of the program. Furthermore, it made attempts to relate program activities to the other programs in the social security field. The government spent about 3 billion guilders (1.5 billion U.S. dollars at that time) annually on the SEP. It was evident that the money flow to the local organizations was paralleled by an information flow under the direction of the CSV Directorate. The program was governed by four important managerial bodies:

- The central CSV directorate that reported to the Minister of Social Affairs who reported to parliament;
- The regional advisors, each of whom controlled several local units;
- The local supervising boards who controlled the work of one local management team; and
- The local management team that ran one local organization.

### 3.7.2 The Problem

The quality of the SEP information system had always been a heavily debated subject. Criticism was directed against its enormous inefficiency and total lack of strategic relevance. Over the years, an excessive information system had been built up in the SEP and its enormous expansion had led to several problems. For example, an unacceptable variety of forms and records were completed, sent, and processed; and rules for distributing or handling the information were unclear or not enforced. Despite these problems, the improvement of the system had been postponed.

In 1986, important and urgent issues finally gave cause to the unavoidable systematic and critical analysis of the information system; parliament forced the SEP to implement a strict budget financing system instead of the open-ended system being used at the time. Because the money flow was dependent on the performance of each organization, its implementation presumed the explicit monitoring and assessment of every executing SEP organization. The management of the central directorate had become convinced that the present management information system (MIS) was not adequate for systematic and honest monitoring and assessment of the local organizations.

The consequence was that an assessment system had to be created based on the wisdom and experience of the stakeholders in this network. Apart from this analytical argument, there was another very important reason for the adoption of a participatory method for the MIS design. The executing organizations were awaiting the introduction of the new budget system with fear and suspicion. Was it not just a budget-cutting tool instead of an improvement process? There were several inconsistencies in the way the SEP law was executed. For example, local organizations were forced to work as efficiently as possible, preferably competing against market prices. At the same time, the idea was to make sure that the best people moved on to the regular labor market, but the ones most likely to move were the ones that enabled a local manager to adopt relatively efficient production processes. It was quite uncertain what parliament would do with the SEP, since there were voices in parliament that felt the SEP had grown much too quickly and had accumulated people who did not belong in the program. There was a great need for discussion among the different managerial echelons concerning how to create a workable, honest, relevant and robust information system. The expectation was that the participation of the several administrative levels would result in more motivation, a more integral MIS and less resistance during the reconstruction of the assessment instruments.

CSV gave the assignment for a participatory gaming project to a team from two universities. The CSV Board was the formal principal and worked closely and continuously with the project team during the project. As an extra guarantee for good teamwork between the project team and the client, a member of the ministry's staff joined the project team. The SWIFT project was executed in 1986/1987. This means that many of the problems discussed here were in a setting quite different from today's (2003) situation.

### 3.7.3 Goals, Purposes, and Objectives

The SWIFT project was intended to set the priorities for the redesign and the re-implementation of an improved management information system for the Social Employment Program. The project had three primary objectives:

- To produce a detailed description of the existing information system within its current organizational setting;
- To assess the current system from the perspectives of the four main managerial levels; and
- To find and integrate options to improve the system in terms of effectiveness and efficiency especially regarding the monitoring and assessment of the local SEP organizations.

### 3.7.4 Why Did the Client Select the Policy Exercise Process?

The gaming/simulation method was more or less "discovered" by a high-ranking staff civil servant. His task was to advise the CSV Board about policy development. He pleaded internally for the application of this method because he expected a great deal from the participatory features. He was convinced that a new and usable information system would only be created if central government started an open dialogue with representatives in the field, something he believed had not been done enough in the past. This methodology was adopted because it had an internal "champion" who used the urgency of the problem and the lack of success in dealing with the prior information system as arguments to convince his internal clients on the relevance of the gaming methodology. That meant that the client had not had any practical experience with this approach, nor had any other form of participatory policy development ever been seriously attempted. Not only was the subject matter (i.e. the redesign of the information system) under a lot of political stress, so was the choice of the way to approach this problem.

### 3.7.5 Specifications for Policy Exercise Design
The exercise was designed for an eight-hour framework that included the introduction, play and debriefing. The game was played three times. Each time, different but comparable representatives of the four managerial echelons were invited to participate. A systematic selection procedure made sure that the participants constituted a pluriform, representative sample of the leadership of the organization. The exercise was run with participants from the four important organizational levels (see above).

### 3.7.6 The Schematic: A Model of Reality
A problem environment schematic was developed in an attempt to create a visual presentation of the information system currently in operation. Although almost everyone had an opinion on the functioning of the current system, a precise overview of the total information system was missing. The schematic was produced during and on the basis of several group sessions and many interviews with the four management levels and several other stakeholders. An important function of this schematic was knowledge elicitation because no individual had a total overview. More importantly, the schematic functioned as a tool for problem framing and as a negotiation vehicle among the parties concerning the questions that were to be the agenda of the policy exercise. For example, the local managers insisted that the information system should take into account that the SEP law put contradictory performance pressures on the local organizations.

For the local managers, the game could only be successful if CSV would accept that the policy exercise should address the question: Are the goals of the law relevant and suitable to use in a monitoring and assessment system? Another item that emerged was the need to define clear rules for the separation of information for "assessment" and information for "policy development." The local organizations made it quite clear they would not volunteer to send relevant suggestions for new policy development to CSV if they ran the risk that this information would be used against them in the assessment phase. Several other differences in perception and micro-political issues emerged and had to be incorporated in the agenda of the exercise.

CSV management considered the schematic an important interim product of this project. The final schematic was used as a basis for deciding what issues and system components were important enough to be represented in the final exercise. A simplified version of the information system schematic is presented in Figure 3.8 (for a more complete understanding of the schematic, see Section 8.2, Step 7).

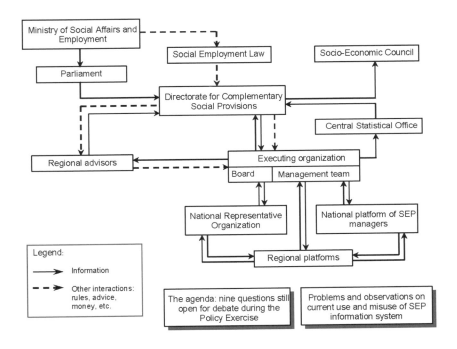

**FIGURE 3.8 | SEP PROBLEM SCHEMATIC (SIMPLIFIED)**

### 3.7.7 Description of the Policy Exercise (The SWIFT Game)

The policy exercise design team dictated the following scenario: a fire had destroyed the existing MIS, and there was only an abstract remaining. The system had to be rebuilt as fast as possible. Therefore, the Ministry had invited the game participants to rebuild the MIS in one day. There were two preconditions: the system must be as compact as possible and it had to be relevant.

In the SWIFT Game, there were four main roles: CSV, regional advisors, the supervising boards and local management teams. All participants played the role that corresponded with the position they fulfilled in the organization. The description of the role stated: "Due to your position inside the SEP, you are an expert on relevant aspects of the SEP information processes. This is why the CSV Board wants your advice about the rebuilding and improvement of the MIS. During the discussions, you are specifically invited to clarify and defend the interests and perspectives of your organizational position."

The participants were divided into teams of three. In the morning, the participants with the same role worked together. In the afternoon, the teams were mixed. In the evening, the participants assessed the results in terms of both utility and robustness. After the game, the participants received a questionnaire about their experiences. This information was used for assessing the gaming process.

The format of the game was role playing and negotiated decision making following a logically ordered set of decision problems presented to the team as semi-structured multiple choice questions on forms and wall charts. The ten questions were addressed using these five steps of play:

- Group discussion
- Group decision
- Group presentation
- Plenary discussion
- Plenary decision

Every question within the game material offered different alternatives. The participants discussed the alternatives, created new options where necessary and made (under some time pressure) a team decision.

### 3.7.8 Major Sequence of Activities

*Pre-Exercise Activities* – One month before the gaming session, all participants received materials to read as well as a workbook to complete. This workbook described the main results of the problem environment schematic, the objectives, the procedures to be followed and the substantive content of the session. The workbook also contained a questionnaire about the decision topics that had to be resolved during the game. The participants completed the questionnaire and sent it back a week before the session. The individual answers were presented on large wall charts in the game room and on the discussion forms each player received.

*Policy Exercise Activities* – The discussion topics in the game covered the important policy tasks of the CSV directorate (assessment of executing units, policy analysis and policy development). Within every subject, the central question was: "What information does the CSV Board need to fulfill its tasks in an effective and efficient way?" The following questions were discussed consecutively:

Morning:

- What information was required for the assessment of the executing units?
- What main objectives of the SEP law have a role to play in the assessment of local organizations?
- Which of 56 characteristics of the performance of local organizations as identified during the systems analytical phase (or other aspects yet to be named) should be used for the assessment?

Afternoon:

General Information
- What kind of methodological criteria have to be fulfilled by the monitoring system?
- How can the chosen assessment aspects be translated into an operational instrument (that fulfills the methodological criteria)?
- How can assessment norms be developed?

Information for policy development:
- What were the relevant indicators and problems with which the CSV Board had to be familiar?
- What additional (external) information was necessary?
- How can a policy development information system be established?

Information for the executing units:
- What kind of information from the CSV Board can the executing units use?
- How can this information feedback be organized?

*Post-Exercise Activities* – The post-exercise stage started with an extensive debriefing of the exercise. The participants assessed the results in terms of usefulness and robustness. The expected and potential changes in the SEP had to be taken into account. Would the information system created in the exercise also be relevant if certain changes in the SEP occurred? Techniques like brainstorming gave the participants a final opportunity, free from the decision pressure of the game, to present their ideas and concerns.

### 3.7.9 The Results
The policy conclusions of the SWIFT project were based on the data collected during the analysis and the three game runs. During the sessions, the information was recorded by means of:

- The discussion forms filled in by the participants;
- Wallboards which recorded the votes of the teams;

- Discussion protocols of each team meeting and every plenary debate; and
- Tapes of all the meetings.

The project identified the following problems as most urgent:

- The current MIS was severely "polluted": it was unnecessarily complex, too extensive and too detailed;
- A transparent structure with consistent rules was clearly missing;
- The CSV Board had a shortage of data-processing capacity;
- Currently, the assessment of the executing units happened in an opaque and one-dimensional (i.e. financial) manner;
- The present information available within the SEP organizations was badly structured and hardly ever used for policy development;
- A systematic and flexible provision for policy assessment was lacking; and
- Because of the poor quality of information, coordination between the executing organizations was absent.

Corresponding to the three objectives, the SWIFT project had the following final results:

- A detailed description of the content and structure of the existing MIS;
- Evaluation of the functioning of the MIS and an agreement on existing problems; and
- Recommendations on how the current MIS could be improved.

The policy exercise resulted in proposals for several profound changes in the MIS. Recommendations were formulated working together with the client, and they were all accepted. The CSV Board expressed its satisfaction with the applied procedures and the project results both verbally and in writing. The SWIFT report was one of the building blocks underlying the white paper proposing an MIS reorganization plan to parliament in the autumn of 1987. The actual reorganization started in 1988.

The questionnaire showed that the participants of the policy exercise were highly satisfied with the process. A large majority, 85 percent, was convinced that the sessions were a good basis for actual improvements to the MIS. They saw the policy exercise as a good investment of time. Half the participants had been involved in the analysis of the system and these interviews required additional time. The personal contact with colleagues from other parts of the organization was highly appreciated.

The SWIFT project was shown to be successful. A major part of this success was achieved by the use of the policy exercise technique: an involving and creative way to redesign a complex institution like a governmental MIS in a participatory and yet efficient process.

## 3.8 Science Policy for the Great Lakes Ecosystem

The IJC case has certain features that are new in comparison to the other cases; the IJC case is more clearly multiparty in nature. Furthermore, although there is enormous cognitive complexity in the other seven examples, in the IJC case, the design team faced the most complicated knowledge household of all. This was a project of the College of Engineering at The University of Michigan; Steve Underwood was the project director.

### 3.8.1 The Client

The client for this project was the International Joint Commission (IJC) on the Great Lakes. A cooperative effort had been underway for many years to protect the Great Lakes of North America. Both public and private agencies had focused their efforts on gaining a greater scientific understanding; the IJC had been central to these efforts. The IJC was established as a cooperative institution of the Canadian and U.S. governments; it is responsible for recommending research policy. The IJC adopted an ecosystems approach to establishing research priorities for the Great Lakes basin. This required a shared framework for discussing and evaluating priorities necessitating an interdisciplinary science-policy dialogue that included both human and natural systems.

### 3.8.2 The Problem

The Great Lakes, located between Canada and the U.S., represent the largest body of fresh water in the world. These lakes, in combination with the St. Lawrence Seaway and other connecting bodies of water, are of global significance. The human population is focused largely along the southern and eastern parts of the Great Lakes (Chicago, Detroit, Toronto, Cleveland, and Montreal). In total, there are about 50 million people located in the states and provinces adjacent to the Great Lakes. These lakes serve not only a large regional population, but through commerce, they provide access to world markets. The economies of both Canada and the U.S. are heavily dependent on these lakes. Another major factor in the economies of this ecosystem is commercial recreation.

The Great Lakes water system consists not only of the ground water flows within the basin, but includes climate factors and underground water flows as well. These lakes are ecologically threatened both because of poor environmental practice within the watershed as well as from the introduction of industrial toxins. Waterborne commerce is a central feature of the Great Lakes with ships from around the world plying these waters. These ships have served as the vehicle for the introduction of exotic species; these pests have caused significant ecological damage and great financial drain on the economies of the area.

Within the Great Lakes ecosystem, the food chain is quite complex. Various organisms at the base of the food chain provide sustenance for organisms that are higher on the food chain; humans are at the top of this pyramid. Persistent organic chemicals such as PCBs accumulate in the various organisms; the highest levels are found in the organisms at the top of the food chain. In some cases, these accumulations of chemicals had become critical. Concentrations in the eggs of some birds had become toxic, preventing their hatching. Concentrations in some fish had made them inedible. These chemicals are produced as by-products of various industrial products; they enter the water through sewer out-falls and other sources. Many of these chemicals are persistent – they retain their toxicity through a very long half-life. As a consequence, poor environmental practices from as early as the 19th century remain an environmental threat in some areas.

The problem was to assist the research community and policy makers in finding a comprehensive, coherent, communicable strategy that provided clear options regarding environmental issues in the Great Lakes/St. Lawrence basin. The IJC had been mostly inward-looking when addressing these issues; often not taking a multi-disciplinary, interdisciplinary, or trans-disciplinary approach to the problems. The interested parties involved in various aspects of Great Lakes research were not communicating or cooperating across boundaries, whether jurisdictional or sector oriented (Underwood, et al., 1994).

### 3.8.3 Goals, Purposes, and Objectives
The goal was to develop an ongoing policy exercise process for the IJC to address the Great Lakes ecosystem; it was to be generic, providing an overview of all relevant concerns. Within the context of this process, the IJC would be able to better evaluate its decisions on individual projects and activities as they related to one another. When completed, the IJC would be able to address a wide variety of specific problems (i.e. toxic waste), one by one. The specific objectives of this framework policy exercise were to:

- Improve communication in a complex environment through the creation of a meta-model that would serve as a framework for decision making;
- Employ an ongoing process and artifact base to illustrate (model) how the integration of issues, information, and actions might be achieved;
- Provide and coordinate access for policy makers to networks of research expertise that could be tailored to provide answers to broad-based (worldview) ecosystem policy questions; and
- Address all aspects of ecosystem behaviors in a comprehensive, coherent and communicable way, such that problems would be viewed in a multi-disciplinary manner and the research approach taken would be interdisciplinary, trans-disciplinary and responsive to the management needs of the policy maker.

### 3.8.4 Why Did the Client Select the Policy Exercise Process?

An interesting situation had developed in the management of the Great Lakes. Very sophisticated new tools were being used to gather highly detailed and sophisticated technical data. These new tools were underused because of the difficulty of providing appropriate access to policy makers. A growing concern was expressed about the need to deal with the myriad of urgent and unforeseen occurrences that crop up unexpectedly.

The IJC held a series of meetings in an effort to determine how best to respond to these concerns (1989, 1990, and 1991; see Figure 3.9). The first of these meetings was a Futures Workshop held in 1989; these discussions were focused on a quantitative, predictive model as the device to be used for discussion of policy concerns. A post-evaluation of this session concluded that this approach was inappropriate to meet IJC objectives. The second meeting, in 1990, was the Ecosystem Model Framework Workshop. The results of this workshop clearly indicated that a hard science modeling approach was beyond the range of current technological abilities for this problem. A third meeting was held in 1991, this was an Ecosystems Framework Round Table; the results of this meeting further demonstrated the need for a qualitative, intuitive approach.

As a consequence of these meetings, the IJC decided to commission a policy exercise that included two elements: an ecosystem game/simulation and a policy seminar. In combination, the two instruments aimed to improve communication among groups in the policy and research communities about the needs within the Great Lakes ecosystem. It was hoped that in combination these two activities would provide an exciting laboratory for the use of multimedia techniques. The objective was to ensure that the establishment of research policy was communicated as a palatable and effective process to the appropriate stakeholders.

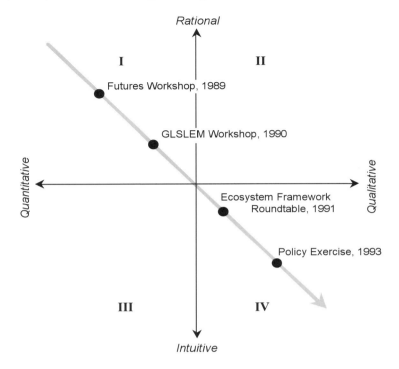

**FIGURE 3.9 | DEVELOPMENT OF IJC MEETINGS**

*3.8.5 Specifications for Policy Exercise Design*
The client anticipated a fairly intense exercise with focused and constructive communication and discussion. Considering the high level of participants, the pace and vitality of the exercise was to be calm and continuous throughout, consistent with the format of a seminar and the style of a serious business meeting. The following specifications were based on the design process described in Chapter 8. The seminar:

- Had to be simple and of high professional quality;
- Had to be visual, dynamic, and interactive;
- Could not appear frivolous or silly;
- Should present a lucid analogy/metaphor of the environment;
- Should avoid professional jargon;
- Should involve participants playing roles other than their real-life characters;
- Should not exceed a day and a half;
- Must accommodate a variable audience size (15 to 45 people);
- Should have documented results available; and
- Should honor a timeline for development.

### 3.8.6 The Schematic: A Model of Reality

The schematic is a visual model of the problem "reality." For the purposes of this exercise, the Great Lakes ecosystem is defined in part as the inter-linkage between the human and natural systems of the Great Lakes. Through a research effort that had extended over two years and which had included interviews with a broad range of ecosystem stakeholders, these two systems had been mapped into a detailed schematic. Close to a thousand variables were represented on the master drawing; it is inappropriate to describe this in detail, but an overview of the schematic is provided below in Figure 3.10, (for a more complete understanding of the schematic, see Section 8.2, Step 7 and the Appendix). The schematic identifies major organizations and/or clusters of concerns and the linkages among them. There were five major clusters: the Economy, Natural Systems, Culture, Institutions and Governments, and Philosophical Approaches toward the Environment. The economy had resource use (both recreational and non-recreational) as its prime focus. The schematic addressed resource management, indicators, industrial activities and production, and various economic concepts. Natural Systems encompassed the Atmosphere, Biosphere, Hydrosphere and Lithosphere and the various indicators used to observe these systems; human impacts and stresses, particularly exotic species and toxins, were also addressed. The stakeholder culture was identified, particularly communications, media, values, and education.

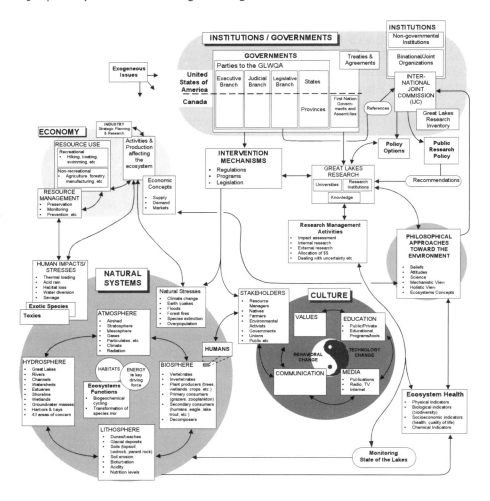

**FIGURE 3.10 | IJC SCHEMATIC (SIMPLIFIED)**

### 3.8.7 Description of the Policy Exercise

This exercise was designed to guide discussion of policy issues. It consisted of a standardized process (the Ecosystems Philosophy Game and the Issues Seminar); a visual map of the problem environment (the schematic); a simple artifact base (the model); and, various reading assignments as appropriate. These elements were modular; they could be combined as needed to address specific concerns of the commission. This exercise can best be understood if viewed as a standard structure for organizing policy meetings: the visuals served as a representation of the larger systems framework necessary to guide policy, and the process governs personal interaction to facilitate communication.

A feature of the exercise was that certain of its components were usable separately for different purposes. For example, the exercise could be adapted as an educational game to be disseminated generally throughout the region. The policy seminar could be used independently under certain circumstances by participants who were already grounded in the ecosystems perspective.

Because an exercise of this type cannot possibly reflect the full complexity of the world, the final product was highly abstracted to illustrate the necessary concerns. The contract specified that three levels of abstraction be utilized: high, medium, and low, with emphasis placed on the top and middle levels. However, the exercise had the flexibility to focus on a greater level of detail if a particular issue demanded it.

The three primary components of the Great Lakes Policy Exercise can be thought of as representing different levels of abstraction, as illustrated in Figure 3.11. At the top of the "cone of abstraction" was the IJC Philosophy Game; this was designed to focus attention on conflicting philosophical positions in order that differences could be revealed and, through the discussions engendered by the exercise, consensus obtained whenever possible. A series of schematic drawings were located in the center of the cone; they put forth in explicit detail the full range of concerns that had been discovered through interviews with a broad range of ecosystem stakeholders. The final activity, the Issues Seminar, is best described as a carefully structured seminar that was used on a continuing basis to address specific issues (e.g. the zebra mussel).

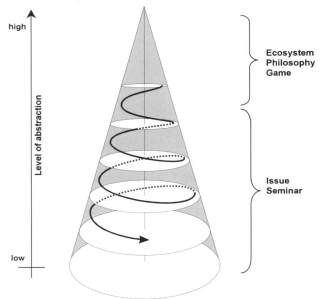

**FIGURE 3.11 | IJC CONE OF ABSTRACTION**

## THE IJC PHILOSOPHY GAME

The Ecosystem Philosophy Game involved a much higher level of abstraction than the Issue Seminar. The game accommodated approximately 21 participants grouped into teams of three; each team had a specific perspective: Alpha Scientist, Omega Scientist, Resource Manager, Resource Conservationist, two users, and, a Philosopher. These seven groups were arranged around a large table. Each participant was provided with a manual that described the perspective of the role and explained how the game was to be played. The players representing the science perspectives had access to a special pair of dice. At an appropriate time during each cycle of play, these teams rolled the dice to simulate research findings. A research card presented the results of the dice roll; the cards gave useful information about the game model. All players were given an event card as each cycle began; it provided clues as to how the underlying model for the game worked.

The game was played on a simple grid board that was divided into 64 cells. This was calibrated to represent two ecological systems that progressed in opposite directions, each occupying half the board. The model had features that were characteristic of a simple ecology, including a highly productive "edge" where the two systems met (e.g. a shoreline). The underlying model progressed through four phases (e.g. spring, summer, fall and winter). Two of these seasons, summer and fall, were active seasons; during this time, the new harvest appeared. The participants were not aware of the significance of the seasons as the game began. Cubes were placed in the cells of the playing board; each cube reflected a circle, a square, or a triangle symbol. These symbols represented basic resources; two were renewable resources, one was non-renewable. The six sides of each cube contained different numbers of each cell; three sides were against a white background and the other three sides had a dark background that represented a degraded resource.

During play, attention focused on these cubes; the top of each cube represented the state of the system as pertained to that resource. As the steps of play progressed, players first revealed their intended actions using their "action cards"; next, the group discussed the implication of the actions; then the actions were either modified or acted on; and finally, the facilitator rearranged the cubes to show the new state of the system. At the end of the exercise, a debriefing was undertaken in order that the rationale behind each action might be better understood.

## THE IJC ISSUE SEMINAR

Participants in the Issue Seminar were organized into seven perspectives: Physical Scientist, Social Scientist, Stakeholders, Research Managers, Program Managers, Policy Makers, and Ecosystem Philosopher. These perspectives were seated at tables in a semi-circle facing a wall where maps were displayed. The facilitator and a computer were situated in the back of the room. Participants were given events to evaluate both as to their probability of occurrence as well as their significance.

### 3.8.8 Major Sequence of Activities

Pre-Exercise Activities – All participants, acting alone, were asked to complete pre-work before attending the Issue Seminar: readings about the topic area, reading their assigned role manual, completing a questionnaire, and rating the various project clusters as to their duration, importance, likelihood of success, peer review information, etc. These ratings were returned to the facilitator prior to the day of the exercise and the assigned values were transcribed to a wall map using a color code. This map figured prominently in the activities of the day.

Policy Exercise Activities – The policy exercise was designed as a two-day exercise that focused on one of any number of important concerns. The zebra mussel, a recently introduced exotic species, was the substantive concern for the first use of the exercise. On the morning of the first day, speakers presented a synopsis of the problem and provided the attendees with the best state-of-the-art knowledge available. In the afternoon of the first day, the IJC Philosophy Game was played. The objective was to induce the participants to consider how their understanding of science could be best integrated into the political context of the problem.

On the morning of the second day, the Issues Seminar addressed the selected problem (e.g. the zebra mussel invasion); all participants adopted a defined perspective (role) and entered into a structured communication process that was designed as a "safe environment" to foster candid discussion of the issue. The afternoon was devoted to a debriefing of the Issues Seminar; during this time real-world concerns were emphasized as the participants resolved the problem at hand.

Post-Exercise Activities – The Ecosystem Framework Committee evaluated the exercise in terms of meeting the mission goals. The participants and audience assessed the exercise in two ways: with respect to its professional utility and the personal gratification it provided; they were also asked to suggest modifications. The policy game was distributed in kit form. Each user had a master copy from which to reproduce materials. The policy seminar was disseminated in the same manner. The IJC distributed the exercise as a monograph with instructions on the use of both the policy game and the policy seminar.

### 3.8.9 The Results

The intent of this project was to develop an ecosystem framework and a process for its use by the IJC in preparing research priorities for a biennial report. The primary criterion for success was whether or not the exercise was of intrinsic value in supporting the IJC activities. Evaluation of the performance of the exercise was in terms of initial goals and objectives as specified in the Concept Report. Evaluation of the game and its impact on the players considered both immediate and long-term benefits.

There were several ongoing activities that related to the exercise. The Great Lakes Information Network was established to provide public access to a variety of lake-related information that was available in digital form. The Environmental Research Institute of Michigan, under funding from the national Advanced Research Projects Administration, was embarking on a major effort to collect current scientific data using state-of-the-art remote sensing equipment. Their objective was to develop a sophisticated database that integrated information from many sources into one coherent and easily accessible resource.

The primary use of the exercise was by the IJC; however, external groups benefited from the exercise as well. For each run of the exercise, depending on the topic under discussion, there was a different mix of representatives from science, the public and private sector (industry, non-governmental organizations, administrators) and elected government officials from both Canada and the U.S.

### 3.9 RESTRUCTURING A NATIONAL HEALTHCARE SYSTEM

This last case study stems from healthcare and was carried out by our British colleagues of the Office for Public Management in London. This case description (the Rubber Windmill) is based on materials provided to us by Laurie McMahon, director of the Office for Public Management. The text below is to a large part based on a public review of the project by one of the managers of the client organization. Media coverage of the Rubber Windmill's findings has been extensive; there was considerable radio and television airtime devoted to the Rubber Windmill exercise. The many press cuttings that accompanied the launch of the report on the exercise were used in this writing.

#### 3.9.1 The Client

The British (Thatcher) government report "Working for Patients" required a radical change in the way in which healthcare would be organized both in terms of the culture and the way of thinking about healthcare. Healthcare in the U.K. traditionally was organized in a centrally planned National Health System (NHS) that was supposed to provide a standard level of care for every citizen. Outside the system, there was an extensive private medical service with insurance and all types of private service and clinics. From its beginning, the NHS had fervent supporters and opponents. The Thatcher (conservative/pro-market) government wanted to restructure this symbol of the centralized welfare state. The arguments presented were: the NHS was not delivering the care it should and it was too expensive, there was not enough innovation, it was bureaucratic and old fashioned, it was bad for the patient, it was demoralizing the providers, and it cost the taxpayer much more than it should.

The remedy was in line with Thatcher's ideology: inject market mechanisms into the system and put government at a distance. The proposals in "Working for Patients" mainly involved the organization of a regional market for healthcare where those people providing and receiving care negotiate with one another. Regional organizations (e.g. Authorities and Trusts) emerged to prepare the new situation and to outline the internal market. It was uncertain how these organizations would cooperate. The consequences of the new (market) relations for care providers, consumers, competitors and local welfare care were far from clear.

East Anglia is a large region in the East of England that includes the cities of Cambridge, Ipswich and Norwich. The East Anglian Regional Health Authority was a pioneer in the construction of the internal market. It had begun the development of strategic performance measurement – both financial and non-financial, including measures of health and quality outcomes and of consumer satisfaction – as the basis for shaping market systems and behavior. It was also undertaking two Department of Health projects to establish managed contracts between districts and units and to trade service provision among health authorities.

The Authority wanted its practical work and thinking to be brought together with a more general understanding of market mechanisms to explore how all these elements would work together. The East Anglia Regional Health Authority started a study together with the Office for Public Management to gain as much insight as possible into the future operation of the internal market. They wanted to test the flexibility of the new organization and also outline possible structural weaknesses and conflicts. A simulation/game was the key element in the project. The study and the simulation were nicknamed the "Rubber Windmill": Don Quixote fighting the wobbly windmill of ambiguity.

### 3.9.2 The Problem

The establishment of NHS trusts and new roles for both District and Regional Health Authorities was in practice being guided by several government working papers and by a number of associated reports and documents emanating from the Department of Health. Each of these new style organizations – provider, purchaser, and market manager – was envisaged as a statutory organization in its own right, led by a Board of Directors responsible for the organization's integrity and success.

The reports defined general conceptions about the future structure and responsibilities of each of these new organizations. However, these conceptions were generally the result of the work of one of a number of separate initiatives, rather than an understanding of the new system as a totality. In particular, there was no consistent view about how these new organizations would interact; these organizations were intended to be the basis for an internal market of health service provision. Providers would compete and sell, purchasers would determine need and let contracts, and market managers would allocate resources and review and arbitrate performance. Unfortunately, the dynamic effects of all these relationships (on providers, on consumers, on competitors, and on the resulting local health) were not really understood to the point where one could project any clear idea about what the internal market would look like in action.

Of course, no one could precisely know what the interactive effects of the new public sector market would be until it was actually put into operation. If considerations of potentially undesired effects were ignored during the pioneering phase, the fear was that one might unintentionally build weaknesses into the structure. Deficiencies might appear in terms both of the responsibilities and behaviors of these new organizations. As a consequence, a significant amount of time might have to be spent remedying them in the future.

### 3.9.3 Goals, Purposes, and Objectives

The goal of the Rubber Windmill Exercise was to be an open exploration of ideas about the probable dynamics of the internal market and to develop new thinking and knowledge in order to guide future development of the market in East Anglia (and, it was hoped, elsewhere). This was to be achieved through the simulation of anticipated market behavior by relevant actors who would be required to examine and refine many of the notions under consideration.

The product of The Rubber Windmill was expected to be a general understanding of market dynamics in the future NHS, not a definition or set of specifications. The exercise was expected to provide broad but practical ideas about how the newly developing organizations of the NHS would interact. It would describe the interaction between parties in the new market and some of the key opportunities, hazards and possible solutions that lay ahead.

As such, the product of the exercise provided additional guidance for the development of new organizations and a basis for continued work towards the opening of "market operations." It helped to gain a better understanding of what the "internal" market would do for health service provision in East Anglia, and thus provided a basis for broader discussion and for responding to questions and concerns that would arise as market mechanisms were developed. As part of an East Anglian demonstration project on internal markets, the workshop provided information and guidance for other health authorities in their efforts to develop similar relationships among providers, purchasers and market managers.

### 3.9.4 Why Did the Client Select the Policy Exercise Process?

The Office for Public Management (OPM) specialized in what it called "open simulations," i.e. complex and often very large multiparty exercises, the design of which goes back to the assumptions and procedures of the free-form war games which we described in Chapter 1. This choice for open negotiation as the basic formatting element of the simulation was consistent with the OPM's views on the nature of decision making in networks of organizations and the role of futuring in the process. What organizations do is not best understood by studying rational planning processes but by using a perspective in which many formal and informal "stakeholders" with differing interests are engaged in *power bargaining and negotiation* to influence outcomes. Such a perception can be gained by using an open simulation in which senior managers are powerful players in a process of restructuring a national system. The eventual direction of organizational change will be a result of the complex web of negotiations among all stakeholders.

The basic views that led the design of the Rubber Windmill simulation can be easily recognized in the assumptions underlying the specifications for the exercise (Section 3.9.5). No matter how simple the logic of introducing the internal market into the NHS, the way in which it would actually work in practice was considered unpredictable. This policy initiative involved a shift in incentives for so many actors in and around the healthcare system that the dynamics of their interactions were extremely volatile. For health service managers, it would be insufficient simply to use current notions of health systems behavior to project the future. Waiting to see what happened and then muddling through was not an acceptable strategy.

This simulation, while not trying to predict the future for the market, specifically helped to identify the range of possible futures by providing a simulated reality in which real actors could model behavior of the interested parties involved. Throughout the simulation, managers were able to make themselves familiar with the schematic; this mapped potential outcomes and helped them better understand the behavior of key actors under changing circumstances as well as the dynamics of the marketplace.

### 3.9.5 Specifications for Policy Exercise Design

To illustrate the OPM's approach a bit further, we quote here some of the core sentences from the original specifications:

> "Given the complexity of the process, there can be an almost infinite number of potential future states. As a result, the simulation must be open-ended rather than bounded by any inherent model or structure. It must reproduce behavior of real actors rather than have people playing out artificially prescribed roles. It must be able to model the diversity and apparent randomness

of real-life and large scale organizational change, rather than limit this by boundaries and rules;

"... this is not a game in any conventional sense of the word. The object is not to play against the rules, because many of the rules (if we are to model reality) must be capable of being renegotiated during the play. Neither is the object for participants to play against each other through the rules. Instead, participants are there to behave as real interests would in the circumstances simulated. Conflicts of interest are modeled, but playing to win via the rules is not;

"In order to produce a realistic context which is well understood by players and by those moderating the simulation, the simulation is based on a part of the East Anglian RHA (the "area")... However, the simulation will not be driven by hard, quantitative data; and ... the play will be observed by the moderators and reporters. Players will also be asked to keep notes of significant interactions to show:

- When (at what stage of the play did the interaction occur)?
- Why (what was their real motivation)?
- What (was the overt content of discussions)?
- Outcome (what was formally resolved and informally secured)?
- Direction (what would you have tried to do next)?"

### 3.9.6 The Schematic: A Model of Reality
A key element in the design process was an interactive workshop two weeks prior to the simulation session. There were (in both the workshop and in the game) about 40 participants, about half of them from East Anglia, many of whom had practical experience within the region. Other participants were invited from the Department of Health and other regions and districts. The Social Affairs correspondent for BBC Radio and the recent past President of the New York City Health and Hospitals Corporation also participated.

The objective of the preparatory workshop was to identify the key issues that the participants wished to test during the simulation. This was achieved by constructing a map (schematic) of the actions which each of the participants in the market would have to take to implement the new arrangements in a way which secured the objective of better value for money and benefits for patients and populations. These benefits were expressed in terms of the East Anglian RHA's commitment to managing public health; they were to be measured in health and quality outcomes in terms of six key values: quality, effectiveness, efficiency, access, appropriateness and responsiveness.

The workshop took the form of participants working collectively to construct a schematic of interactions based on their own knowledge, on actual data (insofar as it could be derived from health service organizations in the region) and on reflection of the mutual and individual organizational interests. This exercise began to expose the key relationships among the various participants and advanced some issues that could be tested in the simulation.

### 3.9.7 Description of the Policy Exercise

The simulation workshop itself was held over three days. The first morning was spent re-examining the schematic, and then introducing participants to the simulation exercise. The participants were divided into a number of groups each identified by colored T-shirts:

- The players (for the most comprised of real managers and clinicians) who would actually operate the market during the simulation;
- The simulation directors and the moderators who supervised the simulation while in progress and between rounds and who took on any additional roles which might be required during play;
- The region's backup team who had prepared data packs and who were available to provide additional information during the simulation if required; and
- The reporters, who recorded events.

### 3.9.8 Major Sequence of Activities

*Pre-Exercise Activities* – The simulation was based on two actual District Health Authorities and the data packs provided a brief synopsis of real facts about those districts. This information was designed to set the context for the simulation; much more important was the information, experience and knowledge of the NHS which the players themselves brought to the simulation. Most players took on a role that was close or identical to their professional role in real life.

*Policy Exercise Activities* – The first round of the simulation took place over three hours covering a calendar year. While the structure and procedures of the simulation had been carefully designed, there were no rules for the play and no rules by which to win. Participants were invited to identify their objectives for that year and to set out to achieve them, recording their interactions and agreements with other players for subsequent analysis and discussion. Almost at once, the purchasers and providers started negotiating over contracts (however, one acute service provider became involved in a protracted argument with its consultants over self-governing status). The region set the budgets for general practitioner (GP) fund-holders and attempted to define and agree on objectives with the purchasers. Financial control was a key issue, particularly with one or two of the providers. At the end of the first round of the simulation, there was a report-back session followed by a discussion and a re-examination and updating of the schematic. One overall observation was that year one had been dominated by the process of setting up the new arrangements with only incidental regard given to service issues.

The second round of the simulation (covering the following year) took place the following morning. Early in the year, the purchasers formed a consortium, (e.g. with the GP fund-holders). The troubled NHS trust applicant overcame local opposition with the help of generous Resource Management Initiative funding. One of the GP fund-holders resigned under protest. Throughout the simulation, one person acted as chief reporter of the East Anglian News regularly writing his stories on an electronic wipe board which produced copies for circulation to all the players; thus, the flavor of real local politics was injected into the simulation.

Following a further report-back and discussion session, the third round of the simulation (covering the third year) took place on the afternoon of the second day. Local authorities were suffering a financial squeeze that was having a very marked effect on services in the community and discharges from the hospitals. The GP fund-holders effectively controlled the whole of the budget for elective admissions in the two districts, and as a consequence, the health authorities found themselves with little room for maneuvering. Hospitals were able to accept only emergency admissions, community trusts with block contracts were being swamped with early discharges, and the region was forced to consider in-year reductions to the GP fund-holders' budgets. These pressures led to a startling phenomenon that had not been anticipated by anyone involved in designing the workshop. Purchasers began to compete for limited hospital services. Being unable to adjust volume or price, *purchasers actually pressed providers to lower quality in order to meet contracted caseloads* and stay within budget.

In the middle of what began to appear as a market crash, the Department of Health was preoccupied with a new set of restructuring proposals and the re-shaping of Regional Health Authorities into Regional Offices of the Management Executive. Bilateral discussions with the Secretary of State for Environment over community care had to be referred to the Cabinet for resolution (with one of the moderators cast in the role of Prime Minister). As the year ended, a delayed settlement foreshadowed a grim 1993/94. The participants adjourned for dinner, exhausted.

*Post Exercise Activities* – Day three of the workshop was reserved for analysis and discussion of what had occurred during the simulations and for a first pass at identifying the actions which would have to be taken to avoid the problems which had been exposed. Everyone agreed that year three of the simulation must not be allowed to happen in reality.

### 3.9.9 The Results

As a learning device, the simulation was extraordinarily effective. The dynamics of the play were influenced to some extent by the starting conditions provided by the moderators – such as the financial climate. Once play had started, however, what occurred was almost entirely in the hands of the players themselves as it would be in reality. They acted and behaved in ways reflecting their own perceptions of the interests of the role they were playing.

These perceptions changed markedly during the three years of the simulation. In year one, purchasers and providers were initially preoccupied with striking a deal, but in a way which largely respected the conventions of existing interrelationships. By year three, the players were much more confident in their roles and were prepared to act much more directly and decisively in their interests without deference to the old levers of authority and structure. The NHS of 1992/93 felt very different indeed – and much more fragmented. One feature which made the simulation seem particularly realistic was the pressure of time. With a month passing every 15 minutes, there was literally no time to think or to plan and players responded to initiatives or events instinctively.

The key issue which began to emerge in year two was the power of the general practitioners on the one hand and the local authority on the other to develop their own potentially divergent purchasing strategies. That in turn began to constrain the district health authority's room to maneuver. This provided the cue for the moderators to set the starting conditions for year three with a local authority financial squeeze and an even more powerful GP fund-holding sector: literally the intention was to test the system to the point of failure.

What was learned from the Rubber Windmill was that negotiations between local authorities and general practitioners of the essential health and quality outcome objectives was not an easy task for these two parties to fulfill. However, it was absolutely essential that the chaos of year three be avoided. In simple terms: *without such a set of negotiated outcome objectives, the new contracting arrangements would not bring benefits for patients.*

Given the political climate prevailing at the time, it was no surprise that much of the massive media coverage focused on the failure of the internal market during the simulation. This initial reaction was replaced by a much more positive attitude. The simulation itself had ceased to be a story in its own right; it became much more usual to see it quoted in the context of other events. Media coverage had two distinct results. The first was to pass on information about the simulation and its specific findings to lay and professional audiences; the second was to enhance East Anglia's general standing as an NHS Region and consolidate its reputation as a leader of the NHS reforms.

It cannot have happened very often in the British parliament since World War II that the honorable Lords and Ladies discussed intensively the results of a "War Game in Cambridgeshire!"

# Chapter 4

## Five Key Criteria and the Case Studies

### 4.1 INTRODUCTION

In Chapters 1 and 2, we developed a line of reasoning which resulted in:

- A definition of what macro-problems are;
- A definition of participatory policy analysis as the generic approach for handling macro-problems; and
- Five criteria for successful participatory policy analysis which capture the lessons from the literature on strategic planning and management and which are corroborated by the literature on policy and decision failures.

The goal of this chapter is twofold. Chapter 1 provided the reader with an introduction to the criteria *(complexity, communication, creativity, consensus,* and *commitment to action)*. These criteria are analyzed in more detail here. Each individual criterion is explored from a policy support or design perspective: how can strategic policy trajectories be structured in order to do justice to a particular criterion?

Next, the case studies from Chapters 3 are analyzed to show how the problem statement of each project suggested a different emphasis on one or more of the criteria; we explain the techniques and provisions with which we tried to do justice to the relevant criteria.

Macro-problems are complex from a cognitive point of view. Framing such a problem correctly is difficult. There are many variables involved, but no one knows how many and what the important variables are. The same is true for the relations between the variables. The causes of the problem are often obscure and so are the future trends. There is no overview or solid past knowledge on how to act vis-à-vis the problem. Usually there are many potentially relevant sources of knowledge available, but the existing knowledge household might prove to be scattered and incomplete, and its elements are often of unequal quality. This information is not available in a format useful for decision making nor is it shared equally by the relevant persons.

There are not many organizations in which one individual has the authority to take strategic decisions alone. Even if a single individual makes the final decision, these top decision makers have to rely on and collect the wisdom of many persons within and beyond the borders of their organization. In complex situations where a group must resolve a perplexing issue, traditional modes of communication prove not to work very well. New methods of communication are needed which provide an overview and stimulate gestalt communication.

Often these problems can be approached with new combinations of proven and well-tested lines of action; but this can only be done when the analysis of the problem leads to the "aha" effect of recognizing the analogy between the new situation and ones that are familiar. Discovering analogies is basically a process of creativity: it needs the playful exchange of perspectives and the retrieval of intuitive or tacit knowledge. Accumulation of experience in a person, a team, or an organization leads to the development of a repertoire of responses to many different challenges. Finding the appropriate response to a challenging issue is not a science, but a craft; it is about combining experience with creativity to find a new, original, inspiring, and adequate pathway into the unknown.

Organizations are always, to a certain extent, balanced conflicts. In most steady-state situations in organizations, conflicts on values and interests are brought to rest. These conflicts have resulted in workable arrangements, in compromises that reflect the existing power balance. But in turbulent times, in periods of transition, and under the strong pressures of major challenges, this consensus will be tested again. There is a need for a new consensus, which should not be the result of a long and costly battle in the period after a strategy has been chosen.

Dealing with major problems needs the concerted action and support of many stakeholders. To move into uncharted territory with many people at the same time presupposes that all individual actors share some capabilities. All individuals must understand the problem, see the relevance of the new course of action, understand their role in the master plan, and feel confident that existing skills or those acquired in time will help them to conquer the obstacles or seize the opportunities ahead. That is why a good process for entry into the unknown has to create a commitment to action in those whose energy and endurance is vital for the success of the strategy.

The message of this section is that each criterion is important, but it has to be seen in conjunction with the other four. Optimizing a process too much in the direction of one criterion will lead to sub-optimal results. For example:

- Complexity – focusing too heavily on the analytical complexity of a problem might lead to all the pitfalls of traditional rational planning: paralysis by analysis, learning by the wrong people, neglecting non-measurable aspects, etc.;

- Creativity – focusing too much on creativity may result in many wonderful plans, but they have to be doable. There is a danger of running in too many directions;

- Communication – a focus on communication that relies on the assumption that the relevant knowledge base and options for action can be found within the set of interacting participants can lead to a too-narrow framing of the problem and to solutions that are too conservative. Certain problems are so complex that the assumption that "the answer is in this room" may not be valid;

- Consensus – when a group of people is brought to a high level of consensus without proper analysis or a stimulus to look beyond the borders of traditional perspectives, the danger exists that only politically feasible solutions will be discussed. In the literature, this is called group-think; and

- Commitment to action – People are action-oriented, especially people who have had a long career in "making things happen." Of course, strategy without action is not strategy and initiatives without the entrepreneurial will to succeed may soon end up on the pile of good intentions. However, a process that only optimizes the will to act will lead to another form of group-think – we believe something because we deeply want it to be true.

## 4.2 UNDERSTANDING COMPLEXITY

### 4.2.1 What is Complexity?

If the readers will reflect on the bibliography of any book on systems analysis, they may become more sympathetic to the task of defining complexity. Many authors, using a variety of logical constructs, have addressed this issue at length. Mathematicians have quite rigorous definitions; social scientists and futurists have less rigorous, but nonetheless compelling, approaches to the definition of complexity. Some of the discussions of the concept of a macro-problem in Chapter 2 illustrate this point very well. In the context of this book, we need not and cannot be complete on the concept of complexity. We will only try to satisfy our need to understand what fruitful suggestions the literature on complexity has to offer to the policy analyst who tries to support those policy makers who face complex policy issues. To find the relevant insights, we look primarily at the experiences with systems analytical techniques over the last half century.

Let us start our short exploration of the concept of complexity by looking at the standard dictionary description of complexity:

"composed of interconnected parts" ... "characterized by a very complicated or involved arrangement of parts" ... "so complicated or intricate as to be hard to understand or deal with" (Webster, 1989).

In Chapter 3, we provided many examples of problems characterized by "complicated or involved arrangement of parts." Look back at Figure 3.10 that contains a description of the parts and interrelations (as far as they are understood) of the Great Lakes ecological and social system. It is interesting to note that the concept of complexity has entered the legal jargon referring to the Great Lakes. The Great Lakes are defined, by law, as

> "... the interacting components of air, land, water and living organisms, including humans, within the drainage basins of the St. Lawrence River at or upstream from the point at which this river becomes the international boundary between Canada and the U.S." The ecosystem of the Great Lakes is defined as ... "the natural system, including humans, and the system of institutional and human constructs created by human society."

Complexity is a relative concept: something is complex in the eye of the beholder. That is, of course, also true for social systems:

> "In such systems the whole is more than the some of its parts, not in an ultimate metaphysical sense, but in the important pragmatic sense that, given the properties of the parts and the laws of interaction, it is a non-trivial matter to infer the properties of the whole" (Simon, 1969 p. 86)."

In essence, this is what most of the projects described in Chapter 3 were all about. Given the properties of the parts and the laws of interaction, it was not only a non-trivial matter to infer the properties of the whole, but it was considered essential for the solution of the problem. Take, for example, the deregulation issue for Conrail. Deregulation is a concept that is highly complex and difficult to comprehend in terms of the specific implications for the relationships between Conrail and its 60,000 customers. The prospect of economic deregulation raised fears among some shippers, communities, and public officials as to the consequences of such public policy – especially a concern for potential economic dislocations.

### 4.2.2 The Role of Systems Analysis

Since the late 1960s and early 1970s, complex societal problems have been analyzed by means of systems analysis and simulation to understand the laws of interaction in complex systems. Formal modeling techniques were used in different, but related, research disciplines such as systems analysis, decision analysis, systems dynamics, and operational research. The methods are grounded in general systems theory, which perceives reality as consisting of many elements which are related to each other in a variety of ways. The traditional systems analytic approach emphasizes the importance of formal (quantitative) modeling, rational planning, and cost-benefit analysis. It is closely linked with the mainstream operational research tradition that tries to find optimal solutions for all sorts of complex problems (e.g. Rosenhead, 1989).

Traditional formal modeling techniques are based on what Rosenhead calls the "hard systems thinking" paradigm. Among the characteristics of this paradigm are the emphasis on a single objective, a single and optimal solution, a single decision maker, and a top-down planning process. It emphasizes the contribution of scientific knowledge to policy making. It is similar to the original forms of strategic or policy analysis which assumed that policy relevant knowledge could be produced in a scientific way, and that this knowledge basis would have instrumental value for rational, top-down, and unicentric decision making (Mayer, 1997, p. 33-37).

The application of systems analytic methods to societal and organizational policy problems was very successful and popular, but serious problems and intense disputes emerged when this paradigm was applied to the type of macro-policy problems that interest us. Problems of validation arose because of the absence of adequate theory and empirical data. Moreover, the practical relevance of many of the modeling efforts was questioned because managers and other policy actors had difficulty understanding and using the formal models (e.g. Watt, 1977). The systems analytic models provided partial insights and solutions for policy problems and these insights were not automatically understandable or acceptable for actors responsible for policy implementation.

We often find ourselves in a position where we work in a large organization which employs hundreds of people who are highly trained in one of the several quantitative modeling traditions. It is only logical that these organizations apply all this experience and thinking power when they face an "abnormal" macro-problem of the type we have described above. However, we find that this leads to disappointments and a postponement of relevant action. In several of the cases in Chapter 3, management had tried a formal/rational approach and had become more or less desperate in finding a more appropriate way of dealing with the problem. This was particularly true in the case of the Social Employment program, but also for the IJC case. Remember what we stated there: The IJC held a series of meetings. The first of these meetings was a "Futures Workshop" focused on a quantitative, predictive model. The conclusion was that this approach was inappropriate. The results of the second workshop led to the rejection of a hard science modeling approach as being beyond the range of current technological abilities. A growing concern was expressed about the need to deal with the myriad of urgent and unforeseen events that occur. The results of the third meeting clearly demonstrated the need for a qualitative, intuitive approach. That is why a policy exercise was chosen that combines an ecosystem game/simulation and a policy seminar.

According to Rosenhead, the crisis in the hard systems methods and practice became widely acknowledged: traditional modeling can only be applied to well-structured policy problems. Because macro-problems are ill-structured or wicked problems, the contribution of the traditional formal models to their solution is very limited. Policy makers' decisions are dependent on many factors other than the variables that can be dealt with in a formal mathematical model. The formal modeling perspective ignores, to some extent, the political setting in which policy making is taking place. An alternative to the hard systems paradigm developed. Under different names, several forms of "soft systems thinking" emerged which challenged some characteristics of the conventional paradigm (for a discussion of this evolution, see Rosenhead (1989), and Eden, Jones & Sims (1983)).

Furthermore, systems thinkers started to argue that a mathematical model is not necessarily the ultimate goal of a systems analytical project:

"... increasingly, models are seen to have different and more subtle roles as instruments to support strategic thinking, groups discussions and learning in management teams" (Morecroft, 1988, p.12, 13).

One relevant innovation was that, during the 1980s, systems analysts realized that much of the understanding of a macro-problem is *generated during the process of model building*. Participation of the policy actors in the model building process could, therefore, be useful. The participation of policy actors would enable the analyst to enrich the model by including subjective sources of knowledge in addition to the objective knowledge derived from theories and empirical studies. Additionally, the communication between analysts and policy actors on the complex problem would be improved. Gradually, group modeling became one of the means of dealing with the problems of traditional systems analysis (Vennix, 1996). The lesson is to involve the client in the modeling process. This is one of the essential features of the multi-step process for game design that we applied in the described cases (see Chapter 8).

When the managers of Conrail, as a group, were presented with the initial schematic that had been pieced together from the bits of information provided by each of them individually, the overall schematic was not acceptable to any of them. The first few months of the design phase were devoted to working with the group of vice presidents. Information was solicited from each member of the group: this information was then processed and abstracted into a model. The model was then presented to the group. The group, inevitably, would break into heated arguments over specific aspects of the model. Through several iterations of this process, the model was refined to a point where all could agree that is was a fairly accurate representation of the central features of the Conrail system.

### 4.2.3 Mental Models – The Big Picture

System dynamics modeling processes are helpful for activating and structuring the vast amount of knowledge that an experienced team shares (see Vennix, 1996). The "soft" modeling techniques emphasize the importance of eliciting different sources of knowledge and the importance of integrating ideas and perceptions regarding the policy problem. Therefore, the definition of what constitutes policy-relevant knowledge shifts from a science-oriented towards a consensual/constructive definition (e.g. Eden & Ackermann, 1998).

The more metaphors one has embedded in the mind, the richer the ability to generate, comprehend, play with, and communicate a meaningful model of complexity. Games are powerful at conveying the totality of a model and the dynamics of a system. Because decision making is not a logical process but rather a gestalt event, the quality of a decision is directly proportional to the systems elements an individual can retain. The more points, nodes, and interactions an individual can carry at a given moment, the better the decision. The more logical and evident the pattern, the greater the ease of comprehending and retaining the gestalt. As a consequence of participation in a policy game, the mind becomes increasingly adept at three things:

- Carrying logical blocks of information (each of which contain numerous particulars – these are sub-models, each of which is understood);

- Aggregating these in some way which is functionally useful (one no longer has to retain all the detail; but only an analogy/metaphor or conceptual model which retains the essence); and

- Making the "great leap" to a decision. This means being able to perceive the totality of the incoming information and comprehend/communicate it. But it also means being able to translate this against some other mental models into a new hybrid model, structure, or perception in which several past structures are blended into a mental map that better suits the need at hand. This is the nature of genius.

In the Pharmaceutical Decision Exercise, it proved essential to capture an integrative (gestalt) perspective of the problem which reflected the mental models of the various stakeholders (see De Geus, 1988). Information about the system and elements of the problem were collected and organized using interviews and a literature review. All the major stakeholders were interviewed to find the problem boundaries; the literature review also helped to determine the boundaries of the problem. This information was converted into snow cards (see Chapters 7 and 8). Great care was taken that the relevant executives were interviewed and the correct external data collected. The ultimate consequence of this thinking is the acceptance among analysts and modelers that their efforts should be directed towards improving as well as integrating the mental models of different actors in a policy network. The term "mental model" refers to the conceptual model that each actor carries in his or her mind to explain the way the business or policy operates.

The first version of the European Discovery Facility schematic (Figure 3.2) was based on interviews with several people from the R&D division. The Vice President of Sales actually started to laugh when he saw this schematic — he saw our representation of how the business worked as a typically closed-minded R&D perspective of the company. For instance, R&D saw itself as the producer of new leads (through internal processes) that resulted in new products to market. After his challenge, the facts revealed that by far the majority of the successful products were the result of partially and/or fully developed products bought in (licensed) from outside companies. The Vice President of Sales framed the idea of a European R&D venture more as a scouting tool for new products than as a complete R&D station. This had a great impact on how the policy exercise was developed and used and the ultimate decision that was taken to exploit a licensing concept while avoiding a "bricks and mortar" solution.

The schematic in the Social Employment project (Figure 3.8) was produced during and on the basis of several group sessions and many interviews with the four management echelons and several other stakeholders. An important function of this schematic was knowledge elicitation because nobody had the total overview. Even more importantly, the schematic functioned as a tool for problem framing and as a vehicle to negotiate among the parties concerning the phrasing of the questions that served as the agenda of the policy exercise. For example, the local managers insisted that the information system should take into account that the SEP law put contradictory performance pressures on local organizations.

In Section 3.7.6, the following was said: "For the local managers, the game could only be successful if CSV would accept that the policy exercise should address the question: Are the goals of the law relevant and suitable to use in a monitoring and assessment system? Another item that emerged was the need to define clear rules for the separation of information for "assessment" and information for "policy development." The local organizations made it quite clear that they would not volunteer to send relevant suggestions for new policy development to CSV if they ran the risk that this information would be used against them in the assessment phase. Several other differences in perception and micro-political issues emerged and had to be incorporated in the agenda of the exercise."

Mental models can be defined as "... networks of facts and concepts that mimic reality and from which executives derive their opinions of strategic issues, options, courses of action and likely outcomes" (Morecroft, 1988, pp. 12-13). In order to deal with the world in which they live, actors develop and shape their mental models via learning-by-doing. These models are linked with their positions in the policy network and, as a consequence, they differ in their level of abstraction. That is why the interrelatedness of actors' mental models can be specified by the analogy of the cone of abstraction – a holistic reproduction of different mental models at points which are located on different levels of abstraction on the cone (see Sections 3.8.7, 7.2.2, and 8.1.1).

The policy analyst must enable communication in a complex environment by creating a language or communication mode which is understandable to the different actors and which is located on a well-chosen level of abstraction. We come back to this important notion in Chapter 5.

### 4.2.4 How Games Master Complexity

Let us summarize what the discussion on complexity in this section and some of the related insights described in Chapter 2 mean for the practice of developing relevant policy exercises. What are the lessons from all this with regard to the process of handling the complexity of macro-problems? What should policy games do to support the process of exploring and understanding the complexity of macro-problems? What are the principles of handling the complexity of macro-problems that we have come to apply in the projects presented in Chapter 3? In our opinion, the best way to summarize these principles is by going back to the conclusions of a study which Geurts and Vennix (1989) made on this subject.

Policy support on macro-problems should be decision-oriented and stimulate broad framing of the policy problem. Knowledge about a problem should be able to be translated into decision consequences of current relevance. In the case of complicated problems, there is a tendency towards premature closure of the problem definition. Since macro-problems mostly press themselves on decision makers as relatively separate policy issues dispersed over time, methods employed towards their solution should help to place a topical issue against the background of the broader policy problem – these problems should be explored from as many different disciplines and perspectives as possible. We believe that the Pharmaceutical Decision Exercise, the case of the Office of the Secretary of Defense and the Social Employment case are good illustrations of the way one can realize these principles in a gaming project.

As stated above, uncertainty is one of the most perplexing features of macro-problems. This does not only hold for cognitive uncertainty but for voluntary (value-related) uncertainty as well. Thus, the translation from scientific statements into policy will unavoidably have strong elements of intuitive judgment and valuation. Knowledge management is currently a popular concept. In part, this can be interpreted as a response to the fact that knowledge has become such an important strategic resource and yet it is so scattered in and between organizations that traditional means for its creation, integration and diffusion are not sufficient anymore. Witness the events of September 11, 2001 – in spite of enormous financial and technical resources, the several agencies responsible for homeland security were overwhelmed with detail and failed to comprehend what was happening until too late!

The cases in Chapter 3 illustrate how much effort has to be put into the integration of all relevant types of knowledge and how prescient Toth was when he characterized the database for long range environmental planning as follows:

"Certain parts of scientific knowledge are solid but, at the same time, not easily available in literature or encrypted in complex models, other parts are uncertain but unfortunately important, some other parts are missing because no-one on the research side realized they are important for policy" Toth (1988, p. 238).

Methods of policy support should allow the elicitation of many different sources and types of knowledge. A good policy exercise is based on a very broad knowledge base in which the mental models of the participants in the exercise have been carefully integrated.

We refer to this ideal of integration by using the concept of gestalt. The primary purpose of any game/simulation is to convey gestalt or an overall perspective of the problem at hand. Many technical devices may be used to obtain this objective. Success is marked by the quality of the discussions that ensue during the debriefing. Although players identify with only one role, it is from this perspective that they gain a perception of the total system conveyed by the game. This is precisely why the board of the University Hospital put their hopes on the policy exercise. They needed to assist division management (albeit with the force of some painful experiential learning) to come out of their too-narrow views of their position and learn to base their actions on the interests of the whole of the organization. The Corporate Culture Exercise (Section 3.6) could never have accomplished its goal without focusing on the system of relationships between all the business functions and the newly acquired independence from the parent company.

Policy support for macro-problems should be based on a well-integrated state-of-the-art overview of available insights. In Rip's terminology: the real art is organizing a robust knowledge household. Rip (1991) defines robustness as the power to withstand attempts at undermining. In our work, we have started to develop the schematic as the tool to test this robustness. Using repeated iterations, we discuss and improve the schematic; saturation is our operational criterion for having reached a state of robustness. Once we cannot elicit new ideas and even the most hesitant opinion makers can agree with the schematic, we go to the next phase of game design. The more highly articulated and accepted the knowledge household is, the more robust or less controversial it will be. The knowledge should be organized in a format that provides a clear and stimulating way to the non-specialist, emphasizing not only what is known, but also what is not known.

## 4.3 IMPROVING COMMUNICATION

### 4.3.1 The Essential Role of Communication

Our basic instrumental assumption on improving the handling of macro-problems is to improve communication about these problems. The policy exercise as a form of communication requires all actors to endorse some point of view, it provides a forum for the integration and consensus of ideas, and it emphasizes understanding vs. prediction. We learn from this approach using the inherent human characteristic of play as a catalyst for thoughtful communication about serious issues.

When we considered policy fiascoes in Chapter 2, we discovered that these might be prevented when the policy design process becomes more iterative, evolving around continuous dialogue about the nature of the problems to be solved and what strategies for resolution solicit the necessary agreement. This requires more and better communication during the policy design process. In Chapter 2, the quotation from Hart (1992) showed how dominant the theme of communication is in the modern literature on strategy making.

The need for communication, especially the need to communicate holistic insights, was clear in every case in Chapter 3. All the clients felt strongly that only through hard investments in communication would there be a chance of handling the big problems they were facing. Given this strong emphasis on communication, we need to explore the enormous empirical literature on how to improve communication on complex policy problems and group decision making. What rules and suggestions does this literature contain?

We are fortunate that Hirokawa and Poole (1996), small group researchers, have asked themselves the same question. They have edited an excellent volume in which several contributors assess the past and current literature. They focus on communication and the effectiveness of group decision making. These authors begin their book by reminding the reader that the tendency in modern organizations to rely more and more on groups to make important decisions, contains some clear risks. Groups can and have made bad decisions in the past, also on very important issues involving war and peace (Allison, 1971 and Janis, 1982). Fortunately, these authors observe that the large body of empirical research shows that groups can improve their decision making via processes and factors which groups can control.

There appear to be four general influences on decision performance (Hirokawa, Erbert and Hurst, 1996: pp. 270-271):

- One factor is the informational resources available to a group: the higher the quality of information available to a group, the better they are able to reach a high-quality decision;

- A second factor for success is the quality of effort in handling the information: decision processes that are characterized by "careful and painstaking examination and reexamination of the information" tend to make better decisions;

- A third factor is quality of thinking: a high-quality decision depends on the group members' ability "to arrive at warranted or appropriate inferences (or conclusions) from decision-relevant information available to them" (op. cit. p. 274); and

- A fourth factor that affects the performance of decision making groups is the quality of the decision logic employed. The authors refer to the work of Senge (1990) to explain that groups who only apply a political logic (selecting the path of least resistance) are less likely to arrive at high-quality decisions than groups who carefully weigh pros and cons of different alternatives. In short, they must apply a rational decision logic. Hickson et al. (1986) found that managers usually weigh three kinds of rationality: problem-solving rationality, interest-accommodating rationality and the rationality of control.

What do our cases tell us about the potential of policy exercises to help realize these four influences on decision quality? The first two points (informational resources and quality of effort) have been discussed in the previous section, so we concentrate here on the last two observations (quality of thinking and decision logic).

Policy exercises can stimulate the formulation of policy options that are creatively different, relevant and internally consistent. Much policy analysis is too limited from a creative viewpoint. When the policy approach involves suggesting futures based on existing trends, the methods used should do more than articulate the probable; for the probable is just one sample out of all possible futures. Underestimating the great variety of possibilities is a danger in this form of policy analysis. Too often, the starting point is just the attainable and not the desirable. There is a tendency towards premature closure; too few alternatives are considered (as Nutt (2002) shows in Section 2.4.3).

The cases presented in Chapter 3 illustrate that gaming/simulations have the ability to present a future's orientation (the representation of any time frame other than the present). Their purpose is to explore alternatives, to develop a sophisticated mental response to "what if" questions, and to permit the formulation of an analogy for the exploration of alternatives where no prior basis exists.

In several of the cases, it is the simulation characteristic of the policy exercise that makes this collective futuring possible. In the Rubber Windmill exercise, the players create the new conditions of the health system step by step by moving from the current reality to the planned new reality. The interesting lesson here is that the participants were not, even on the basis of their best effort and knowledge, able to find operational strategies consistent with the optimistic and ideological principles supporting the plans.

The Conrail case has a strong simulation character: a future is created step by step. On the one hand, the future emerges via preset external trends and realities (the scenario and the events), and on the other hand, the decisions and actions of the players (as processed via the accounting system of the game) create, in part, new and often unexpected realities. In Section IV, we describe a discipline for making these exercises realistic and workable.

The simulation format in policy games allows the manipulation of complex information from a policy perspective. That is, this format allows the derivation of statements that are beyond logical dispute. These statements describe the relationship between policy options and their consequences, and require that both short-term and long-term consequences be weighed. The Systems Dynamics and Decision Analysis schools have especially enriched the policy analytic instruments with thinking aids to appraise complex and uncertain knowledge. Experience has shown that a human being can discover structures in complexity reasonably well, but that it is very hard to trace the dynamic characteristics of an outlined structure without suitable aids (e.g. Forrester, 1968; Sterman, 1988). The work of Dörner (1996) shows that our cognitive pitfalls disturb all stages of policy making, but particularly when drawing the right conclusions from available knowledge (see Section 2.4.2). Policy exercises offer provisions like the thinking aids from the modeling disciplines to help participants overcome these mental pitfalls.

The results from the empirical studies support our conclusions on how to handle the complexity of macro-problems (summarized at the end of Section 4.2 above). They also help to put our emphasis on communication in proper perspective. According to Hirokawa, Erbert and Hurst (1996, p. 273): "the existing literature reveals a very confusing state of affairs regarding the relationship between group communication and group decision making performance."

Many seem to believe they can prove that the quality of communication is the most important determinant of the quality of the decision. Others find proof of the fact that the final outcome of a group decision process is mainly explained by pre-session input variables and that weak communication is merely a loss of efficiency in reaching that outcome. However, Hirokawa, Erbert and Hurst (1996) find several generalizations from communication research that have particular relevance for our topic: group communication on complex issues. They organize their observations under four headings: structures, modalities, procedures and behaviors, as summarized below. To do justice to these authors' carefully structured overview, we have to warn our readers that the three authors add to this summary a deep analysis of the unavoidable limitations of much small group research.

### 4.3.2 About Communication Structures

Several researchers (e.g. Shaw, 1981) have compared the effects of different communication structures on decision performance. Four structures are famous:

- The circle (every member can communicate with only two other members, the first will communicate with the last);
- The chain (the circle without the closing at the end);
- The wheel (one pivotal member is linked to all others); and
- The all-channel (every member can reach all others).

Interestingly enough, there is a strong contingency effect: the complexity of the task determines which structure gives the best results. Centralized structures like the wheel are better in situations where the task is relatively simple. But when a group faces a complex problem that requires a lot of sub-decisions, a decentralized structure (like the circle) appears to perform better. As we shall show in the remainder of this book, the key communication concepts with which we describe the ideal of open and multi-actor communication is the multilogue concept (Duke, 1974). This all-channel concept is introduced and further defined in Chapter 5. In the games described above, a conscious choice was made on when to use what communication structure for what purpose or task in the game. In this context, many different modes of structuring, both centralized and decentralized, were used.

For example, in the University Hospital exercise, the participants started the first round with a role-specific brainstorm session in teams of three. Subsequently, each team had to give an opening statement, so that the participants were informed about the others' point of view. The next round was a process of deliberation and negotiation. The participants had the opportunity to meet other teams bilaterally or create small ad hoc meetings of several parties. Important aspects of this part of the session included continuous consultation, lobbying, and decision making.

Next, a meeting of the Hospital Board and division chairpersons took place. The other players were the audience who could intervene with written questions. This "fishbowl" technique was difficult and illustrative, both for the spectators and for the players in the "fishbowl." In the afternoon, every original team met again and gave a new interim statement. For the second time, the participants had the opportunity to meet other teams. Another meeting then took place between the Board and division chairpersons, with the other teams as the audience. The purpose of the last round was to learn and evaluate. Each team was required to put a summary of their experiences on an overhead sheet. These were used in the debriefing session among the players and the consultants. This fast alternation of teamwork, open market communication, and plenary (or sub-plenary) meetings was considered a very strong asset of the exercise. Of course, such a communication fiesta needs careful planning and good facilitation. For the players, it must be an intense but natural experience. For the facilitator, we have a double lesson: nothing works without proper prior planning, and the best improvisation is well-prepared improvisation.

### 4.3.3 About Communication Modalities

In the empirical literature, Hirokawa, Erbert and Hurst (1996, p. 275) have discovered an interaction effect between modality and performance. The more complex the task, the less restrictive the mode of communication has to be (i.e. more open, more mixing of verbal and other forms of communication). Less restrictive modalities offer more opportunities for the group to make optimal use of the available information.

A well-designed game realizes this aspect of multilogue by offering many different modes of communication. The situation-specific language that a game creates is not only transmitted via written or spoken words – a good game consists of many different symbols that support communication among the players: these are visual models (many kinds of cards, game pieces and other paraphernalia can be used). For example, see the multiple symbols that were created for the Ecosystem Philosophy Game (Section 3.8.7, The IJC Philosophy Game).

A fundamental thought regarding communicating about complexity has been ingrained in every schoolchild: "A picture is worth a thousand words." This saying attempts to convey the notion that words in sequence are less powerful than an iconic image; or, more properly, words and pictures combined can more readily convey a totality and therefore speed up the understanding of a rich environment. We want to show that properly conceived and executed, "a game is worth a thousand pictures" (Duke, 1974) when used in context with words and pictures as a rich hybrid communication form. From this logic derives the following communications-oriented definition of gaming/simulation:

> "Gaming/simulation is a gestalt communications mode which contains a game-specific language (the jargon used to describe components of reality), appropriate hybrid communication technologies (e.g. wall charts and/or a microcomputer), and the multilogue (multiple simultaneous dialogue) interaction pattern" (Duke, 1974, p. 55).

### 4.3.4 About Communication Procedures

There exist many kinds of techniques to guide a group through a discussion and decision process, e.g. Delphi, nominal group technique, etc. Many rely on Dewy's idea that a group needs help in reflective thinking. Again, the nature of the task is an important contingency variable. "As the difficulty of the decision task increases, ... formats that encourage vigilant and systematic face-to-face interaction tend to result in higher-quality outcomes..." (Hirokawa, Erbert and Hurst, 1996, p. 276). A second interaction effect is caused by what is called "the functional potential" of the discussion format:

> "... studies indicate that any discussion format that encourages a group to analyze a problem thoroughly, to establish criteria for a good solution, and to evaluate the positive and negative qualities of alternative choices in the light of those criteria leads more often to higher quality decisions than do formats that do not permit the group to perform those functions ..." (op. cit. p. 277).

The policy exercises in this book stimulate this "vigilant and systematic face-to-face interaction" via the combination of role-play and rigorously tested steps of play. Vigilance means hard work for the participants, as the flow of activities in the Social Employment Game illustrates. First of all, the pre-game workbooks had to be filled in; they were used to show differences and similarities of initial perceptions on the prepared wall charts. The format of the game itself was role-playing. Management Information System decision making is predicated on a logically ordered set of decision problems presented to the team as semi-structured multiple-choice questions (using forms and wall charts). Each of the ten questions in the policy exercise was handled in the same way: group discussion, group decision, group presentation, plenary discussion, and plenary decision.

Every question within the game material offered different alternatives. The participants discussed the alternatives, created new options where necessary and made (under some time pressure) a team decision. The participants were divided into teams of three. In the morning, the participants with the same role worked together. In the afternoon, the teams were mixed. In the evening, the participants assessed the results in terms of utility and robustness. After the game, the participants received a questionnaire about their experiences. Techniques like brainwriting and brainstorming gave the participants a final opportunity to present their ideas and worries without the decision pressure of the game.

### 4.3.5 About Communication Behaviors

By manipulating certain aspects of communication behavior, many researchers have tried to establish a link between behavior and performance. One conclusion is:

"… groups experiencing low-quality communication … led to decisions of significantly lower quality than was the case with groups characterized by high-quality communication (i.e. precise statements, internally consistent statements, positive reinforcement statements, relevant statements, and statements emphasizing cooperation and teamwork) … groups making high-quality decisions displayed higher-quality leadership, more open communication, and a higher proportion of active participation… the more attention a group must invest in discussing the procedures it will follow, the less attention it will focus on other functions necessary for reaching effective solutions" (Hirokawa and Poole, 1996, p. 277, 278).

The difference between open and closed games is relevant here. If, as in the Pharmaceutical Decision Exercise, the focus of the game is on finding a satisfying and well-tested solution, then the structure of communication should more or less force the players into a mode of problem solving by looking at and deliberating all the realities. However, this must not take too long! The timetable of the game and the processes of communication are very strict: "It is decision time, ladies and gentlemen," was a phrase heard several times during the day of the game. In fact, the same was true for the Social Employment and other games. Communication in these games was the means, not the end.

The University Hospital game was much more concerned with mimicking and improving communication behavior itself; as a result, communication processes were the focus of the simulation. This was also the case in the Rubber Windmill exercise. In both cases, the central theme was "communicating about communication." And of course, a much more spontaneous, albeit sometimes very ineffective, set of communication modes was provoked and allowed via the game plan. It was exactly this aspect of ineffectiveness that had to be discussed and improved during the debriefing.

We interpret the four sets of generalizations from empirical small-group research as important rules for the design of effective communication in policy exercises dealing with macro-problems. In fact, we devote Chapter 5 entirely to describing our conceptualization of policy games as a special form of communication; the concept of multilogue: the simultaneous dialogue of multiple actors in pursuit of a greater understanding of the topic at hand. The multilogue mode, when functioning during the actual play of a game/simulation, creates a problem-specific language.

Policy gaming, when done correctly, is a well-prepared and carefully structured group process. It provides the participants an opportunity to approach a topic from any perspective that seems relevant; inquiry is permitted at the level of abstraction that seems appropriate to the respondent. A good game will display, make explicit, and permit the recording of linkages among major segments of a holistic imagery. It helps the participant to understand the many feedback relationships among the segments. As an alternative (issue, problem, or new fact) is pulsed through the game, the participants should obtain, through both direct and serendipitous means, an awareness of the complexities involved.

## 4.4 STIMULATING CREATIVITY

### 4.4.1 Gaming and the Creative Environment
There are hundreds of definitions of creativity. The subject has attracted many writers from many disciplines who have tried to bring some order into this field. Our discussion of creativity below is eclectic and selective, because, like our dealings with the criteria of communication and complexity, we are neither interested in, nor capable of, writing the full overview of the relevant literature. We searched this literature from a pragmatic point of view. What should and can games do to stimulate creativity? That question is the leading topic of this section.

Isaksen (1988) refers to Welsh (1980) who proposes the following definition on the basis of his survey of the literature:

> "Creativity is the process of generating unique products by transformation of existing products. These products must be unique only to the creator and must meet the criteria of purpose established by the creator" (quoted in Isaksen, 1988, p. 258). Isaksen (1988, p. 259) also shows the link between problem solving and creative thinking: "Creative problem solving involves a person producing a novel response that solves the problem at hand" (Welsh, 1980, quoted in Isaksen, 1988, p. 258).

From Isaksen, we learn that, apart from the discussion on what constitutes a creative response or product, there are three other areas of research on creativity:

- Understanding the creative personality;
- Describing stages in creative processes; and
- Knowing how to design environments that are conducive to creativity.

We are especially impressed by the way Isaksen (1988) has ordered his insights on the latter topic. He formulates 12 suggestions on how to shape an atmosphere conducive to creativity. He warns the reader that this list is incomplete. His suggestions are necessary but not sufficient conditions for creativity. Because the list contains so many suggestions that are directly relevant for game design, we include it here (Isaksen, 1988, pp. 261-262):

- "Provide freedom to try new ways of performing tasks; allow and encourage individuals to achieve success in an area and in a way possible for him/her; encourage divergent approaches by providing resources and room rather than controls and limitations;

- Point out the value of individual differences, styles and points of view by permitting the activities, tasks and/or other means to be different for various individuals;

- Establish an open, safe atmosphere by supporting and reinforcing unusual ideas and responses of individuals when engaged in both creative/exploratory and critical development thinking;

- Build a feeling of individual control over what has to be done by encouraging individuals to have choices and involving them in goal setting and the decision making process;

- Support the learning and application of specific creative problem-solving techniques in the workplace and on tasks that are appropriate;

- Provide an appropriate amount of time for the accomplishment of tasks; provide the right amount of work in a realistic time frame;

- Provide a non-punitive environment by communicating that you are confident in the individuals with whom you work; reduce concern of failure by using mistakes as positives to help individuals realize errors and meet acceptable standards and providing affirmative feedback and judgment;

- Recognize some previously unrecognized and unused potential; challenge individuals to solve problems and work on new tasks in new ways; ask provocative questions;

- Respect an individual's need to work alone or in groups; encourage self-initiated projects;

- Tolerate complexity and disorder, at least for a period; Even the best organization and planning using clear goals requires some degree of flexibility;

- Create a climate of mutual respect and acceptance among individuals so that they will share, develop, and learn cooperatively; and, encourage a feeling of interpersonal trust and teamwork; and

- Encourage a high quality of interpersonal relationships and be aware of factors like: a spirit of open cooperation, open confrontation and resolution of conflicts and the encouragement for expression of ideas."

We think that the links between this list and the case studies are quite evident. So a few comments and references to the cases will suffice.

One of the first points that strikes us in this list is the emphasis on trying novel ways to perform a task. Maybe one of the most creative steps in all the cases was the fact that all clients moved away from existing routine and tried an unknown process called gaming/simulation, something that was often received with suspicion and doubt. For example, the IJC faced a myriad of urgent ecological concerns. Having focused unsuccessfully on a quantitative, predictive model as the device to resolve policy issues, they came to the conclusion that this approach was ineffective. They elected, instead, a policy exercise that combined an ecosystem game with a policy seminar. This combination improved communication among the various groups in the policy and research communities concerning the needs of the Great Lakes ecosystem.

In the Conrail case, it was not so much the game but rather the innovative participatory preparation of the game that led to the creative switch in that project. The process of designing the Pharmaceutical Decision Exercise resulted in a new insight: product development could not be viewed properly from the sole perspective of R&D. The subsequent re-framing of the problem resulted in a new and innovative solution that resulted in faster, more effective results with less risk.

Creating an open, safe atmosphere and supporting and reinforcing unusual ideas and responses of individuals are themes that are part and parcel of the gaming disciple. Play makes people free, and we have witnessed the power of gaming in this respect in almost all cases in the book. The many parties involved in the Rubber Windmill accepted the invitation for this revolutionary and politically sensitive experiment exactly because it was a game. In the Social Employment game's evaluation, the fact that people were allowed to role play and thus "get heard" was considered very valuable.

The data from the questionnaire in the Pharmaceutical case indicated that the participants perceived the policy exercise to be successful in accomplishing most of the stated objectives. They were particularly satisfied that the exercise created a positive atmosphere for open discussion of sensitive issues. All the participants felt free to contribute their perspectives. Furthermore, it was their overwhelming opinion that the exercise was an enjoyable process for formulating company strategy. They felt that the policy exercise uncovered aspects of the problem that they were unaware of before and that they themselves had come up with some new ideas.

Safety is not something that is guaranteed automatically. Role playing may provoke certain people to say things they might later regret. In the run of the EDF game, there was one young R&D manager who, in his role as marketing manager, made such fierce statements (repeatedly), that the facilitator started to worry about the effects of the exercise on his career. Small interventions and hints from the game operator helped to relieve some of the tension and, in fact, quite a few of his ideas were accepted.

### 4.4.2 Creativity, Play and Learning

Isaksen's list not only contains many practical suggestions for designing games as environments for creativity, it puts forward two points we need to elaborate on:

- The first four items on the list are a reminder of the fundamental connection between games and creativity; and
- Several items on the list make the connection between creativity and learning.

As stated before, the Dutch philosopher Huizinga emphasized the relation between games and creativity very strongly in his famous book *Homo Ludens* (1955). Also, the creativity expert De Bono (1971) makes the connection between play and creativity in his book on lateral thinking:

> "Why do children stop playing? ... It could be that play is actively discouraged by logical adults who point out its uselessness and define growing up as the responsibility to behave usefully. During play, ideas suggest themselves and then breed further ideas. The ideas do not follow one another in a logical progression, but if the mind makes no attempt to direct the ideas and is curious enough to pursue them, there will always be enough ideas – often there will be too many. The ideas may not prove useful immediately, but have a habit of turning up later. Even if no specific idea turns up, the general familiarity with a situation which is provided by playing around can prove a most useful background for the development of future ideas" (pp. 111-112).

Something seems contradictory here: play is an activity that is an end in itself and yet games are designed for serious creativity purposes. But just as people devise games for their own and others' amusement, they also manage to develop games in which the learning and creative effects are aimed at a consciously chosen goal which is "beyond the play."

Let us now look at games, creativity and learning. The essence of some of Isaksen's remarks in his list is that there cannot be creativity without some of the phenomena we normally associate with learning. There are many stage or phase models of learning. A clear inspiration for many of these models is Dewey's (1910) five-step model of individual reflective thinking: becoming aware of the situation or problem, making an assessment of the situation, suggesting solutions, assessing solutions and testing solutions. For gaming, the message of this family of models is that a good game offers the player a chance to go through several of these reflective cycles.

Many authors on creativity have tried to improve this core model. Under the heading of "creative problem solving" or "creativity techniques," several improvements have been suggested, tested and found to be useful. Jarboe (1996) finds that these innovations improve the traditional reflective model in four ways:

"Attention is granted to arousing interest, motivation, and effort for the task, reflecting the belief that individual reactions to the problem situation are relevant to effectiveness…";

"A second difference is the incubation phase, where nothing to do with the task is scheduled … creative models aver that this is an important step that must be programmed into the process for a 'creative shift' [to occur]";

"Creative models use more explicitly techniques for 'imagination'"; and

"Creative models attend to the social dimension. The concept of having fun is an important part of being creative, as many studies reveal" (all quotes: Jarboe, 1996: p. 353.)

The eight cases we have presented show that the policy exercise must incorporate creativity-enhancing techniques such as brainstorming, brainwriting, synectics or lateral thinking. The creativity-stimulating power of gaming is also in its very nature. Creativity presupposes fun, motivation and effort. Gaming is fun, it is one of the most involving and liberating social technologies for making group work productive and enjoyable. That is not only true because of the kinds of creativity advantages Huizinga has seen in gaming; it is also true because gaming puts the players in a situation of "experiential learning." Kolb's learning cycle (Figure 4.1) describes this form of learning very well (Kolb, 1984).

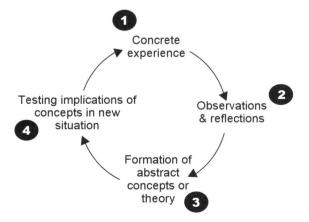

**FIGURE 4.1 | LEARNING CYCLE (KOLB, 1984)**

In a game, a player discovers a concrete, realistic and complex initial situation. The gaming process helps the player to work through the situation by going through Kolb's cycles several times. But there is more. As Lane (1995) explains, policy gaming stimulates "learning how to learn." Argyris and Schon (1978, p. 27) introduce the concept of second order or deutero learning. In other publications, one finds a distinction between single-loop and double-loop learning. Characteristic of single-loop learning is "learning by doing." Improved responses to a problematic situation develop out of the accumulation of positive and negative experiences. Double-loop learning happens when people reflect on and change their style of learning, and when they innovate their repertoire of responses to deal with a perplexing situation. David Lane presents Figure 4.2 to show that this concept of double-loop learning in fact adds a cycle to the learning cycle of Kolb.

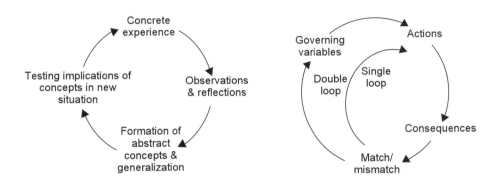

**FIGURE 4.2 | THE LEARNING CYCLE AND SECOND ORDER LEARNING (LANE, 1995)**

Double-loop learning is difficult because it quite often assumes fundamental reflection on the player's system of intuitive knowledge. Systems of intuitive knowledge are hard to change, not only because they have been built up over long periods of time, but also because we often are not aware of our biases and preoccupations. For "many managers and professionals uncertainty is a threat; its admission a sign of weakness" (Argyris & Schon, 1978, p. 247).

In a well-designed game, phases of learning by doing alternate with reflection and discussion phases and activities to stimulate double-loop learning. A game is a cyclical event in which the progression through these two learning cycles can be much faster than in real life. In the game, one learns to develop an overall view of connections and rules in a system and to influence and renew one's behavioral repertoire. A child learns through play. When a child has learned all it can from one toy, another one then becomes the favorite for a time. Games and toys are, to use a term from the Tavistock Institute, "transitional objects." In the simplified and safe world of the game, the child practices essential living skills. The linkage between playing and learning is also stressed in the management literature. De Geus (1988), the former Shell futurist, points out that models and simulations can perform this function for managers. They are transitional objects; they fulfill the temporary function of providing a safe learning environment.

### 4.5 THE NEED FOR CONSENSUS

#### 4.5.1 Three Ways to Look at Consensus

Consensus for action demands involving the right people as a basis for action. Typically, policy makers require the big picture before they can feel comfortable with their decisions – but beyond achieving this, they have the task of ensuring that their cadre understands and supports their actions. This is particularly true when a major shift of policy or critical decision takes place that puts existing practices and relationships in jeopardy.

The purpose of this section is to illustrate the problems associated with establishing consensus. We still have some doubts on what the most fruitful name for this fourth of our five Cs should be. There are at least three alternatives that suggest the kind of gaming contributions we want to explore in this section. Consensus is the first, the second is conflict mediation and the third is collaboration. We discuss all three in this section. Again, our main purpose is to explore what games can do to support the search for productive and feasible approaches to macro-problems.

In several sections of this book, we refer to a network or multiparty model of organizations. When policy issues can only be solved by the interaction of members of different organizations, the relevance of this perspective seems immediately clear. Also, it can be very useful to approach intra-organizational issues from this multiparty perspective. Organizations are not single-party, single-goal systems. Organizations are more or less structured/coordinated networks of individuals and groups that have different stakes in the organization. During times of great pressure and changes, the integrating function of shared values and goals may become weakened. Serious differences in perspective often emerge on how the organization should proceed. In these cases, the members of the different sections perceive a separation of interests and it becomes clear to them that not all aspirations can be achieved simultaneously. There is a need to redefine the hierarchy of goals. Cyert and March

(1963) have explained that organizational goals are the product of negotiations between the members of dominant coalitions. They introduce the "concept of dominant coalitions" implying that individual participants do not have equal power in decision making and that the preferences of some will receive more attention.

It is striking to discover that all eight of the clients in our case studies specifically listed the need to achieve consensus as one of their top priorities. In terms of Hickson et al: the political rationalities were in a state of change, but the rationality of control demanded that management take an integrative initiative, almost a peacekeeping mission, to keep the network intact. Some excerpts below illustrate this:

> Conrail – "... the client was interested in creating a simulation that would reveal to top-level managers what the political reactions to various systems alternatives would be. The managers could then form a consensus on an alternative that, though less than perfect from a management point of view, would be politically feasible."

> The Great Lakes – "... the Great Lakes Policy Exercise can be thought of as focusing attention on conflicting philosophical positions in order that differences can be revealed and, through the discussions engendered by the exercise, consensus obtained whenever possible."

> Office of the Secretary of Defense – "One of the primary objectives of the OSD Policy Evaluation Exercise was to reach consensus, where possible, on recommendations to be included in the final report."

> Corporate Culture Exercise – A central objective of the exercise is to "... provide an opportunity to develop strategies, build consensus and determine the effects of decision before implementation."

> Pharmaceutical Decision Exercise – "... the aim was to have a consensus-building activity that would draw upon the wisdom available within the organization to help management reach a consensus on the optimum siting of a new facility..."

### 4.5.2 Conflict Mediation

A conflict is a perceived difference in interests and a perception that different aspirations cannot be achieved simultaneously. In this definition lies the first conflict-mediating role policy gaming can have – a game can help explore whether or to what extent a conflict of interests really exists. Vennix (1981) explains very well why perceptions of differences in interests have to be challenged and how participatory methods like group modeling (and, as we will show, also gaming) can be of help. Vennix mentions the following reasons why conflicting interests might turn out to be something else:

- Differences in interests can sometimes be reduced or clarified by having the participants develop a broader, more holistic causal understanding of the relevant processes; when framed in a broader, more systemic context, differences might prove to be very relative and common interests might be more visible;

- Some perceived differences in interest might become understood as differences in meaning or importance that different persons give to the same phenomenon and often these different meanings correlate with different organizational positions and/or different professional backgrounds; and

- Differences in perceived interests might prove to be the consequences of different styles of information acquisition and thus reflect that different people have a different filter in selecting information. They may have different mechanisms to incorporate new information in their mental models, have different strategies on how to cope with missing information, and have different selective mechanisms to "forget" information that was once known to them.

The case studies make clear how the process of game design and use can assist with conflict mediation. For example, because of the design process used in the Pharmaceutical case, it was possible to redefine perceived conflicts of interest between R&D and the other business functions. It was discovered that product development as seen by R&D was only part of the picture. This led to a re-framing of the problem, and in the play of the exercise, a new and innovative solution was conceived that involved not building a new R&D center at all.

One of the important functions of group exercises like gaming is to explore where conflicts really exist and to what extent a sense of conflict might be a reflection of other, more cognitive, differences. In fact, this goes back to all the functions of games we have mentioned in the sections on complexity and communication. Several cases show that games are productive tools to combine the discussions on cognitive aspects of a problem with realistic clarification and exploration of micro-political realities. Games have proven to be useful in having representatives of many different interest groups show each other what the probable outcome would be for a process of collective bargaining that mimics reality.

The Rubber Windmill is probably the most relevant example of this. This "early warning" exercise showed that, given the current distribution of power resources, interests and know-how, the resulting outcome of the new legislation might be politically unstable, unsatisfactory to most, and even not very helpful to those who seem to be the short-term winners. The participants discovered they have certain interests in common and found that the responsible political institutions had to develop a more balanced process in order to avoid the results that the early warning exercise produced.

### 4.5.3 Collaboration

Even after intensive endeavors to clarify issues and positions, conflicts on how to proceed might still exist. The parties now understand clearly why and where they differ. They know that certain interests cannot be pursued at the same time and that value tradeoffs have to be made. So they are in a position of consent: they agree to disagree. In many conflict-ridden situations, there can be tremendous value in reaching such an understanding (via a supported group process). But the questions still remain: How should the conflict be handled? How should the value tradeoff be settled?

Pruitt and Carnavale (1993) distinguish three broad classes of procedures to deal with conflicts:

- Separation of action in which the parties go their own way and act as independent decision makers;
- Use of a third party to decide, (i.e. the boss, the judge, a referee); and
- The start of a collaborative process of negotiation and mediation, the latter being negotiation with the assistance of a third party.

Poole et al. (1991, p. 29) quote Ruble and Thomas who distinguish three modes of negotiation behavior:

- "Distributive behavior: parties pursue their own interest, without regard for others' need or interests; they conceal information and behave competitively, indicating a closed attitude to the problem and to alternative courses of action;
- Avoidance: parties seek to flee or to smooth over the conflict; [and]
- Integrative behavior: parties attempt to work with other parties, ideally to find a solution that realizes the interests of all concerned. This behavior is transparent in that the parties' interests are clear, and there is openness to other points of view and solutions."

Ottenheijm (1996, p. 40) finds in the conflict literature a general acceptance that integrative behavior is the most productive way of handling conflict:

"Integrative behavior leads the group towards a win-win situation, where the outcome is a synergy of the people and ideas involved. Distributive behavior either increases the conflict or leads to a kind of false agreement based on one party using its power over the other(s). It leads either to a victory of one of the parties or a simple compromise. ... Avoiding does not resolve anything either, because a conflict does not disappear by ignoring it."

Integrative behavior is the more constructive way to behave. Organizational psychologists call this the stimulation of "multiparty collaboration." Vansina, Taillieu and Schruijer (1998) quote Gray (1989, p. 5) who defines collaboration as "... a process through which parties who see different aspects of a problem can constructively explore their differences and search for solutions that go beyond their own limited vision of what is possible." However, the authors criticize this definition because it seems to make any well-intended conversation a process of collaboration. The authors themselves stress that collaboration is a work process in which participants engage because they belong to other groups.

It is interesting to note that Vansina, Taillieu and Schruijer (1998, pp. 159-81) use a simulation to study the dynamics of multiparty collaboration. One of the most striking conclusions is that just "bringing all stakeholders in the same room" and relying on procedures to "hold the collaborative efforts in focus" is not enough. "Self organizing and self-management does not lead to collaboration just by the absence of traditional management" (op. cit. p. 3). Their multiple simulation runs show that, when left to themselves, the participants prove to have very little mediating skills and a lack of role models to know how to structure multiparty collaboration in a successful way. This behavior has to be learned and it is obviously not something managers learn in their regular management education. Vansina, Taillieu and Schruijer (1998) show that a game can be a valuable tool to teach these skills.

Multiparty collaboration is more than bringing people of good will together. It has to be structured, it needs to be learned and it requires facilitation by a skilled mediator. Some of the cases show how games have been used as pre-decision negotiation tools. In retrospect we discovered five lessons in these cases which illustrate how to support conflict management which Ottenheijm (1996) initially derived from the negotiation literature.

- The focus should be on the problem rather than on the personal or emotional issues. Separating the person from the problem can be achieved in several ways. It is sufficient to point to the most important mechanism: people play a role, they defend a perspective, not their own position. What they say in the game, they say because their role forces them to do so. The EDF example showed that this impersonal presentation of some of the difficult messages that had to be delivered was a very important factor in the success of the game.

- The wider the range of alternatives considered, the more likely it is that a negotiated result can be found that satisfies all interests. Several of the case studies illustrate that a well-prepared game can offer a wide variety of alternative policy options the chance to become generated, presented and evaluated in an efficient and transparent process. Games can be good devices to avoid premature closure. The Social Employment story illustrates this point rather well.

- Integrative behavior needs a cooperative climate. As we stated before, a game can offer a safe environment in which people feel at ease and in which they enjoy a collaborative effort.

- The more clarity and order in process and roles, the better the negotiation result will be. In this respect, a tailor-made game will reduce uncertainty and fear because it is prepared with members of the organization and is clearly presented to participants prior to its usage. Clear role descriptions, well-tested and clearly announced steps of play, lucid agendas, and a facilitator to support the debriefings are some of the ingredients that make policy games good environments for pre-decision negotiations.

- It is important to avoid artificial conflict-reducing devices such as voting or relying on a leader to make the final decision. Poole et al (1991) state: "If members believe the issue will come to a vote, they have little motivation to compromise. ... Those in the majority know they can force their will, while minorities may take principled, but losing stands." As the cases show, there are many ways to circumvent this problem: polling, multi-criteria tasking, role switching (from advocate of a policy to a victim of it), etc. As an example, consider the research clusters used during the discussion of the zebra mussel in the IJC issue seminar: biology and life history, control and mitigation, socioeconomic research, migration patterns, etc. These clusters were described using a variety of factors: objectives of the project, research approach being considered, the disciplines involved, other related ongoing research, knowledge gaps of concern, cost of the proposed research, ecosystem influences, etc. Each of the participants is required to rate the importance of each of the criteria. This is done using simple scaling techniques; the results are printed as pie charts by the computer (individual decisions are combined into an average for each team of three players). These perspectives, of course, differ from one another; as differences are revealed through the pie charts, they become the basis for discussion and negotiation concerning the final criteria to be employed.

As in the sections on complexity, communication and creativity, the main goal of this section was to collect a set of operational ideas that specify general criteria. The ideas presented above give some guidance when structuring a game that should be helpful as a pre-decision negotiation tool.

### 4.5.4 A Review of Consensus

So, what happened to the idea of consensus? The following is the standard dictionary definition of consensus (Webster, 1989):

"... harmony, cooperation, or sympathy especially in different parts of an organism... group solidarity in sentiment and belief"

"... general agreement unanimity, accord... collective opinion: judgment arrived at by most of those concerned. AGREE: To be of one mind"

Are we looking for consensus in this dictionary sense of the word? We are not proposing that organizations should always try to find consensus on all strategic issues. However, we are strong supporters of what Steven Saint and James R. Lawson (1994) have to say in their book: *Rules for Reaching Consensus, A Modern Approach to Decision.* For these authors:

> "Agreement does not mean conformity, where all group members think alike. Nor does it mean that a majority of the members agree or that everyone in the group agrees about everything. Mutual agreement does mean that members share the sentiment or belief that all legitimate concerns have been addressed. It is felt more than it is measured." Another way of stating this is "consensus is the mutual feeling that all concerns have been addressed. What is required is that everybody has been heard and understood. Time lost in collective decision making is regained at the implementation stage. The net increase in productivity is significant and synergistic."

Due to the divisional structure of the University Hospital (see Section 3.2), participants often showed defensive strategies when their interests were at stake. Reaching consensus was not possible in every situation. However, their basic attitude towards working from the perspective of the entire hospital was affected positively by the exercise and a joint problem definition was reached.

Gaming is one way to realize what has been so optimistically stated in the "procedural justice theory": when people feel they have been taken seriously, they are even willing to support policies with which they do not really agree (Vennix, 1998). This brings us to the subject of how to guarantee commitment to action.

## 4.6 COMMITMENT TO ACTION

### 4.6.1 The Two Faces of Commitment

Interestingly enough, "showing commitment" has been described in the strategy literature both as a positive, desirable state of mind and as risky and potentially harmful. Words of support about commitment can be found in publications on organizational development and participative management, but the warning signs are predominant in writings on decision making. It is worthwhile to unravel in this section this seemingly contradictory status of one of our five key criteria.

Let us first establish that commitment is essential to decision making. Noorderhaven (1995, pp. 7-8) correctly explains that the concept of decision has to do with selection and commitment: "if a purpose or plan is selected as the best, but the decision maker does not feel committed to it, for all practical purposes no decision has been made." Commitment is part of the definition of decision because it is the voluntary and emotional element in decision making. It is the positive willingness to implement a selected path of action. However, commitment does not imply immediate or constant action. Commitment shows itself whenever an irrevocable allocation of energy, time, talents and/or other necessary resources has to be made to the selected alternative.

This definition makes clear why strategies can suffer from too much and too little commitment. Too much means sticking to a line of action when another path should have been selected. With too little commitment, one is not really willing to fully implement the selected path even when there is no other option. Too much and too little commitment are phenomena which have been reported at all levels of decision making relevant for this book: individual, group and organization. The prescriptive literature on decision techniques and decision processes is full of tips and tricks on how to guarantee the one and avoid the other. In the remainder of this section, we will explore some of these prescriptions and analyze our cases and the gaming discipline from the perspective of supporting the search for the "right amount" of commitment. We will first deal with the warning side and then move to the "how to get more of it" literature.

### 4.6.2 Preventing Escalation of Commitment

Escalation of commitment is a key concept in the decision literature. It refers to the tendency of decision makers to not stop or mitigate a failing policy but, on the contrary, reinforce it (Noorderhaven, 1995, p. 85). Popularly known as "throwing good money after bad," the process of escalation has much to do with the famous inability of many persons to disregard sunken costs. The amount of money or energy already spent on a project is often not positively related to the probability of future success. However, the need to justify past behavior and to seem rational in retrospect, may explain why it is so difficult for individuals, groups, and organizations to stop a failing and strangling strategy.

Ross and Staw (1993) have put together an interesting overview of the determinants of escalation of commitment. The summary below will make clear that, in almost all our cases, some of these determinants posed a possible threat to the quality of decision making (we paraphrase the summary of Ross and Staw from Kreitner & Kinicki, 1995).

Psychological and Social Determinants – Individuals perceive facts in such a way that they are in line with previous decisions. We take more risks when a problem is framed in a manner that focuses on the negative rather than the positive outcomes and we tend to become too devoted as champions of our own decisions and projects. A social climate that punishes mistakes by gossip, loss of face, or other negative sanctions may make it very difficult for a manager to change an unproductive course of action even when he or she has lost faith in the current strategy. The prospect of "sure loss" (i.e. negative public exposure) will seem less attractive than the risky shift of pushing harder in the direction of a very improbable outcome.

Organizational Determinants – Unfortunately, communication in organizations tends to break down when a bad message has to be delivered. Organizations are also frozen conflicts and each strategy has internal supporters and victims. It may be more attractive to push ahead towards a threatening future than risk the short-term rebalancing of power that may result from a change of strategic direction. Information collection and processing are often slow in complex organizations. Many other factors add to what is called organizational inertia and it is this inability to "get the act together" that can and will often result in the continuation of policies that create disaster (see Bovens & 't Hart in Chapter 2).

Characteristics of the Problem – Any decision problem that scores high on the process criteria described earlier runs the risk of resulting in escalation of commitment. The more complex a decision proves to be, the more communication and negotiation it will take. The more creativity and emotion people have to put into it and the fiercer the internal battle, the more difficult it will be to acknowledge that a decision has to be reconsidered. An element of complexity that is especially contributing to escalation is the discovery of delays. Understanding that one should be patient because an investment might take some time to turn into a profit, is in principle an element of wisdom. But knowing when patience turns into foolish stubbornness is very difficult.

Contextual Factors – Changing an unproductive strategy is more difficult when powerful outsiders and stakeholders fear a potential loss if an organization should change direction. Media, pressure groups, professional organizations, governments, bureaucracies, competitors, suppliers, clients, politicians, in fact the whole network of external parties, may push an organization to continue on a road that the organization itself might want to leave.

Escalation of commitment is a very human flaw (see Dörner in Section 2.4.2); it cannot be easily remedied by a single technique. Staw and Ross (1990) recommend several ways to avoid escalation, some of which are clearly supportable through the use of gaming/simulation. For example, these authors' idea of having different individuals make initial and subsequent decisions about a project fits very well into the war room technique in the Conrail case, as does their advice to provide more frequent feedback about the progress of a project. The IJC case study is a good example of combining participative gaming with continuous feedback.

The pharmaceutical example can be interpreted as a warning against the phenomenon of escalation. Staw and Ross suggest that one should encourage decision makers to become less ego-involved with a project, and that is exactly what went wrong in an earlier internationalization strategy for this pharmaceutical company. This adventure (expansion into an Asian market) escalated in the wrong direction. This happened because a few people involved in that decision process were isolated; they were seduced into continuing work on a strategy that should have been stopped earlier. And when it failed, the penalties were harsh – the Director of International Affairs was sent home. Staw's and Ross' advice to reduce the penalties of failure should have played a role here.

One of the best remedies for this "fear of failure" is to broaden the base of responsibility. The CEO in the pharmaceutical R&D decision adopted this strategy by involving as many people as possible in the second (European) strategy project. Popular wisdom would call this a "cover your rear" strategy, participative management calls it "shared responsibility" or "collective ambition development." In fact, in all the cases in which management brought together a great variety of people to prepare a decision, this idea of sharing responsibility played a role ("I will make them my accomplices"). In several cases, even outsiders were invited, most clearly in the Rubber Windmill exercise. This highly political, super-complex restructuring of a national healthcare system is an example where all the factors potentially causing escalation of commitment were present.

### 4.6.3 The Road to Positive Commitment
Let us now look at the literature that promotes tools and techniques to actively stimulate commitment. In Chapter 2, we quoted several authors that belong to or describe the "involvement" schools in strategic management. Hart (1992) describes the rise of commitment through involvement in the strategy literature and Hickson et al (1986) empirically discover that many strategic processes, whether they are sporadic or fluid, involve interaction among many parties, both formally and informally. We mentioned the stakeholder approach that looks at involvement in strategy beyond the borders of the organization.

Many arguments for "commitment through involvement" prevail in the literature. One is that both strategy making and its implementation are often convoluted actions: they are fragmented, extended, iterative, interrupted and delayed. Convoluted actions take a relatively long time while many interests and parties compete for attention; they have many sub-steps and sub-cycles, and the search for solution requires many different specialties (e.g. McCall & Kaplan, 1990, pp. 73-77). Of course, the major danger of convoluted action is that it evaporates without solving a problem or seizing an opportunity.

The literature suggests that these processes need a "champion" who keeps the process alive and all the "noses in one direction." Powerful as this may be, in this age of job-hopping, the functional lifetime of a champion may be too short to stay on top of the strategy for the required time-span. For example, the strategic maneuvers essential to success in the University Hospital case and the Pharmaceutical case required many years. In addition, the people who were to run the show in the coming years were the ones in the second or third hierarchical level below the CEO. "I want them all involved," said a CEO who started the simulation project, "because ten years from now, many more people than just myself will still have to want what we want today and remember why we wanted it in the first place." One reason to adopt gaming in these cases is to use the power of experiential learning to create a whole network of confident champions.

Extra arguments for this quest for collective commitment can be found in publications on a wide array of topics such as the de-layering of organizations, the professionalization and knowledge intensity of work, and the need to find new ways of keeping talent in the organization by other than financial rewards.

There seems to be one healthy combination of two reasons for adopting a gaming process that clients often mention to us and their intuition is positively supported by empirical research. This kind of group work is selected most often and has proven to be most useful when one can *take advantage of the expertise of many different persons* and one *needs the commitment of many different stakeholders to implement a policy* (Noorderhaven, op cit.; Beach, 1997).

Participation does not automatically lead to quality decisions. Groups need to be stimulated to adopt and support a broad framing of the problem. In the cases described in Chapter 3, the game design processes in combination with the multiple role interactions make sure this happens. Group processes can also result in pseudo-commitment because there is always the danger of passivity in group discussions, a phenomenon also labeled as "free rider" behavior. The strict and balanced distribution of tasks and activity of all the participants as planned in the steps of play in a gaming/simulation is a safeguard against this non-committing abstinence.

Participation makes a decision process complex and time consuming. Participation certainly has its risks, and some of these have been described in this chapter. The ideal is a process that allows a client to harvest the positive contributions of participation while avoiding the negative activities. Not too much commitment, not too little, but exactly the right degree of the right people on the right decisions. But there are no perfect predictions in strategic analysis and there are no perfect processes in strategy making. Besides, who would want the surprise-free, totalitarian social engineering of Orwell's 1984?

## 4.7 CONCLUSION

### 4.7.1 The Important Notion of Contingency
The cases show that macro-problems in certain contexts need a different "process architecture" than problems in other situations. In the strategy and organization literature, this observation is usually linked to the important notion of contingency. We searched the literature on this link between participation and contingency with three questions in mind that seem very relevant for the design of policy exercises:

- Which characteristics of a policy issue suggest a participatory instead of a non-participatory process, i.e. when does one refrain from applying the concepts regarding participatory policy analysis and the five criteria?

- If a participatory policy analysis type of approach seems relevant, how can one decide on the exact role one should give to participation; in our terms: how does one decide on the correct objective and problem statement for a gaming process?

- How can one assess the degree of attention the process design should pay to each of the criteria and how can it be ensured that the actual policy process does justice to this analysis?

The notion of contingency has been in the strategy and planning literature for a very long time. In ancient times, Sun Tzu tried to convince his readers that a wise general's response to a strategic challenge should be contingent on certain characteristics of the situation. This idea has been fully recognized in the non-military planning and strategy literature. Increasingly, it has become clear that this contingency thinking is relevant not only for the content side of strategic debates; it is also important for the design of appropriate strategic processes.

The design of the process involves more than just the choice and design of one key method. There are many choices to be made if a process has to be contingent on the characteristics of the macro-problem. Strategic trajectories involve many design decisions, e.g. timing, number of participants, subject matters, tools, forum formats, etc. As explained earlier, these are often perceived as being identical to one central methodological element, e.g. a strategy workshop, a game, a scenario discussion, etc. In fact, the quality of this key tool can only explain part of the success of a strategy process. That means that the general criteria for strategic trajectories are:

- Effectiveness (or relevance): the process has to support the problem solving around the issue at hand;

- Consistency: each element in a process (trajectory) has to fit into the overall pattern that leads to the goals selected;

- Integrality: a good process design takes all the parameters of choice into account;

- Efficiency or Parsimony: a strategic trajectory should not include elements that do not contribute to the goal;

- Realism: a logical criterion is whether a process architecture (sometimes costly) can be realized: does it have enough commitment from the parties involved, is the necessary expertise available and are there sufficient resources?; and

- Flexibility: can the process plan be adapted when the strategic need or context changes?

Strategic trajectories can thus be analyzed as consisting of tools, processes and formulas all of which have to support the effectiveness, consistency, efficiency, and legitimacy of the whole trajectory. Much research has to be done to understand the many design parameters involved and the way these can be combined into effective, integral, consistent, parsimonious and realizable trajectories.

### 4.7.2 A Model for Participative Management

One of the earlier models to help decide on the degree of involvement of groups of employees in decision making was developed by Vroom and Yetton in 1973 and expanded by Vroom and Jago (1988). Kreitner & Kinicki (op. cit. p. 318) quote several empirical studies supporting the earlier work of Vroom and Yetton and one empirical study to support the more recent work of Vroom and Jago.

The authors distinguish five styles or process strategies regarding participation and eight problem attributes that can be combined into a decision tree to help match the style with the attributes. The five styles are:

- **Style 1** – Individuals at the top decide, using available information;

- **Style 2** – Subordinates (or clients in other situations) are merely involved as informants in the data collection; the decision is taken at the top;

- **Style 3** – Broad bilateral consultation both on information and solutions between top level and individual relevant subordinates (i.e. stakeholders) but the decision is taken at the top;

- **Style 4** – Sharing the problem with subordinates as a group, collectively obtaining their ideas and suggestions, but the decision is still taken at the top; and

- **Style 5** – Leadership and subordinates in a group together share information, generate and evaluate alternatives and reach consensus on a solution. Leadership accepts the decision that emerges from the group.

Strictly speaking, only the first strategy is non-participatory and the four others seem to form an ordinal scale of participation. Gaming is essentially a group process, and one can easily find in our cases different examples of Styles 4 and 5. The Pharmaceutical case is probably closest to the most intense form of participation one can define according to Vroom et al.: the CEO of the R&D division did accept, defend, and implement the result of the EDF policy exercise. However, the public policy example (the IJC case) illustrates that the Vroom model Styles 3 and 4 can be supported through gaming. The participants are invited as informants and/or experts; all parties accept the fact that players in the exercises form pseudo-groups, bringing in the perspectives of relevant social categories or collectivities. In those examples, the added value of direct interaction is not sought in commitment or consensus building but in complexity reduction (analysis and integration of multiple perspectives) and creativity.

> It is interesting to see how Vroom et al. combine these process styles with the problem attributes. Although their wording is different, the reader will easily recognize the congruence between the concepts Vroom et al. use and our five criteria. To explain the Vroom model, we will describe an example. The model indicates that full group participation (style 5) is adequate for different combinations of the eight problem attributes each representing different categories of strategic issues or challenges.

In the Pharmaceutical case, the assessments in favor of group participation (style 5) are reflected in Vroom's eight problem attributes:

- The technical quality of the decision has to be high;
- Requires the commitment of the subordinates;
- Management lacks sufficient information;
- The problem is ill-structured;
- Subordinates share the organizational goals that are at stake in this issue;
- A top-down decision on this issue would lead to serious acceptance problems in the organization;

- Employees have enough information and expertise to make a high-quality decision; and
- This issue will not reveal nor provoke conflicts among the members of the organization over the preferred solution.

This Vroom model gives us a conceptual basis for the empirical observation from the case studies that gaming/simulation is a multi-functional strategy tool. It illustrates that statements about the problem attributes and the understanding of their interrelations are in fact results of assessments and interpretations. That observation has to be kept in mind, because it has serious consequences for a game design process to be used in a strategy process. One critical comment on the Vroom model is that it does not directly relate participation to the strategic challenges as they come along (e.g. the environment in which an organization has to live). As we said before, it is a model not so much of problem attributes but of interpretations of attributes in terms of process criteria.

### 4.7.3 Participation as a Strategic Competence

Hart (1992) has much to offer here in that his theory and research on strategic processes give us a much better understanding of the interaction among environmental characteristics, strategic process mode and strategic success. Hart, not unlike Vroom et al., defines five modes of strategy making, i.e. the command mode, the symbolic mode, the rational mode, the transactive mode, and the generative mode. The first three modes are non-participatory or participatory in the sense that subordinates only provide information to the decision makers at the top.

Hart's transactive mode is participatory in that lower level members of an organization are given a chance to be active in policy development. It is also a learning style, in that processes have many iterations, much multi-functional communication and feedback. Hart's generative mode puts organizational members on a higher step of the "participation ladder"; in part they become individual entrepreneurs with some degree of freedom in their decisions. In this mode, one enters new territory via small experiments which creative groups and individuals have been allowed to develop in safe and stimulating environments. Again, it is not difficult to fit our cases into the two participatory modes Hart defines. The transactive mode is easily recognized in several of the cases.

Hart takes an overview of the strategy literature to formulate which modes will be found in what environments (i.e. facing what strategic challenges). One of his central hypotheses is that, when strategic actors find themselves in a situation with many stakeholders and many different interests, they tend to adopt (at least within their organization) a participatory strategy to learn about and involve stakeholders. In a situation where the environment is turbulent, dynamic and complex, actors seek to survive by relying on intra-organizational participatory or entrepreneurial forms of strategy making while, at the same time, restructuring the organization into a flatter, more network-like form. Hart's understanding of prior research efforts supports the contingency perspective on strategy making; not only the strategic response, but also the mode of strategy making varies in successful organizations with the challenges of the environment.

Hart and Banbury's (1994) empirical study of 285 firms supported many of Hart's (1992) hypotheses. Hart and Hart & Banbury introduce a modern and important element into the thinking about strategic processes or modes. The authors show these modes are "capabilities" or "strategic competencies." When a company has mastered these skills in difficult environments, this competence will offer the chance to do better than the competition. Because participatory modes are hard to install and hard to keep up, skills in these modes will, in certain situations, be an important asset. Modern companies tend to be active in many markets across the whole globe and their environments change in unpredictable ways. As a consequence, Hart and Banbury clearly find in their data that companies which have skills in more than one strategic process mode will outperform companies that only rely on a single mode (see Brews and Hunt, 1999 for similar empirical results.) Hart and Banbury are confident in concluding that the process matters; multiple skills in complex strategy modes help companies to be successful in what we have called "entering uncharted territory." Participatory (learning or experimenting) styles of strategy making are essential skills for a modern company.

### 4.7.4 Beyond the Borders: Stakeholders and Networks
In several of our cases, participation in a policy exercise goes far beyond the borders of the initiating organization. In a recent monograph, Mayer & Veeneman (2002) bring together a collection of gaming projects regarding inter-organizational chains and networks in the public utility and infrastructure sectors. These cases are witness to the rise of the "network society." Participation in inter-organizational settings has gradually received more attention in the literature. Many publications on this topic have emerged which try to describe how to manage inter-organizational relations. In the publications that concentrate on the private sector, this field is called "stakeholder management."

In the public policy-oriented literature, one comes across the comparable concept of "network management." Three of our last four cases are examples of the strong need that organizations feel to bring together representatives from very diverse backgrounds in order to discuss a problematic issue with them. These cases are, according to modern understanding, practical realizations of "stakeholder" or "network management." In order to grasp what this current literature has to offer as hints for game design, we will first look at the stakeholder theory and then describe some relevant elements of network theory.

In their extensive review of the literature and relevant case material, Savage et al. (1991, p. 61) developed the thought that "an effective organization strategy requires consensus from a plurality of key stakeholders about what it could be doing and how these things should be done." In line with contingency theory, Savage et al. explain that the identification of relevant stakeholders will depend on the specific strategic issues (or challenges) an organization faces. Moreover, whether an organization holds the potential for threat or cooperation depends on the specific context and history of the organization's relations with that stakeholder and the key stakeholders influencing the organization (op. cit. pp. 64-65).

Savage et al. have developed a classification of stakeholders into four categories together with four generic strategies for addressing the stakeholders:

Type 1 is the supportive stakeholder with high potential for cooperation and low probability of becoming a threat. The natural strategy to interact with these stakeholders, according to Savage et al., is to involve them in relevant issues, thus maximizing their cooperative potential. The intra-organizational strategy of decentralizing authority and stimulating the decision-making participation of middle management and/or employees fits into this strategy.

Type 2 is the marginal stakeholder – neither highly threatening nor cooperative. The authors mention, as examples for medium to larger organizations, stakeholders such as interest groups, stockholders and professional associations of employees. Certain issues might emerge (e.g. safety, pollution, etc.) which could activate these stakeholders. Thus the appropriate stakeholder strategy is "monitoring" and taking action when a marginal stakeholder might be affected by a strategic decision.

Type 3 stakeholders have a high potential for threat and a low probability for cooperation (e.g. competitors, sometimes also unions and media), which creates a situation of dependence for the organization. The logical strategy here is defensive: the reduction of dependence.

Type 4 is the mixed blessing stakeholder whose capability for threat or cooperation is equal (e.g. employees with strong labor market options but also customers or clients). This type of stakeholder might migrate to Type 1 (supportive) but also to Type 3 (non-supportive). This type of stakeholder, according to Savage et al., might best be approached with a collaboration proposal. Joint ventures are one way of filling in this strategy.

Savage et al. stress that for each of the "non-attractive" types of stakeholders, an important fundamental strategic option is to try to reform the relationship with the stakeholder in a more favorable direction. Rather than accepting a continuing situation of defense, it might prove much more productive and less energy and resource consuming to transform the relationship into a more cooperative strategy.

Stakeholder management concerns underline the role of top managers as brokers or facilitators of network relationships. A game like the one developed for Conrail functioned later on as a tool in this brokerage process. The typology of Savage et al. can have several functions in game design. For example, early on in the game design process, it can help to define, with the client, the objectives of an exercise more precisely, including whom to invite to the exercise. Later on in the actual game design, it can help to check whether one has defined a set of roles to be played which does justice to the diversity of the actual policy environment. In public policy, one can find a comparable line of argument around the concept of network management.

In network theory, policy making means the creation of networks and influencing the rules of the game in these networks. Our IJC case is a clear example of this modern form of public policy making. De Bruijn and Ten Heuvelhof (1995) point out three key structural elements of networks: "pluriformity" (diversity), autonomy and interdependency. Consequently, these authors define network management as "changing interdependencies, autonomy and diversity in a network and altering the substantive and temporal whimsicality (capriciousness) in order to create governing options for a governing actor" (op. cit. p. 32). The concept of whimsicality refers to the unpredictable or chaotic nature of the policy processes in a network. Public agencies often try to influence the transparency and predictability of the policy processes in a network, both with regard to timing as well as definitions of content. It was one of the goals of the Rubber Windmill to bring organizations together at such an early stage that unwelcome surprises in the action and interactions in the healthcare system could be prevented.

The above excursions into strategic process theory and into the literature on stakeholder and network management illustrate the importance of the contingency perspective on gaming trajectories. An event like a policy exercise has to be carefully integrated into a well-planned trajectory and this has to fit into the overall process strategy which an organization adopts for a certain strategic issue. Finally, the process strategy has to fit the nature of the policy issue and the micro-political realities of the social positions around that issue, and this is true whether these are intra or inter-organizational stakeholders.

# Section III

## *Theory and Research*

**INTRODUCTION TO SECTION III**
Chapter 4 established the link between strategy theory and the applications of gaming/simulation described in Chapter 3. Our objective was to clarify why and how gaming is relevant for strategic management.

In Chapter 5, we direct the reader's attention to the phenomenon of gaming/simulation itself. The chapter summarizes our theoretical perspective on the nature of the processes we call policy games. The thoughts expressed in this chapter have helped us over the years to understand "what this profession of ours really is all about." The chapter reformulates our interpretation of gaming/simulation as a language for complexity and it proposes concepts like "multilogue" to help typify the communication patterns that are unique to gaming/simulation.

Chapter 6 describes several lines of empirical research associated with policy games. Apart from the functions of research to prepare the content of a game, it explores past efforts and potential new research designs that help to evaluate the contribution of gaming to strategic management. The chapter also describes the interesting use of gaming as an environment to study the policy making behavior of individuals and groups in an experimental fashion.

# Chapter 5

## Multilogue - a Language for Complexity

Note: This chapter relies heavily on *Gaming: The Future's Language* (Duke, 1974)

### 5.1 INTRODUCTION

In the process of muddling through complexity, it is often relatively late that a client comes to understand that a macro-problem must be addressed; by that time, many different types of methodologies may have been set in motion. Typically, this will include a variety of traditional investigative approaches pursued with increasing urgency and overlap. Each approach will tend to emphasize a segment of the problem; overview will become clouded; the communication forms employed will have inherent limitations.

This book intends to show that, in appropriate situations, the proper use of gaming/simulation offers strong promise for establishing the comprehension of totality necessary for the intelligent management of complex systems. As long as we are dependent on communication forms that are sequential, time-constrained, imprecise, dry, and cumbersome, it will be difficult to comprehend the complexities of macro-problems, and we will continue to apply piecemeal solutions to problems that should be solved holistically.

Rhyne has made a trenchant statement about this. While describing the need for holistic communication, Rhyne states (1975, p. 16): "there is a macro-problem, an interweaving of adverse conditions that is more extensive, more richly structured by interior lines of interaction, and more threatening than any circumstance faced before by all mankind." Rhyne's article was formulated "to stimulate exploration of the means whereby appreciation of complex wholes may be more quickly and more reliably told to others." He rejects our ancestral language forms as inadequate to the task and argues that new forms must be invented. He sees decision as a gestalt event and not a logically determinable process; he believes that citizens, policy researchers and decision makers must first comprehend the whole, the entirety, the gestalt, and the system, before dealing with the particulars. Rhyne suggests a variety of approaches to this problem and alludes to gaming/simulation as having a particular potential.

### 5.2 MODERN TOWER OF BABEL

We have made it quite clear that we view gaming/simulation as a form of communication. In 1974, the first author of this book put this thesis forward in his book *Gaming: The Future's Language* (Duke, 1974). Since then, the information age has arrived. Communication is in a state of revolution. Fortunes are made and lost in the communication business. And everyone who has some experience in this area knows that change has only begun!

Not only many years but also many gaming projects have passed since the writing of *Gaming: The Future's Language*. The more we have built up experience with applying games in policy contexts, the more the image of gaming as a form of communication has become imprinted into our minds. In this chapter, we want to restate some of the thoughts on gaming as a language to deal with the future. We are aware of the fact that we are neither trained linguists nor communication theorists. What we have to offer is theory from practice, developed through observation of the applied use of policy exercises. These thoughts have proven useful to us in explaining a new communications phenomenon, the policy game. We know this chapter contains speculation, but the concepts in it have inspired us over the years. We put these thoughts together to form a contribution to the professional discussion concerning how to assist organizations using policy exercises.

Before attempting a definition of a policy exercise in a communication context, it is necessary to review some of the central characteristics of the various forms of human communication. The unique ability of gaming/simulation to convey the gestalt of complex systems is described below, and gaming/simulation is defined in this context.

Policy makers who are forced to address macro-problems have the difficult task of thinking well into the future while communicating with each other, with a myriad of specialists, and with their constituencies. They are required to visualize alternatives and to evaluate probable results, including unintended consequences. To avoid these, and countless other misadventures, policy makers must learn to "reminisce about the future" (Duke, 1974), to explore "what if" questions in involved and highly speculative environments if they are to ensure higher quality decisions. Management of such an environment requires a holistic perspective that cannot be obtained through traditional sequential communication forms. It also requires the maturity of understanding to recognize that the sophisticated techniques of science sometimes need an assist in solving these macro-problems.

Those in responsible positions face additional difficulties in that many individuals want to be effectively part of the dialogue; there is a growing urgency to communicate effectively because any solution that might be selected is certain to constitute an intrusion into someone's life. Communication incident to the management of these macro-problems takes place in the modern equivalent of the biblical Tower of Babel. The current "Babel" does not result so much from the world's many different languages (German, French, Arabic, etc.), but, rather, the problem lies in the differing perspectives, styles, and vocabularies (jargon) of the many disciplines typically brought to bear when resolving complex issues. Review Figure 1.4 The Policy Game Paradigm and consider the many types of jargon that are implied. As a consequence, efficient communication is impeded among the several specialties which must investigate the macro-problem, and further difficulties are encountered between these specialists and those responsible for managing related management decisions. The need for conveying holistic thought is urgent, and the coming decades will increase this urgency considerably as new information is generated exponentially and the problems of the world grow more complex.

## 5.3 COMMUNICATION MEANS LANGUAGE

The central assumption behind our reasoning is that man thinks in images, in a gestalt; but we transmit this imagery by means of language. This requires that we translate a holistic image into a sequential string of component descriptions, and that the listener attempt to reconstruct the image: "a picture is worth a thousand words." Sequential language is sufficient as long as the listeners can hold initial components as they receive later ones; this requires that the gestalt be simple. Because a mental holding process breaks down very quickly under the strain of today's complexity, another method of transmitting information must be developed.

One of the strongest components of language is the use of analogy. Through analogy, we are able to modify associations derived from past phenomena. If we are to select that future which best serves humankind, we must now develop analogies that are based upon conjecture, but which can be used to formulate hypotheses about the future, thoughtfully, carefully, and in realistic detail.

Moore & Anderson (1975) identify four characteristics that are central to any learning environment; these also appear to be central to any environment where true communication is to occur. These principles are paraphrased below, as they address the communication environment:

- The sender must succeed in motivating the receiver before information is transmitted;

- The receiver must be an active rather than a passive participant in the process;

- The communication flow (information) must be individualized so that the pace for the receiver is correct; and

- The receiver must have prompt feedback in the dialogue so that messages can be challenged and differing opinions expressed.

These considerations are sometimes difficult to achieve in the case of two individuals attempting to communicate about a simple topic; they are always difficult when a group is trying to address a complex environment. Gaming is a spontaneous solution by many people in varied situations to the problem of developing a gestalt communication form; they have developed a new language, a form that is future-oriented. Such a perspective begins to explain the wide diversity of materials that appear as games; it becomes a useful guide to the development of effective games. The development of the gaming/simulation technique offers extraordinary opportunity for sophisticated and rapid communication; it will assist humanity in coping with the inevitable kaleidoscope of new imagery that must be confronted.

## 5.4 THE CONCEPT OF COMMUNICATION MODES

To gain a true sense of the power of the policy exercise, attention must be directed to the significance of how the concept of communication modes links to the communicative nature of gaming/simulation. There is a wide diversity of communication modes; one is not necessarily better than another, but certainly one is often more appropriate than another. It is particularly important to establish that gaming/simulation is appropriate to a given situation before embarking on its use. A communication mode is defined as being composed of three components: a language, the pattern of interaction among the respondents, and the communication technologies employed (see Figure 5.1).

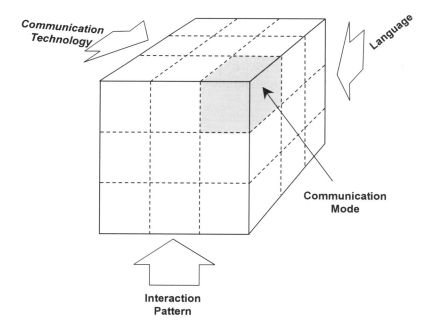

FIGURE 5.1 | A COMMUNICATIONS MODE

The transmission of any message entails the use of a language, defined for our purposes as a symbol-set and the conventions governing its use. A language may be standardized and in conventional use (English, mathematics), or it may be specially created for a restricted situation. Professionals develop a jargon for use within a given field (e.g. law, medicine), and in the vernacular, a layman might say that they "speak a language of their own." This problem-specific jargon occurs naturally during gaming events. If the game designer prepares properly for the jargon, it can facilitate good communication during the game.

The structure of a language may not be readily apparent or formalized. Typically, the user will be unknowingly trained in the use of the rules of the language. Learning such a rule structure is an intellectual exercise distinct from the operational use of a language. As a consequence, most people learn and use language without being consciously aware of its structure. This phenomenon exists in games where participants are confronted by game-specific language that they learn, use, and discard without having been intellectually aware of the process.

Communication technology is defined here to include both natural and man-made devices for transmitting a message from sender(s) to receiver(s). Natural phenomena (the human larynx and ears) are frequently coupled with artificial devices (printing, telephone, film, slide projection equipment, email, the internet and so on). The more complex the message, the more specialized are the communications technologies required; as a consequence, it is likely that natural phenomena will be supplemented by man-made devices in increasingly sophisticated configurations. Although communication technology has advanced rapidly in recent years, the pattern of interaction is still archaic for most modes of message transmission. Messages are still frequently highly sequential, static, one-way and non-interactive; this hinders any effort towards depth of communication; frequently, the receiver is not viewed as an active participant in the process.

A communication technology is defined as a tool for encoding, transmitting, and decoding a message; these technologies may be quite elaborate, with multiple synchronized channels as in the use of television or film. Communication technology may be used in various elaborate formats to assist in conveying complex messages; often this requires that the recipient be passive. Patterns of interaction among respondents also vary from the simple to the complex (see Figure 5.2).

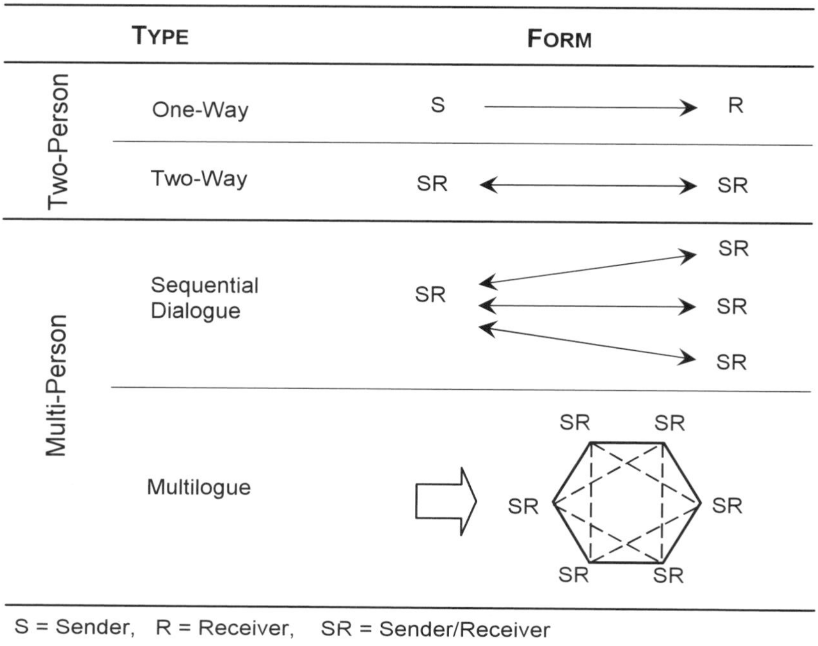

| TYPE | | FORM |
|---|---|---|

S = Sender,   R = Receiver,    SR = Sender/Receiver

**FIGURE 5.2 | PATTERNS OF INTERACTION**

The simplest forms of communication are two-person exchanges, in either one-way or two-way dialogue exchanges. Multi-person exchanges become more involved. While there are many possible patterns of interaction in multi-person exchanges, two forms are germane here: sequential dialogue and multilogue. Sequential dialogue has been selected to represent the pattern between a central figure (lecturer or speaker) and an audience. This pattern is found in conference sessions, classrooms, public meetings, technical sessions, and so on, and is the most common and presumably the most efficient pattern. It is used to exchange ideas or information focused on some area of interest by a group varying in size from less than 10 to more than 100 persons. It is characterized by an initial statement by a central figure followed by a series of remarks from respondents which are directed back to the leader of the meeting (comments directly between the respondents tend to be disruptive and are usually prohibited). The leader may present his or her information in its entirety before the discussion, or may present it in a series of logical units interspersed with questions, answers and comments. Because the leader is not prescient, the remarks from the respondents arrive in no particular order. This tends to create confusion and makes for an inefficient exchange of ideas.

In summary, a variety of communication modes can be employed. These may be perceived as falling along a continuum ranging from simple to complex. As they become more complex, their three basic components – language, communication technology, and pattern of interaction – become more sophisticated both individually and in their combined patterns (see Figure 5.3). The policy exercise is at the most sophisticated end of the continuum, and typically uses multiple "languages" (including a game-specific language), multilogue, and a sophisticated, interactive combination of communication technologies.

| MODES<br><br>COMPONENTS | PRIMITIVE | ADVANCED | INTEGRATED | |
| --- | --- | --- | --- | --- |
| | | | MULTIMEDIA | FUTURE'S LANGUAGE |
| LANGUAGE | Few symbols<br><br>Simple conventions | Many symbols<br><br>Complex conventions | Multiple sets of symbols<br><br>Parallel complex conventions | Multiple sets of symbols<br><br>Some newly created<br><br>Parallel, complex situation-specific conventions |
| PATTERNS OF INTERACTION | One-way<br><br>Two-way | One-way<br><br>Two-way<br><br>Multiple Dialogue | One-way<br><br>Two-way<br><br>Multiple Dialogue | One-way<br><br>Two-way<br><br>Multiple Dialogue<br><br>Multilogue |
| COMMUNICATION TECHNOLOGY | Few, Simple | Many, Complex | Sophisticated combinations | Sophisticated combinations<br><br>Interactive |

**FIGURE 5.3 | COMPONENTS OF COMMUNICATION MODES**

From this logic derives a communication's definition of gaming/simulation: a gestalt communications mode which contains a game-specific language (the jargon employed to describe components of reality), appropriate communication technologies (e.g. wall charts and/or a computer), and the multilogue (multiple simultaneous dialogue) interaction pattern.

## 5.5 FORMS OF COMMUNICATION MODES

The various modes of communication currently in use range from primitive to sophisticated; these can be divided into four major categories: primitive, advanced, integrated-simulated, and integrated-real. In a sense, the two extremes of the continuum can be viewed as being linked, in that two parties fully sharing a reality need no overt communication or can suffice with primitive modes. The greater the communications gap and the more involved the reality to be confronted, the more elaborate and sophisticated the language must become.

| EXAMPLES | 1 | 2 | 3 | 4 |
|---|---|---|---|---|
| | **PRIMITIVE** | **ADVANCED** | **INTEGRATED** | |
| | | | **MULTIMEDIA** | **FUTURE'S LANGUAGE** |
| COMPONENTS | **SIMPLE, ONE-WAY COMMUNICATION** | **TELEPHONE CONVERSATION** | **MULTI-PERSON SEQUENTIAL DIALOGUE** | **COMMUNICATION THROUGH GAMING/ SIMULATION** |
| **LANGUAGE** | Sign language<br><br>Grunts | Spoken English | Spoken English with visuals | English, math, game-specific language |
| **PATTERNS OF INTERACTION** | One-way | Two-way (Dialogue) | Multi-person sequential dialogue | Multilogue (Multi-person simultaneous dialogue) |
| **COMMUNICATION TECHNOLOGY** | Larynx<br>Sound waves<br>Ear | Telephone | Voice<br>Microphone<br>Slide projector | Voice<br>Telephone<br>Wall charts |
| **EXAMPLE OF MESSAGE** | Come here! | Can you come tomorrow if it does not rain? | Discussion of impact on a community of ethnic group in-migration | Discussion of impact on a community of ethnic group in-migration |

**FIGURE 5.4 | POSITIONING A FUTURE'S LANGUAGE**

*Primitive forms* (Figure 5.4) can be divided into informal (grunts and hand signals) and formal (semaphore or navigational lights); in both instances, they are ubiquitous. In situations that are simple and transitory, the former will suffice; but as communication needs become more important, more involved, or more consistent, these rudimentary types become formalized. Primitive forms are characterized both by limited message content and immediacy to experience. Hand signals and body language can be used to locate basic necessities in any country; international road signs using standard signals have found their way into formal usage throughout the world. In spite of this basic universality, these primitive modes can only be used to convey relatively simple messages. They are generally used in face-to-face contact. For example, a cry of warning is almost universally understood by people of all cultures. Its function is to alert someone to a danger; it is effective only in so far as the person warned shares the other's perception of current reality, i.e. he or she is in the same place at the same time and is knowledgeable about the environment.

*Advanced forms* of communication include spoken languages, written languages, emotional forms (art, acting, role-playing) and technical forms (pictures, mathematical notation, musical notation, schematic diagrams, etc.), which are often used as supplements to other advanced forms. It is quite common, of course, to use these in some combination (for example, slides with a lecture), and such uses can be viewed as rudimentary forms of integrated languages. Of these, integrated-simulated is characterized by deliberate combinations of media (film and television) or by hybrids (gaming/simulation) which employ all prior forms in any combination which best enhances the transmission of some reality. Advanced communication modes can be used to transmit complex messages. These forms of communication abound.

*Integrated forms* of communication entail the coordinated usage of two or more advanced forms. Integrated forms of communication result from humankind's efforts to go beyond the limitations of the various individual advanced modes. The use of integrated forms of communication flows from special needs not successfully met by the advanced forms employed individually; the effort to "integrate" always entails more cost and effort. Integrated forms can be used to convey very elaborate messages with special nuance. Inevitably, a given usage has very specific limits of application.

To show how the concepts of language, pattern and technology help us understand the differences between our vision of a future's language and other modes of communication that we find often in policy processes, we have developed Figure 5.5 below.

| MODES OF COMMUNICATION | | EXAMPLE |
|---|---|---|
| **PRIMITIVE** | **INFORMAL** | Grunts<br>Hand Signals |
| | **FORMAL** | Semaphore<br>Lights<br>Flag at half mast |
| **ADVANCED** | **SPOKEN** | Conversation<br>Lecture<br>Seminar |
| | **WRITTEN** | Telegram<br>Letter<br>Book |
| | **TECHNICAL** | Mathematical & musical notation<br>Schematics |
| | **ARTISTIC** | Acting<br>Art<br>Role playing |
| **INTEGRATED** | **MULTIMEDIA** | Film<br>Television |
| | **FUTURE'S LANGUAGE** | Flow chart<br>Highway map |
| | | Iconic models<br>Architectural scale model |
| | | Gaming/Simulation |

**FIGURE 5.5 | A COMMUNICATIONS CONTINUUM**

In the next section, we explore more deeply how communication modes differ along certain dimensions that are relevant for the topic of this book, i.e. strategic problem solving.

## 5.6 DIFFERENT ABILITIES OF COMMUNICATION MODES

Human communication needs are infinitely varied and, consequently, many formats (modes) are employed. To better understand the unique function of the major types of modes, several common characteristics have been identified (see Figure 5.6). These characteristics vary across the communication continuum.

| MODES / CHARACTERISTICS | PRIMITIVE | | ADVANCED | | | | INTEGRATED | |
|---|---|---|---|---|---|---|---|---|
| | INFORMAL | FORMAL | SPOKEN | WRITTEN | TECHNICAL | ARTISTIC | MULTI-MEDIA | FUTURE'S LANGUAGE |
| SEQUENTIAL/ GESTALT | Highly sequential. | | Basically sequential but various devices employed to ease this constraint. | | | | Least sequential; most capable of conveying gestalt. | |
| UNIVERSALITY/ SPECIFICITY | May be employed for a broad array of subject matter. | | Standardized modes suitable for in-depth usage with a limited range of applications. | | | | Mode specifically tailored to a communication need. | |
| SPONTANEITY | Natural, easy, convenient. | | Special skills required, Sophisticated uses often "dry". | | | | Special effort required to initiate. Spontaneous in usage. | |
| MUTABILITY | Readily adaptable to the situation at hand. | | Formalized structures; changes evolve slowly. | | | | Specialized constructs adapted to specific situation; often can be adapted while in use. | |
| RANGE (CATHOLICITY) | May be employed by a broad range of people. | | Application limited to those skilled in a particular mode. | | | | When carefully constructed, suitable for a diverse clientele. | |
| MESSAGE CHARACTERISTICS | Only rudimentary message can be conveyed. | | Sophisticated messages can be conveyed. | | | | Can convey sophisticated message in a gestalt context. | |

**FIGURE 5.6 | CHARACTERISTICS OF COMMUNICATION MODES**

*The Sequential/Gestalt Constant* reflects the inherent ability of the communications mode to convey gestalt or holistic imagery. Sequential communication exists in all communication modes to some extent, and inhibits the transmission of some types of messages. As we move along the continuum (see Figure 5.5) a variety of devices are used to ease this constraint. For example, in the primitive mode employing semaphore flags, the message recipient is required to accept the symbols one by one, and can only interpret the message after a logical string of symbols has been received. Contrast this with written English, where the reader can skip forward in the text at will, and is normally aided in comprehending the meaning and significance of a particular passage by a variety of stylistic conventions (table of contents, sections, chapters, paragraphs, schematic material to illustrate the linkage of ideas). In spite of these devices, the basic sequence of a book is very pronounced. Letter follows letter to make words, words string into sentences, and so on.

Selecting a more technical mode further along the continuum, such as flow-charting, we discover greater freedom in conveying gestalt. The users of a flow-chart can, to some extent, select their own route through the structure, and are also permitted to double back and select alternate paths. A flowchart is a picture of a certain logical set, and although it is inherently sequential, (if condition "x" go to box 36) it is particularly valuable for conveying the logic of a system.

The primary motivation for the development of the various integrated communication modes is to increase the ability to convey gestalt, to escape the cumbersome sequence of simple modes. Contrast the imagery transmitted by a film abstracted from a Russian novel with that derived from a reading of the text. The text will certainly give more detailed information, but even the most diligent of readers, buffered by a detailed logical mapping of the emerging developments, cannot as quickly obtain the sweeping overview provided by the film.

However, a device can be created for each specific future's language to assist in establishing and retaining an imagery of the big picture – the total scheme under consideration. Such devices are often graphic (drawings, diagrams, schematics) and frequently will be three-dimensional (perspective drawings, architect's models), but may be supplemented by sophisticated computer simulations which, upon proper inquiry, will reveal the dimensions of the system. The introduction of role play and the use of scenario are still other devices used to assist in conveying gestalt.

*Specificity-Universality Constraints* determine the degree of flexibility inherent to the language form in adapting to new substantive material. As one moves to the right along the continuum of communication modes, each particular mode becomes more subject-specific, and, therefore, less suitable for a broad array of purposes. The various forms of communication suggested under the integrated modes are elaborate constructs devised to meet highly specific communications objectives. Gaming/simulation is located to the extreme right of the continuum because each given product employs a specially contrived jargon (game-specific language).

Some communication modes are "frames" into which content must be added. For example, flowcharts or crossword puzzles may be suitable as techniques for a wide array of content. Once the content has been added the product has only limited usage. There are numerous frame games that meet this description.

All future's languages are problem-specific and as such must be designed to meet the need of a particular client. As a consequence, the range of sophistication and, therefore, the methodology employed will be enormously diverse. Fortunately, many future's languages lend themselves to basic structures, or frames, which can be used repeatedly in different situations by altering the content (e.g. the rules of flow-charting are consistent, but the content will vary in each application.)

*Spontaneity of Use* represents the ease or relative freedom with which a user can employ a given mode. The ease of use of the various modes of communication ranges from the spontaneous cry of warning to the technological jungle associated with a television or movie production. In the latter instances, the creation of the specific mode (film, videotape) may be very complicated; however, the completed product may be quite simple to use (reading a book versus writing and publishing it). Note that the spontaneity of use of games will vary tremendously; it is a function of the techniques and the design employed. Because they are used to facilitate discussion about complex subject matter, the various future's languages tend to be somewhat complicated in construction. When completed and placed into operation, their ease of use varies considerably.

*Mutability* refers to the ability of the communications mode to be altered while in use. There is a broad diversity among the various communication forms in terms of the user's ability to change them. The simplest modes have little formal structure and can change upon the agreement of the two corresponding parties. Written English follows certain formalized conventions, but these yield through time. The more precise technical forms are even more resistant to the whimsy of the user; mathematics, musical notation, and computer programming languages derive their great value in part from their relative constancy. To the extent they are directed toward a passive receiver, the more sophisticated forms such as books and films are essentially immutable in any specific instance; a given mode (films) will change readily through time. Gaming/simulation as a communication form employs active sender/receivers, and as a consequence, a specific game can be altered while in use. Future's languages are basically transient in format to permit the restructuring or more careful articulation of the problem as viewed by those participating in the dialogue. They are dynamic communication forms; they must respond during use to changing perceptions of the problem.

*Range of Audience* in Figure 5.6 refers to the width of the array of potential users for which a given mode of communication is suitable. The relative catholicity of the various communication modes, like the characteristic of mutability, can be perceived as somewhat U-shaped; that is, those at either end of the continuum will find a greater array of potential users. Everyone can grunt or point and most adults, even the illiterate, can participate successfully in a serious game situation. The advanced modes in the center of the continuum inevitably are restricted to those with the necessary specialized skills (mathematics, computer programming, and so on). Each gaming/simulation is a special construct for a given purpose; to be successful, the primary audience must be defined before construction begins.

Policy games can be designed to accommodate groups using a specific jargon, and those which have an inherent diversity of jargon and/or markedly different levels of sophistication. Games have a basic catholicity of design. There is hardly an audience for which a game has not been designed; high school students, university students and faculty, business leaders, community groups, military strategists, diplomats, and so on. This is best illustrated by the incredible profusion of examples currently on the market. Some require nothing more than a sheet of paper or a blackboard and can be completed by a wide array of participants in a short time. Other games, designed to meet more sophisticated audiences, are used for training and in actual decision making contexts.

*Message Characteristics* refers to the nature of the message that can be conveyed, including but not limited to such characteristics as complexity, analogy, qualitative thought, quantitative thought, subtlety, permanency (ability to re-establish), precision, intangibles, time constraints, and systems characteristics. In general, the more primitive the mode, the more rudimentary the message conveyed. As communication needs become more sophisticated, distinct message characteristics emerge, these influence the mode of communication selected. Emotional messages may be presented through the various art forms; highly precise and/or theoretical constructs may rely more heavily on mathematical notation. If there is a strong need to convey a sophisticated message in a gestalt context, an integrated mode will be selected. Because games are specifically constructed for a particular communication problem, the individual game construct will take a unique form – only then can the idiosyncratic needs of conveying a unique message be satisfied.

Common to all games is a pulsing of thought or inquiry. This takes several forms, the most common of which are cycles in which players make their decisions sequentially. Games are almost invariably cyclical, and each cycle permits iterative questions that must be resolved in the total context of the game. The common use of issues, problems, or an iterative decision set in games illustrates this point. This process is frequently modified by the inclusion of events that are either pre-programmed or triggered by circumstances that develop and/or by random events which focus the players' attention on some new problem or aspect of the situation at hand.

## 5.7 CONCLUSION: GAMING AS A FUTURE'S LANGUAGE

The continua in the figures in this chapter used the term "future's language" for those modes listed at the right-hand extreme. This usage is meant to imply that these forms will prove of greatest value in those circumstances where the need to convey gestalt is urgent. It is not suggested that they are the "language of the future"; nor is it suggested that future's language is limited to gaming/simulation. Other examples exist and more are sure to be devised. What is suggested is that gaming/simulation, properly conceived and employed, is a powerful tool both for discussing the future by conveying gestalt and for addressing alternative future situations that could not otherwise be explored. The unusual ability of gaming/simulation to provide a holistic imagery is its central characteristic.

In the sections above, we have conceptualized a future's language as being a hybrid mode which employs other forms in any combination which best enhances the transmission of some complex reality. Future's languages permit the pulsing of specific, tangible inquiries or alternatives in correlation with a holistic image. There is a correlation here with the strictly sequential traditional communication forms. Both spoken and written language, even in their sophisticated forms, advance through a strict sequence (sentence follows sentence, thought follows thought). The sequential pulsing of inquiries through a future's language is more sophisticated in that a pulse in itself becomes a logical and coherent proposition, independently formed, evaluated, and comprehended. As such, it provides the focus of inquiry as it is tested against the gestalt or holistic image provided.

To conclude: there are several characteristics available to analyze the various modes of communication and these help to explain the character and special utility of gaming/simulation. These relationships are abstracted in Figure 5.7. This diagram illustrates the relationship between the several communication modes and the central characteristics of the strategic communication tasks in complex environments we have identified in earlier chapters. The message of Figure 5.7 is this: multilogue is appropriate when there is complexity in an open system; the organization has little control over the decision variables and it cannot avoid or postpone taking decisions that have a long-range impact on the system. As we move from the left to the right of the continuum (Figure 5.7), the mode becomes richer in its potential to overcome perceptual differences. However, a price must be paid for this sophistication: as we move to the right along this continuum, the modes become more difficult and expensive to use. The important insight here is that major groupings of communication modes can be defined in terms of several central characteristics:

- The ability to convey gestalt;
- The range of subject matter which can portrayed;
- Their ease of usage;
- The ease with which the form can be changed while in use;
- The range of audience that can be accommodated; and
- The characteristics of the message.

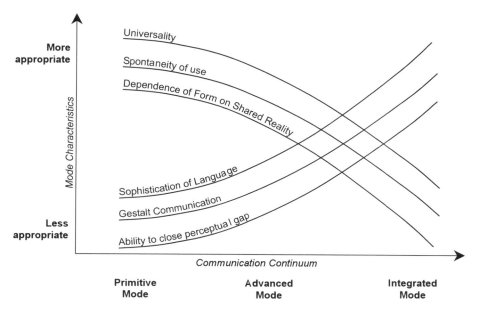

**FIGURE 5.7 | VARIATIONS OF MODE CHARACTERISTICS**

*One caution is required.* The policy exercise is a costly mode of communication in both construction and use. It is incumbent upon the potential user to consider alternative modes carefully. Before proceeding with the gaming technique, every effort should be made to ascertain that the client's need cannot be met by some less cumbersome mode.

Ill-conceived uses of gaming/simulation in the past have not been helpful. The technique has not been well understood and enthusiastic proponents have used it beyond its capability. Gaming is not a predictive device or a panacea to be plugged into the problem of the moment. It can be useful for gaining perspective on complex issues; it is particularly useful for guiding speculation about future circumstances. The policy exercise approach can more readily convey a totality and therefore speed understanding of a rich, complex, environment.

There are five criteria used to explore the nature of the policy exercise, in terms of a "future's language":

- The primary purpose of any policy exercise is to convey gestalt or an overall perspective of the problem at hand. Many technical devices may be used to obtain this objective. Success is marked by the quality of the discussions that ensue during the debriefing. Although players identify with only one role, it is from this perspective that they gain a perception of the total system conveyed by the game;

- Policy exercises are problem-specific; that is, they address a particular situation and, in any given event or play of that exercise, the subject matter is explicit and unique. Unfortunately, many games have been used inappropriately, out of their intended contexts. One response to this problem has been the invention of frame games that are specifically designed for a fresh loading of content for each application;

- The policy exercise, properly employed, is inherently spontaneous. Participants who overcome the early difficulties associated with start-up procedures become deeply enmeshed in the activity;

- Policy exercises have been designed for a wide array of audiences: business leaders, community groups, military strategists, diplomats, and so on. Some games require nothing more than a sheet of paper or a blackboard, while others require trained facilitators, computers, and sophisticated facilities; and

- The policy exercise has the ability to present a future's orientation (the representation of any time frame other than the present). Their purpose is to explore alternatives, to develop a sophisticated mental response to "what if" questions, and to permit the formulation of analogy/metaphor for exploration of alternatives where no prior basis exists.

In terms of the concepts developed above, gaming/simulation is defined as a gestalt communication mode, a future's language that combines a game-specific language and appropriate communication technologies with the multilogue interaction pattern. This pattern, properly coordinated with other techniques, is central to the game's ability to display gestalt. This combination of components is unique among the various communication modes – especially when one considers that it is presented to the participants in an interactive mode (as contrasted with the unidirectional pattern of film or television).

Figure 5.8 attempts to show the different stages of the communication process in the gaming mode. The top of the figure visualizes reality as a polyhedron rather than a plane, since the typical problem will be multifaceted. This reality is abstracted into a cognitive map via a process in which, usually and preferably, the future participants in the game are involved. Through an intensive communication process, the game and its starting conditions (Game T1) becomes a tangible model (artifacts) that represent a conceptual model. This is an open model (the game) in the sense that players may change it during use. The facilitator has the role of introducing events (new items on the communication agenda); these prompt discussion (multilogue) and induce changes to the initial model. As the players go through the different cycles of the game, new realities are created and explored as cyclical play advances. A critique following each cycle and a debriefing at the end of the game links the models employed in the game to the participants' perceptions of reality.

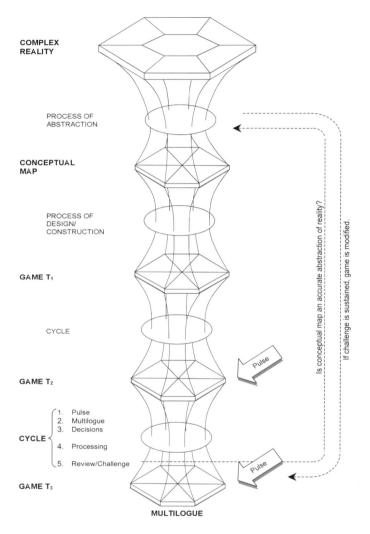

**FIGURE 5.8 | CHALLENGING THE GAME MODEL**

Several items of significance must be emphasized. First, the players are engaged in different roles with differing perceptions of the reality modeled by the game. Because they are simultaneously engaged in the process, the message interchange pattern contains many concurrent dimensions and the term dialogue is insufficient to describe the process. Rather, it should be thought of as many parallel and simultaneous dialogues (multilogue), all pertaining to some aspect of a complex phenomenon. Serendipitous occurrences, both during the play of the game and in the organized debriefing which follows, will heighten the significance of these message exchanges in terms of what they convey to the player about the nature of the complex reality.

As stated, communication through a gaming model entails not only multilogue among the players, but also communication between players and designers. The game is iterative, involving cycles of play each of which mimics some actual time phase, but which varies in focus depending on the pulse of information used to trigger multilogue. Discussion is followed by decision; decision by processing. These results must be reviewed; during the debriefing, players must be encouraged to focus on the reality that the game model attempts to represent. If there are challenges by the players, these must be resolved by offering evidence to sustain the model, or through the modification of the model to more accurately reflect the new understanding of reality. The discussions obtain their focus both from the basic model represented in the game and from the pulse, which is a device for organizing the progress of the discussion. Because the pulse may be either pre-specified or introduced as a result of participant need during play, there is considerable latitude both in setting the agenda for discussion as well as in establishing the sequence of deliberation. This permits some escape from the rigid sequence of the formal lecture, which must go logically from beginning to end.

The multilogue model used in a game/simulation creates a problem-specific language (Figure 5.9). The game-specific language is a critical element in the gaming process; it implies the thoughtful invention of jargon as part of game design. The jargon employed to describe components of reality becomes the symbols that are unique to the problem being explored. It must be sufficiently complex to improve discussion about a specific problem, but simple enough to be learned during the normal course of play. The behavior of the participants creates a set of conventions governing the use of the symbols used in the exercise. The symbols used in the game/simulation acquire specific meaning for the participants through their experiences in the exercise. This problem-specific language may be deliberately designed or inadvertently created by the players as jargon.

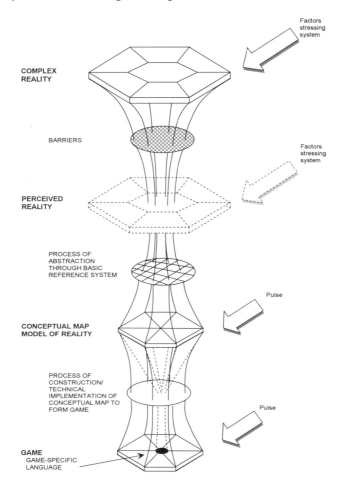

**FIGURE 5.9 | A MODEL OF COMMUNICATING THROUGH GAMING**

It is specifically suggested that the game model, when functioning during the event of a game, is the basis for a game-specific language. The jargon employed to describe roles or components of reality that are modeled become symbols that are unique to the game. The basic game structure or model, including the constraints of message potential between decision units as well as the behavior of individual decision units in response to the message, becomes the set of conventions governing the use of the game-specific symbols. These two, in conjunction, constitute the game-specific language. The ambience of the game provides the context for learning, in an operational sense, the meaning of the special symbols used to represent the abstracted reality.

One of the central theses of this book is that gaming is a "future's language," a new form of communication. It has the potential of great impact in many disciplines and problem situations. This is an extremely effective communication technique that allows participants to safely explore diverse issues and choose alternative solutions to today's complex problems. The future will in all certainty differ dramatically from the past, and the languages that have passed to us from antiquity will no longer suffice. The problems that must be faced in the future differ from those of the past because of their relative complexity, the rapidity of their occurrence, the newness of their character, and the systemic origin of the basic problems involved. Gaming/simulation is a hybrid communication form. It is not well understood, sometimes poorly used, and its use for solving macro-problems is still in its infancy. Nonetheless, there is convincing evidence that, when it is treated with the same precision and understanding as traditional forms of communication, it proves to be very useful for solving the wicked problems many organizations face today.

# Chapter 6

## Empirical Research and the Policy Exercise

### 6.1 INTRODUCTION

The three pillars underlying this book have been the *case studies;* the *theoretical constructs or topical conceptualizations,* albeit from fragmented and diverse sources; and *theory from practice,* i.e. the summated learning-by-doing of gaming practitioners.

In most areas of applied policy and organization science, there is hardly any separation between application and *explanatory or evaluative research.* This is true for policy exercises; research efforts have to be interwoven with the uses of games in applied settings. As a consequence, most empirical research on policy gaming is a compromise and it is often quite limited from a research-design perspective. Empirical study of gaming in policy settings proves to be difficult. If one were to apply the classical paradigm of empirical social science to most academic gaming publications, the result would most certainly be somewhat disappointing. As we shall illustrate, even the bravest of our Ph.D. students have to struggle hard to develop and execute empirical studies that come close to realizing the handbook demands on classical experimentation and cross-sectional or longitudinal designs.

### 6.2 "IT WORKS" — BUT IS THAT ALL WE HAVE?

As two academics who have devoted much of their professional time to executing and coaching empirical research on gaming/simulation, we wish this book could document that the empirical foundations of this field have made a quantum leap during our professional years. This is not the case; however, empirical work around gaming/simulation has certainly grown in the last three decades. Somewhere in the early 1970s, the first author of this book made a strong (but not cynical) statement regarding the empirical base supporting the gaming-discipline at that time: *"It works, that is all we have."* The phrase was not so much a reassuring description but more a call for action. It was a plea towards academics in the gaming discipline to do more research, share their results and jointly build up gaming/simulation as a true academic discipline. Since then, much has happened on the gaming-research interface. In this chapter, we want to review a small part of that activity, namely selected examples of empirical research that have connections with the main topic of this book, i.e. the use of gaming/simulation for strategy and policy.

An academic discipline can be characterized as having, apart from a successful practice, a distinct theory and methodology; its body of knowledge should, at least in part, be brought forward through empirical research. We think this volume contains some strong arguments for the claim that gaming/simulation is developing the characteristics of an academic discipline. We hope to enforce this argument with the contents of this chapter.

Within the collection of empirically oriented publications on gaming/simulation which have links with strategy and policy, a large part has to do with empirical evaluation of the intended and unintended effects of management games in training situations. We do not discuss this class of research here. However, there is more interesting research than the important evaluation of training games. Below, we use a simple word game to sketch five different interconnections between research and gaming:

*Research for Gaming* – The first is research for gaming, i.e. all the empirical research that can and often will go into the preparation of a game. Since we will devote all of Chapter 8 to game design, it is important here to explore and explain what this game-design process shares with and distinguishes from research that follows the traditional empirical approach. We will describe this category in some detail in Section 6.3.

*Research with Gaming* – A second relevant category of empirical studies is research with gaming, constituting the surprisingly varied uses of games as research stimuli or observation contexts to test and develop hypotheses on policy- relevant behavior. This category is very broad and quite interesting to the student of policy and strategy. It could easily fill a separate academic monograph and thus deserves more space than we can give it. In Chapters 2 and 4, we discussed the work of Dörner and Vansina et al. Section 6.4 shows some of the variety and relevance of this category.

*Research on Gaming* – The third category is research on gaming, meaning the potentially very broad class of systematic evaluation studies that empirically assess the uses of games in real-life strategy and policy trajectories. As far as we know, this type of evaluation is scarce. It is hard to do, because the conditions for fruitful research are difficult to create. We will explore some aspects of this topic in Section 6.5 of this chapter, but, given the current state of affairs, this section will be more programmatic than summative.

*Research in Gaming* – Sometimes one comes across a fourth connection, research in gaming. In this case, designers build a role (e.g. the outside observer) into their games for some of the participants to temporarily assume. This might be done to collect some data to draw the attention of all the players to selected social science concepts which might help to clarify the dynamics of the interactions among the policy actors in that game session. For this, the game materials might offer a topical checklist or scoring scheme derived from a relevant academic discipline to secure the validity and utility of this activity. Geurts et al. (2000) described some examples of this interface between research and gaming and we limit ourselves here to referring to that source.

*Research through Gaming* – A fifth connection between gaming and research that should be mentioned here is research through gaming. The IJC Great Lakes case is only one example of many games that are used as tools to "get research going." This use of gaming can vary considerably, e.g. from the limited role of a generic game as an ice-breaking and creativity-stimulating device in a research start-up to the very elaborate application of a tailor-made gaming process for strategic R&D management. Several cases in this book have links with research and technology planning. We believe that the cases and concepts from Chapters 3 and 4 suffice to explain this particular research function of gaming, so this chapter will not have a separate section to reiterate our thoughts.

We warn the reader that our categorization of the activities along the gaming-research interface has problems when used too strictly. Researchers are creative people and they often discover several ways of "playing with" and interpreting their data. The same data set collected during a game might support propositions on cooperative behavior in multiparty settings and shed light on the effectiveness of the game in which the data was collected. The rather limited aim of this chapter is to show the varied and potentially fruitful relations between gaming and empirical research. We cannot be exhaustive in the description of this interface nor can this chapter assess the value of all research examples. Many different disciplines use games in their research and so the contributions to theory and method of these efforts have to be assessed within those disciplines. This chapter should be read as a call for action: the use of gaming/simulation as a process of participatory policy analysis will benefit from more solid empirical work.

## 6.3 RESEARCH FOR POLICY GAMING

Chapter 8 will explain the steps in the process of designing policy games as we have come to use and disseminate them over the years. In this section, we want to draw the attention of the reader to the systems analysis phase of game design. A methodological reflection on this step will help to clarify how our routines for this phase relate to the empirical traditions in the strategic and policy sciences and how game design can be fed with different cognitive inputs and various empirical research formats.

### 6.3.1 Participatory Model Building

The combination of inductive and deductive systems analysis that we use to prepare for policy gaming (see Chapter 8) can be recognized as a procedure that belongs to the broad class of hybrid and systemic model building routines that have emerged since the advent of modern systems theory. These family relations and their history have already been explained in earlier chapters, especially in Section 4.2, Understanding Complexity, where we talked about organizing a robust knowledge household. A key feature of our technique is to involve the client in our model building. Many of the modern versions of system dynamics or strategic decision analysis and other related group-based strategic consulting processes have a similar approach (see for example Morecroft & Sterman, 1994).

From a methodological perspective, any preparation, running, and evaluation of a policy game is a special way of achieving the three phases of modeling (i.e. abstraction, deduction and evaluation/implementation.) Figure 6.1 (originally from Hanken and Reuver, 1976) shows this basic model cycle.

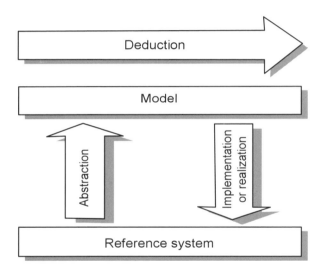

**FIGURE 6.1 | THE MODEL CYCLE (HANKEN AND REUVER, 1976)**

Geurts & Vennix (1989) explain how both gaming/simulation and many forms of computer simulation have evolved in such a way that their uses as strategic consulting tools can be interpreted as taking a client organization through a process of participatory modeling. The developments since 1989 have brought us further integration and the development of hybrid strategic process tools. We believe that the Geurts & Vennix "model of participatory modeling" from 1989 is still a relevant and valid concept for understanding current methodological synergies in simulation-based strategy consulting (see Geurts et al., 2000). For example, with Figure 6.2, Geurts & Vennix show how modern simulation schools place the phase of abstraction into operation to transform cognitive inputs from many sources into a problem-specific conceptual model that guides the construction of the simulation tool.

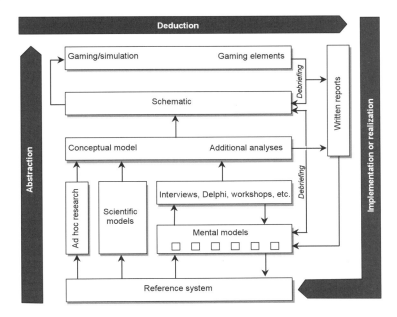

**FIGURE. 6.2 | GAMING/SIMULATION AS PARTICIPATIVE MODEL BUILDING**

In this figure, the reader will recognize the different elements of communication through gaming as described in Chapter 5. Figure 5.8 shows how the mental models of different persons are elicited and confronted. There is an endless variety of interview and discussion techniques that can be used for this purpose. Most professionals use their own favorite tools, but many of these are direct descendants of traditional data collection techniques from empirical social research (e.g. open or closed face-to-face interviewing, questionnaires of many different formats, focus group interviews, panel studies and the related Delphi techniques). Figure 6.2 shows how models from academic disciplines and ad-hoc empirical studies can have a role in this phase of abstraction. We illustrate this concept a bit more in the following paragraphs.

*6.3.2 Framing the Problem*
The analysis of our eight case studies in Chapter 4 has shown both the strategic importance and the potential variety of theoretical and empirical inputs of game design. In several organizations that we helped with macro-problems, we came across a silent assumption that "our people know everything there is to know

about the world." It is fair to say that their track record shows they have often proven to be right with this assumption. Unfortunately, there is always one issue or challenge for which the trusted, internal sources will give us the wrong information, and it is very hard to know when such an issue presents itself. It has been consistently our role, quite often with the overt and sometimes with the silent support of leaders within an organization, to force groups to be open to unknown or disregarded channels of information. In retrospect, there is a kind of tension at work here, engendered by a dilemma. One really needs the inputs from the actual players. Most modelers have accepted by now that there is both a validation and a legitimization motive to make sure that a model is well grounded in the internal expertise of the client organization. But there is also validation and legitimization involved in making sure that one has made the data collection as broad as possible. The organizations in some of our cases had a history of not looking beyond familiar horizons and, as a consequence, prior strategic moves had ended in a dead man's valley. If such a history becomes apparent, good professional ethics requires that one only accepts a contract to help find a way out of the wrong valley if the database can be made much broader. New perspectives and data from outside research, independent experts and/or scientific theory can be beneficial to any part of the strategic problem-solving puzzle.

First of all, startling new perspectives or astonishing data can help *or even force a policy problem to be re-framed*. For example, the Dutch Social Employment project needed a systematic, albeit more or less classical, empirical evaluation study of the current information system by independent outsiders before the vast limitations of that system became obvious. What started as an informal rumor or complaint and as a worry for a few people became an issue that everyone wanted to see on the policy agenda. The framing changed. It became clear that an ineffective and inefficient information system was a problem beyond the central government ("let them deal with it"). The intermediary and executing organizations also saw how much this system could harm their own positions, especially when the new budget financing was introduced ("I might be digging my own grave by filling in all these forms").

The framing of a macro-problem (which is usually an ill-structured problem mess, see Section 2.3) is decisive for the type of solutions that will be generated. Dunn refers to other grand old men from policy analysis who signal this "error of the third type." Dunn (1981, p. 97) begins his excellent chapter on problem structuring with a warning from Russell L. Ackoff (1974):

> "Successful problem solving requires finding the right solution to the right problem. We fail more often because we solve the wrong problem than because we get the wrong solution to the right problem."

The process of transforming a notion about a problematic situation into a formal and substantive (and may we add: acceptable) representation is subjected to many forces that may lead to serious distortions. The problem-structuring literature suggests rules and remedies for avoiding these pitfalls; it supports the interactive, stepwise, and pluralistic procedures that we have adopted in our gaming projects.

Worldviews, ideologies and popular myths all play a role in problem conceptualization, and Dunn (op cit., p. 108) correctly observes that all three are usually partly right and partly wrong, and thus partly useful and partly dangerous. Scientific research and well-tested theory have to be mobilized to get past these dangers. Einstein's famous saying: "there is nothing so practical as a good theory" describes very well what science can do here. That is why we put so much effort into what we will call the "deductive" element in systems analysis (see Chapter 8). The best research for game design is *past research*, i.e. the accumulated *explanatory theories* of the empirical disciplines.

To the novice, it might be a disappointment to discover that no academic discipline will provide a grand theory that will fully and without creative reinterpretation deliver the conceptualization of macro-problems. Rip is absolutely correct about the unfortunately strong correlation between unsolved scientific disputes and long-lasting controversies in policy making (see Sections 2.4 and 4.2). However, library research and conversations with specialists quite often helped enormously in our projects. We discovered perspectives that were new to us and to the clients and we found useful classifications and typologies. We were glad to absorb limited but powerful generalizations about cause and effect relationships, and many other fruitful empirical "statements of invariance" or "theories of the middle range," to use concepts of Robert K. Merton (1957).

### 6.3.3 Scenarios and Forecasts

Trend studies and scenario projects are very important types of "research for gaming" because they are essential contributions to the adventure of charting out the "terra incognita." They help to systematically explore the future as a threat or an opportunity. Trend studies usually focus on what is "likely," scenarios broaden this focus and bring in the "possible." Quantitative trends and forecasts try to make the uncertain certain. They focus on the measurable and strive for precise statements about the (near) future. On the other hand, scenarios explore uncertainty and help the policy maker by "drawing a map" of possible future states. Usually, they take a longer time horizon and accept both qualitative information and quantitative data. Because of these characteristics, scenarios have quickly become very popular in strategy and policy analysis because they can be produced in interactive workshops, e.g. as preparatory steps in developing a simulation (see e.g. Becker, 1983; Schwartz, 1991; van der Heyden, 1996; Mayer, 1997; Maani & Cavana, 2000).

A note on terminology is appropriate here. In the gaming literature, and in the chapters of this book, the term "scenario" has a meaning that differs somewhat from the one above. As a product of a futures study, a scenario is a set of stories that hypothesize alternative futures that a social system might face in the coming years. Central to this concept is that there is never one future, but many futures; the possibility of alternatives draws attention to the openness of the future.

Gamers refer to a scenario in a somewhat different way, as can be seen in Section 7.2.1 and in the case studies of Chapter 3. In this context, the game scenario refers to all the information that is brought together to set the stage for the game. Game scenarios define the artificial world the players will enter. They are carefully structured stories, supported by different material, but with the essential feature that they leave the future open to the participants to create. However, Chapter 7 will make clear that a futures scenario can be made part of the gaming scenario – for example, when the designer has prepared sets of exogenous events (outside the control of the players) that "come true" at certain moments in time. On the other hand, a futures scenario can be the intended policy-relevant product of a gaming project, i.e. when different sets of players use the same game scenario to "play out" different futures.

It is important that policy games offer the participants a mature, realistic, and up-to-date testing ground for their strategic moves. To achieve this, we use a seemingly simple but challenging, five-point checklist when seeking and organizing the broadest possible set of data and concepts that can be related to the future. The key concepts in the checklist are all adjectives to characterize a statement about the future. The five concepts are:

- The possible future;
- The thinkable future;
- The likely future;
- The desirable future; and
- The malleable (or doable) future.

The interesting thing about this list is not its labeling. Rather, it is the triple intellectual and imaginative challenge it proves to contain for almost everybody who is participating in the policy debate, whether it is during the design or the run of a game. The triple challenge is:

- To define each of the five concepts as empirically, operationally and clearly as possible when addressing the unique policy problem at hand, using all the data and ideas one can obtain.

- To make sure that one understands and can formulate how each of the five concepts relates to the other, not only in theory (see Figure 6.3), but especially in this particular problematic puzzle. It is important to ensure that the participants do not run away from the dazzling number of relevant combinations one might discover.

- To do justice to the fact that even the simplest of futuring debates will soon prove to bring to the surface sharp differences among persons. The exercise must try to define them and not cover them up; but it should also try to harvest these without formulating meaningless "Hallelujah" statements.

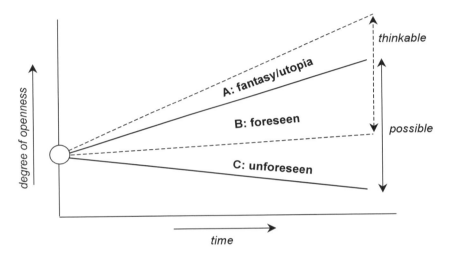

**FIGURE 6.3 | THE FUTURE: A SPACE OF POSSIBILITIES**

Figure 6.3 maps out some of the most important relationships among the five key concepts. The checklist is an elaboration on the perspective of the philosopher Carl Jaspers who has characterized the future as a space of possibilities. But these possibilities can only be partially foreseen. The only future for which we can make policies is the future we can imagine. Area A in the figure shows that much of what we think of now will later prove to be nonsensical (a pleasant or troublesome fantasy that did not belong in the realm of possibilities). It should be kept in mind that the future might turn out to be better or worse than we initially held possible. Area C symbolizes these unforeseen futures.

One of the attractive features of gaming/simulation for the development of strategy is that it can help people to stretch their minds, i.e. to widen the space of the thinkable futures (see the dotted arrow in Figure 6.3). Surprising data from outside research and/or deviant opinions of outsiders (a friend calls them "exotics") will help to make the game content more open to this mind-stretching effect. It is sometimes useful to invite these "exotics" to the formal game sessions. In the bureaucracies of large organizations, it is hard to find people who, through their personality and background, will "look over the fences" that others take for granted.

What about the futures in area A, which are thinkable but considered not possible? How much attention should a game devote to these? How intensely should one search for data and ideas to fill this category during game design? At this point it is useful to look for different statements about the *desirable* future and relate them to area A.

If the desirable future happens to be somewhere within area A, then it can be called a utopian vision: desirable and thinkable, but impossible to create. These utopias are especially interesting when some participants see the likely future as unattractive. In that case, it will not be too difficult to find candidates for a fierce debate on how to make the impossible possible. It is safe to assume that those who find the likely future attractive or at least acceptable will argue for realism and incremental strategies. A game is a good environment in which to have these "malleability" debates. Those who present careful arguments might show that they are right: what some people want cannot work (see the Rubber Windmill story)! On the other hand, motivated utopians might inject some of their commitment into the debate: "we can do it, if we only want to" (e.g. aligning strategic behavior, as in the individualistic culture of the University Hospital).

Debating the thinkable-but-not-possible relates in another fashion to value statements or desirability. We refer here to extremely unlikely situations that are so dangerous that they never should be allowed to happen (see Section 2.4.3 for Weick's view on high reliability organizations). If the improbable happens, one should have contingency plans at hand to fight the consequences and keep disastrous effects as small as possible. Here we enter the border area between strategic and disaster management; gaming is one of the few techniques that has consistently shown to be helpful for these purposes.

An important way of handling uncertainty and risk and to warn for the potential of disaster is monitoring via the installment *and use* of good information systems. Both our Pharmaceutical case and the Social Employment Program case show how difficult it is to keep information systems in place that are truly strategic. In the latter case, a strategic war gaming session was needed to redirect the monitoring system which had gone completely off track. However, it is hard to keep management motivated to spend a lot of energy on an early warning system in times when the skies are clear and the sun is shining. Maybe that is the time to run a policy exercise the outcome of which scares everyone to death (did anyone really take terrorism seriously before September 11, 2001?).

### 6.3.4 The Power of Content

We have used the themes of policy framing and futuring to explore the relationship between game design and empirical research. Other elements of a problem-solving cycle that are brought into a game (e.g. defining the policy alternatives), can be supported by research in much the same way. The message here is that a game has to be developed in a process that forces the designer to organize the knowledge household in such a way that the participant will recognize it as valid and relevant. In addition, a good database for a game should surprise, even entice, the starting player. In order to be able to do this, a first requirement is that a policy game has its feet on solid ground. Information systems, surveys, observations, workshops, personal interviews and written documentation – all these channels of information have to be searched and used during the systems analytical phase of game design.

Sometimes one has to put game design on hold and give priority to preparatory studies. It can be a waste of expensive management time to invite busy people to a game when the knowledge base is not up to the experience and talents of the participants. A game that misses the punch of powerful content will not achieve what it should do: stimulate the disbelievers to jump into the ring and sweat for a while in terra incognita.

### 6.4 POLICY RESEARCH WITH GAMING/SIMULATIONS

A wide variety of social scientists have used policy and strategy games for the explanatory study of human behavior. Policy-relevant behavior of a person, a group or even a rather complex organization can be observed and manipulated in games under circumstances that are hard to find or control in real-life situations.

The policy and organization sciences draw from several parent disciplines, especially psychology, sociology and economics. The uses of games for research bear witness to this diverse background. It is not at all difficult to bring together examples of games used for testing a gamut of hypotheses that these sciences can generate. Past research examples include: the study of individual managerial behavior, the interaction of small groups in a policy process, and the dynamics of larger groups and organizations (up to inter-organizational collaboration and negotiation).

This section is devoted to a single in-depth description of one recent empirical study. We thought the content and method of this study to be particularly interesting in the context of this book. We can illustrate the advantages and the problems of using games for policy research by diving a bit deeper into one research project.

### 6.4.1 Research Example: Do Decision Aids Matter?

As many policy scientists have discovered, empirical evaluation of the relevance of policy development tools and processes is notoriously difficult (see e.g. Mayer, 1997, Bongers, 2000, Heyne, 2000). We will come back to this later. The study of gaming/simulation is no exception when it comes to conquering the practical and conceptual difficulties of empirical evaluation under normal field conditions.

In order to achieve a degree of experimental control, researchers have begun to use gaming/simulations creatively as a policy environment in which they introduce a decision aid in order to observe its use and assess its relevance. For example, Meinsma et al. (1998) report on the exploratory use of a policy game to measure the impact of a formal, visualized (animated) simulation model on the quality of the communication among policy makers in a multi-actor problem-solving process.

An elaborate example of this type of research design is the Ph.D. project of Ellie Roelofs (Roelofs, 1998; Roelofs, 2000). She too, looked for an experimental answer to the question: "Do decision aids matter?" Roelofs' project was, in a very intriguing way, balanced on the borderline between experimental research with gaming and an evaluation study of gaming. We describe the efforts and results of Roelofs' work at some length because it offers excellent insight into both the possibilities and limitations of combining research efforts with running gaming/simulations in a professional environment.

Roelofs developed a relatively rare opportunity to control, manipulate and compare several runs of a very complex policy game. The subjects were not policy novices such as students but experienced civil servants from six municipalities in the Netherlands. In half the runs, the players used a problem-structuring technique while, in the other runs, problem structuring was not specifically stimulated nor aided but left to spontaneous processes in the game.

Problem structuring is a very important part of policy development. Roelofs defines it as the "activities of representatives of various organizations which are directed at influencing the definition of an issue" (Roelofs, 2000, p. 173). Roelofs stresses that problem structuring does not only take place at the beginning of a policy trajectory, but the (collective) definition of an issue can be at stake at any moment in a policy process. As time goes on, one can observe varying levels of activities aimed at influencing the definition of the issues, although it is likely that, at the beginning of a new trajectory, the frequency of these kinds of activities tends to be highest.

### 6.4.2 Measuring the Complexity of Policy Issues

Like us, Roelofs is interested in complex issues. She draws on the policy sciences, including literature reviewed here earlier, to define the concept of "complexity" and to do the hard work of developing operational measures to assess the quality of problem structuring which a group of policy actors (players) realizes during the experiment. Roelofs concentrates on three dimensions of the complexity of policy issues. The first is *cognitive* complexity, i.e. the extent to which an issue involves substantial and/or specialized knowledge together with large numbers of variables that interact in such a way that policy consequences are hard to predict. Issues that are *socio-politically* complex involve many actors in social networks who have different institutional interests to defend. *Normative* complexity is the level of contention among the actors about the norms and values with which they regard the issue. Each dimension requires two criteria to be placed into operation. For the reader, it will not be difficult to recognize the strong correlation with our five criteria, but it would take us too far from Roelofs' research to try to theoretically reconcile the differences between the two approaches. The six criteria are (all quotes: op. cit. p. 174):

*For cognitive complexity:*

- Aspect differentiation: "the richness of ideas the policy makers hold about the issue."

- Aspect integration: "the extent to which the various issue aspects are ordered and linked to each other to form clusters of ideas which add meaning and transparency to the policy actors' understanding of the issue."

*For socio-political complexity:*

- Balancing interests: "the way in which the various interests involved in the issue are being considered and addressed."

- Participation: "the extent to which stakeholders actually contribute to the process in terms of money, time and energy."

*For normative complexity:*

- Communication: "the level of cognitive and mutual understanding amongst the policy actors."

- Process management: "the way the debate among the actors is organized and structured."

### 6.4.3 A Decision Aid within a Policy Game
The gaming/simulation BANS is used by Roelofs as the empirical environment to apply these six criteria to problem-structuring activities. BANS simulates pub-

lic policy making within a local community. It is a two-day training tool for local civil servants who want to develop their skills in "interactive policy making." The 14 participants play policy-relevant positions such as: government, citizen, business, not-for-profit representative, etc. These parties are brought together to create, in an interactive way, policies for five very real-life policy issues which cover matters like public safety, infrastructure, environment and welfare.

BANS is a relatively open game process; however, it has several pre-structured elements like a scenario, events, steps of play, decision forms etc. It is not necessary here to describe them all; suffice it to say that the game has several periods where participants meet to discuss the issues and/or to create collective "products." The steps of play demand these products (and partly pre-define them), e.g. a timetable and agenda for involving the public-at-large in the simulated debate. The order and chairing of these meetings are left to the participants to settle. Roelofs uses this standard version of BANS in three runs. For the three other runs, she adds more structure to the game, first by introducing a new role, i.e. that of the external consultants/facilitators; this role is played by three trained outsiders. These facilitators coach the group meetings in the game and they use a specially developed discussion tool for that purpose. It is this tool that introduces the assisted problem structuring into the game.

Several intervention methods have been developed to contribute to the quality of problem structuring in multiparty settings. Eden et al. (e.g. 1983, 1992, 1998) have been very active in this field with a technique called "oval mapping" which these authors use as part of their well-known process of Strategic Option Development and Analysis (SODA). Roelofs selected this oval-mapping technique for her experiment; however, given time constraints, she had to develop a shortened version.

### 6.4.4 The Experiment: Design and Results
Roelofs' study could be classified as a post-test design. The municipalities were randomly assigned to the experimental and control group. Checks on potentially confounding factors were conducted afterwards by comparing background data. Although the teams from the municipalities were alike in many respects, the small numbers made it unavoidable that certain differences did emerge between the control and experimental groups. For example, in the experimental group, there tended to be more people that Roelofs characterized as "doers" from line departments, whereas in the control group, a more reflective and self-critical attitude was apparent.

Roelofs used questionnaires as well as observation methods to assess the six quality criteria for problem structuring. The players filled in the questionnaires after the group meetings. This gave Roelofs the opportunity to study how the perceptions of the participants towards the quality of their own problem structuring developed during the game. Three to four trained observers followed the groups during all their meetings and created elaborate observation and discussion protocols that were pre-structured according to the six criteria.

Each of the six runs of the game resulted in a long text (45 pages) with observation notes. It is impressive to read how disciplined and creatively Roelofs used techniques from content analysis to reduce the observation data into an analyzable format. In the end, she was able to categorize and compare the data, with both statistical tools and qualitative statements, along several important dimensions:

- The experimental versus the control group;
- The observation versus the questionnaire data;
- Each of the six individual runs;
- Each run at several points in time; and
- Each of six different policy issues that were discussed in each run.

In her analysis, Roelofs can relate the scores on the criteria to the content of the policy products the players created during the game as a way of comparing differences in problem structuring with differences in policy outputs.

It is beyond the scope of this book to relate every valuable insight Roelofs derives from the data. In summary, she found less pronounced effects of the problem structuring method than she had expected. The intervention with oval mapping seems to result in a positive but rather narrow effect on aspect integration and differentiation. There is only a limited effect on the criteria relating to socio-political or normative complexity; the effect is mainly cognitive. Roelofs concluded that oval mapping has a striking positive effect in preventing "loss of quality" in aspect differentiation. Although, initially, the technique hampered the flow of ideas by forcing structure, the ideas did not get lost because the map of the ovals functioned as a collective memory; the policy process seemed to be accelerated by the technique. The control group needed more time to get through the policy processes in the game, but Roelofs had to keep open the possibility that this difference is at least in part due to the differences in composition between the two groups ("doers" versus "reflectors").

Roelofs reported on some striking differences between the observation and the questionnaire data: quite often they are not in accordance with one another. The relatively simple and subjective scores of the participants sometimes contradicted the more detailed and objective findings from the observation protocols. Since complex and difficult-to-grasp concepts such as "aspect integration" seem to get a better chance of being measured when one takes time to reflect on the results of an oval-mapping exercise, Roelofs put more trust in her observation than in her questionnaire data.

A very important methodological warning can be attached to Roelofs' observation that post-process questionnaires are usually the only evaluation methods applied in the study of decision aids (including gaming/simulations). If one sees the observation data as a means for criterion validation of the standard questionnaire approach, then one can only support Roelofs' statement that a closer monitoring of the reliability of this standard evaluation procedure is desirable. "A satisfied customer who has expressed his appreciation for an intervention with a problem-structuring method may not necessarily have experienced any other change than that of his or her own feelings regarding a particular issue or instrument" (op cit., p. 185).

### 6.4.5 Advantages and Disadvantages of Using a Game for Policy Research

Looking back on her study, Roelofs supports some of the clear advantages of games as environments for policy research. For many reasons, complex inter-organizational policy processes are very hard to observe and record in real life. Roelofs' study confirmed again that it is possible in a game "to follow policy makers around and write down their actions and conversations both in formal and informal settings. It has thus been possible to follow, to a certain extent, the dynamics in the way various participants approached an issue, took position and tried to convince others of their perception" (op. cit. p. 186). Similar advantages of gaming/simulation for policy research have been reported and positively used by other researchers, like Vissers (e.g. 1994).

Another clear advantage of gaming for Roelofs' research problem was the possibility of offering identical policy environments to the experimental and the control group, while at the same time, structuring the stimulus for the control group in the desired fashion. The steps of play and the "policy products" the players produced made it possible to plan and test data collection in advance and to make sure the data sets for all runs were comparable. Combining content analysis of products from the policy process with data from questionnaires and observations is usually not possible in real-life situations. The extensive observations and the detailed protocols of conversations seem to be the exclusive benefit of the gaming situation. Normally, observing the interactions in comparable policy processes would suffer from seriously biased viewpoint effects because the researchers can never be present at all events at all times. That is easier in a game, but this nearness of the observer can be "too close for comfort" and create an unknown and hard-to-avoid control effect.

Control effects and their generalized impacts are, of course, Roelofs' main methodological concerns, as they would be for any researcher using an experimental design. Roelofs has been so careful as to ask her (expert) participants what they thought of the degree of reality of BANS. She interpreted the results of these questionnaires using the typology for validity of gaming that Raser developed in 1969 and Peters, Vissers et al. annotated (Raser, 1969; Peters et al., 1996; Vissers et al. 1998). Roelofs had the following to say about this assessment:

"These outcomes suggest that BANS does differ from real-life experiences. However, it captures a number of characteristics of real-life policy making processes that are realistic in the eyes of the players. The interactions between the various policy actors evoked by their position on the issues they are involved in, resemble those of the world the game-simulation tries to simulate. BANS provides a context for policy making which is familiar in terms of the issues and interacting interests. The psychological and process validity BANS provides seems quite acceptable, as does its structure validity, albeit to a lesser extent. Its predictive validity appears to be limited" (op cit., 80).

In her final conclusions, Roelofs summarized two disadvantages of her research design. First, the "artificiality" of the gamed situation may be a problem, even though, as Roelofs explains, the game BANS had many features to guarantee external validity. Of course she does not know how much the behavior in the game differed from real life. She is right when she says that only the combining of experimental research with longitudinal field research will shed more light on this issue.

Second, there remains the question of the correct way of placing the chosen decision aid (Eden's oval-mapping technique) into operation. Remember that the conclusion was that she could not find much effect from this decision aid. Not only did it prove difficult for Roelofs to give the technique enough "space" in the existing BANS game structure, but it is this basic BANS game structure which caused the differences between the control and experimental groups to be relatively small. BANS was certainly not a free-form game of the kind used, for example, in the University Hospital case described in Chapter 3. On the contrary, BANS was designed as an educational tool and accordingly it contained many different structuring elements to guide the learning process. The game also stimulated "interactive policy making." Consequently, as Roelofs said: "participants were probably inclined to pay positive attention to various interests, involving various actors, and to try to be sensitive to the needs of fellow policy makers. Hence, participants were already inclined to show some of the behaviors problem-structuring methods aim to evoke of their own accord" (op. cit. p. 187). Of course, the answer cannot be found within Roelofs' data. In the future, repetitions of her interesting research design with different games, in combination with field evaluations, may bring more clarity to the matter.

From an application or professional point of view, one could perhaps re-frame Roelofs' study as the systematic comparison of two variations of the same game. Participants were invited to play a game and they did, obviously with a lot of enthusiasm and positive learning experiences. Half of the groups (the experimental condition) stepped into a game process with somewhat more structure than the other half (the control groups). What Roelofs saw as a decision aid study that used a game as the research environment, can be re-framed as a comparative *evaluation* of two versions of the same game. In such a study, one could have asked whether both of the gamed formats positively affected the policy-structuring behavior in real life, or neither of the two, or only one of them.

Looking at this study from this perspective takes us into the realm of evaluation studies that we will discuss in the next section. As the reader will discover, the analysis of Roelofs' intricate and intelligent research has prepared us to understand many of the difficulties facing the evaluation of policy gaming.

## 6.5 RESEARCH ON GAMING: THE EVALUATION PERSPECTIVE

As stated in Section 6.1, this section on evaluation will not go into empirical studies that focus on the assessment of teaching and training games. Educational uses of policy and strategy games are outside the scope of this book. However, for this section, that choice threatens to leave us somewhat empty handed because the vast majority and most systematic evaluations of policy and strategy games are clearly in the educational realm. However, we will not enter a field that we had better leave to colleagues who are more knowledgeable about this type of application. We refer to the many publications for this purpose by members of various professional groups (see Keys & Wolfe, 1990). These include the International Simulation and Gaming Association (ISAGA), the Association of Business Simulations and Experiential Learning (ABSEL), the North America Simulation and Games Association (NASAGA), and the Society for the Advancement of Games and Simulations in Education and Training (SAGSET).

In this section, we briefly discuss an example of various endeavors to evaluate the policy relevance of gaming/simulation. The main part of this section is programmatic: we define a series of research lines that are possible in the evaluation field, most of which need much more attention than they receive at present. A second inspiring example that looks at evaluation research on tailor-made gaming in the related practice of organizational change appears in the last paragraphs of this section.

### 6.5.1 The Harvest: Some but Not Enough

We have conceptualized the gaming/simulation approach to policy making presented in this book as a form of participatory policy analysis. Consequently, we want to discuss the evaluation of gaming/simulation from that same perspective. Reviews of the literature by members of the Tilburg research program on participatory policy analysis have indicated that there is less empirical research on the conditions, utility and relevance of trajectories and tools within the field of participatory policy analysis than one would expect. This is unfortunate, given the frequency and importance of participatory policy analysis trajectories in modern policy practice (Geurts & Mayer, 1996; Mayer, 1997; Bongers, 2000; Heyne, 2000). To date, research into the impact and effectiveness of participatory policy methods has focused mainly on the cognitive effects of participative modeling, scenario techniques and group decision support (GDS). For example, in the studies by Vennix (1989) and Verburgh (1994), the effectiveness of group modeling is measured by a quasi-experimental design employing a technique developed by Axelrod (1976) to trace and assess the quality of the cognitive maps of the participants. Roelofs' (2000) study discussed above falls into this category. Mayer (1997) and Heyne (2000) both compared a wide variety of participatory policy analysis trajectories that used structured and scenario workshops, but none of them can really be called policy exercises of the type described in this book. Bongers (2000) is one example of a productive and international stream of publications in which the policy relevance of GDS is evaluated.

The general conclusion on the state of the art of evaluation in participatory policy analysis has to be that most of the reported evaluation studies are case studies: in-depth descriptions of the "why-what-how" of a project. Often one comes across post-hoc satisfaction surveys among participants and sponsors. Without much hesitation, we will declare this conclusion on the state of affairs of participatory policy analysis evaluation also true for the assessment of policy gaming. There is a "mea culpa" argument involved here. In Chapter 3, we presented eight cases studies and, in these projects, empirical evaluation remained limited to satisfaction measurement. Of course, post hoc questionnaires are important as ventilators of immediate reactions and as tools to reach closure on a project contract. However, as Roelofs (2000) shows, satisfaction and impact are two different things.

A relatively recent indicator of the scarcity of systematic evaluation studies of policy games is the harvest of the 28th annual conference of ISAGA held in Tilburg in 1997. The topic of that conference was specifically set to be "gaming/simulation for policy development and organizational change." Of the 120 papers presented, less than ten described an empirical study and of those ten, less than five seemed to be evaluating the policy relevance of a game (Geurts et al., 1998; Joldersma & Geurts, 1998).

### 6.5.2 Example: the Impact on a Policy Makers' Mind

An example of an evaluation that is more sophisticated than usual was presented at the 1997 ISAGA conference. This was reported by Rouwette et al (1998). MARCO POLIS is a game used to introduce employees of housing associations to new market conditions. Similar to the processes described in the Rubber Windmill case, not-for-profit housing associations have become more market dependent and have had to find a new balance between their social goals and the need for competitively securing their financial continuity. The game was tailor made and commissioned by an association of housing associations. The content of the game is generic; it simulates a typical housing market in a fictional small town.

The game was used by at least 15 professional groups consisting of 15 to 50 people. As Rouwette et al. (1998, p. 95) report: "On most occasions, both facilitators and participants judged the game to be highly successful in making the demands of the new situation clear." But the producers of the game wanted to deepen their understanding of what this judgment meant so they started a more systematic evaluation study. We refer to the original text for the results of the study; here, we only pull out of this study some observations on the research design. One run with 49 professionals was studied in a way that deserves credit for several reasons:

- The assessment of the impact was governed by a clear and well-tested theory, i.e. Azjen's (1991) theory of planned behavior;
- The theory was translated into a multivariate model and four very relevant and testable hypotheses which linked participation in the game to changes in beliefs, attitudes, perceived behavior and behavioral intentions;
- Data was collected both before and after the run, making pre-post test comparisons possible;
- Measurement instruments were derived from well-proven procedures; and
- The data analysis used appropriate multivariate statistical techniques.

As one can expect, if a researcher looks into a gaming project in such a systematic and detailed way, the interpretation of the results will demand care and discipline. Rouwette et al. do exactly this; certain expectations of the game design phase are corroborated by the data, but others cannot be proven. If we look at this study from the broad perspectives of both evaluation methodology and participatory policy analysis, then the limitations of this study are clear. We make the following observations on Rouwette's study as stepping stones to the next part of this section; they are not intended as criticism of Rouwette's work:

- The impact of the game was sought only at the level of the individual; other consequences, e.g. on institutional policy, were not in focus with this study;

- The measurement of behavioral effects was limited to intended behavior that was verbally expressed via questionnaires filled in at one point in time after the game. A longitudinal assessment of actual policy behavior could have been a next step; and

- One might discuss whether this game was used for professional training purposes or as a step in a policy process; we will come back to this issue. But this much is clear: the generic game MARCO POLIS was produced *for and not with* the participants and its use was less "in the middle" of a specific organizational policy struggle than most of the cases we presented in Chapter 3.

An interim conclusion: evaluating policy games during a professional application is not easy; we can derive some reasons for this:

- The client has to perceive evaluation as important and a clear agreement between the client and the team has to be reached in advance, because evaluation and confidentiality can easily be perceived as conflicting with one another;

- Evaluation will need data that, in general, cannot be collected without asking extra effort from the participants;

- It is sometimes necessary to run the risk of a control effect, i.e. influencing the game process by observing it;

- Evaluation forces a team to mobilize and accept the input from empirical disciplines because, without a good theory and an excellent design, the cost/benefit ratio of an evaluation will be disappointing. It takes careful planning and a disciplined attitude to accomplish a serious evaluation; and

- Those doing the evaluation have to accept that many of their ideas about research design will not work in practice. Instead, they will have to be creatively placed in operation according to the rule "if it cannot be done as it should, we should do the best we can." This means that results will have to be interpreted with great care.

### 6.5.3 Evaluation Research along Eight Lines

The positive side of the discussion so far is that our short analysis of Rouwette's study shows how empirical designs can be interwoven with professional applications of gaming. It illustrates that a mature program for empirical evaluation of policy games will necessarily be diverse in focus and design. There is a need for effect evaluation, process evaluation, cost-benefit types of studies, and long-term impact studies.

The Tilburg group on participatory policy analysis research (e.g. Geurts & Mayer, 1996) suggested eight types of relevant evaluation research on participatory policy analysis trajectories. Each type has a different focus on criteria and methods. This classification is relevant for the programming of the assessment of policy games; we describe these eight types below.

### Type 1. Process evaluations

The goal of process evaluation is to assess the quality of policy gaming as a sequential and structural set of activities. Process evaluation can focus on the whole trajectory or on a specific step. This can be done *during* the process, immediately *after*, or *both*. Relevant criteria for the quality of the trajectory of an evaluation tool have been suggested previously (see Chapter 4). Several data collection methods are available: observation by experts (if necessary in a quasi-participation role), interviews, and/or structured questionnaires. The goal is to learn from successes and mistakes. Process evaluation helps to derive the reconstructed logic from the logic-in-use. Process evaluation is indispensable for the growth of the methodology of policy exercises.

The next three types are all forms of "effect" or "output" evaluations that aim at the measurement of the intended, realized, and unintended (more or less immediate) outputs of a gaming effort. As in the policy sciences, it is useful to distinguish "output" from "outcome" in this discussion. Output refers to the direct results that can be measured after the game. It has to be distinguished from the strategic use or impact on the strategy of the initiator and/or the other stakeholders involved. This is usually referred to as the outcome of the effort. We will deal with strategic or outcome evaluation later (Types 5 through 8).

*Type 2. Effect on individuals*
When it comes to forcing a new issue or perspective on the policy agenda, the intended role of the policy exercise might be to influence the cognition, attitude or values of the individual participant. Type 2 research that tries to measure these outputs is usually quasi-experimental in nature. Some of the studies described above have shown that this line of research can be productive but complex because of many conceptual and methodological difficulties. Apart from that, often there are serious practical difficulties. As we explained, it takes much careful planning not to disturb the gaming process while collecting data for the evaluation. It is therefore no coincidence that, for example, Bongers (2000), finds in his review of effect evaluations of computer-assisted group meetings that detailed experiments are often done with students as subjects. Experimental control (e.g. by varying the game for research reasons) in field applications is often impossible. The usual alternative is to rely on ex-post subjective assessment by the participating individuals.

*Type 3. Effects on participants as a group*
Several of the stated goals of the policy exercises in Chapter 3 aimed not only at changes within individuals, but also focused on characteristics of the participating groups. A frequently defined goal is to create a shared "cognitive map" or knowledge household among the participants. Some initiators of gaming projects hoped to create consensus on the need and direction of strategic actions. Some strategic gaming is intended to better link different organizations; the game is used to stimulate a willingness to form a nucleus or a lasting team for coordination.

These objectives suggest that the unit of analysis for evaluation is not the individual but the group. The appropriate research design to assess these objectives will be quasi-experimental. However, compared to the assessment of individual changes, measurement instruments, data collection and data interpretation are more complex.

*Type 4. Product as output*
A strategic gaming trajectory is quite often concluded with a written document (a report, white paper, etc.). These papers are either written by the participants themselves or by assisting staff. A logical line of output evaluation is to study the quality of these products. Are the ideas generated new and valuable? Is the information relevant and complete? Is the final document a valid and comprehensive summary of the ideas and views exchanged by the participants? Content analysis, reviews by participants, experts or stakeholders are the logical routes to collect the relevant data for this type of evaluation.

*Type 5. Dissemination*
Let us now introduce the strategic or outcome evaluations that look beyond the active phase of the gaming trajectory and look further ahead in time than the output evaluations described above. Each policy exercise is a strategic move or instrument within a stakeholder network. A strategic perspective on the role of the policy exercises suggests the next four evaluation types.

Many gaming initiatives do not focus exclusively on the participants or the initiating client organization. Majone's observation seems particularly valid for public sector projects: "In principle any reader of a policy study may be considered a member of the analyst's audience. ... it is possible that by the time the analysis is completed, the original client will have been replaced, key elected and appointed officials will have left the office, and other actors will have moved to another problem" (Majone, 1989, p. 41).

Type 5, or a dissemination type of evaluation, focuses on the diffusion of information generated in a gaming process. An attempt is made to determine what audience is reached by the project, by what information (or insight) and via which channel. Research designs and methods from mass communication research are appropriate here. This type of research might have been done after the Rubber Windmill project, potentially involving a review of the coverage of the conference in the press, on TV and radio. The window for this research is usually limited to a few weeks immediately after the event.

*Type 6. Effect on network*
Policy games are often intended as stimuli to improve network interaction and cohesion. One way of assessing the probability of success of a policy exercise in

this respect is to measure the relevant attitudes and action plans within the group of participants immediately after the sessions (see effects on participants as a group, above). However, whether good intentions are put into lasting action is another matter. It is theoretically possible that an immediate measurement of intentions does not reveal an inclination to act, but that, after a while, former participants will stimulate joint action among the stakeholders they represent. This example makes clear that this type of research has at least two basic difficulties: (1) changes in soft network characteristics are hard to measure, and (2) attributing the observed changes to the stimulus will be complicated by many contributing factors.

*Type 7. Use in decision making*
These two difficulties of outcome evaluation research also complicate research focused on the use of simulation results in decision making. The vast empirical literature on decision making in public and private network settings illustrates that the reconstruction of strategic decision making processes is certainly possible, but it demands extensive and multi-method research designs. Cause and effect relationships in the "messy" processes in which strategic decisions are taken are hard to establish. That means that isolating the effect of one single event, i.e. a strategic gaming trajectory, is not a simple task.

The "utilization of knowledge" school, mentioned in Section 2.5, has contributed much to the development of relevant concepts and the understanding of conditioning factors of one form of reporting the results of policy analysis (e.g. written reports or comparable documents). This school has found three forms of use of these reports by policy makers: instrumental use, conceptual use and persuasive use (as an advocate). *Instrumental* use of policy research refers to the direct translation of results into policy measures or programs. Research has indicated that instrumental use is not common. More often, policy reports are found to alter the way of thinking about social problems. This is called the enlightenment or *conceptual* function (e.g. Weiss & Buchavalas, 1980; Caplan, 1983). The term *persuasive* refers to a legitimizing or symbolic use of policy analysis.

Instrumental use is often restricted to operational decisions. Conceptual use that does not involve immediate and direct application of new knowledge to decisions can gradually bring about major shifts in awareness and reorientation of basic perspectives. Instrumental use seems to be particularly rare when the policy issues are complex, consequences are uncertain, and a multitude of actors are engaged in the decision-making process.

For the evaluation of the contributions of policy tools like gaming, it is relevant to keep in mind the ideas of "decision quality" as a possible focus for evaluation research. Inevitably, one cannot escape the need to make a decision; at that moment, one does the best one can. A good decision does not automatically lead to a good (desired) result because, unavoidably, strategic decisions will encounter surprises during their implementation. This distinction between "decision quality" and "result quality" suggests several interesting questions for research:

- Is it possible to define measurable decision quality criteria for a policy exercise without resorting to result criteria? ("We do not know whether this decision will help us to get where we want to be, but it is the best decision we could make").
- Is it valid to ask decision makers whether their decision was improved by a gaming effort (e.g. "Yes it helped me a lot," "Yes, it prevented me from making a mistake," etc.)?
- Perhaps the impact of gaming on decision quality has to be defined primarily as the ability of such a trajectory to stimulate the progression of a decision process (e.g. "At least it got us out of a decision deadlock," "It helped us to settle one question and that is enough").

*Type 8. Impact of gaming on policy program effectiveness*
Indeed, establishing the causal link between a policy development game (via its impact on decisions) and the actual results achieved by a strategic policy program is generally beyond the reach of empirical science. The long time horizon, the many confounding factors, the dynamics in all the factors involved and the limitations of comparative research, are just a few reasons why this form of evaluation is not often done. The maximum result is likely to be a case study with limited comparability and evidential power.

### 6.5.4 Games and the Implementation of Strategy
Training games can make a very important contribution to strategic management. Simplistic distinctions might be misleading. In the practice of working with clients in organizations, it is sometimes harmful to press too hard on the distinction between the training and the policy development applications of gaming. Conceptually, classical dividing lines between corporate training programs and strategy consulting trajectories are under serious review. Management practice and management sciences have discovered *learning* in organizations as both a strategic challenge and an opportunity for competitive success. (See Section 4.4 about the link between learning and creativity). It is not useful to consider "learning how to make policy" a simple training activity while, at the same time, using elevated language from the learning paradigm to re-conceptualize strategic failures as top moments for organizational learning.

Games are used increasingly as elements of carefully structured implementation processes to help organizations implement strategic changes. In this book, the Corporate Culture Exercise serves as an example (Section 3.6). Sometimes these interventions are called training, sometimes organizational development, and sometimes a strategic re-orientation. "Off the shelf" games are regularly used in these contexts. Several companies redesign classical games for their own businesses.

The book *Changing Organizations with Gaming/Simulation* by Geurts et al. (2000), shows how organizations create and use tailor-made games for complex structural and cultural changes. The purpose and the context of use of the examples presented differ from the majority of the cases we describe in this book. However, the participatory methodology of design is the same and so is the practical need to weave the gaming activity carefully into other new or ongoing activities within the organization. For the uninformed outsider, even many of the processes in the finalized games will look the same. In the games Geurts et al. (2000) describe, one can see players making policy, i.e. they collect data, exchange opinions and information, and make decisions.

We emphasize this relative comparability because it implies that the challenges for systematic evaluation are highly comparable. To put it simply, the evaluators of policy gaming and of gaming-for-change can learn a lot from each other. As far as we can see, the empirical evaluation of games-for-change is somewhat ahead of the games-for-policy. For example, consider the comprehensive study of de Caluwé (1997) which combines a process evaluation with output and outcome evaluation (also reported in de Caluwé & Geurts, 1999 and in Geurts et al., 2000).

In the example, Delta Lloyd is a well-respected insurance company that employs more that 2800 people. Its competitive performance had become disappointing and management saw serious threats for the future. After a non-gaming but highly interactive phase of strategy development, a set of turn-around decisions was taken. One was to lay off some 600 people and another was to start two organizational revolutions. As a consequence, the company became extremely de-layered (300 management positions disappeared) and, at the same time, all the company's processes were handled by multi-functional teams. The "new" Delta Lloyd was basically a network of 140 teams with a relatively small management structure at the top.

Creating the structure was one thing, making it work was another. For the members of the organization, working in teams meant a serious cultural change: everybody had to behave differently in the future. What was sanctioned to be good behavior in the past might now turn out to be dysfunctional. New reference behavior had to be developed and new reward systems and internal heroes had to emerge.

It was decided that everybody (from the CEO to the facility staff) would participate in a change training program. De Caluwé shows how this program can be characterized as a set of interrelated decisions on 22 design parameters. Choices were made on the content, structure, actors, mechanisms and certain pre-conditions of the intervention. A two and a half-day training program, several forms of follow up, and a very visible and active management were the key characteristics of the intervention. A tailor-made game was used for training and, over four months, about 140 teams played the game. Imagine the logistics of such an enterprise.

De Caluwé's evaluation of this project is probably unique. In full cooperation with the client, he was able to collect a massive set of data. He used document analysis, questionnaires, in-depth interviews with managers and trainers and written observation protocols. He was able to administer the same questionnaires measuring attitude towards teamwork at five points in time: before and immediately after the game, and also three, 12 and 18 months later. These measurements produced a remarkable wave-like curve. After the game, there were very positive attitudinal effects; these subsided during the first year but, after that, tended to become positive again. De Caluwé sees this as a learning curve. The new behavior that was adopted in the safe environment of the game proved difficult to continue in real life; it can only be mastered (internalized) after a period of some frustration. In general, de Caluwé concludes that the impact of the program has been positive and lasting.

From a methodological point of view, it is interesting that de Caluwé tries to do justice to the fact that such a game-based change program is a stimulus consisting of many different design elements. Even his extensive data set does not allow the isolation of the positive results of one element, i.e. the game. His expert interviews and other qualitative sources do allow him to identify (post hoc) effective elements in the intervention. The use of the tailor-made gaming/simulation came out as one of the effective elements. De Caluwé finds clues for which characteristics of the game caused its effectiveness. He mentions ten features of the game, e.g. the strong similarity to reality (created by the tailor-made design) and the fact that the steps of play forced the players to go through the learning cycle repeatedly.

### 6.5.5 Application is Evaluation, but We also Need Research

We have described some examples of the relatively scarce empirical evaluation studies; however, we have neither been able to summarize the accumulated results of empirical evaluations nor their implications for the development of our discipline. In some of the cases, we have been in the position to stimulate empirical evaluations; we have tried to implement what we learned from these projects into our methodology for the design and use of policy games. In that sense, the chapters on theory and methodology are our summary of what we have learned from past empirical evaluation research.

Most knowledge on policy games develops through systematic and inter-subjective testing in carefully planned and executed policy interventions and consulting processes. The explanatory practice theories and prescriptive methodologies which lead the professionals in their work are tested, rejected, improved, detailed, accumulated, etc. while being used in servicing a wide variety of critical clients. In a constructivist's view on science, this developing body of knowledge can be considered as being subjected to continuous and rigorous scientific testing.

This testing through professional application does not take away the need for specific empirical evaluation research on policy gaming. The research is necessary for scientific reasons and for improving gaming practice. In this field of applied science, the selection of procedures and tools is often determined by waves of fashion. There is the constant threat to act like the proverbial child with the hammer: "give a child a hammer and everything in its surroundings will look like a nail." Well-structured evaluation studies can contribute much to a more informed and contingent selection process: we want to know what works, where, and why.

With this chapter, we wanted to show the varied and potentially fruitful relations between gaming and empirical research; we hope that it will function as an effective call for action. Solid empirical work will help to improve policy gaming as a process of participatory policy analysis and as an instrument for policy research.

# Section IV

## *Designing Games for Strategy*

The case studies and their analysis have shown that, for strategy making, the policy exercise is a multi-functional tool. The policy exercises presented differed significantly in objectives and format. This brings us to the question of how to design games for strategy and policy. The next two chapters will describe our theory and methodology on game design and construction as they have developed over the years.

The purpose of Chapters 7 and 8 is to address the methodological underpinning of the discipline of the policy exercise. Chapter 7 describes the elements that serve as the basic building blocks used in the construction of a policy game, and Chapter 8 describes a process of design. The materials presented here are predicated on empirical observation of the play of many games; these observations are supported by theoretical evidence presented elsewhere in this book. Since 1964, the authors have designed several games a year (a total of more than 100) which have addressed a broad range of subjects throughout the world. During this period, we have endeavored to define the design process with increasing precision. These chapters represent a rethinking of our past efforts as well as an integration of various works by other authors.

We have stated earlier that the participatory practices of game and model design have developed quite separately from the reflective and empirical literature on participation in strategic processes. In retrospect, one can find many ideas in the process literature supporting various pragmatic rules and recipes from game design. This literature provides useful thoughts and generalizations that help in gaining an understanding of why and when games work for strategy; this deeper understanding is vital to the further maturation of the gaming discipline. The game design process presented reflects many of the tips and rules that derive from this process literature.

Many different kinds of products are called games and/or simulations; yet no accepted definition is in universal use. A central reason for confusion about the proper definition and use of policy games is that they *tend to be viewed from the perspective of the substantive interest of the design team.* They are seen as a tool being utilized by a professional whose primary interest lies with substantive content, rather than with the techniques of gaming. As a consequence, authors define terms and concepts against the backdrop of the unique substantive needs of the moment. The resulting confusion creates resistance to the evolution of a discipline. The professional gaming community has not achieved a basis for a careful distinction among these phenomena; this derives primarily from a lack of clarity of understanding of their underlying structure.

One approach to the resolution of this problem is to identify the explicit components of these instruments. Our inspection of a large number of these exercises revealed a wide diversity of styles; however, we discovered that they hold many elements in common. An understanding of this underlying structure is essential to ensure effective professional use of these tools. The terminology presented in Chapters 7 and 8 is offered as a standard set of conventions to be employed in the construction of policy games; this can be thought of as an initial effort toward a "manual of style" for the professional. Consistent use of these terms and concepts will improve communication among professionals and facilitate more useful gaming products. This consistency will improve our ability to help the client with a better understanding of the policy gaming technique.

A policy game is comprised of a number of basic and distinct elements; they may take a wide variety of forms, but in appropriate combinations they are essential to a complete exercise. Most of these elements will be found in a properly designed game; they may be more or less rudimentary, depending on the nature of the problem being addressed. These elements, presented below, are the basic building blocks from which the exercise is constructed. They fall into three major categories: content, structure, and process. As defined by Webster, they are:

> Content – "... that which is to be expressed through some medium, as speech, writing, or any of various arts."

In the case of the policy exercise, this includes the substantive content (scenario and events), and the image (theme or analogy/metaphor) of the exercise, and the participants and their decisions.

> Structure – "... the relationship or organization of the component parts of a work of art or literature; a systematic framework"

Structure in a game can be thought of as the physical characteristics of the exercise (format and basic referent system), the procedures of play, (policies, rules, scoring, steps of play) and the simulation (model, data, and accounting system) that will be used to process player decisions.

Process – "... systematic series of actions directed to some end"

Process can be thought of as the presentation of the exercise (facilitation and the three primary phases of a game), game artifacts (visuals and paraphernalia), and the evaluation of results (documentation, etc.).

# Chapter 7

## Understanding the Policy Game Construct

Note: Chapter 7 and 8 are envisioned as being used independently of the rest of the book. As a consequence, there is some redundancy to ensure clarity for the reader. You may also find the Detailed Design Tips located in the Appendix to be helpful.

### 7.1 INTRODUCTION

This chapter describes the basic elements of a game under three main headings: content, structure and process. They are presented through the logic that governs their usage rather than in alphabetic order. Game elements must not be confused with the 21-step game design process (described in Chapter 8). Proper understanding and use of the game elements is critical to the development of a successful game. The objective is to use these elements in such a way as to achieve a carefully structured seminar in a game-like environment.

Elements must be addressed initially as part of the process of developing the design specifications and finalized during the design and testing of the prototype. These components are offered as suggestions to help clarify the phenomena, not as hard and fast rules that must always be followed. However, when game elements are used appropriately in conjunction with the 21-step design process, they assist in the rational development of the policy exercise. In the final analysis, policy games should be simple but elegant – part proper preparation, part artistry, part genius, part group activity, part hard work, part proper preparation and part luck.

The elements are the building blocks used during construction. However, the result of the design process is a *construct* that has to be *used*; it only becomes meaningful during actual use. It is like a box of Monopoly® waiting to be opened – the game only exists while being played. This leads to potential problems with language, e.g. roles are designed for intended participants; if the exercise is used for a group other than that originally intended, the players will bring different knowledge and skills to the game. This will modify the content of the actual game. The same is true for process. The game construct will have process-guiding tools and instructions, but, as described in Section 8.2.5, Step 18, the actual game process only occurs when the participants interact during play with a facilitator trained to conduct this exercise (see Figure 7.1).

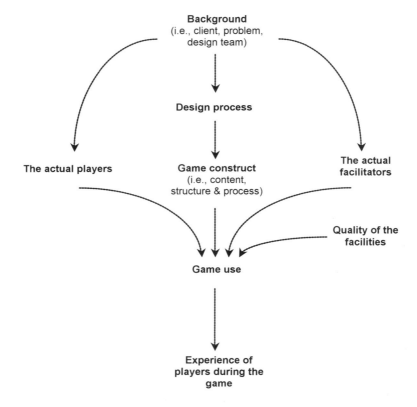

**FIGURE 7.1 | FACTORS AFFECTING THE GAME EXPERIENCE**

## 7.2 CONTENT

Webster's definition of content, "that which is to be expressed through some medium, as speech, writing, or any of various arts," is useful for game design. Content can be thought of as having three major components: substantive content (scenario and events), imagery (theme and analogy/metaphor), and the participants and their decisions (roles, perspectives, and decisions). These concepts are discussed below.

### 7.2.1 The Substantive Content

The substantive content providing context for the game is presented through the scenario and the events (and related materials such as workbooks, etc.). Serious games are typically presented in a real-world context (or hypothetical equivalent); this may be set in the past, the present, or the future. It is in this context that the payoff from the game will be achieved. It is essential that the substantive content be both accurate and relevant.

Scenario

The scenario (as used in conjunction with the policy exercise) is the story line (history, present situation, and appropriate speculations about the future) that all participants are given as the game begins. This provides a good background for the game and gets all participants off on an equal footing. It is normally lucid but brief; more detail will be presented to the participants as the game continues through the events and other material presented during each cycle of play (see the Conrail example, Section 3.4).

The exercise is typically presented to the players through a series of significant and relatively discrete problems that must be addressed in the context of the total system being studied. As the game proceeds, these problems follow one upon the next; and in complex games, several may be initiated simultaneously. Often referred to as "issues," these become tangible handles that the player can use to enter into and explore the substantive problem. The facilitator must understand the sequence of messages that will be used to guide players into productive confrontation with the emergent realities of the problem. In developing the scenario, several questions must be addressed: How abstract or detailed should it be? Does the scenario have to mimic some existing source document? Can the participants modify it during play?

The use of the scenario parallels its use in a novel or in the performing arts. In each case, it becomes an integral part of the technique for conveying the plot. The scenario may be presented as a text, but frequently it will be supplemented with various devices to illustrate the present state of the system, including workbooks, functional interaction diagrams, flowcharts and other graphic materials. Frequently, brief role descriptions will be included for all participants to establish initial points of reference, and thereby establish a basis for discussion.

Events

Events are incidents presented to specific players, often in the form of a "newsletter," at the beginning of each cycle of play to re-focus the attention of the player on a particular aspect of the problem. They are used to update the scenario as the game progresses; they initiate changes in the focus of the game and force players to make decisions. Events provide new information and this serves to make the game dynamic; they contribute information to the problems that players must solve. Events are very useful in helping the players to stay focused; they serve as a guide to program the discussion and keep the participants on track as real time passes during play.

Events can be of three types: programmed, triggered, and random. Programmed events are pre-designed to happen automatically during specific cycles of the game. Triggered events happen in response to some action of the players; they are precipitated automatically by the accounting system. Random issues represent a set of typical problems that might be productively explored, but their presentation to the players will depend on chance; the facilitator can also employ them if the discussion or play of the game lags.

### 7.2.2 The Image

The game designer must develop a mental image of the subject matter that the exercise is intended to mimic. The image refers to the primary impression to be conveyed by the game. Because games are used to address complex issues, the substantive content can be extensive (see Section 8.2.2, Clarifying the Problem). Two devices that can be employed to maintain focus for the discussion during a game are the "theme" and the "analogy or metaphor."

### Theme

The theme is defined as the substantive focus to be addressed by the game; it may be manifest as a major theme and/or as appropriate sub-themes. A major theme may be so all-encompassing that the game will not be useful unless specific sub-themes are employed for different stages of the exercise (for example, see Section 3.3.8, the Pharmaceutical Exercise). A game that is heavily loaded with situational content as a device to present a conceptual framework may be low on the cone of abstraction. As a consequence, the game may not convey a sharp sense of how the specific conceptual components are to be used.

### Analogy/Metaphor

At some point in the design of every successful game, there comes a moment when purely technical constructs are transcended. It can be argued that games are part artistry, part technique; the key is to determine how best to inspire the "moment of magic" that brings the game alive! Through some combination of inspiration, experience and luck, a game construct is hit upon that conveys, as a lucid analogy, the heart of the problem being gamed. From this basic bedrock, various layers of technique can be added to meet client requirements.

An analogy/metaphor can be defined as one or more similes employed in a game to facilitate the gaining of insight. This can be thought of as imagery conveyed to the participants that increases motivation, enhances insight, improves communication, and adds a bit of fun. It increases the efficiency of idea transfer. An analogy may be represented by a series of small things or a single artifact or concept. In some cases, the initial artifact has limited capacity but is so designed that it can be increased in sophistication as play progresses (moving down the cone of abstraction).

The use of an analogy/metaphor assists with the ability to frame and retain concepts, (models, interactions, structures). These permit the mind to logically sort, store, and recall the significance of minutiae and to use these to create a new generic model that fits the situation at hand. Analogies permit the participant to look at a complex environment and develop a perspective (gestalt) that lets one assimilate the available knowledge and, as a consequence, to create a new operational model.

The primary objective of the game design team is to identify a powerful and appropriate analogy/metaphor (a "model of a model") that the participants will recognize and endorse. This must capture the essence of the client's problem. A prime benefit of the use of analogy/metaphor in games is that participants do not get sidetracked into working with trivial details. To illustrate, one client had a group attempting to redesign their physical workspace. They were working with detailed floor plans and there were endless arguments (because they knew too much about the specifics). A metaphorical game was designed that required the construction of an abstract space model; this distracted the staff from technical details and successfully focused their attention on interpersonal networking issues (the client's primary concern).

The Rubber Windmill (Section 3.9) serves as another example. The simile employed mimicked the organization as a marketplace: there was supply and demand, payments and barter, market sharing of ideas and information, etc. Every design decision supported this metaphor, even the multi-colored T-shirts that the participants wore (which made the game room look like the floor of a stock exchange.) The Social Employment case (Section 3.7) also provides a metaphor, in the form of a decision tree with many branches. Each team had to select a path by collectively solving the puzzle.

The analogy/metaphor serves as a tool that can be used to encourage learners to transform information into new meanings for their own use. An analogy can enhance retention and make learning more memorable – participants often remember a game event of 20 or more years ago because the analogy used was simple and stayed with them. As a consequence, when the experience is debriefed, the questions relating to the transfer and application of insights gained from the analogy are the most important elements to be gleaned.

### 7.2.3 The Participants and Their Decisions

The essence of a policy game is the interaction of appropriate stakeholders (as roles in the game) through an appropriate model of the system being explored. The world frequently has too many interests (actors) to be represented in full detail in the game; as a consequence, some must be represented generically, while others must be excluded. During the development of the exercise, it is necessary to resolve which stakeholders will be represented, the needs and responsibilities of each role (task assignments, decisions, etc), and the level of personal experience required of each participant.

The concept report (see Chapter 8, Step 13) should include a detailed section specifying the characteristics of the intended participants; it should note any characteristic of the participant group that would have a bearing on game design. This should address: age, level of sophistication, prior training, previously shared experiences, professional status, educational background, the primary motivation for participation, etc. Other factors to be addressed would include group size (the number of participants expected to participate in the game), prerequisites (e.g. computer skills) required before being permitted to play the game, etc.

The design specifications should address the desired degree of participant involvement (this can range from an emotional emphasis to a more intellectual presentation). Design of a game requires a prior knowledge of the participant's expectations. If players are highly motivated on arrival, the game need not be designed to entice them to participate. Other participants may require a more appealing design structure to achieve the suspension of disbelief necessary for full participation. A variety of incentives can be used to get participants to participate actively and enthusiastically.

A policy game is more occasion-specific than many other forms of communication. It is imperative for the designer to understand the audience's motivation for participation and the typical conditions for use of the exercise. The more precise the understanding of the intended audience's characteristics and motivations, the more effectively can various design considerations be employed to ensure a successful game.

Roles
Roles provide the primary actors with an appetizer to suggest what is possible in the "real world." They are an essential element in achieving the suspension of disbelief that is required for productive communication in a game. Roles describe a hypothetical set of interests, knowledge and responsibilities that are attributed to a given participant (or team). They serve as a device to minimize the injection of the personalities of the participants into the game and to provide some freedom of action to players. The identity of a given role may be a person, a corporate structure, a public entity, or some abstract phenomenon. The roles in the games interact with each other and with the game environment. Players interpret their roles through the model, the decision feedback mechanisms and through interaction with other roles. Many experienced game designers advise that players not be given specific instructions about playing a particular role as it is too easy for them to later deny responsibility for their actions (they may blame the constraints of the role). Similarly, it is generally accepted that assignment of attitudes and values along with the role should be avoided or minimized.

The game designer must give careful thought to role selection. Material that is being created from various components of the game (e.g. a simulation) must be directed to the proper role; conversely, information that is obtained from a given role must be processed rationally through the accounting systems. The output from all decision points must have a specific target(s). Roles will generally be limited in number to those most central to the system. Descriptions of roles should be predicated on known real-world counterparts. By deliberately structuring a role so that players are required to deal at a strategic level, or by placing the role under constraints not normally found, the occupant of the role can manipulate the system from a new perspective. Frequently, roles are incorporated into a game to permit the participant to experience the system from a context not available to the player in the day-to-day activities of the organization.

There are three types of roles: gamed (real players making decisions), simulated (theoretical players), or pseudo (present, but their decisions do not enter into the accounting system):

*Gamed Roles* are personally present at the time of the gaming activity; they represent decision makers selected from the client's environment. They are required to interact with the other players and to make decisions that are processed by the accounting system.

*Simulated Roles* are not represented by a human player; rather, they are represented in the mechanics of the game through a simulation, the model, the accounting system, and/or other mechanisms. They are used to generate output useful to gamed or pseudo roles. A simulated role can be more useful than a gamed role because it successfully avoids the idiosyncratic response of an individual player; it can also be used to represent a broad class or category of data.

*Pseudo Roles* are distinguished from gamed roles in that they interact with the participants as "experts"; their decisions may influence players but do not enter into the accounting system. Pseudo roles are frequently "on the spot" inventions (played by the facilitator or a guest) to assist in circumstances not provided for in the original design. They can be used as a tool to be used judiciously to solve unexpected game developments.

Players may be organized as individuals, coalitions, or teams, as appropriate. Roles present the viewpoint of a single individual; perspectives (roles structured as multiples) are designed to present the perspective of an interest group. The decisions, however represented, are the heart of the game – they must be explicit and systematically evaluated by the accounting system; their outcome establishes the ultimate value of the game.

*The Rule of Three* argues that individual decision makers (roles) should be used sparingly. When possible, three roles should form a team with a single perspective; this group must work together to make a single decision. This device requires a richer and more thoughtful investigation of the information at hand; the resulting decisions are inclined to be less arbitrary than those from an individual acting alone. These coalitions should be predetermined during the design of the game. Teams may be formed as parallel entities, identical in structure (whether competitive or cooperative), or teams may be distinct groups, each charged with a separate function. The success of a game is heavily influenced by player organization.

In addition to these roles of an operational nature, there are individuals present during the course of the game associated with the administration of the exercise. From an administrative standpoint, facilitator(s) will be needed; there may also be observers, role adviser(s), a bookkeeper, and other specialists (see Chapter 8, Step 18 – Facilitating the Exercise).

Role manuals must be available for each player type; these must give the participant a clear sense of the nature of the role, the activities they are to complete, their relationship to other players, etc. Some of the content of each manual can be duplicated (e.g. a drawing showing how all players relate to each other, steps of play, etc.). Role manuals range from a single sheet of rules to a volume; both extremes are uncommon and probably somewhat ill-advised. The role manual should present, in abstracted form, some of the central questions addressed in the concept report (See Chapter 8, Step 13). The role manual should include a statement of the game objectives and an overview of the big picture, using flowcharts, tables and overview schematics as appropriate. The role manual should also introduce the game-specific symbolic structure, the steps of play, an introductory scenario, and one completed cycle of decision forms (this helps participants understand the process and gives them a starting point for the exercise). Materials that will be used frequently for reference purposes throughout the game should be included as part of the Appendix. These may include maps, data tables, and charts or other graphics that help in maintaining a perspective of the total system.

Decisions
One key to a successful policy game is the requirement that all participants make and defend decisions. Decisions are defined as the irrevocable selection and/or allocation of actions required of roles during each cycle. The actual mechanisms for obtaining these decisions vary from role to role, but may include completing decision forms, negotiation, developing and implementing strategies, nominal group techniques, Delphi-like techniques, and/or voting (avoid voting whenever possible - strive for consensus instead).

A good game will require players to commit themselves to decisions at the earliest possible moment; this process of commitment should grow in complexity and precision as the game progresses. Decisions must relate logically to the roles/perspectives as well as to the model being investigated. The participant must be held "publicly" accountable for the decision(s); this serves as the trigger for an exchange of ideas. Decisions should be structured based on the system schematic (see Chapter 8, Step 7). When the specific decisions are being developed, it is important to focus on role-specific decisions (number, clarity, etc.); sequence of decisions (orderly progression from step to step); and the linkage of decisions (orderly progression from player to player).

Decision points may be simultaneous or in rotation. If decisions are presented as a series of player "turns," the play is more sequential than if simultaneous decision making is used. Desirable practice involves simultaneous play, with all teams reaching decisions at about the same time. Nonetheless, there may be good reason for sequential decision making (e.g. having each team focus on the activity of other teams). After the initial cycle, as the players become more proficient with their own decision making process, they become increasingly aware of what other players are doing. This facilitates the conveyance of gestalt about the system. The real world rarely presents us with circumstances in which the players perform in turn, permitting the others to observe. Quite the contrary, things usually happen more or less simultaneously; it is only through a great deal of experience that we gain the "maturity" that permits us to understand complexity.

## 7.3 STRUCTURE

Webster's definition of structure, "the relationship or organization of the component parts of a work of art or literature" ... "to construct a systematic framework," is useful for game design. Structure can be thought of as having three major components: the physical characteristics of the game (format, basic referent system); the procedures of play employed to ensure a logical progression of activities (policies, rules, scoring, steps of play); and the simulation (model, data/information, the accounting system, indicators).

### 7.3.1 The Physical Character of the Exercise

The game will be manifest through its physical character – the format and the referent system. The physical characteristics of policy games vary widely; familiarity with the literature and experience in the field will assist the designer in developing a range of technique from which to draw.

Format

Format is defined as the physical configuration (the documents, visuals and artifacts) of the game as well as the various processes that the participants encounter in the game; it is the environment the players will experience. It is important for the format to mimic the client's environment as much as possible. The game is intended to be a playful, safe environment. The game format must encourage innovation and risk taking as a means of opening communication among players in the various teams as well as among the larger group during the critique and debriefing activities. As in any good negotiating situation, arguments can be transferred to the thing (format) rather than being focused on personalities. There are an infinite variety of formats that can emerge; the designer should avoid the mistake of copying an existing game format – let a new style emerge from the process! It should be clear, appropriate and powerful.

Frequently, a game combines role playing (based on the central figures from real life) with a physical setting that gives structure to the interaction (a board, map or flowchart, room arrangement, etc.). Participants are required to make decisions that are comparable to real-world decisions (e.g. run a hospital). As play begins, these activities are structured to simulate the present system; the players will "discover" that the system is sub-optimal. Success in the game will be indicated by their improved communication resulting in various alternatives being brought forth and evaluated; consequently better quality decisions will be achieved.

Game boards exist in three basic types: edge, grid, and patterned. One of the best-known "edge" boards is the commercial game Monopoly®. A second common board pattern is the "grid" board (a coordinate system that produces a series of cells that can be identified spatially by referencing the X and Y coordinates – this is well illustrated by a chessboard). The "patterned" board takes a great variety of shapes (e.g. the player progresses by moving symbols through an existing flowchart). In some instances, the players may be permitted to modify the flowchart as the game progresses (a more sophisticated example as used in a policy exercise might be the map of a region defined by its ecology; see Section 3.8).

Basic Referent Systems

The basic referent system is defined as one or more frames of reference that underlie and give order to the policy exercise. These reflect the intellectual discipline or set of substantive ideas that influence basic decisions about design. The selection of the basic referent system is extremely important because it must be in harmony with the objectives of the client and the characteristics of the participants. If these are properly matched, the task of getting the players quickly into the exercise will be much simpler than if they are forced into an alien referent system. A policy game requires a team of players, in an artificial environment and under severe time pressure, to deal with extensive substantive information in the context of a sophisticated conceptual referent system. There is a great deal for a player to assimilate in a few hours; it is a lot to squeeze into a game! It is not possible to give full treatment to this topic here; however, referent systems often reflect one or more of the following orientations: resource allocation, group dynamics, geography, demography, politics, business concerns, economics, sociology, psychology, anthropology, history, systems exposition, and others. Examples of basic referent systems reflected in the cases include Conrail (geographic/market place), Social Employment Program (decision tree), Employee Orientation Simulation (initially a silo, subsequently a matrix organizational structure) and the Rubber Windmill (the marketplace). The basic referent system is often a "board" (see the preceding paragraph).

### 7.3.2 The Procedures of Play

Procedures of play can be thought of as various facilitation mechanisms used to ensure a logical progression of activities; they can be classified as policies, rules and steps of play. There are a wide variety of procedures that may be presented as rules (not subject to change within the game) or as policy that is subject to player modification. The character and utility of a game are heavily influenced by the rules and policies employed. The game design may create a constrained or free environment as best meets the needs of the client specifications.

Policies
Policies can be defined as participant-imposed constraints controlling play. Players should be able to interact with the game in ways not initially perceived by the designer. When players are permitted to alter, amend or enrich procedures within the basic gaming structure (for example, moving from a nonexistent definition of acceptable player behavior to an advanced articulation in successive cycles of play), they can maximize learning without the unnecessary specification of an elaborate rule structure.

Player-generated policies appear quite frequently in virtually all policy games and are to be encouraged because their very formation implies a coherent consolidation of player purposes and objectives. They often deal with negotiations among players, teams, coalitions, and/or the game operator. They take an endless variety of forms, simple or complex, fixed or varying, from cycle to cycle. It is often necessary for the game operator to play the role of judge in overseeing these player-generated policies. Policies permit players to mold their simulated world into a more useful model during play. Negotiation should be used to address policy disputes; it is a good idea to require that policies be written down.

Rules
Rules are important tools that permit the designer to transform the client's environment into the focused and abstracted world of the simulation. Rules are best defined as specific facilitator-imposed constraints that govern play. Players must obey rules; they cannot be changed by the participants. Rules must be stated clearly by the facilitator; *they should be few in number*, lucid, and essential to the logical progression of the game. These are not to be confused with rules for win-

ning as defined in competitive games. Rather, they *are a set of conventions that participants are asked to adopt for the duration of the game.* Generally, rules as such should play a relatively minor part in a game. Nonetheless, some are inevitable and they must be addressed. They are of two types: those dealing with the accounting system and those controlling behavior during the course of the game. Rules dealing with accounting systems tend to be rigid to permit ease of quantification of results. Rules controlling player behavior have a greater degree of latitude than those governing the accounting system.

Games should be human driven rather than rule driven; the philosophy should be "it is your world, you solve it." There has been undue emphasis on rules in gaming simulation, perhaps as a result of the strong heritage of rigid war games and game theory. The concept of rule use in the policy exercise is poorly defined in the literature; further, rules are often not explicitly stated in actual policy exercises. Because of game design considerations, certain conditions may be inviolable (for example, the requirement of iterative cycles and the calculations inherent to a particular model). A much more productive concept is "procedures," intended as a flexible term to cover all mechanics of play, including any rule structure. A key skill of a talented game designer is the ability to create a game with rules that feel natural to the players *and,* at the same time, create a simulation that is doable, focused and structured.

Scoring
Scoring is defined as a system of penalties and rewards reflecting the results of decisions taken by the players; specific feedback must be developed for each role. Parlor games typically have a clear-cut scoring procedure. However, winning or losing is almost always an invalid concept when using the policy exercise; rather, the concept of win-win is appropriate. Win or lose scoring detracts from communication; the idea conveyed by scoring should be to illustrate what is possible to achieve in the client's environment. For this reason, formal scoring mechanisms are typically not provided in an exercise; the "indicators" (see Section 7.3.3) are intended to serve this function. The indicators enable players to evaluate their own performance; specific feedback must be developed from the indicators to each participant. Indicators and scoring are closely linked concepts; a well-designed exercise lets the participant judge his or her own progress rather than have an artificial and meaningless number imposed as a score.

Steps of Play
Steps of play are defined as the sequence of activities that players must follow during each cycle of play. All games should consist of a series of cycles, which are iterative and which become more complex cycle by cycle. Within any given cycle, there is a standard set of steps that are confronted by the player. Steps of play are discrete activities that govern participant behavior; they must be quite simple, and

each step should be a single action. This is essential if the participants are to understand what to do next and the facilitator is to control the timing of the game. Naturally, the first cycle is unfamiliar, and consequently takes longer than the following ones because the participants must be oriented to their environment. Steps of play will emerge during the construction of the game prototype. Figure 7.2 provides an idea of how activities might be structured in a typical policy exercise.

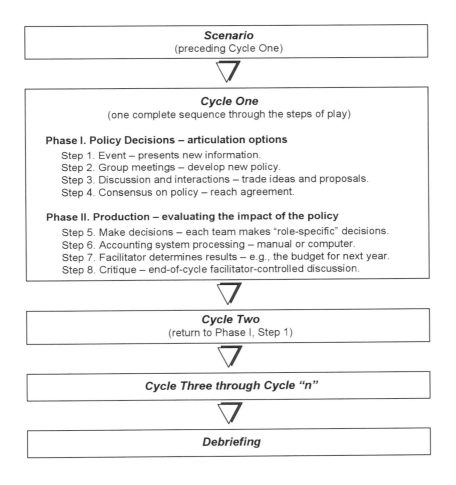

FIGURE 7.2 | TYPICAL STEPS OF PLAY SEQUENCE

The first step of play in a given cycle is the event; in turn, there is a discussion and interaction between the roles and the facilitator. Discussion should focus on reviewing the material (output) resulting from the start-up data or from the last cycle. Further discussion should be addressed to seeking information, forming coalitions, developing strategies and improving communication about the problem. In some instances, the game facilitator is obligated to initiate discussions. Examples include the formation of an ad hoc group to consider some problem, question, fact, or alternative at the request of the facilitator and to subsequently report to the assembled game participants.

Next in each cycle are the decisions which may be of both an inter-team and intra-team nature. The concept report will define the sequence in which these are to be made and give reasons for the sequencing. Generally, decisions should be made under reasonable time pressure.

Finally, the decisions must be processed through an accounting system, whether manual or computer. Regardless of the character of the processing system involved, it is extremely important for the game facilitator to review the decisions made by the players (before processing them) and to ensure that they represent the actual intention of the player. More importantly, the facilitator must check that they do not go beyond the capabilities of the game itself. It serves no purpose for a facilitator to process a decision knowing that the result will be an embarrassment to the player and an obstruction to progress in the game.

### 7.3.3 The Simulation
The simulation can be thought of as the quantitative components of the policy exercise; it consists of the model, a data/information system, the accounting system and the indicators. These will vary from highly simplified to rather complex components depending on client need.

### Model
The model becomes explicit through the design sequence (in particular through the schematic – see Section 8.2.2, The Design Sequence, Step 7). It must correspond to the underlying systemic structure of the problem; it will mimic the client's environment that is presented through the game. This simulated world will be used to process player decisions; it can be thought of as a formalized system for capturing the primary substantive focus of the exercise. At the start of the game, the model is typically presented to the players as an analysis of the situation in both its quantitative and qualitative respects. For example, in the Conrail Exercise (Section 3.4), a quantitative model was used to simulate the results of player decisions.

Games use different types of models: resource allocation (e.g. limited availability of municipal funds, competition by group members for budget, competitive bidding for land ownership), group dynamics (role-playing and/or interpersonal relationships), and system specification (the explicit expression of a complex system, its roles, components, and linkages). Many gaming/simulations reflect all three of these considerations but typically one theme will be dominant. This does not mean to suggest that other types of models cannot be applied to a broad selection of gaming/simulations.

The model that the game is intended to convey may be *implicit* (assumed to be known by the participants); *explicitly* presented to the participants in the game materials; or *integral*, becoming evident to the participants as they participate in the game. However presented, this model will be used to process player decisions. Depending on the purpose of the game, the model may be either descriptive or prescriptive. Most policy games will be based on a descriptive model (e.g. an estimation of probable voting behavior of various interest groups); however, this is often supplemented by a prescriptive model (e.g. budget model). If a descriptive model is used, the use of analogy (both physical and/or symbolic) is quite common. If a prescriptive model is used, it will be based on a structure of law, natural phenomena, and/or various man-made or scientific phenomena.

The model should represent an explicit expression of a complex system; it is useful to document the theoretical basis for the model in the concept report. If the theoretical basis is weak, this concern should be presented with equal candor so that those dealing with the problem will have some notion of where reality ends and fantasy begins. When dealing with the multidimensional world of gaming, the art of muddling through is essential. In gaming, data that is artificially generated can become a source of strength if it is presented with candor rather than through subterfuge.

Data and Information
The game is a device for exploring gestalt. To achieve this, players must be permitted to pursue any dimension of the subject from any perspective that seems relevant to them at an appropriate time. They must be provided with both a total systems overview and sufficient detail. For this reason, an important component of any game is a clearly referenced set of information at both general and detailed levels, as well as a carefully articulated information flow procedure. The information provided, in terms of quantity and depth, is dependent on the communication purpose, the sophistication of the players, and the conditions of play.

A significant factor in the development of a game is the loading (what, when and how to present data to participants) of data and information. During the first cycle of play, it is quite common to watch players grow increasingly apprehensive. This is inevitable because a great deal of information is being presented rapidly in an unfamiliar context. To counter this, players should be given no more information than is essential at any given moment. As a game progresses, each cycle becomes successively more involved and deals with an increased amount of information. As involvement and commitment increase, a self-generated need for information increases. Once a player is motivated to raise questions, he or she is able to assimilate surprisingly large quantities of information. As each cycle passes and the sophistication of the player increases, succeeding rounds become increasingly challenging.

The game should maintain a consistent level of abstraction, not only within a given role but also between the different roles and components of a game. When one role demands attention to detail and another role deals with questions of strategy and planning, communication between these players will be minimal. Equally important, the level of abstraction should permit the players to address the questions that are inherent to the policy objectives of the game. Games should not permit players to become too involved in detail –there will be no time to think about questions of strategy. If one is dealing with managers or other professionals, the level of abstraction in the game must permit analysis and synthesis of useful heuristics.

Information will generally be in one of three categories; reference materials, output from the accounting system, and information from participants. Reference information will include any relevant material dealing with the subject matter. Standard reference materials should be roughly the same ones the participants would choose if they were to make their own library search for supporting material. It is a mistake to generate greater detail than the average player can readily assimilate; an over-saturation of information may make the game harder to understand than reality. In an on-the-job situation, one at least has the ability to make on-the-spot judgments as to what information to retain and what to avoid. In a game where the setting is controlled by the facilitator, the player will assume that it is appropriate to attempt to comprehend and deal with any information presented during the exercise; an overload or poor selection by the developing team can create problems.

A glossary is a useful item as it sets forth the definition of terms employed. Another value of the glossary is that it serves as an indication of the degree of complexity of the game. Other reference materials that can be displayed visually should be provided. In many games, a variety of wall charts need to be posted showing the progress of different variables, cycle by cycle, as they are computed by the accounting system. Any reference material that will facilitate communication among players should be provided.

The most important use of information in any game is during the discussions (both inter-team and intra-team) and during the critique at the end of each cycle. The values of these discussions cannot be overemphasized, for it is through them that much of the information to which the player has been exposed is synthesized. Specific data that documents themes, issues and/or alternatives must be made available to players as they make their decisions.

Obtaining a thorough and valid empirical database on which the game message is formulated can be a costly and time-consuming process. There is a serious obligation on the part of the designer to document the source and validity of the data in the concept report. Parsimony is central when developing a database for the participants – too much detail will drive the game lower on the cone of abstraction; as a consequence, players may miss the big picture and spend their time fruitlessly debating detail. Tests for data include the relevance to the model, an acquisition plan, a careful file structure and storage system and a coherent and readily available list of variables that are used.

Accounting System
The accounting system is the process by which player decisions are captured and recorded, processed to ensure accountability of the roles, and the results reported back to the player to engender discussion. There are an infinite variety of accounting systems which may be invisible to the players. The accounting system may be formal (embedded in a computer model) or some less rigorous approach. A central question to be addressed by the design specifications is whether a computerized accounting system is desirable, necessary, and/or practical. Transparency of the model is essential for a successful game; an elaborate computer model can cloud the picture. This is especially true in those cases where complexity, time, and lack of proven science prevent predictive models. If a computer is used, care must be given to facilitator training and providing access to appropriate technology during the use of the exercise.

The accounting system consists of a system of accounts and underlying model(s). Systems of accounts become fixed procedural agreements, whether or not known to the players, by which decisions of the players are processed and forwarded to another component of the game. Design specifications should determine what information flows are to be provided during the exercise, and which are to be monitored, recorded, and preserved beyond the exercise for purposes of evaluation.

A well-designed game obtains the commitment of the players by requiring explicit decisions that are processed through the accounting system. Even the casual observer can see the anxiety that is generated when players must first commit their position to paper. At this point, the players become involved and want to know whether their decision is valid. The results of player decisions become one of the most important sources of information and dynamics during the game. Players will be frustrated by the failure of the game mechanics to give an accurate and rapid response. Most policy games require a relatively formalized accounting system that deals consistently with player decisions. The EDF exercise required that players have access to a wide variety of factual information; the accounting system made extensive use of graphic displays, indexed notebooks, and computerized database capabilities (see Section 3.3).

An important element in game construction is the establishment of the order of processing through the accounting system. Most games deal with systems that are complex and nonlinear; in reality, the problem being addressed entails many simultaneous activities. However, in a game, the accounting system is inevitably rigidly sequential because of mechanical constraints. In some cases, many simple accounting components are linked together into a totality that is quite complex. The order of processing of various models, components, or decisions will inevitably be artificial in some sense.

After decisions are processed (by hand or by computer), the results will be of two basic kinds: player specific and general information. Player-specific information is delivered to individuals; general information should be posted for all players. The accounting system should continuously illustrate relationships among the actors. It requires sophisticated judgment by the designer to ensure that the participant experiences the results of the accounting system as an overview rather than as disconnected fragments of information.

Indicators

To the extent that a formal accounting system is used, it is necessary to focus the results of the decisions on the central aspects of the model under investigation; indicators are useful in this regard. Indicators are defined as a few specific outputs of the accounting system (presented through graphs, charts, etc.) that are available to the players as feedback of the results of play. These indicators should focus discussion on the accounting system results that address the most important aspects of the problem.

## 7.4 PROCESS

Webster defines process as "a series of actions or operations directed toward a particular result." Process within the policy game can be thought of as the mechanisms through which the roles in the game interact with each other and with the game environment (e.g. artifacts, environmental processes). The facilitator is responsible for controlling both the roles and the environment during the game. Process includes the presentation of the exercise (facilitation, the three primary phases of a game); the game artifacts (visuals, paraphernalia); and the evaluation of results (documentation, etc.).

Game processes can be thought of as the mechanics of the game. There are a variety of facilitator-generated tasks (e.g. forms, voting, etc.) as well as player-generated tasks (e.g. negotiation, developing and implementing strategies, etc.). Game processes have a structure that is important in establishing communication within the game. They are subject to modification during a given game as the players create a jargon of their own and as procedures are abbreviated for the mutual convenience of the participants.

*7.4.1 The Presentation of the Exercise*

The purpose of a policy exercise is to assist participants in gaining insight into a complex issue. The presentation of the policy exercise (facilitation, visuals and paraphernalia) is critical for success.

Facilitation
It is always necessary to have one clearly defined central figure facilitating the game whose word is beyond dispute. This does not mean that the facilitator is not subject to challenge and interrogation by the players during the critiques. Rather, it means that, during the normal operation of a cycle, the players must submit to the instructions of the facilitator. In addition, role advisors are used in games that are so complex that the start-up time would be prohibitive without them. Subject matter specialists may be introduced at any time to aid the facilitator in transmitting factual information to establish the nature of the system; they can assist players in learning both the function and the mechanics of the role.

To ensure proper use, a well-designed policy exercise must include detailed instructions for the facilitator. A good game design team will give careful consideration to the utility of the game as an environment for self-instruction. If the game is so rigid that the player cannot alter characteristics which seem unrealistic, irrelevant, or restraining, or which prohibit the player from exploring some alternative future that is of interest, the game has failed. At the same time, a game provides an environment for the player to confront the total system. A game is a failure if a player leaves the exercise understanding some aspect well, but having failed to improve his perception of the linkage of this aspect to the totality.

Techniques can be employed to involve the players emotionally in the consequences of the decisions they have made (e.g. public disclosure of the results of decisions). Another technique that can be used to maintain player involvement is the use of a roving reporter to reveal players' actions or strategies. It must be emphasized that the objective of the game is to increase dialogue and not to embarrass the players. Successes may be reported; if it seems necessary to reveal a failure, the facilitator should go to some pains to give the player some way to save face (the concept of a "safe environment" is central to the design and use of a policy exercise).

Primary Phases of a Game
A policy game has three primary phases: introduction prior to play, the play of the game itself, and the final debriefing. This sequence of activities is required to initiate, conduct, and conclude the exercise.

*Pre-Game Activities*

A variety of pre-game activities are required of the facilitator prior to arrival of participants. This includes logistical concerns (room arrangements, technology, etc.) as well as distribution of player materials. Chairs should be comfortable and arranged to be conducive for player interaction. When possible, distribute materials beforehand to properly prepare the participants for the game. The pre-game handout serves several purposes: it identifies the day's objective; provides a brief scenario and role descriptions; and gets players focused on the game activity. The sequence and timing of the distribution of these materials is situation specific, but the materials might well include:

• A letter of invitation with the particulars of the logistics, an explanation of the purpose of the game, a description of what is expected of the participant, a description of the activities that will be associated with the game experience, and a phone number or other contact information;
• A brief document that presents in summary the basic materials with which the participant is expected to be familiar;
• Selected readings that will establish the proper frame of reference for the activities pursued by the game; and
• A workbook that requires the participant to make explicit decisions before arriving at the game (including a brief questionnaire if appropriate).

*Game Activities*

Once the participants are present, game activities begin. It is necessary to familiarize participants briefly with the intent of the game, the structure, procedures, and the initial scenario. The game progresses through several cycles; each cycle consists of a sequence through the steps of play. These cycles fall into three phases: learning how to play the game, dealing with the substance of the game, and the "happy ending."

The introduction takes many forms; it may be presented to players either before or upon their arrival and a variety of media may be used. In some contexts, it is quite desirable to have lectures or readings precede the game as preparatory material. It is a mistake to have an elaborate introduction as play begins; this can overwhelm the participant. Inertia is reduced if presentation to the players is accomplished quickly. The initial presentation requires a coherent and relatively simple characterization of steps of play, symbolic structure, game mechanics, time scale, information flows, game components, and the primary linkages among players. Players will inevitably enter a game with a minimum of information; however, they will move to a fuller level of comprehension through the device of increasingly sophisticated cycles of play.

The scenario should be addressed briefly at the outset so that the players share some common sense of the problem that they are about to address. In most cases, this should be brief (a five-minute introduction or a brief two-page statement). More detail on the scenario may be presented during the later cycles of play.

As the session begins, a series of formalities are conducted. These might well include introductions, a restatement of the purpose of the meeting, etc. The first cycle is typically a bit more involved than the following ones because the participants must be oriented to their environment. The best way to familiarize the participants with the structure of the game is to walk them through the first cycle introducing the particulars as they go through the steps of play. They are required to make decisions and follow all procedures; these activities are kept as simple as possible. These steps are repeated each cycle; after the first cycle, the participants are familiar with the process and the pace will increase.

*The first phase* acknowledges the initial inertia that inevitably results when players encounter a game for the first time. During this time, the players may feel distressed and attempt to escape participation in the game. Only essential materials should be presented. The participants should be directed through the forms in careful sequence as rapidly as possible so they can gain a general sense of what is going to happen and can gather some perspective for their own roles, other roles, the various components of the game, and the general gestalt. Each role should address the simplest possible set of materials and decision forms. In later cycles, complexity can be introduced as required.

Each cycle is followed by a short critique; *this is the last activity in each cycle.* The critique is a facilitator-controlled discussion at the end of each cycle designed to assist participants to gain insight into the game. It signals to the participants that a cycle has ended and that they will soon get another chance to explore a new set of ideas. This must include a review of the results from the cycle just ending. It is important to permit players to challenge any aspect of the game that they may find to be troublesome.

*The second phase* of playing the game, usually from three to five cycles, requires the players to develop and test their strategies. Events are introduced to generate exogenous problems that create cross pressures. Players are then forced to find solutions. The operator should be as inconspicuous as possible, administrative procedures should be as smooth as possible, and the processing of decisions *should be as rapid as possible.* Participants should be permitted to explore the limits of the system. The only exception to this rule would occur if a breakdown of gaming activities were about to take place because the decisions went beyond the limits of the technical capability of the game.

The "happy ending" cycle is *the final phase* of the exercise which is run primarily for the purpose of permitting players to establish a logical conclusion to their strategies. The facilitator must be alert to the possibility that the participant may attempt to use "end-of-game" strategies (defined as making unrealistic decisions in an attempt to "beat the game").

*Post-Game Activities*

The debriefing is the primary post-game activity; it is to be conducted while players are still present (don't postpone this to a subsequent meeting, because memory fades!). The debriefing is a systematic end-of-game discussion to evaluate the exercise; it provides the participants with an opportunity to escape from the game. If the game has been carefully designed, the players will be deeply involved. Players need an opportunity to complain about errors or flaws that they have encountered and, conversely, to glow about their successes. It is important that they be given a brief opportunity to go through this phase. The debriefing serves two purposes:

- It gives the participants an opportunity to vent, to clarify, and to explain or defend their behavior; and
- It gives the facilitator an opportunity to interact with the participants to ensure that they are comfortable with the evolution of the exercise. Players need the opportunity to confirm their understanding of the significance of the content as it relates to the real world.

Debriefing is defined as a systematic facilitator-controlled discussion at the conclusion of the exercise to evaluate initial objectives. The primary function of the debriefing is to refocus the participants on the client's environment. This should be a serious review session that:

- Permits the participants to vent their emotions;
- Provides feedback on the game;
- Interprets results of the game in a real-world context;
- Enriches the game experience;
- Validates the experience;
- Reviews the advantages of simulation and gaming; and
- Acknowledges the limits of the technique.

If a game is successful, the extensive final debriefing will be a rough-and-tumble session during which players, committed to their beliefs, challenge the underlying model(s) and evaluate how this links to the reality they are addressing. They should be encouraged to pursue with diligence any ambiguities, errors, or undocumented postures which seem invalid to them. Since there is not just one perspective represented by one player but multiple roles addressing the same problem from different perspectives, a debriefing can develop exceedingly sharp discussions about the character of the client's environment.

*The debriefing should be entered through a deliberate announcement* that the players are leaving the game and entering into a period of analysis. There should be a summary statement about the systems, models, roles, linkages, scenario and other components of the game, and discussion by the players about the construction of the game, its message, its successes, and its failures. This should generally be brief and somewhat perfunctory since those players who really wish to pursue these questions can be sent the concept report. The availability of the concept report in a well-designed game permits this stage of the critique to go very quickly (see Step 13, Section 8.2.3).

During the course of the debriefing, players must be permitted to challenge any aspect of the game. Games are typically not constructs of hard science but rather abstract presentations of such phenomena. Participants may have suggestions that could lead to the improvement of the exercise. The challenge provision ensures that any player who has serious doubts has an opportunity to express his or her challenge and offer alternatives.

Finally, *the debriefing should focus the players' attention on the substantive problem* under discussion. This review should be permitted as much time as possible. The purpose of the review is to concentrate on the problem and capitalize on the understanding now shared by the entire group. This review should take from 15 to 20 percent of the total time available for the play of the game.

### 7.4.2 Game Artifacts
Inevitably, policy games require a variety of artifacts to aid the process. These can vary widely, but judiciously used, they can be quite valuable. Two primary types of artifacts are visuals and paraphernalia.

Visuals
Visuals assist participants in gaining insight; artwork is an important consideration when creating the desired feel and image for the exercise. Graphics, when properly employed, are vital as one element in the suspension of disbelief that must be achieved if the exercise is to have its full impact. Symbols and paraphernalia should look sharp, clean and businesslike; concepts that are central to the discussion should be visible in chart form. Some suggestions for materials that may be useful include a typical accounting system sequence, typical computer output, data file layouts, flow-charts, functional interaction diagrams, linkages among the roles, overview schematics, player activity charts, room layout, rules, the schematic, steps of play, tables, technical graphics, wall charts, etc.

Paraphernalia
The system of gaming elements and system components described in Section IV creates the basis for forming an interactive and composite structure, both in

terms of their possible forms and how to design them. The choice of materials (paraphernalia) follows logically from the nature of the model and the game objectives. Paraphernalia are the various artifacts required by the facilitator to mount the game. They are inevitable, but a well-designed game will use a minimum, and *each artifact will have an explicit purpose*. It is important to select the correct stage props and keep them at an appropriate level of detail. Designing a stage setting for a Broadway play presents a comparable problem: *Oklahoma* required an elaborate stage setting, while *Waiting for Godot* required a bare minimum of props.

The initial design specifications (see Chapter 8) should determine the constraints to be imposed on materials used in the game (e.g. the need for portability, reproducibility, storage requirements, etc.); the number of "things" employed should be reasonable when measured against the game objectives. Abuse through overabundance or lack of clarity can destroy the effectiveness of a game. Parsimony is the watchword for good game design.

A mockup of all game materials prepared during the development of the prototype can be quite useful; it permits the client to evaluate the level of detail and the final character of the game. It is important to maintain an up-to-date list of paraphernalia required for the game. Some things to keep in mind: color coding of materials, computer requirements, cost, documentation required, other media required, portability, quantities of materials required, sources of game components, and standard vs. custom-made materials.

### 7.4.3 Evaluation of Results
When the exercise has been concluded, it is important to be able to establish whether the objectives have been met. The client will need evidence of the results; hence, mechanisms need to be thought through while the Concept Report (see Section 8.2.3) is under development; this evaluation must be focused on the initial objectives. This will permit specific mechanisms and procedures to be developed during the construction sequence.

There are two concepts associated with evaluation that must be distinguished: evaluation of the exercise, and evaluation of the results of its use (see Chapter 6). Ironically, there are situations that result in a good game producing bad results (as a consequence of poor facilitation, the wrong participants, inappropriate distractions during play, etc.). The reverse may also be true (a good facilitator can sometimes save the day, an audience that has an intense interest in the topic may forgive flaws in the game).

When considering the game itself, an evaluation of each of the specific game elements is the most appropriate way to proceed. If criteria were developed during the evolution of the Concept Report, the elements can be judged separately. Of course, the elements must also be evaluated in their totality. It is important to establish procedures to establish efficacy of the game in terms of validity, reliability, and utility. The evaluation should also look for unexpected outcomes, either positive or negative.

In some cases, a follow-up questionnaire may be sent to participants to serve one of two purposes: The objective may be to ascertain how much the participants learned from the game or the objective may be to have the participants critique the game. It is important to distinguish between these two objectives.

Documentation
Often, the client will require a final report documenting the exercise design, use, and results. It is also useful to provide the participants with materials that summarize the happenings of the game. This serves as a set of notes, but the document can also be circulated to confirm impressions derived during the game. It can serve as a further commitment of the participants to the process, by reinforcing the "message" from the experience.

# Chapter 8

## *Designing the Policy Exercise*

Note: Chapter 7 and 8 are envisioned as being used independently of the rest of the book. As a consequence, there is some redundancy to ensure clarity for the reader. You may also find the Detailed Design Tips located in the Appendix to be helpful.

### 8.1 INTRODUCTION

The purpose of this chapter is to describe a professional process for the design and use of the policy exercise. It draws heavily from *Gaming: The Future's Language* (Duke, 1974). The methodology for the design of tailor-made exercises has been developed and tested over a period of 40 years. Many public and private organizations have used this methodology to assist management in handling complex problems (Duke, 1974; Greenblat & Duke, 1975, 1981; Geurts et al., 2000).

For many, the process for designing a policy exercise has been somewhat ad hoc and has not been well documented. This chapter explains the design process for policy games as it has developed over the years; it consists of deriving a theory of real-world behavior, constructing a theoretical model and converting it into a policy exercise. Each of these activities can and will increase the overall accuracy and validity of the model relative to the actual system under study. This has been an evolutionary process – it remains a work in progress. The approach described here is the result of stimuli and feedback from many tests in practice and accordingly it reflects the wisdom of many of our clients and colleagues. There are five phases to the process we employ; each of the phases will be described later in this chapter:

| | | |
|---|---|---|
| Phase I | – | Setting the Stage for the Project |
| Phase II | – | Clarifying the Problem |
| Phase III | – | Designing the Policy Exercise |
| Phase IV | – | Developing the Exercise |
| Phase V | – | Implementation |

In recent years we have witnessed a proliferation of decision techniques to aid planning and management in large organizations. Two major styles of decision aids have developed. One set of techniques has its history in applied mathematics, econometrics, operations research, and systems analysis, focusing on the use of formal models and algorithms for policy development; these are most effective when dealing with Quadrant I situations (see Figure 8.1).

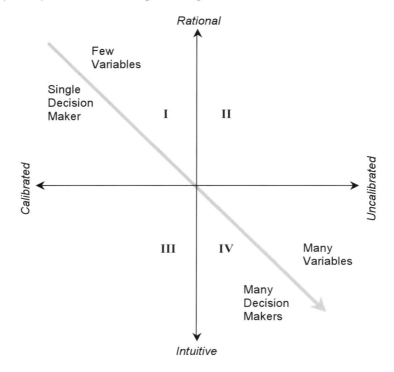

**FIGURE 8.1 | MACRO-PROBLEMS ARE QUADRANT IV SITUATIONS**

Although many applications of these techniques have been successful, their limitations, when applied to strategic level problems, have also been well documented. Criticisms of these formal strategic policy tools include over-simplification, over-emphasis on easy-to-quantify aspects, too much dependency on incomplete scientific theory, problems with data, that they are overly time-consuming, and most importantly, that they require that the users accept the results of a "black box" (the underlying model).

A recent example of the debate on formal modeling shows Alan Greenspan, Chairman of the Federal Reserve, answering his critics who accuse him of blending formal analysis too much with intuition. While many experts advocate the use of increasingly sophisticated models for managing the economy, Greenspan relies on a more hybrid type of "risk management." In a speech quoted in the *Asian Wall Street Journal*, September 1, 2003, Greenspan is quoted as saying "Every model ... is a vastly simplified representation of the world that we experience with all its intricacies on a day-to-day basis." Greenspan explains how the Federal Reserve also uses what we have called scenarios. "Our knowledge base is barely able to keep pace with the ever increasing complexity of our global econo-my". This means, he said, "The Fed doesn't just set interest rates according to the most likely economic forecast but also considers less probable outcomes with potentially dire consequences".

This example shows that a second set of decision techniques that have received much attention can be labeled "judgmental;" these are most effective when deal-ing with Quadrant IV situations (see Figure 8.1). Originating from disciplines like cognitive and social psychology, these techniques focus on intuition, creativity, dis-cussion and communication as stepping stones to strategic policy formulation. They have proven to be useful in many policy applications; however, the criticism of these techniques is also undeniable. Their limitations can be characterized by concepts such as: subjectivity; reliance on incomplete mental models; neglect of data, theory and expert opinion; and too little capacity to deal with the complicat-ed causal processes which affect the future outcomes of planned policy.

In our discussion of participatory policy analysis in Chapter 2 and through the cases in Chapter 3, we have made our position clear that an optimal approach to strategic policy formulation should try to combine the best of these two approaches. A basic characteristic of a design process is that it should facilitate a form of participatory policy analysis that combines the rigor of systems analyti-cal techniques with the creativity and communicative power of structured group techniques. This process has to result in an operational model of a very complex system. Reality is simulated through the interaction of role players using non-for-mal symbols with formal, computerized sub-models (where necessary). We see the technique of the policy exercise as one important contribution to the creation of a family of hybrid decision techniques.

From a methodological point of view, the intended end product of the design process is an operating model of a real-life system. In the game model, people in different but interrelated roles create, at least partly, the dynamic behavior of the model. Gaming/simulation can generally be distinguished from free role-playing; it is true that roles form a part of the simulation, but a policy exercise also has other components. In addition to role descriptions, a designer also uses scenarios, a series of prescribed actions for operator and players as well as carefully select-ed symbols and paraphernalia: game boards, cards, etc. The policy exercise is more formalized than role playing and, in the design, there is more emphasis on portraying reality.

Games are also different from computer simulations as used in operations research. In a computer model, all aspects of a system are described with mathe-matical or logical symbols. It is the computer that works out the dynamic behavior of the programmed model structure. In a game, reality is simulated through the interaction of role players, using non-standardized symbols. Computer models are quite often a part of a game in the so-called interactive or man-machine games.

The design process presented here can be clearly distinguished from that employed by many past applications of the policy exercise by its flexibility and sensitivity to the problem at hand. The dichotomy of tailor-made versus off-the-shelf games may help to clarify the distinction. The discipline of gaming/simulation, as it emerged from the military and moved into fields like management and urban planning, has produced a library of "off-the-shelf" exercises which are used frequently and successfully in professional training programs and university courses worldwide (Horn and Cleaves, 1980; Elgood, 1984). Because most of these games describe generalized or ideal-typical situations in non-existing organizations, they have limited value as policy development tools. The macro-problems that we described in Chapter 3 are so unique that the policy exercises we build for them had to be client specific.

The design process has to guarantee the on-time delivery of tailor-made products under severe time pressure. It has to be very transparent and trustworthy. Many people are involved, all of whom have a high economic and emotional stake in the process and who usually are going through the process for the first time, sometimes with a degree of insecurity. The method has to be reliable and flexible at the same time; it has to help in creating the in-between and end products as planned but it also has to be able to allow for step-by-step learning. The design process has to be the reliable compass for the project team. Otherwise, they may get lost in the struggle with the different complexities of the macro-problem. The design process and its list of preplanned in-between deliverables helps the designers find their way back if they go astray. Usually they discover that they have skipped one of the steps in the process and must go back and follow the process in the intended order.

### 8.1.1 Key Design Features

There is a correlation among principles, communication, complexity, knowledge, and the policy exercise that avoids the partition of the solution process. The policy exercise approach uses a sequence that combines many management elements: issues, structure, content, policy, planning, decision making, problem solving, enabling, implementing, managing, process, elements, relations, dynamic conclusions, and frequent feedback loops to ensure validity. This approach is very effective for investigating the complexities of important, non-reversible decisions (Gordon, 1985). The technique provides an understanding of the complex structure of decision-making processes of the real world.

Well-designed gaming/simulations are transient in character; they permit the restructuring of the game during play. Evidence of this can be obtained by taking any given game and running it with different participants. The more thoughtful games deliberately structure mechanisms that encourage and facilitate player or operator modification during play.

Game design is a combination of a disciplined design approach with a mimicry of existing game formats and styles; it is an elusive but real "art." Some principles of design are reasonably well articulated; others are just beginning to emerge. The game designer should have an express and coherent purpose or message to guide the construction of a game. Only the clear articulation of this purpose permits the rational selection of gaming as the appropriate communication mode. Skilled professionals have learned the art of gaming from experience; over time, using inspiration and imagination, they have built repertoires that permit the establishment of meaningful reference systems for policy discussions.

Gaming is best understood as a communication form: an analysis of the various communications media indicates that each game is very specific to some particular communications purpose (see Chapter 5). This specificity of purpose, as well as the high cost of the technique, become convincing arguments for precision in the design and parsimony in the construction and use of the game. When considering resources for game design, both cost and time are significant factors. The resources required to design, construct, test, and disseminate the game must be considered, as well as the cost encountered each time the game is used.

In determining the primary communications purpose to be achieved by the game, it is useful to review the primary purposes on which the exercise should focus. In establishing these, consider the cone of abstraction (Figure 8.2); this is useful in clarifying what can realistically be achieved with a specific technique (See Section 3.8 for an example). The product should be developed at an appropriate level to meet specific objectives. The exercise could be designed to:

- Transmit information to an audience;
- Serve as a questionnaire to extract information or opinions from the players;
- Establish dialogue among players;
- Motivate participants;
- Provide an environment in which creative ideas will spontaneously develop;
- Create awareness of a complex environment;
- Assist in decision making; and
- Achieve consensus.

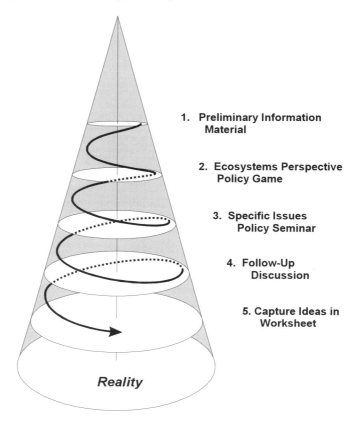

1. **Preliminary Information Material**

2. **Ecosystems Perspective Policy Game**

3. **Specific Issues Policy Seminar**

4. **Follow-Up Discussion**

5. **Capture Ideas in Worksheet**

*Reality*

**FIGURE 8.2 | CONE OF ABSTRACTION (WITH REFERENCES TO THE IJC CASE)**

### 8.1.2 Basic Characteristics of the Discipline

The creation of a game requires the successful interaction of several different groups (representatives of the various stakeholders, content specialists, structural modelers, etc.). All games are basically iterative in their structure; repetition through many cycles of play facilitates learning. They are best thought of as an environment for improved learning, achieved by successively defining the totality of the problem in increasing detail. Players commit themselves, and their decisions receive prompt feedback. Additional iterations introduce more detail; this progression helps to establish a context that is broad and structural. Games attempt to reproduce the appearance of reality but the security of the artificial is always present. If their preparation is thoughtfully designed, the style will naturally evolve.

A central concept for the policy exercise is that of a safe environment. This technique is employed for group model building and the clarification of alternatives. The function of the design team is to help the participants establish a future-oriented "vision" that permits the evaluation of alternatives.

The policy exercise is designed using the concept of "neutrality of design"; it is rational within the bounds of the human condition. The emphasis of the design team will be on defining opportunities, impediments, and alternatives. The technique is used under the presumption of "people of good will" motivated to engage in productive confrontation of the issue at hand. Because the policy exercise is problem specific, each instrument should fit the particulars of a unique problem environment. The game design process is explicit; each step addresses a specific client need. All methodologies have limits, and the proper use of gaming requires precision for effective results.

### 8.1.3 Why a Deliberate Process is Required

The design phase (resulting in a Concept Report) is the most crucial stage in the development of a policy exercise. Often, designers skip this step and begin with construction. This is comparable to starting to build a house without a blueprint. The steps described below derive from both theory and practice; they have the redeeming quality of ensuring a successful project. In practice, they may sometimes be truncated to meet the needs of a given client. However, a sequential process is demanded, and all the concerns implied by the full sequence of steps should be addressed.

*Games require a melding of differing perceptions of reality; as a consequence, they are best if designed by groups rather than individuals.* Working with a group generates a richer game. Given that the design and use of a successful game is somewhat akin to putting an organization through psychological analysis, resistance can be expected from those who feel threatened by the process. Integrity and clarity of the design process ensure that a consistent framework is evident to all those who may be involved (design team, client, and final participants); the process also creates an environment in which "truth" is forced to surface. Viewpoints at variance are exposed and confronted; a sharper perspective is reached through negotiation among the respondents. As the process proceeds, step by step, distracting issues can be set aside and a sharp focus maintained on the macro-problem. The process, employed relentlessly, will not only achieve agreement on the problem, but on the alternatives available as well; in most cases, consensus for action can be expected.

*If a deliberate process is used:*
- All staff time and energy are used to create an evolving prototype. Substantive knowledge may be initially flawed; however, each of the rule-of-ten runs (Section 8.2.4) provides an opportunity for specific content to be challenged and modified. Components are increasingly made to fit together using a trial and error process;
- Staff meetings achieve one of two objectives: either they reach agreement on some aspect of the exercise, or they identify the specific problem(s) that can be resolved by staff work. Each team member is obliged to raise concerns in a tangible, explicit way. Discussion is controlled toward this objective. The "complex system" is teased out, one aspect at a time. Progress is slow, but deliber-

ate; the team can judge where they are in the process;

- Because artifacts (e.g. the schematic) are used to capture ideas, the current state of knowledge is captured; as a consequence, it can be challenged in a systematic way;

- There is self-evident project memory. The accumulating artifacts (game materials) serve not only to remind the team of where their thinking was at the last gathering, but the prototype serves as an excellent way to get feedback from outsiders in both impromptu and structured ways; and

- The focus is on the product (game) rather than a diffuse problem; this is central to the task; many safeguards are built in to ensure that content of the final product is valid.

*If a deliberate process is not used:*
- Staff time and energy may be diverted to pursue substantive knowledge; because this is infinite, the task can never be completed (literally). The more they learn, the more they must learn to make every thing fit together. There is no imperative to focus attention on that which is most relevant;

- Meetings tend to be cyclical, ending more or less where they began. This derives from the fact that the subject is a truly complex system – each speaker struggles not only to articulate his or her thoughts but also to understand the comments of others. The words employed are sequential, but the system under discussion is a web. This results in a paradox – the more sophisticated the participants, the more convoluted becomes the discussion! Progress is hard to judge; the team has no established guideposts;

- Because artifacts are not used to capture ideas, content cannot be challenged in a systematic way;

- There is no project memory. There is no process that permits insight gained from a discussion to be deliberately and efficiently re-articulated on the occasion of the next meeting; and

- The focus is on content rather than on the product (game).

*8.2 The Design Sequence*
The process of design falls into five broad phases; 21 specific steps are nested therein. The steps will be presented in detail in the remainder of this chapter. They are listed in Figure 8.3 in abbreviated fashion to provide the reader an overview of the process.

**Phase I. Setting the Stage for the Project – Complete the essential preliminaries.**

Step 1.   Administrative set-up – Organize the project.
Step 2.   Define the macro-problem – What prompts this exercise?
Step 3.   Define the goals of the project – What are the primary objectives?
Step 4.   Project objectives/methods employed matrix – Is a game appropriate?
Step 5.   Specifications – Constraints and expectations.

**Phase II. Clarifying the Problem – Define both the focus and scope.**

Step 6.   Defining the system – Content, boundaries, interrelationships.
Step 7.   Displaying the system – Create a lucid cognitive map.
Step 8.   Negotiating the focus/scope with the client – Set a clear target.

**Phase III. Designing the Policy Exercise – Create a blueprint for the exercise.**

Step 9.   System components/gaming elements matrix – A model of a model.
Step 10.  Definition of gaming elements – Describe each module.
Step 11.  Repertoire of techniques – Don't re-invent the wheel.
Step 12.  Select a format for the exercise – What style is appropriate for this client?
Step 13.  Concept report – Document the working drawings.

**Phase IV. Developing the Exercise – Complete the rule of ten test runs.**

Step 14.  Build, test and modify a prototype exercise – Put the pieces together.
Step 15.  Technical evaluation – Ensure an efficient and effective tool.
Step 16.  Graphic design and printing – Develop a professional presentation.

**Phase V. Implementation – Ensure proper use by the client.**

Step 17.  Integrate the exercise into the client's environment – Make it fit.
Step 18.  Facilitating the exercise – Practical use by the client.
Step 19.  Dissemination – Deliver the policy exercise to the client.
Step 20.  Ethical and legal concerns – Protect the client and the designers.
Step 21.  Final report to the client – Ensure proper closure.

**FIGURE 8.3 | THE DESIGN SEQUENCE**

As stated, the process of game design is a mix of adherence to the discipline, the development of logic for each case, proper reference to a repertoire of techniques, intuition and inspiration. The design process combines logic and serendipity; creating the simulated environment is an artistic challenge. Selecting the correct stage props and keeping them at an appropriate level of detail requires skill. The challenge is to retain verisimilitude while creating an interesting model that will mutate and evolve. The design process described below fulfills this function.

The policy exercise, first and foremost, is an abstraction of reality. It should serve as a valid and efficient model of a complex environment for communication purposes. It should capture those aspects of the problem that are central to the discussion at hand – but, equally important, it should be parsimonious. Too much detail, and/or a confusing presentation can obfuscate rather than clarify. The process described here, if faithfully followed, provides a clear, logical basis for capturing the essence of the problem environment and translating it into an appropriate exercise.

Experience shows that this is a replicable, disciplined process to guide the development and use of policy games. Twenty-one distinct steps allow the design team to proceed systematically; this permits the client to follow the progress of the work and to judge, explicitly, if the product meets the initial specifications. One of the strengths of the step-by-step process is that it supports stakeholder communication throughout the design effort. The process is designed to direct a sequence of activities that involves formulation of the initial situation, articulation of a conceptual model, design, construction, and running a gaming exercise, and capturing the insights that emerge.

In the abstract, the game design process is viewed as sequential; the game designer proceeds logically from point to point. In practice, the designer may attempt a somewhat more simultaneous solution and may adapt the order of progression if required to meet the client's needs.

### 8.2.1 Phase I – Setting the Stage for the Project
Phase I has five steps that must be carefully addressed at the outset of a project. Steps 1 through 5 should be viewed as an iterative process. For example, as the effort to clarify the problem becomes more precise, the specific objectives to be achieved can be more clearly articulated. The initial steps serve to guide the remaining development process. Those who ignore these five activities do so at their peril; the remaining activities rest on this bedrock.

### Step 1. Administrative Set-up
The purpose of this step is to ensure that the project is properly authorized and that the chain of command, review of progress, and administrative details are appropriately organized. Attention to administrative detail is required for any project; the standard concerns are well known; however, there are special concerns that need to be addressed, unique to the development of a policy exercise.

A clear definition of the client is essential; there are many situations in which this is not immediately evident. Someone within an organization may identify a problem of concern, fund a policy exercise to address the issue, and authorize it to begin. Experience shows that this may be initiated at any of several administrative levels (the CEO, a vice president, a department head, etc.). However, given the murky nature of these problems, the true locus for a policy decision to resolve the matter may ultimately prove to rest elsewhere within the organization. The study team may quickly realize that the problem is set in too restricted a fashion. For reasonable success, it may be necessary to negotiate the focus to a higher level. Needless to say, this requires tact; more importantly, it requires strict attention to the sequential (but iterative) completion of the design steps. Problems of this kind will become evident in Step 2 (Problem Definition); they will be resolved by the completion of Step 8 (Negotiating the Focus of the Exercise).

Proper authorization for the project is a must! It is common for these types of projects to be launched under great time pressure; the initial client representative may attempt to bypass internal procedures to get underway quickly. This can prove to be a fatal mistake for the project. It is necessary to arrange for the orderly conduct of business at three levels: the client, the organizational unit controlling the project, and the project team. This includes all the activities of the client and the consultant receiving proper authorization for the project. This initial step will vary significantly among organizations.

The successful development of a policy exercise requires, as does any project, a careful delineation of responsibilities and lines of authority. Care should be taken to follow standard contractual arrangements (e.g. fees, budget, specifications, expected results, procedural agreements, contractual obligations required of the client, deadlines, go/no-go decision dates, expected deliverables, sign-off required, etc.). These, and other appropriate administrative matters, should be fully resolved before the substantive material is addressed.

A "designated agent" *must be identified to represent the client as a key contact* or project manager. Responsibility for different aspects of the project may be delegated among several people (e.g. financial, access to data and information, graphics assistance, etc.), but it is crucial to specify one individual who is to be the central contact person for the design team. This agent should have sign-off authority or clear and quick access to someone who does. This agent is the one responsible for approving any major budget or technical changes as well as the finished product. Through this agent, the client will formally sign off by approving each major phase of the project (this protects against conflict at later phases of the project).

A project of this kind typically requires several types of personnel: various experts (content specialists, computer specialists, facilitator, etc.), game designers, and administrative staff. This may require negotiation to obtain an appropriate project mix. Typically, the client has the ability to provide both content experts and administrative staff; however, it will be the rare situation in which in-house game-building skills are available. The client must choose between three alternatives: completing the project internally, using a consultant to assist client staff, or contracting the project to an outside group. Specific concerns to be addressed include the need for objectivity (difficult for client personnel to achieve!), gaming expertise, confidentiality (hence the need to limit information to in-house staff), cost (it may be more cost-effective to contract the project out) and other client-specific concerns.

The utility and perception of the final product will be a function of good communication as the project proceeds from beginning to end. The urgency so typical of these situations demands proper procedures to facilitate quick and uninhibited communication by the policy exercise design team. This demands a clear chain of communication both within and beyond the organization. Within the organization, both vertical and horizontal lines of communication should be cleared to permit the team to cast a very broad net, particularly during Phase II (Problem Clarification). Communication that extends beyond the organization may be essential; this may require special procedures for clearance. Because egos are involved, many participants may feel threatened during the design phase; as a consequence, negotiation procedures should be worked through in advance.

Step 2. Define the Macro-Problem
The purpose of this step is to establish a sharply focused problem statement that defines what the game is to address. It is important to clarify the problem with precision at the outset of the design process. This should capture an overview of the problem that reflects the perspectives of the various stakeholders who must be interviewed to find the perceived problem boundaries. The initial problem statement has to be acceptable to all participants in the process. This statement should articulate both the technical aspects of the subject as well as any specific communications objectives (participatory decision making, communication of policy to staff, corporate culture, etc.) that are to be achieved by the exercise. The problem statement (accompanied by the specifications) should be sufficiently detailed to permit evaluation of the success of the game when completed. This statement will be redefined and clarified several times as consensus is established regarding the definition of the problem and the objectives of the exercise.

Only a clear problem statement will guide the selection and the active involvement of concerned parties in understanding the complexity of the issues involved; identifying, creating, analyzing, and selecting alternative solutions; and assessing the impact of proposed alternatives. A problem definition consists of three distinct statements: *background information, the problem statement,* and *further elaboration* as may be required.

*Background of the Problem*
This statement should provide a summary of the characteristics of the problem

environment (e.g. stakeholders, organizational structures, issues, etc.). This description usually elaborates on several components of the problem: its history, characteristics (scope, cost, size, etc.), technical aspects, how it affects the organization, how solving the problem will benefit the organization, etc. The need, conditions, or circumstance that prompted consideration of a game should be stated; it should be convincing to a neutral observer and as concise as possible. This background statement will lead into a summary statement of the problem that will be central to the creation and evaluation of the exercise. It will support a detailed analysis of actors (needs, objectives, and responsibilities) as well as of the problem environment (internal and external) that will take place during the schematic development phase of the design process (Steps 6, 7 and 8).

*The Problem Statement*
The problem statement is not a description of the amorphous big picture, but rather *a narrowly defined concern that the exercise is to address*. If properly achieved, it enables the active involvement of concerned parties to focus on:

- Understanding the complexity of the issues involved;
- Identifying, creating, analyzing, and selecting alternative solutions; and
- Assessing impacts of proposed alternatives

The problem should be reduced to one succinct statement that is acceptable to both the design team and the client; it should be no more than a few sentences long. This task is difficult to achieve, but if successful, it makes it possible to bring the goals of the project into sharp focus (Chapter 3 provides eight examples of problem statements.) *The final product will be evaluated against this problem statement and the specifications that accompany it.* Typically, there will be a need to redefine the problem statement a number of times.

*Further Elaboration*
In some cases, it is appropriate to extend the problem statement with further detail; this should be added at this point. It would include an elaboration of subject matter (substantive content), specific alternatives to be considered, and the themes, issues, and/or problems that are to be stressed. The substantive material that is to be dealt with by the game should be defined as explicitly as possible.

Step 3. Establish Goals and Objectives for the Project
The purpose of the exercise must be clarified at the outset! Failure to resolve this will result in confusion during construction. In turn, this leads to time and cost overruns as well as a poor quality process and product. The purpose of Step 3 is to define exactly what the intended contribution of the project is to strategic problem solving. Gaming/simulation can fulfill three classical functions of strategic management when used in a consulting project:

- Pre-decision Analysis – Discovering problems, formulating and ordering problems, developing and clarifying alternatives, evaluating alternatives and developing plans of action;
- Decision making – Negotiating, building consensus, reaching decisions; and
- Implementation – Motivating and building awareness, educating, training and synthesizing perspectives.

If the problem has been clearly established, goals can be articulated and the steps through the design process can then be optimally adapted to the project goals. Chapter 4 – Five Key Criteria, suggests many ways to formulate the contribution of gaming/simulation to strategic management. For a successful design process, *a single primary purpose should be specified*. If more than one of these purposes applies, each should be stated explicitly, and *they should be clearly placed in order of priority*. The policy exercise can be used as a structured meeting environment to gain understanding of the big picture, envision desirable long-term futures, identify related issues, facilitate discussion of issues, develop evaluation criteria, provide a structure for documentation of results, and facilitate the distribution of results. Typical objectives that have been central to past policy exercises can be found in Chapter 3. Here are a few more that relate to strategy making in the "sustainable corporation":

- Encouraging innovation in technology and behavioral change;
- Teaching the impact of manufacturing on the ecosystem;
- Creating awareness of the concept of sustainable production;
- Demonstrating the interconnectedness of sustainable development issues;
- Forcing consideration of environmental issues;
- Requiring organizational views to interlock with a worldview;
- Focusing on long-term consequences of current business practices;
- Catalyzing ideas for new programs of strategic initiatives;
- Motivating participants to achieve a sustainable corporation;
- Promulgating a new corporate culture; and
- Gaining consensus for action on a major decision.

Goals should be broken down into a specific set of objectives to serve as progress markers during construction and evaluation. The objectives of the exercise should be realistic and appropriate, based on the problem being addressed. Typically, a multiple set of objectives will be listed; some will be clearer than others, and some may be in conflict. These need to be winnowed down and prioritized into the few that are most central to the concerns reflected in the problem statement. Objectives need to be presented in a sufficiently flexible form to accommodate the concerns of participants that may arise during the exercise.

Step 4. Project Objectives/Methods Employed Matrix
The purpose of Step 4 is to review a broad range of methodologies to ensure that

gaming is appropriate. A basic ground rule to apply when making the decision to use a policy exercise is to consider other alternatives. Clients should be effectively engaged in making this choice to ensure their full knowledge of the policy exercise technique vis-à-vis other approaches that might be used. Games and/or simulations are only one of several options available when addressing the client's needs. Because of the client's unique characteristics, it is important to carefully weigh the pros and cons of each situation to substantiate the validity of the policy exercise approach. This forces consideration as to which form of communication is most effective in meeting the client's objectives. Ultimately, effective evaluation of the project should start with an honest response to the question: "Is a policy exercise appropriate in this situation?"

The project-objectives/methods-employed matrix is used to define what devices are to be used when addressing a macro-problem. Handbooks on policy and strategy document a wide variety of research designs, decision aids, and communication procedures relevant for strategic problem solving. They include competitor analysis, market research, modeling techniques, computer-assisted group sessions and even outward-bound team motivation sessions. Because a policy game is hybrid and occasion specific, it is important to select and/or combine the appropriate methods for this client.

It is necessary to ascertain that the client's needs cannot be met by some less cumbersome mode. Some questions need to be carefully addressed: Why was a policy exercise chosen in the first place? What benefits are to be derived exclusively from this approach? Will the game completely satisfy all the client's objectives? What areas may not be fully covered? Note that the exercise is expected to meet only specific, limited, readily evaluated objectives; it is a mistake to expect a broad array of objectives to be met.

Step 5. Specifications for Game Design
The purpose of this step is to establish clear technical specifications; this is a natural extension of the development of the problem statement. They provide an opportunity to make objectives and constraints explicit during the phases of design, construction and use. The specifications become a pragmatic list of concerns that the game designer should address during the construction of the game. The objective is to delineate constraints and expectations for the project and also to raise and address specific questions that anticipate the conditions that will govern the design and use of the exercise. The responses, if carefully delineated, provide detailed specifications at the outset of construction against which the final product can be evaluated. It is important to consider each of the design steps and to anticipate what specifications will be required to ensure that the design process progresses smoothly. When writing specifications, it is a good idea to review all of the 21 design steps; pay particular attention to Steps 1, 6 and 11 through 21.

The specifications should spell out the chain of command, project management procedures, budget and financial arrangements, deadlines, critical dates, personnel arrangements, procedure for reporting changes, deliverables, sign-off authority, and similar concerns. Ground rules should be established for the circulation of reports (who receives them, confidentiality concerns, deadlines for response, etc.). Clarity and completeness here will contribute to a smoothly run project.

Particular care should be given to the financial resources available for the development and use of the exercise. The budget for the project should be specified separately for each of the major phases: setting the stage, clarifying the problem, designing the policy exercise, developing the exercise, and the implementation activities. Final game costs often exceed initial estimates, particularly when precise goals are not stated and approved by the client before construction begins. Similarly, the cost of using a game may vary greatly. With costs so difficult to estimate, it is incumbent on the client and designer to agree on what resources will be made available during construction and for normal use of the game. A product may have reduced utility because the unit cost per run is beyond the capacity of the organization to sustain. If each use of the game has a new set of participants and/or a new game facilitator, the cost will be high. In those instances where the game will be used frequently by the same highly trained facilitator and where audience characteristics are consistent, the cost of each run will drop markedly.

Allocation of time is no less important than dollars both in the development and use of a game. The time required for the development of a game will be the product of the clarity with which the problem has been stated, the appropriateness of gaming for the problem, the clear specification of goals in the concept report, and the range of skill and experience of the game designers. Careful task scheduling is required (timeline for the project – design, construction, testing); this demands the identification of critical due dates. The design of a serious game is an evolutionary process; as a consequence, procedures for reporting changes in the direction of the project to management should be established at the outset.

These notions are intended to suggest a reasonably comprehensive set of questions that the client and designer should specify before a game is commissioned. Since each game is to fill a specific need, these thoughts can only be used to prompt a careful search of conditions appropriate in a particular context. Specifications should be signed off by the client before beginning construction of a game.

### 8.2.2 Phase II – Clarify the Problem
The purpose of Phase II is to complete the cognitive mapping process (interviews, literature review, snow cards, schematic).

Games attempt to assist with decision making under uncertainty. Participants understand the need to improve the exchange of information among themselves about differing perceptions of the future as well as the need to develop and evaluate alternative scenarios. Games can be very powerful for this purpose. People find games memorable and valuable (memories from games have proven to be vivid after 25 years). They provide data as information that is structural and logical; this serves as a framework that permits the storage of information. The artifacts employed make imagery more memorable.

A lucid problem statement will contribute to the process of creating a format for the game (form follows function). If the problem is defined with care, the game design follows readily. Because this is so important, we recommend that no less than a third of the available resources (time and money) are devoted to clarifying objectives, developing the problem statement and developing the concept report (prepared in Step 13, it summarizes the findings of Steps 1-12).

Step 6. Defining the System
The purpose of this step is to investigate the underlying substantive nature of the macro-problem. Only a rigorous systems analytic procedure will be able to capture the problem environment in its entirety. It is essential to grasp an integrative (gestalt) perspective of the problem as it is reflected in the mental models of the various stakeholders. Information can be collected and organized using a wide variety of procedures: interviews, a literature review and workshops. All the major stakeholders are to be interviewed to discover their perception of problem boundaries. The literature review is to determine problem boundaries as reported by prior research. Care must be taken that not only the relevant internal executives are interviewed but also that external experts and data are explored.

The subject of a game must be specified in a precise way before construction begins. The specification of substantive content may take the form of written reports, abstracts and/or a detailed subject outline. Without such documentation, the final product may not be relevant. This document should capture and present logically that which is known about the problem environment; of equal importance, the document should identify that which is unknown – specific concerns for which no data, theory, and/or past experience are available.

The findings of the research should be captured in a model of the organization; this should be described in a short text. Identify the major actors: their goals, activities, and resources, and the interactions among them. The model should be simple, consisting of a limited number of key statements, a thumbnail statistical sketch and the major constraints affecting the organization. This is required both to guide the development of the exercise as well as to assist participants during play and in the critique. However abstract, this model should be defensible.

A systems analysis ensures a rational and thorough approach to game design. Without this step, assumptions may go undetected, variables and relationships may be unnoticed, and the resulting simulation may be unrealistic.

Information about the system and elements of the problem can be collected and organized using interviews and a structured workshop during which participants create "snow cards." Additional snow cards may be generated from a literature review. (One client had a large number of these cards arranged on a tabletop. On return from lunch, team members opened several windows simultaneously. Wind blew the cards about the room and someone called out: It's snowing! Thus the name "snow card" was born).

Snow cards are ideas, variables, problems, flows, relationships, models, laws, stakeholders, decisions, etc. that appear significant. Only one thought is committed to a single card, and this thought is kept as cryptic as possible (without loss of meaning). Each card captures a brief statement or a word that represents an issue or variable uncovered during the analysis. This process tries to find all the problem variables and how they interact; it uncovers the boundaries, actors, and the inputs and outputs of the problem. The snow card process is described in more detail in the Appendix.

The system may be defined from one or more conceptual referent systems (group dynamics, resource allocation, geographic, demographic, political, economic, social, psychological, anthropological, historical, etc.). It is common to have several hundred cards when analyzing a complex problem environment. The development of a set of snow cards is best done through a team effort using a freewheeling brainstorming approach. This inductive form of analysis is intended to be inclusive – if anyone thinks it might be important, it should be included. These cards are converted into a working schematic that should convey all the concerns expressed by the snow cards. The schematic is for staff use at this stage, not for the client. This is the most critical part of the process – if the boundaries are too tightly delineated, significant alternatives may be ignored.

Often, we divide the team into two groups. The first group works with members of the organization and their stakeholders using interviews and workshops. They concentrate on the "logic in use," i.e. the diverse mental maps of the persons who live in the system. The second group seeks to find conceptual models and generalizations from multidisciplinary, academic and professional literature, statistical data, and if relevant, outside experts; they look for potential frames of "reconstructed logic." In team meetings, the results of the "top down" and "bottom up" analyses are contrasted and one perspective provides the homework for the other group (see the concept of robustness in Chapter 4). Saturation is the criterion used to stop this process. When no new ideas, frames and/or perceptions emerge, it is time to go to the next step: the consolidation of these insights into a schematic. Of course, the criteria of saturation is only valid if one can guarantee that the teams have put forth a maximum effort in approaching the system from as many sources and perspectives as possible.

The teams must select sources (books, articles or people) with care. In all cases, they look for pithy statements that reveal a significant aspect of the problem. For example, if there is a journal article by an expert that addresses the problem, this should be searched for the major areas of concern – e.g. finance, geography, actors, science, fact, interrelationships, etc. Remember – you are trying to play detective and piece together clues that let you discover the system in its full flavor. Avoid the trap of taking too much from one source (as this may give you a distorted view). When exploring the system, there may be bewildering amounts of data, much of which is irrelevant or misleading. Take time to understand and identify the key elements in the system, otherwise you cannot successfully simulate it, even in highly abstract form. What one should look for is:

- Action triggers and their mode of operation;
- Major flows, stocks and delays (input, throughput, output) in the system;
- Areas of clarity and areas of ambiguity;
- Congruency and conflict in organizational perception;
- Decision-making levels;
- Key elements in control systems (feedback);
- Major decision points and factors influencing them;
- Major players;
- Patterns of interrelationships and points of interaction;
- The pattern of organizational politics; and
- Theoretical evidence (natural, man-made).

Step 7. Displaying the System
The next objective is to develop a graphic that contains an overview of all the considerations that are significant to the policy issue being addressed by this process. This should proceed through two primary steps: the working schematic and the final schematic. Schematic presentations of complex problems exploit the advantages of visual communication. They do so by simultaneously expressing the "big picture" as well as the significant issues required for understanding the problem environment. For the schematic to be able to convey an overview of the problem quickly and simply, it should be organized in such a way that it is clear not only to those building the game, but also to those participating in the exercise.

Every stakeholder will view the problem environment differently. These differences should be confronted and negotiated to the point that a single explicit visual conceptualization is agreed upon. Inevitably, this will be a complex rendition of the relationships of several hundred (possibly in excess of a thousand) variables (previously developed as snow cards, see Step 6) that are of interest to various stakeholders. All stakeholders should be able to locate the central features of the world as they view it within this schematic. The schematic is improved using repeated iterations; saturation is our operational criterion for having reached a state of robustness. Once we can no longer elicit new ideas and even the most hesitant opinion makers can agree with the schematic, we go to the next phase of game design. The more highly articulated and accepted the knowledge household is, the more robust or less controversial it will be. The knowledge should be organized in a format that provides a clear and stimulating path for the non-specialist, emphasizing not only what is known, but also what is not known.

*Definition of a schematic*
A schematic, as used in the development of a policy exercise, is a drawing that represents a model or overview of the system being investigated. It calls on the results of Step 6 (Defining the System). The drawing will show major system components (e.g. actors, processes, data files, etc.) and the primary relationships among them. The drawing will show any important sequence(s) of activities; however, this is not its primary purpose. Each system component should be described by a few primary attributes that help to define the processing sequence of the completed exercise. A well-designed schematic is an effective way to:

- Engage a group of professionals in the discussion of central issues;
- Provide the group with the big picture; and
- Help the group develop solutions that reflect the various interdependencies.

A schematic illustrates a much richer interpretation of the problem than one person can conceive alone. Most clients find the process of creating a schematic to be very useful for clarifying assumptions and perceptions of key decision makers and actors. The resulting schematic, therefore, takes on its own value and serves other purposes in addition to guiding the creation of the simulation. Many clients have volunteered enthusiastic endorsements of the final schematic. In more than one case, the client has indicated that this drawing alone was worth the price of the entire project!

*The Working Schematic* (Map of the snow cards)
The initial description of the situation usually comes forth in discrete, partially organized, and sometimes conflicting pieces. It is the task of the research team and the client to synthesize these elements of the system into an integrated and explicit model that can be easily described and discussed. The snow cards and other results from Step 6 are arranged into a working schematic. This should identify and schematically describe the major system characteristics and linkages (endogenous and exogenous factors, relationships, flows, tables, etc.). This

initial effort should be presented on a single large sheet of paper, of any conven-
ient size (typically very large). The result of this early trial schematic is an inclusive, but rough, approximation of the problem environment that should convey
the bulk of the concerns expressed by the snow cards. It is a working document
used by the staff to capture ideas and to organize them into a preliminary sketch
of what the game might look like; as it progresses, it must be reviewed by the
client.

*Final Schematic*
Eventually, the necessary abstractions, omissions, and re-definitions are undertaken and the entire configuration is committed to a final format (such as a colored graphic). This is a condensation of the original working schematic into a
formal document for delivery to the client. As such, it will have been reduced to
those factors considered most relevant within the constraints of the problem
statement. This iterative process of selection will be done in the context of an
ongoing dialogue with the client; it should evoke discussion resulting in consensus about the final drawing. This discussion should clarify variables and uncov-
er gaps, assumptions, and disagreements about how the problem is perceived.
The final document should retain enough detail to adequately represent the
problem environment; it should communicate the central aspects of the problem
visually and quickly. The schematic ensures that the team includes key components and excludes components that are not central to the simulation; it will be
changed repeatedly as the team works towards consensus. Abbreviated examples
of final schematics can be found in Chapter 3. An example with more detail is
included in the Appendix.

Step 8. Negotiating Focus and Scope with the Client
The purpose of this step is to select the systems components from the schematic that are to be included in the systems components/gaming elements matrix
(Step 9). Because the system has been diagrammed in its entirety, the team can
make rational choices about what to include or exclude. The complete problem
set (as initially perceived by the significant actors) is often too broad and inclusive. As a consequence, the schematic, when reviewed and accepted by the client,
will normally contain more factors than need to be incorporated into the final
game. Through dialogue with the client, the design team should interpret the
original objectives, problem statement and specifications against the final
schematic and select those factors of primary concern that must be represented
in the gaming vehicle. The process guarantees that the game meets the specifications developed in Step 5. It is also imperative to ascertain the appropriate level
of abstraction at this stage. If this step is done well, the final exercise will be situation specific, lucid, and relevant. The client has a serious obligation of review
at this juncture; the objective is to set a clear target for the exercise.

### 8.2.3 Phase III – Designing the Policy Exercise

Many professionals have had the experience of developing a "great" game (enjoyable for participants) that did not dovetail well with the client's actual need. In these cases, a retrospective view typically reveals that the problem was inadequately defined at the outset. *Another mistake is to start with a preconceived game format instead of following a deliberate process* (and allowing form to follow function). This results in wasted resources as the team attempts to force a fit between the problem and a preconceived gaming format. Phase III entails the creation of a blueprint for the exercise; this takes the form of a concept report. To achieve this document, four steps are required: the systems components/gaming elements matrix, a definition of gaming elements, a review of a repertoire of techniques, and the selection of a format for the exercise. This process is described below.

### Step 9. Systems Components/Gaming Elements Matrix

The purpose of this step is to transform systematic thought of the substantive system into systematic thought of the policy exercise, component by component. The system (as represented in the schematic) must be transformed from a model of the problem to a model of the game. This demands an orderly, replicable process. The task here is one of capturing creativity, identifying and incorporating the best ideas into the game. Because the process is demanding of the design team, adequate time should be scheduled at the outset and appropriate facilities must be provided.

To avoid a nonproductive state (indicated by iterative comment, hostility, or disinterest), the process should be allowed to emerge as a "happening" around the central theme (ideas can be inserted in any cell at any time). A display area is organized with clusters of descriptors arranged on a large tack board surface (see Figure 8.4). The columns reflect the systems components (selected in Step 8) and row headings reflecting the game elements (from Chapter 7 – roles, rules, scenario, format, step of play, etc.). The cells are completed in a matrix conversion process that shifts the analysis from a schematic model of the problem to a procedural and symbolic model of the gaming exercise. This matrix fosters a creative process; it provides an effective tool to accomplish this task. The process followed is a series of brainstorming sessions by the design team, where the team addresses each cell of the matrix, making conversions where appropriate.

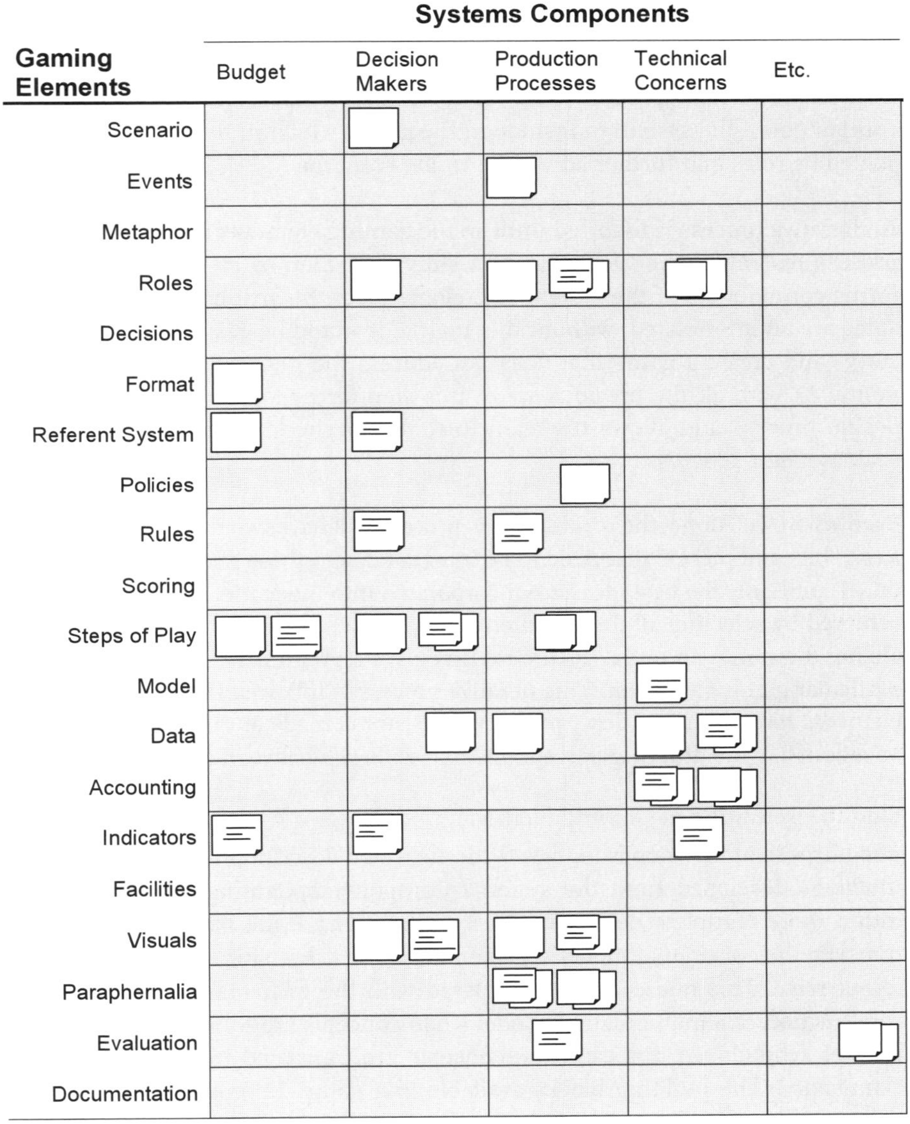

| Gaming Elements | Systems Components | | | | |
|---|---|---|---|---|---|
| | Budget | Decision Makers | Production Processes | Technical Concerns | Etc. |
| Scenario | | | | | |
| Events | | | | | |
| Metaphor | | | | | |
| Roles | | | | | |
| Decisions | | | | | |
| Format | | | | | |
| Referent System | | | | | |
| Policies | | | | | |
| Rules | | | | | |
| Scoring | | | | | |
| Steps of Play | | | | | |
| Model | | | | | |
| Data | | | | | |
| Accounting | | | | | |
| Indicators | | | | | |
| Facilities | | | | | |
| Visuals | | | | | |
| Paraphernalia | | | | | |
| Evaluation | | | | | |
| Documentation | | | | | |

FIGURE 8.4 | SYSTEMS COMPONENTS/GAME ELEMENTS MATRIX

This approach permits the logic to develop from the standpoint of the system (down), from the standpoint of the game (across), or at random (brainstorming any cell at any time), dependent on the insight and motivation of the staff. *No attempt is made to correlate or rationalize the various cells one with the other at this time.* The notes in a given cell may well contradict those of another; this will be resolved in the next step. Ideas for each gaming element should be captured in the matrix; the team must determine how each systems component will be addressed. For example, if an R&D process were being simulated, a research team might be a component of the system to include in the game, which in turn, could be represented by roles and further addressed in the scenario.

An iterative process is followed until all the gaming elements are described. This process resembles the "weaving" of a story line. Step by step, the team transforms components of the system into elements of the artificial world. The variables are all interrelated; without this matrix, it would be easy to "get lost in the story" and create a game that does not address the necessary systems components. As with all the previous steps, this step forces logic and clarity into the design process and allows the team to routinely check their effectiveness and evaluate their progress.

Even when well done, the results of this process will have two flaws: the ideas tend to be "bits and pieces" that need to be integrated, and these need to be winnowed down until only the best ideas are incorporated into the game. This refinement is achieved by selecting all those content cards (ideas) from a given row and rationalizing these into an initial document that gives a preliminary description of that particular gaming element. This iterative process is followed until all the gaming elements have an initial description. No attempt is made at this time to correlate or rationalize the differing perceptions that will exist between game elements.

Step 10. Definition of Gaming Elements

The purpose of this step is to transform the initial description of the gaming elements as developed from the systems Components/Gaming Elements Matrix into a more complete definition. These elements are the building blocks that translate the conceptual model represented by the schematic into a working policy exercise. This phase can be compared with the formalization phase in the construction of a mathematical model when concepts are translated into mathematical symbols. In this case, the concepts are translated into proper gaming "language." The building blocks available to a game designer include the elements: scenario, events, theme, analogy/metaphor, roles, decisions, format, basic referent systems, policies, rules, scoring, steps of play, model, data and information, accounting system, indicators, visuals and paraphernalia (Duke, 1981). Chapter 7 describes the gaming elements in detail.

The theoretical basis for each element should be carefully described, with particular attention paid to the quality of empirical data. Finally, the output to be generated by each component should be described (both its character and purpose). The object is to create an explicit model of reality; in the process of creating the simulated environment, it is important to select the correct stage props and keep them at an appropriate level of detail. The central problem is the elaboration of a game "environment" wherein flexibility and realism are maximized. Usually, many modifications are necessary to bring a good game together, this often necessitates compromise with the original specifications or objectives. (The concept report (Step 13) should include provisions for reporting such changes and obtaining client approval).

After each gaming element has been described, the next step is to integrate ideas vertically to ensure logical consistency among the various elements. As these elements are developed, no matter how inadequate they may seem, they are committed to a report that gives a description of an early prototype of the full exercise. A test run of the prototype cannot be completed until these are available at an initial level of development. This draft document will be changed during the test runs; it provides an opportunity to give an initial description of the exercise to the client.

A preliminary mockup of all game materials is very useful at this stage; it should include diagrams of graphics, decision forms for player use, etc. These initial materials may be sketchy; however, if successfully presented at this stage, the client can be more certain that the level of detail is appropriate. Attention should be focused on these materials during the review process because they reveal a great deal to the client about the final character of the game.

Step 11. Repertoire of Techniques
The purpose of this step is to review a broad range of experience and select techniques appropriate for this client. Repertoire is defined as known gaming techniques (paraphernalia, basic styles or referent systems employed, various graphics, interpersonal dynamic mechanisms, etc.) which might be incorporated into the exercise. The admonition here is: Don't re-invent the wheel! The design team should have familiarity with a broad range of techniques. These "tricks of the trade" can be derived from a review of the literature and professional practice. A review of previous gaming efforts can be undertaken in order to obtain a set of ideas that might be used in the development of this exercise. A major difficulty facing the team will be ready access to a complete library of related games.

Artistry comes into play at this point. Schon has made the point that artistry consists of the ability to invent, as needed, a method suited to the difficulties being experienced (Schon, 1986). It is clear, in the design of a policy exercise, that form follows function. If the process has been followed with care until this point, the selection and/or invention of technique will come readily to the design team. The techniques employed need to be reviewed with the client to gain a sense of those that will be most appropriate in this situation.

Step 12. Select a Format for the Game
The purpose of this step is to determine an appropriate format for this particular client. The format (style) can be thought of as the physical environment and the processes through which the exercise will be presented to the participants.

There are many styles of presentation that may be used to present a complex model; the selection requires a melding of various techniques to accomplish the client's objective. The object is to try and find group process techniques that facilitate the communication objectives of the game. These exercises range from very volatile, fast-moving, emotional kinds of exercises, to very scientific, thoughtful man-machine interactive types. The object in each case is to develop a format that will be palatable to the people who will be participating and to create a format that is logically related to the problem at hand. The primary objective is to identify an analogy or a "model of a model" that can be used to improve communication among the participants during the actual use of the game. This is a critical element: the exercise must seem an acceptable environment to the stakeholders.

The selection of a format or style for the game is a creative process. Because designers use differing frames of reference, the framing of problem situations into a game format varies widely. Some common formats include role playing, board games (edge, grid, patterned), constraint cards, flowcharts, and computer simulations. Several client-specific variables influence game format; they should be examined for each situation. They will govern decisions about format and style of play as the exercise is developed: group size, purpose (goals and objectives), organizational context, time available for play, character of the participants (age, homogeneity, etc.), function of the exercise (policy decision, project evaluation, training, etc.), and substantive content.

The format can be thought of as the core of the model upon which the game will be built. The design team should wait until Step 12 to choose a format; this ensures that the team does not become overly committed to an idea before they have completed a thorough and rational research process. A review of existing formats is also helpful. The choice should further be based on personal preference, production constraints, and simplicity with respect to the objectives.

Step 13. Concept Report
The purpose of this step is to document design agreements that will govern the exercise, consolidate ideas into a workable blueprint and obtain client sign-off. No large-scale project should be undertaken without an agreed-upon plan. Just as an engineering team will formalize their blueprints before beginning construction, the policy exercise design team must capture their plans in a concept report. This ensures that they have communicated clearly with one another as well as with the client. Unless amended with the agreement of the client and the designer, the final game should conform to this document.

This report is a detailed statement that will guide the development of the exercise. As in the previous steps, the report is developed using an interactive process in which the client and the design team exchange ideas and negotiate a document that describes the nature of the desired product. After submission of the preliminary report to the client for critique and modification, the concept report becomes final. Any changes past this point require the joint approval (negotiation) of the client and the game design team as changes may have serious consequences in timing, cost, and/or effectiveness of the final product.

The concept report should describe the problem environment (schematic) and the proposed method of game presentation. It should address the initial specifications (e.g. characteristics of the participant group that would have a bearing on game design – age, level of sophistication, homogeneity, prior training, prior shared experiences required before being permitted to play the game; etc.). In addition to the synthesis described above, the concept report should outline the procedures for construction, including:

- Individual components, including their purpose;
- Data to be employed and its specific use;
- Order of sequence of any processing that will take place, (with or without a computer);
- Macro and micro cycles of play;
- Flowcharts of sufficient detail to adequately guide the building of individual components; and
- Detailed descriptions of each gaming element.

If the concept report is carefully prepared and reviewed, construction should be routine and uneventful; a thorough report will enhance the quality of the final game. The completion of the report can be thought of as the end of the planning/programming stage of the project. As with most planning efforts, the more energy given to this stage, the higher will be the quality of the resulting product and the more efficient will be the design process.

It is tempting to bypass the first three phases of game design (setting the stage, clarifying the problem, and the concept report) and to jump headlong into construction. Yielding to this approach will result in a failure to achieve precision of design, the careful engineering of the construct to meet a communication need, and almost certainly, a loss of parsimony in the construction activities themselves. There is a tendency for teams to begin in the middle of the design process and to avoid the hard work required in answering the questions that must be raised to complete the concept report. The difficulty is compounded by the element of risk inherent in making a written commitment that might later serve as an indictment of the team. The process of constructing a game inevitably forces the designer to confront these questions anyway, although in a less systematic way. Part of the art of good game construction lies in the ability to achieve a solution while juggling many variables; an orderly and sequential concept of game design will benefit the design team.

### 8.2.4 Phase IV – Developing the Exercise

After a concept report has been authorized, the team goes through three stages of design (building a prototype, technical evaluation and graphics design). The game elements must be fashioned appropriately, one by one. These initial modules must be fitted together and further developed during the rule-of-ten runs (see Step 14). The client should recognize that many different runs are required before the game itself is completely calibrated. Depending on the primary purpose of the game and the character of the system involved, there may never be a time when a final game exists. If an exercise is used in an ongoing context, there may be continuous modifications after an analysis of each game run in order to adjust the construct to meet the clients' needs. Metro/Apex (Duke, 1966), a game for training students to cope with urban systems (municipal budgeting, air pollution, etc.), is still in use at a number of universities after 35 years; users maintain a monthly newsletter to report on evolutionary changes (additional models that have been integrated, new technology, etc.).

### Step 14. Build, Test, and Modify the Prototype

The purpose of Step 14 is to construct an initial prototype that contains all gaming elements in rudimentary form. This trial and error method progresses logically, one game element at a time. The prototype evolves through ten test runs, each being progressively more rigorous. The "rule of ten" argues that a series of ten increasingly more precise rehearsals should be undertaken before the product is presented to the client. This requires about five test runs undertaken with staff (constructing and assembling the various components, and rough calibration) and a second set of about five runs with professional participants (final calibration). This iterative process ensures that the initial objectives are achieved; the procedure may be truncated, but this entails the risk of an immature product.

This initial prototype should be built quickly and with flexible materials to enable easy modification. In games of any complexity, there are numerous components that should be separately designed, constructed and assembled. These should contain rudimentary versions of each game element (scenario, events, roles, decisions, format, policies, rules, scoring, steps of play, model, data and information, accounting system, indicators, visuals, paraphernalia). These individual components should be created before attempting to assemble a prototype. All elements should be identified and any linkage with another game element should be described. A mockup of all elements at this stage will permit the designers to be more certain that the level of detail is appropriate and that it will provide the client with a preview of the final exercise.

The prototype should be carefully subjected to calibration before release to the client. If the game has much complexity, the final assembly and trials will reveal a variety of omissions, overlaps, inadequacies, trivia, redundancies and possible errors. Special attention should be addressed to the formulation of the final five test groups. The client may have a responsibility for participation during testing as spelled out in the specifications. Incremental changes in the construct reflect the learning obtained through these tests. Participant time can be squandered with immature products; this can result in the unnecessary aggravation of a captive audience. This phase requires that attention be directed to the original game objectives in order to maximize the final fit of the game.

Step 15. Technical Evaluation
The purpose of this step is to systematically compare project specifications and objectives with the proposed game structure using a technical matrix to ensure parsimony of design. A "game objectives/game elements matrix" is completed to cross check that the product under development conforms to the original specifications (as developed in Step 5). This matrix compares the carefully delineated objectives of the exercise on one axis against the gaming mechanisms employed on the other. The cells have language indicating how the specifics of the project have been met by one or more gaming elements. To the extent that a discrepancy exists, further refinement is required. This matrix not only ensures that objectives remain valid and are met by the product, it also assures that parsimony has served as the watchword and that no gimmicks remain in the exercise. The goals of the evaluation include checking on the generic criteria of validity, verisimilitude, playability, operability, and the specific objectives in terms of the five Cs (see Chapter 4) as well as the game content as described in the specifications. If a replicable, systematic process is used during construction, the rule-of-ten runs should establish validity.

Because the policy exercise approach is still in its infancy, clients have difficulty knowing what to expect from the final product and how to evaluate it when it is put into use. For this reason, it is important at the outset of a project to define the criteria that will later serve as the measure for the technical evaluation of the product. A set of descriptive criteria will help the clients and the participants understand the exercise. These would include the circumstances that induced the game, the availability of game kits, the character of the expected participants, the type of player involvement; the time required, the steps of play and plot outline, and the main dynamic of play.

Step 16. Graphic Design and Printing
The purpose of this step is to focus attention on the need to develop a professional presentation when transforming the prototype materials into a finished exercise. Graphic materials (visuals, paraphernalia, etc.) are used throughout the

entire process of developing a policy exercise. The schematic (Step 7), the Concept Report (Step 13) and the final prototype require finished materials of a professional quality (in contrast to the prototype materials that tend to be expedient). Three issues come into play when considering graphic design and printing.

First, these materials will be evolving throughout the process; several people will have a hand in developing the prototypes. This can result in a lack of visual coordination among the materials. Unless a clear policy is established, materials can be prematurely brought to a final graphic stage resulting in unnecessary cost and delays. No commitment should be made to final graphics/paraphernalia until Step 16. Another concern is that these materials might best be contracted out to another division of the organization or to an independent contractor; this may be the most efficient way to obtain materials of professional quality. There also may be a requirement of the client to ensure that company policy is met concerning logos, copyright, etc. Finally, time delay at this stage is common, particularly if the materials are contracted out. If Step 16 is acknowledged as part of the total process from the outset, an appropriate time allocation can be made and retained in the schedule. This is particularly true if some software product has to be written and debugged.

### 8.2.5 Phase V – Implementation

The purpose of Phase V is to ensure proper use of the exercise by the client. At this interface, the game leaves the designer's world and makes the transition to the client's world. The game is no longer the responsibility of the designer (except in those cases where responsibility for facilitation rests with the design team); however, the team should oversee this stage by means of participation and staff training until the client feels comfortable with the product. If the initial objectives are to be fully achieved, the exercise should become vested; that is, the stakeholders should view the product as legitimate, non-threatening (within reasonable limits), and of immediate pragmatic value.

The successful use of the game by the client is crucial. Steps 17 through 21 are designed to systematically guide the design team and the client through this final stage. A number of concerns should be addressed here, including integrating the game into the client's environment, facilitation, dissemination, ethical and legal concerns, and appropriate reports to the client. The design team should be present to the extent required and within the limits of the budget.

Step 17. Integrate the Game into the Client's Environment
The purpose of this step is to ensure the proper integration of the exercise by the client. The objective is to make the exercise "fit" into the client's environment. This requires that the client and the designer cooperate in anticipating the conditions under which the game will normally be used. This stage includes the

tasks necessary to transfer the game to the people responsible for its use, facilitation, and maintenance. Organizations facing crisis will be preoccupied; the game should fit readily into their environment if it is to be used effectively. This is achieved by completing any refinements to the game and providing appropriate training to members of the client organization.

When defining the Specifications for Design (Step 5), i.e. its objectives and characteristics, careful thought should be given to the context of use of the final product (see Section 4.7 on contingency and the strategic process). Most games will be of greatest value when used in a format integrated into some larger context (e.g. a seminar). Specifications should determine the conditions that govern game use. A number of questions should be addressed: Under what conditions will the game normally be used? What follow-up circumstances are anticipated? Will the same group run the same exercise repeatedly? What considerations (social, political, technical, etc.) are anticipated relative to its use?

Even when the game is primarily designed for a one-time use, the client will often want the final product to be maintained and facilitated by a specific division (e.g. strategic planning and training). The process of transferring the game should ensure that those responsible for the re-use of the product have: a knowledge of the nature of the theory behind the exercise; familiarity with the concept report; and intimate knowledge of the particulars as may be required to facilitate the exercise.

A cultural translation towards the end of testing and before the game is given to the client may be necessary to achieve a better fit within the client's corporate culture. Cultural translation refers to the adjustments required to fit the client's environment (e.g. the inclusion of company or industry-specific jargon, adopting corporate procedures, the application of a company logo and artwork, etc.). It may also mean the removal of political red flags or problem areas identified during testing. In cases where the client's language is other than English (or, as in many cases, the client intends to use the product in several countries), a language translation should be done in conjunction with the cultural translation.

Step 18. Facilitating the Exercise
The purpose of this step is to ensure that the client has access to proper facilitation skills for the exercise. A game of this kind is very demanding in several ways. Even if designed with care, a game requires a great deal of time commitment from participants as well as the cadre that facilitates it.

It is necessary at this point to distinguish between the designer and the facilitator (in some cases, one team serves both functions). During the final use of the game, the designer can no longer be held accountable; the game facilitator becomes largely responsible for its use. In many strategic implementation projects, the facilitators will not have been privy to the thought that went into the development of the concept report; as a consequence, the facilitators need to be familiar with this document before attempting to run the exercise. The specifications (Step 5) should have addressed the questions of facilitation (who will facilitate, what skills are needed, what training is required, and whether there are any debriefing considerations to be made mandatory for participant protection). In strategic projects, we strongly advise that the intended facilitators participate in the whole sequence of the design activities.

The facilitator assumes a considerable responsibility in undertaking a run of the game. He or she is responsible for the accurate completion of all accounts, communication exchanges and other interactions that occur. Facilitation also includes the activities required to ensure appropriate processing and evaluation. The process should ensure that participants are appropriately informed of content, structure, process, and the mechanics of the exercise. All the work that goes into an exercise of this type can be in vain if care is not taken to ensure that it is properly used. Facilitation is an art unto itself; but no matter how skilled a facilitation team may be, they should be provided with cogent materials to assist them in interpreting and using the exercise. The facilitator should use the exercise for the purposes and in the manner for which it was designed. A novice facilitator may resort to gimmickry to make the game more fun or to establish the game as more relevant to their particular ends. Arbitrary changes without full knowledge of their implications can do serious damage and may violate basic ethics of game use.

*The facilitator should let the game proceed with a minimum of intervention.* The various roles that have been established are part of a carefully coordinated system to permit an audience to address a problem. An overly strong facilitator, failing to understand the need to let communication occur spontaneously, can stifle interaction. The basic concept underlying the use of the game is to facilitate communication. Because the players are well informed, they do not need to be taught, but rather to confront each other and the issues in a productive and interactive style. Never attempt to defend the game as a predictive exercise or as a true replication of the world! It is neither. The game is to serve only one purpose – to prompt players to think about reality in new ways.

The participants need to be introduced to the role and function of the facilitator, with an emphasis on the point that a successful game run requires that procedures need to be followed. It can be damaging to engage in public disputes about particulars of the game and/or to let an ambitious player become too dominant. It is important to have one clearly defined central figure as the facilitator of the game whose word is beyond dispute. *The facilitator must be the boss!* This does not mean that the facilitator is not subject to challenge and interrogation by the players during the critiques and the final debriefing. Rather, it means that during the normal operation of a cycle, the players should submit to the instructions of the facilitator.

In addition to the facilitator and the roles embedded in the exercise, there are often other individuals present during the administration of the game; these might include role adviser(s), a bookkeeper, and/or other specialists. Generally, role advisors are used in games that are so complex that the start-up time would be prohibitive without them; they can assist players in learning both the function and the mechanics of the role. Subject matter specialists may be introduced at any time to aid the facilitator in transmitting factual information about the system.

No visitors should be permitted in the room during any part of the game. The presence of casual observers during the course of a game will be disruptive to the facilitator as well as the players. There is a tendency for observers to become enmeshed in the activities of the game, but in highly tangential and sporadic fashion. The result is that bona fide players, rather than being engaged in the primary dialogue that has been carefully established, are likely to find themselves in a secondary conversation. Casual observers may have neither an intense interest in gaming as a technique nor in the subject matter at hand, but simply a general interest in the proceedings; *they are a deterrent to good communication and should be excluded.* Casual observers in a game are invariably negative factors.

In some cases, scientific observers may be present to make observations of player behavior during the game relative to information processing, group dynamics, or other experimental activities. The presence of such observers raises ethical questions. Prior arrangements should be worked out that ensure no ethical codes are violated by the experiment or by the presence of the observer. If permitted in the game room, severe constraints should be imposed: absolutely no talking to the facilitator or any players, no interference with the activities, and a minimum of activity signifying their presence. Another type of legitimate observer may either be qualified on the basis of their interest in games or their interest in the subject matter; they can be included in the run of the game as assistants to the facilitator. These observers need specific tasks, materials and instructions that let them do their work without interfering with the game; communication with the facilitator or the players should be minimal.

Step 19. Dissemination
The purpose of this step is to deliver the policy exercise to the client and to ensure continued use of the exercise (if appropriate). The client's successful exploitation of the product (if intended) requires that the original specifications anticipate the dissemination method to be employed as well as how facilitator training will be achieved. The concept report should detail appropriate techniques to minimize

cost and complications. The non-commercial nature of policy games creates difficulty when preparing packages of the completed game for distribution; this is rarely a profit-making venture. Some designers have transformed a successful game into a product capable of commercial dissemination, and some publishing houses are making efforts to produce game kits. The task of reproduction and distribution of game paraphernalia is as important as that of training operators. There is both a strong ethical and professional need to reserve sufficient funds in the project budget to meet both functions.

A properly devised exercise can be quite revealing and can confront management with options not previously considered. As a result, the client may wish the exercise to be made available to a wider audience than originally specified. For example, the strategy game used in the Pharmaceutical case was transferred to the training division and used for internal courses. If the exercise is to be accessible, it should be transferred to a specific division to be properly maintained and facilitated. A basic information set should be made available to interested parties; this would include: title, date, client, designer, and description (content or subject matter); purpose (intended use); dynamics of play (participant, information, player involvement, time considerations); kit availability; and a basis for evaluating the exercise.

### Step 20. Ethical and Legal Concerns

When developing a policy exercise, it is necessary to protect the participants, the client, and the design team against both legal and ethical pitfalls; there is a serious ethical responsibility for the product, both in its design and non-manipulative use. The policy exercise should be a safe environment for learning. If ideas are to flow freely and new insights to be gained, old shibboleths should be vigorously challenged and participants must be protected from retaliation.

*Ethical Concerns*

The designer and the operator share responsibility for any ethical problems that emerge during the use of the game. Several of these concerns have been addressed in our description of the design steps, we re-emphasize a few here. The design team has an obligation to provide the client with a clear conceptual statement of the characteristics of the process and the product. A game should only be designed and conducted if this seems to be the best and most appropriate way to address the problem. Often, the designer will not be the facilitator; therefore, the designer has an obligation to provide the facilitator with information that will allow the game to be used intelligently. This requires an accurate portrayal of the game (concept report, literature accurately describing the game objective and particulars, instructions for a mandatory debriefing for player protection, evaluation form, etc.) as well as ensuring that all materials are fully operational. A policy exercise is not a sufficient substitute for reality to permit an employer to use it as the exclusive measure of evaluation of an employee's performance. This approach would be quite unfair, since people who perform very well in a real-world context (where personalities and the specifics of the situation are familiar) might behave differently in the game.

Inevitably, the policy exercise deals with sensitive issues within an organization. Because major policy issues will be involved, it is important that agreement be reached at the outset as to how sensitive materials will be handled. Procedures should be put into place permitting freedom of thought while providing adequate protection. All materials need to be treated with confidence; the process, and any products resulting from the process, are typically for internal use only. These internal reports are prepared for each aspect of the game; they should not be released without the express approval of the client. The benefit of these internal reports is that a written record is formulated as the game takes shape; they become invaluable when questions arise about the character of work undertaken.

Legal Concerns
If appropriate, it is important to consider the exploitation of a successful product as the specifications are developed. Legal precedent is probably adequate for any commercial versions that may be involved. Design specifications should address the issue of the ownership of the exercise (client, designer, or public domain), leasing arrangements, logo, patents, copyright, royalties, and the rules governing the retention, release or transmission of results. In the case of games that are essentially in the private domain, legal questions seem to be resolved by mimicking those procedures associated with the production of books and similar materials. Copyright, patent, trademark laws, and general procedures for royalties already employed for books can readily be transferred for use with games. Royalties and financial arrangements yield readily to standard convention.

Step 21. Reporting to the Client
The purpose of this step is to ensure proper closure for the project. The exercise is not complete until appropriate documentation of the results has been prepared reflecting the several stages of the design process and the results of subsequent use. As a minimum, there should be the original proposal (if contracted) or a prospectus (if in-house), a concept report and a final report to the client. An early agreement should be reached as to how these should be circulated (To whom will they be routed? How much time allowed for response? How to resolve differences that emerge?). In addition, the final product should be documented as appropriate; this may take the form of manuals for the game facilitator and participants, final graphics and artifacts, etc.

In many cases, a final "white paper" will need to be developed. This text should capture the results of the game for any reporting requirement that may exist. It is often useful to provide the participants with materials that summarize the happenings of the game. This document can also be circulated to the participants to confirm impressions derived during the exercise. Proper follow-up can serve as a further commitment of the participant to the process, by reinforcing the "message" from the experience. In some cases, a post-exercise evaluation may be required.

Games are notoriously hard to evaluate (Chapter 6 and the Appendix discuss evaluation in more detail). The criteria and methodology to measure the effectiveness of the exercise should be established in the concept report. The selection of an appropriate validity test is imperative; this should be done in accordance with the original goals, objectives, and specifications. Evaluation undertaken by a subject matter specialist who knows little about gaming as a disciplined activity may present a danger. When a formal evaluation of the exercise is undertaken, the initial specifications should determine whether the exercise will be measured against the judgment of experts in the context of use, the judgment of professional gamers and/or the reaction and evaluation of the participants.

Whatever method is chosen, after some experience with the final product, an evaluation is prepared. The goal is to develop a written description of the objectives of the exercise, the character of the product, the nature of the intended use, and a summary of the results of the game. This report must capture the main arguments, majority and minority opinion on these issues, and any agreements or decisions that may have been reached. If gaming/simulation is going to fulfill its promise, our profession should place a stronger emphasis on the need for improved evaluation methodologies (see Chapter 6). Failure to clearly define our methodology places the discipline at risk.

As stated before, a successful exercise often reveals opportunities not previously addressed (e.g. the client may find the product of potential value as a public relations tool). In many cases, it has been useful to devise extensions of the initial product to focus on particular situations and/or to be aimed at a particular subset of decision makers who are attempting to achieve change within the organization. Insofar as the client finds it helpful, it may be important in this phase to make presentations within the company to explain the policy exercise approach so that the results are fully understood beyond those who actually participated. In the case of the pharmaceutical company, the original version of the exercise was presented to the Board of Directors; a somewhat simplified version was run for middle management.

## 8.3 CONCLUSION

The design process for creating a policy exercise is well defined. The process consists of deriving a theory of real-world behavior, constructing a model to reflect this theory, and translating this model into a game. Each of the 21 steps will contribute to the accuracy and validity of the model relative to the system it is intended to represent. In the previous sections, we have tried to document the many advantages to the employment of this approach. First and foremost, the design team can communicate with each other efficiently throughout the process with no fear of becoming lost. In addition, the team can communicate effectively with the client from the outset – there is no need to hide behind a professional screen or to make magical giant leaps requiring the client to "have faith." There is no magic, just hard work. The process permits the client to become and to remain informed as a series of decisions are taken in an effort to represent their world in an effective decision model.

When used faithfully, the following benefits will derive from employing a deliberate process of game design:

- Validation of the initial decision by the client to proceed with a game;
- Clarity in the initial organization of the project;
- Protecting the client and the design team from misunderstandings;
- Defensible budgeting arrangements for resources: time, money, staffing;
- Efficient, step-by-step approach;
- Meeting all deadlines, built-in checkpoints to ensure staying on target;
- Efficient teamwork, no getting lost;
- Retaining the client's understanding and confidence as the process unfolds;
- The effective clarification of the client's needs;
- Ease of communicating with the client;
- Efficiency, cost savings, etc.;
- Effective structuring of the problem;
- Development of a prototype exercise;
- Testing and modification of the prototype;
- Timely delivery to the client; and certainly not least,
- Establishing the validity of the evaluation process of the final product.

When using this design process, it is important to have reasonable objectives and adhere closely to them; it is also important to use teamwork effectively. Remember that games serve well as devices for communication, so it is incumbent upon the designer to identify who is trying to communicate with whom, and quite specifically, about what specific substantive content. Finally, games are situation specific – if a game is well designed for a specific client, it should not be expected to perform well in a different environment.

# Section V

## Conclusions

**INTRODUCTION TO SECTION V**

This book has been written with two goals in mind. The first was to contribute to the further development and dissemination of gaming/simulation as a method of strategic problem solving. The second was to improve communication between this discipline and related policy and organizational disciplines.

As an epilogue, the last chapter of this book tries to restate in a condensed form the main insights we have acquired during the process of working towards these goals. We have called this review "The Potential of the Policy Exercise." We are confident that the reader will agree that we have succeeded in showing that policy gaming has proven its power and that it holds even more promise for the future.

# Chapter 9
## *The Potential of the Policy Exercise*

### 9.1 THE EMERGENCE OF POLICY EXERCISES

Games are as old as humankind. They are used for different reasons – to entertain, to educate and, in some instances, to find a solution to a policy problem. They provide a planned, safe environment where participants temporarily remove themselves from reality. Within the artificial reality of the game, it becomes possible to deal with problems such as uncertainty and risk in a playful, relaxed and functionally focused way. Perspectives can be taken which are not possible in a serious day-to-day setting. Historically, gaming was a tool of the military that was adopted by business schools and the applied social sciences. In the past three decades, the technique has been employed with growing success in non-military strategic policy making. The potential of these applications is far from exhausted; the most exciting developments still lie ahead.

As a form of applied science, the concept of the policy exercise did not come out of the blue. It evolved from techniques widely referred to in the literature as gaming, operational gaming, gaming/simulation, simulation, and decision exercises. Evidence of the presence of these techniques dates back to the 1800s in their use by military strategists to develop mental discipline; other games of strategy date from a much earlier time. Recent uses of the discipline have extended far beyond their original military purpose and far deeper than their role as a social pastime; indeed, gaming is now common practice in the social sciences, public policy, business, management science, and a host of other disciplines.

### 9.2 MACRO-PROBLEMS AND STRATEGIC MANAGEMENT

Large organizations are now using policy exercises for strategic management purposes to elicit a shared vision of the unique and confusing challenges we have called macro-problems. This book concentrated on these latter applications. In Chapters 1 and 2, we described and analyzed the macro-problems that organizations confront. The causes of the underlying problems are varied; exogenous influences are usually important causal factors. However, organizations also often contribute to the negative impact of these situations through a variety of reasons, including:

- Management may lack an adequate, shared perception of the problem; this results in decisions being taken predicated on tunnel vision;

- Whatever organizational structure may be in place, the pressure of a macro-problem is often coincident with the emergence of a value dilemma, a lack of mutual trust, avoidance of productive discussion and/or open conflict;

- Macro-problems tend to create urgent situations that demand attention *now*; as a consequence, managers tend to respond to short-term considerations. Some fear the consequences of their actions and lack commitment to the decisions taken; others display hubris, resulting in an escalation of commitment to disastrous policies;

- Hundreds (sometimes thousands) of variables are in play in a given macro-problem; this is bewildering to even the most dedicated management team. In these situations, they may postpone a decision and be forced to act when confronted by a crisis; and

- The reasons cited above contribute to another problem – the failure to consider enough alternatives and/or create adequate novel strategies; as a consequence, sub-optimal decisions are taken.

Unable to attend to all the factors and their interrelationships over time, individual managers and other stakeholders focus on the few aspects that appear to be the most influential or hit the closest to home. However, by selecting a limited set of variables, each individual is also establishing a unique conceptualization of the situation, leading to different perspectives on the formulation of effective strategies. Personal values and human cognitive limitations generate different interpretations of the same situation. Other factors that contribute to variations in individual perspectives include perceptual and cognitive biases, personality, individual competence, and organizational or social roles.

Macro-problems typically involve implicit or explicit disagreement about actual or potential strategies, reflecting competing views on the nature of the decision environment. The issue is usually partially the result of prior disputes internal to the organization or in conflicts concerning the definition, classification, and evaluation of a problem at the interface of the organization and its environment. Individuals with different professional, cultural, and divisional backgrounds are likely to view a strategic situation differently, reflecting their own values, interests and perspective on how the world operates. These internal differences are another source of dispute that is as much of a problem as are issues originating as clashes between the organization and its environment; both have the potential for igniting brush fires with similar results.

In earlier chapters, we documented these and other characteristics of the intellectual, political and cultural crises that macro-problems create. The difficulties organizations experience in dealing with these challenges can be thought of as a single underlying problem best described as a lack of synthesis of the knowledge and aspirations of the individual members of the organization. In turn, this is the result of the lack of any reasonable communication format to address these situations.

The multi-dimensionality of these "messy" macro-problems demands hybrid strategic processes which, in accordance with Ashby's law of requisite variety, can do justice to the unique and seemingly chaotic constellations of factors and forces. We have summarized the demands on such a process with the five Cs: *complexity, communication, creativity, consensus* and *commitment to action*. These process criteria are recognized by many experienced strategists and in leading publications on strategic management. However, they are very hard to make operational in one and the same process.

Traditional management methods need to be integrated and supplemented in situations that have macro-problem characteristics. The new approach must be faster, employ a team, be reasonable in cost, be flexible, and be capable of assimilating a very large number of variables that derive from both exogenous and endogenous environments. Policy gaming is such an approach. We characterize it as scoring high on a "scale of strategic power." By this we mean the ability of a decision aid or process technique to put the five Cs into operation in a fast and efficient process. The policy exercise employed must be precisely responsive (in terms of the five Cs) to the uniqueness of the macro-problem.

## 9.3 POLICY EXERCISES AND THE FIVE CS
This book has shown that the extremely complex strategic issues we call macro-problems can be clarified through the use of carefully constructed policy exercises. This process of policy gaming helps decision makers as they attempt to creatively find a way through the "terra incognita" of the macro-problem they confront.

Gaming is not only strategic thinking, but also strategic action. The property of games to remove the participants temporarily from daily routines is very helpful in keeping them focused on a strategic issue. Participants are sheltered from political pressures and from the stifling effects of etiquette and protocol found in real-life situations. The interactive situation and "virtual reality" created by the game can quickly convey enduring structural information. In that sense, a game is a communication mode that is capable of linking tacit knowledge to formal knowledge by provoking action and stimulating experience.

Policy gaming, as described above, shows that there is no essential difference between learning and problem solving. As a consequence, when confronting uncertainty, an experiential learning process can be very powerful, especially when it can be combined with a scientific (systems analytical) approach. The process presented here of designing policy exercises as dynamic, open models of a problem situation incorporates features from both learning theory and general systems theory. Problem solving requires creative experimentation. Policy gaming is a realistic but sheltered experimentation within the system of complexities in which the problematic situation is embedded.

The power of games is that they organize and convey a holistic perspective on a given problem in a format that allows the direct translation of these holistic insights into orchestrated strategic action. At the same time, games help to develop new knowledge because they allow participants to experiment with behavior and strategies never tested before. For the most complicated strategic macroproblems, policy exercises translate existing knowledge into action and potential action into knowledge. It is this determining property of the kind of gaming described in this book that makes it a major tool to assist policy makers in coping with the increasingly complex problems that confront organizations and societies today.

Within the context of a game, one develops a highly organized jargon or special language that permits the various participants to talk to each other with greater clarity than they might through traditional communication modes. At the beginning of the last century, ships at sea still communicated brief messages to their land base via carrier pigeon. Carrier pigeons are no longer used; rather, computers, radios, and satellites keep a continuous surveillance of all ships. As the communication forms of a previous era (e.g. telegrams), have given way to improved forms over the past century, it is inevitable that still more sophisticated forms must evolve. Both role-playing and expert panel games can facilitate effective communication within diverse groups (multilogue as opposed to dialogue), encouraging consensus building and bridging communication gaps

Another feature of the gaming approach is the conflict resolution and consensus seeking that is facilitated by the multilogue communication process (Chapter 5). The game works as a vehicle for transmitting and clarifying the various perspectives and interests among the participants. Through their participation in the game, the stakeholders have an opportunity to present their perspectives and encounter others of which they were unaware. During the joint experimental action in the game, value debates become focused, sharpened and placed into operation in such a way that value tradeoffs can be negotiated. This increases the chance that the views of many different stakeholders will be considered in the formulation of a strategy and that these stakeholders will understand the rationale behind the strategy that finally emerges. This communication of perspectives and the establishment of a value tradeoff is desirable to eventually secure consensus and thus acceptance of and commitment to the emergent strategy.

As they move collaboratively through the game adventure and towards the assessment of possible impacts of major decision alternatives, the participants become involved, reassured and motivated. However, in a positive sense, the game is, at the same time, a startling and demystifying experience. The process of objectification that takes place in a game helps to reinforce memory, stimulate doubt, raise the right issues (disagreement forces further discussion), and control the delegation of judgment (those who are affected can check the logic of action). This "virtual look into the future" also helps to explore the unfortunate situations and conditions in which an elected strategy got off track and/or became a fiasco. All this fosters the power of these "exercises in explicitness" to prevent escalation of commitment. The exercise places the potential of failure on the policy agenda and that makes it much easier to redirect a failing strategy in the future. Games serve as vehicles to develop realistic, mature, and well-grounded commitment.

In summary, the policy exercise is a versatile method for dealing with complex and ambiguous issues; it has established itself both theoretically and practically as a valid means of portraying complex realities and of communicating coherent overviews of those realities. The technique conveys sophisticated information with novel perceptions of the interrelationships involved. In a pragmatic sense, the power of this approach derives from several underlying concepts (defined above). When carefully integrated in an exercise designed for serious purpose, gaming techniques:

- Are relatively quick and inexpensive (compared to the limited number of alternative methods available);
- Are palatable and somewhat seductive; this derives from the well-documented fact we humans are "game playing animals" (Huizinga, 1955);
- Permit the creation of a safe environment for learning where risky notions can be explored under controlled conditions; and
- Induce the suspension of disbelief among participants that is required if new ideas are to be given a fair hearing.

### 9.4 POLICY GAMING AS A STRATEGY PROCESS

Policy gaming is more than attending a policy game. In our view, policy gaming is an integral participative strategy process. Its architecture has been described in Chapters 7 and 8; there are five broad phases in which 21 specific steps are followed. The actual run of the policy game is only one, albeit important and highly visible, step in this collective process of inquiry and communication.

The gaming process is an interactive and sequential process to help sharpen the problem statement and the specific objectives to be achieved. The 21 steps guide the client organization through a series of collective inquiries and communication activities producing interim results that help the organization to arrive at a holistic understanding of a complex problem. As understanding improves, more detail is added and the developed exercise becomes a professional seminar with a playful and involving character. It also has an effective and efficient content and format.

Previous chapters have shown the conceptual roots of this methodology. Like any innovation, the process architecture of policy gaming is a hybrid, a new combination of techniques. It combines, functionally, ideas and tools from a wide variety of relevant disciplines, such as systems theory and modeling, learning theory, strategy theory, participative management, communication theory, group dynamics, organizational behavior and project management. We have used several analogies and comparisons to explain how the different steps in the process form an integral and consistent whole. For example, we have referred to interactive modeling, participatory policy analysis, and multi-loop learning. All these references help us to explain our choice for the step-wise, cyclical and interactive format of the process of policy gaming described here. Concepts like "cognitive map" and "knowledge household" have been introduced to convey the ability of policy gaming to accommodate an enormously wide variety of substantive inputs. In modern academic terms: our approach supports the pleas for a constructivist and discursive approach to strategic management.

The eight cases presented and analyzed in Chapters 3 show the 21 steps in action. Some of the insights about this process are summarized below.

The process guarantees on-time delivery of tailor-made products under severe time pressure. The process realizes ideals and demands of good project management under the very difficult conditions which macro-problems create for clients and supporting professionals. The value of this feature of the process cannot be underrated – the kind of problems described in this book inevitably cause chaos and confusion.

The process facilitates contingency. In each of the eight cases, a different gaming approach was needed and created. For that purpose, the method has several provisions and tools that help to explore, frame and analyze a problem from the perspective of the five Cs. Parallel to the substantive analysis of the problem, the approach helps to establish what the necessary contribution of the gaming process should be. A unique profile of process ideas emerges that is summarized in the specifications for design and tested in several other steps.

Each of the five Cs has several anchor points in each of the phases of the gaming process. The resulting impact on the five criteria is reached step by step when progressing through the gaming project. For example, the mastering of complexity is made possible by provisions in almost every step of the process. Commitment is definitely not only the result of participation in the game but also the product of many different involving and motivating elements in the chain of events. Similar observations hold for communication, consensus and creativity. We consider this cumulative, progressive character of the process one of the important factors explaining the success of the projects described.

An effective overall strategy is critical to the organization's successful day-to-day operations. This point was made by Peter Drucker when he suggested that it is more important to "do the right things than to do things right." Moreover, strategic decisions on macro-problems are synonymous with high stakes because many of these decisions require large commitments of capital over long periods of time. Incremental decision making and allocation of resources may not be an option. The combination of internal and external constraints may force the organization into high-risk decisions that would normally be avoided. The risk is especially great when high stakes are combined with a high level of uncertainty about the outcomes of a strategy; this is frequently the case when the decision is made in a turbulent environment and lacks precedent within the organization.

It is often true that one individual has the final authority to set policy for an organization; however, that person is usually well advised to seek the counsel of close associates. This book attempts to document the evolution of a new and powerful process architecture designed to assist those groups who are responsible for collaborating on the creation of policy for their organization. In Chapter 4, we have shown how empirical research supports the idea that, for certain turbulent environments, an interactive form of strategy making is the most desirable. Research also suggests that the internalization of such a form of strategy making is a strategic (i.e. competitive) competence for an organization, especially when combined with the skill to alternate between process styles.

An increasingly complex world has required that professionals concerned with strategic management develop and disseminate generic interactive techniques that can be quickly applied in a disciplined, professional manner to assist top management in orienting itself to rapidly changing situations. Policy exercises are most often used in exceptional situations to engage busy managers, support staff and experts to confront and negotiate issues, and to elicit a shared vision or plan for the organization in those situations where precedent is of little value. It seems worthwhile for an organization that has once used this process with satisfaction to install the skills and procedures to make policy gaming a lasting part of its strategic repertoire.

In Chapter 5, we have conceptualized gaming/simulation as a hybrid communication form, as a language for complexity. Mastering this language is an important strategic skill for organizations. One could also call it essential to modern society because of the complex nature of policy issues, both public and private. It is essential that these multi-dimensional issues be addressed in their totality as a gestalt phenomenon. Serious games have evolved as a form of human communication centering on situations that are symbolically represented in a relatively safe context. As its point of departure, gaming takes the view that man is a grammatical being (Campbell, 1982). Thus, gaming is instrumental in extracting the dynamics of communication and inter-subjectivity, and hence helps to reveal and capture the essence of thought and behavior as it is exhibited in complex situations.

As with every language in its infancy, the structure (grammar) of the policy exercise has not yet been rationalized (most people who use a language do so without an explicit understanding of the inherent rules of that language). The technique of gaming/simulation urgently needs thoughtful attention to this structure. However, even in its current stage of development, the technique provides leadership with a realistic method to integrate a diversity of skills and understandings; when effectively internalized by an organization, it serves as an ongoing forum for inventing the future.

Properly designed games can be viewed as abstract symbolic maps of various multi-dimensional phenomena. As such, they serve as basic reference systems to assist in the formulation of inquiry from a variety of perspectives. If these constructs are properly elaborated, they can represent not only a present reality but also alternative futures. In this era of data overload, there is an urgent need for the acquisition of heuristics, a flexible set of highly abstract conceptual tools which will let those responsible for the strategy of their organization view new and emerging situations in a way that permits comprehension and in-depth discussion with others.

Rephrasing Drucker's famous expression will make clear how we position this strategy process we call gaming. It is true that it is most important to "do the right things." But it is not easy to find out what they are. Our book strongly supports the claim that, when confronted with macro-problems, policy gaming is the right way to discover "the right things to do."

### 9.5 THE DISCIPLINE OF GAMING/SIMULATION

The two goals that motivated us to write this book (to contribute to the development and dissemination of gaming/simulation as a method of strategic problem solving and to improve communication between this discipline and related policy and organizational fields) have much to do with our personal conviction developed during our professional careers. An important and realistic task remains to be done: gaming/simulation must be further developed as an applied scientific inter-disciplinary field.

We believe that this book is one illustration of the fact that gaming/simulation has its own body of knowledge, its own research tradition, its own professional practice and its own forum and that it learns from systematic reflection on its professional practice. And, of course, we also hope that the future might show that this book has become a well-appreciated link in the chain of progress in the discipline. We are optimistic about the future of gaming/simulation, but we also think there is much to be done. One important task is to better understand, internalize and communicate what the discipline of gaming/simulation really is.

A well-established discipline, especially if it positions itself on the more applied end of the theory-practice continuum, will develop a permanent interaction and dialogue between application and research. Both activities are relevant forms of knowledge acquisition and both help to develop the principles and theorems of a discipline. For such an interactive progression to work, one needs a professional culture of openness and critique and an environment that brings together the professionals and academics in the field.

Gaming/simulation is an inter-discipline because it develops in part through the internalization of knowledge from other disciplines. The 21 design steps, for example, put into operation insights from several academic disciplines. However, from the point of view of professional application, each individual gaming project is always a multi-disciplinary effort. As the cases in Chapter 3 show, each project needed substance that had to be drawn from many sources usually including several academic disciplines. In this sense, the interdisciplinary process know-how of gaming/simulation functions as a "supporting science" to organize and realize major multi-disciplinary applied studies – in our case to support strategy and policy. Framing the nature of our work in this way has many consequences, particularly with respect to the professional attitudes and skills of the individual gamer.

For example, professional gamers need to have a very open mind and a broad, albeit not necessarily deep, overview of many different fields of science. They also have to be able to work productively together with many different and highly specialized individuals. Their cognitive skills have to be in lateral and integrative thinking, their social skills have to make them team players and coaches, and their aspirations have to stimulate them to serve and facilitate.

An analogy that uses the evolution of statistics would be useful here. Statistics is very much an art and a science (as is gaming). There are a variety of methodological issues, approaches and techniques within the discipline of statistics; but, overall, statistics is used to serve other disciplines (forecasting, model building, etc.). Statistics is clearly defined and, as a consequence, it is very much an acknowledged and respected discipline; however, the discipline had to struggle to overcome the impression of being "just a technique." Practitioners of gaming/simulation would do well to reflect on the difficulties encountered by the successful discipline of statistics.

Clarity and communication about this conception of gaming/simulation as a "supporting inter-discipline" might take away part of the confusion about the various phenomena called games. The most central cause of the confusion is that games are typically viewed from the perspective of a particular substantive discipline; they are seen as a tool being utilized by a professional whose primary interest lies with content, not technique. This confusion is an obstacle to the evolution of the gaming discipline; authors continue to define terms and concepts from their own disciplinary perspective and against the backdrop of the unique substantive needs of the moment.

This is especially true when thinking about the demarcation between gaming/simulation and the different disciplines that study policy and organization. For example, social psychology with its successful studies in group dynamics contributed a great deal to the body of knowledge that is incorporated in the gaming processes described above. On the other hand, social psychologists are very active users of games, both for their research environments to study social behavior and in their professional practice, e.g. in role play and social drama. And again, social psychologists are also often consulted during the systems analytical phases of game design to give their professional inputs for the diagnosis of the strategic situation of the client organization.

Gaming is a relatively new profession that has grown in a topsy-turvy fashion; opportunities to use gaming products have come rapidly. It must be acknowledged that, as professionals, gamers have been slow to become attentive to the need to establish a well-grounded foundation through which their products and processes can reasonably be evaluated. Designers tend to believe (with passion) in the efficacy of gaming that is predicated on an internalized model of validity of the games. Unfortunately, neither the gamers nor their clients have consistently demanded rigorous evaluation (as Chapter 6 has documented).

Problems within the gaming discipline are certainly compounded because gaming professionals are scattered around the world and, as a consequence, communication is limited and intermittent. Clients present subject matter that is extremely diverse; this results in products that are quite dissimilar in their characteristics. Few gamers have had formal training in this area; they have academic degrees in a wide array of fields. Specialized academic nuclei in the gaming discipline are limited to a very few. On the other hand, there are several professional organizations that we have mentioned (ISAGA, ABSEL, NASAGA and SAGSET). The professional journal *Simulation & Gaming* is now 34 years old and, in our opinion, better than ever.

However, if the gaming profession is to achieve its goals, gaming professionals must intensify their efforts to communicate the above concepts about the nature of gaming/simulation to our contemporaries, clients, and fellow professionals. We hope this book contributes to improved communication along the interface between gaming and policy making.

## 9.6 CONCLUSION

"Today's generation has to solve, in real time, situations for which there is no precedent. These situations cover a wide spectrum of problems. They all have characteristics of complexity, a future's orientation, the lack of a clear paradigm for action, the need for a dynamic communication process within and beyond the affected organization, and finally, the need to transmit a clear image beyond the organization of any policy decision that may be taken" (Duke, 1987, p. 6).

The management of macro-problems is like a fourth-dimensional problem we three-dimensional beings cannot comprehend. We are unable personally to encounter these complicated and chaotic phenomena, and therefore also unable to communicate with one another, even at elite levels, about possible management schemes to solve some of the "messy" problems of today. We need to relax the constraints on our communication. This means moving to the gestalt end of the communications continuum. Here, through the proper use of gaming/simulation, we find very strong promise for re-establishing the comprehension of totality that is necessary for the intelligent management of any complex system.

This is especially true with certain public policy issues. For example, how shall society, in its search for more peace, freedom and justice, deal with the new terrorist threat? Serious questions must be addressed for which we have no functional precedent, yet society is pushed relentlessly into action. There are also many private sector concerns (e.g. how shall private industry adjust its functioning to accommodate to the reality of a global economy?). Gaming/simulation has proven successful in meeting similar needs.

Dramatic and fundamental changes in society over the past century are permanent, irreversible, and profound. These changes require humankind to alter its languages to permit thoughtful and rapid speculation about a many-faceted future, and to permit policy makers to venture decisions for which there is no precedent. The complexity of these issues points out the urgent need for conveying holistic thought. In particular, the elaboration of the concept of systems, the dramatic improvements in computers, and the rapid evolution of related technologies have generated information networks beyond ready human comprehension.

Recent trends indicate that a new growth period for gaming is about to begin. A world growing in complexity combined with the development of a discipline of gaming/simulation and the information and communication revolution may indicate a renaissance. The base of knowledge and experience from the last 30 years provides a good foundation for further development of policy gaming into a direction that most probably will surprise even the current specialists. The modern high-tech entertainment games with their virtual reality and their worldwide (internet) participation and dialogue suggest one of the sources from which the new generation of tools for the "language of complexity" might emerge.

As we suggested before, we are not Orwellians who believe in or aspire to a surprise-free future. It is a technocratic illusion to think that any process or technique will provide a policy maker the mythical crystal ball. Preparing for the future is a managerial responsibility, knowing the future is not. We wanted to bring across that there are better ways of taking on that responsibility. *Decision quality* is an ethical category. It refers to the situation in which those who had to take a dramatic decision and those who assisted, can without doubt and remorse say:

> "We took the best decision we possibly could *and* we did everything in our power to prepare for its successful implementation."

Gaming/simulation techniques hold considerable promise for improving decision quality. They have the ability to abstract phenomena to humanly meaningful terms, to facilitate the internalization of a model of a complex system, and to enable the player to operate in a dynamic environment which requires periodic decisions, the results of which are emphasized through various feedback techniques. Policy gaming is an appropriate process for dealing with the increasing complexity of policy environments and the problems of communication within these environments. Designed for organizations facing crisis, the technique provides a multiple-perspective, small-group problem-solving and decision making approach for organizational strategic management.

# Supplemental Hints

## *Steps of Design*

These notes are intended to serve as Supplemental Hints for Chapter 8 – Designing the Policy Exercise. Tips are presented for Steps 6, 7, 13, 14, 15, 16, and 18.

**Step 6.** Defining the System – Hints on Using Snow Cards
"Snow cards" are an effective device for organizing complexity and allowing its abstraction to a level that facilitates game design. They are used as the first step in the process of building a schematic. An extensive list of issues relevant to the problem and its environment is generated; each issue is recorded as a brief statement on a separate "snow card" (small slip of stiff paper, typically 2"x 3"). These snow cards are generated through a review of documents, discussions with significant professionals, and group brainstorming sessions; all respondents have a vested interest in the particular problem. During these sessions, the participants discuss the problem and record ideas perceived to be important. The snow cards should reflect all aspects of the problem and its environment considered significant by any respondent.

The project plan should give careful attention to the question of "who should be involved in the project and for what reason?" The client and project team should agree in advance on who can and should be approached as informants during this phase of the systems analysis. As stated in Chapter 2, we usually employ a "top-down" and "bottom-up" process to optimize both the interactive and the systemic character of this modeling phase. The top-down team looks for (partial) theories, models, generalizations, etc. to help in structuring the problem. The bottom-up approach is more constructivist. It starts by collecting and then comparing and linking the perceptions of the persons involved. Usually this is done via "narrative" interviewing; however, group discussions also prove very useful here. The snow carding technique can be applied both in the top-down and the bottom-up process.

When interviewing people, there are three "rules":

1. Select With Care – Seek those who have a stake in the argument and/or are equipped with power to act. This may be the CEO, vice presidents, department heads, external stakeholders, etc. Those with expert knowledge are useful – but they may obfuscate with detail (remember, you are after the "big picture"). Additional snow cards may be generated from interviews with key people in the field (outside the organization). Don't question respondents in a formal way; rather, prompt them to talk about the problem/system from their own perspective. The ideas that come most readily to their minds tend to be quite important. Use snow cards and capture just enough words to permit the later reconstruction of the conversation. For prompts, use ideas and concerns that others have raised as well as any other logical concerns. Try to get them to address (in no particular order; let them ramble) people, places, relationships, economics, science, problems, events, policy, alternatives, etc.

2. Believe What They Say – You are not there to judge, correct, challenge, admonish, instruct, or criticize. "Believe" everything they say, and capture it in the spirit of what they present - don't distort their response with pre-conceived notions of your own. The reality check comes later (when the schematic is developed and reviewed by the client). This follow-up schematic review process has inherent confrontation; it will not only reveal distortions of individual perception, it will also prompt "aha" moments of new discovery.

3. Have Respondents Jot Down Ideas – often, they will write down thoughts that they do not express orally (they may have a deep concern but are reluctant to express it out loud). This is most likely to occur during an interview with two or more people present (it is best to limit the number of participants during these interviews).

Following the interviews, a snow card session is held with the design staff and client representatives present. To be successful, facilitators of the process have to stimulate new ways of thinking. They must ensure that all participants follow a set of rules:

- Criticism of the notions advanced by others is prohibited, because such criticism may hinder innovative thinking. The objective is to foster the attitude that "anything that you feel is important must be recorded;" minority views are encouraged and dominance by strong personalities is to be minimized.

- Imagination should be turned loose, encouraging participants to suggest any idea or concern that comes to mind. "Wild Cards" are encouraged, because many times such a proposal may bring out an exogenous concern and/or an innovative idea.

- Participants should assume differing, carefully constructed perspectives from which to view the problem. Role playing can be used at this stage to ensure that the problem is viewed from many facets.

- In addition to contributing ideas of their own, participants should seek to improve and integrate previously generated ideas.

All matters raised during these activities must be recorded as snow cards. Color-coding (of the cards) may be used to identify the various "roles" being used; how-ever, the donors remain anonymous. A snow card should survive the culling process based on its content, not because of the identification with the person who generated it.

Once the snow cards are generated, they have to be given an initial rough sorting and classification by the design team. During this process, the snow cards are placed under some general headings and sub-headings; these emerge naturally and may change, but select those that seem logical at the moment. Information from the top-down approach will be useful here (Chapter 2). This process of sort-ing and re-sorting should continue until a satisfying structure begins to emerge (all duplicates should be thrown away). A draft is repeatedly presented to inter-ested respondents to gain consensus.

**Step 7.** Displaying the System – Hints on Building a Schematic
The model of the system being gamed is represented by the schematic. It will be used to structure player decisions and interactions. The schematic governs the construction of the game. The system should be clearly presented in text and graphics that can be reviewed before design activities begin; it is also useful to make this available to the participants in the final exercise.

Step 6. (Defining the System – Hints on Using Snow Cards) typically results in a large number of cards (several hundred to a thousand). Not all of these ele-ments have to be taken into consideration in order for the schematic to be an appropriate presentation of the problem. The following categories are common-ly used in building a schematic; they can be used separately or in logical combi-nation. They are not necessarily independent and/or mutually exclusive:

- actions
- aspects
- concerns
- events
- goals
- needs
- problems
- solutions
- trends

- activities
- characteristics
- decision makers
- forces
- information
- objectives
- questions
- strategies
- resources

- alternatives
- components
- decisions
- future considerations
- issues
- plans
- roles or actors
- themes
- etc.

These cards are converted into an inclusive but rough schematic of the problem environment that must convey all the concerns expressed by the snow cards. This is a critical part of the process – if the boundaries are too tightly defined, significant alternatives may be ignored.

On some appropriate space, preferably a large table or a wall with a tack board surface, the clusters of descriptors are arranged in temporary fashion, group by group, as seems appropriate. In the initial stages, the clusters will be quite small, consisting of only three to five descriptors that are logically related. As the process continues, the clusters will become increasingly large. In this phase, the display area is organized conceptually as a graphic that represents a totality into which all of the clusters must logically be inserted. This inherently forces the squeezing of some ideas into lesser significance and the inevitable discovery of gaps (a significant category with too little detail).

As individual clusters are formed into larger groupings, arguments will develop about the appropriateness of a given descriptor set. These concerns are addressed through discussions that result in clarification of the organization's worldview. The process described is iterative, and should continue until the group performing the task is satisfied that the drawing is an accurate reflection of their perception of the reality being abstracted. Throughout the entire process, new content is generated to fill in gaps that may be recognized by the design team. Inevitably, the final drawing will be a complex rendition of the relationships of several hundred variables that are of interest to one or another stakeholder. Each stakeholder must be able to locate the world as they view it within the final schematic. For an example, see Figure A-1, City Budget Schematic; prepared by Prof. Tsuchiya of the Chiba Institute of Technology, Chiba, Japan. In this figure, it is easy to recognize the results of both the top-down and bottom-up systems analysis. Each word or symbol in the text refers to one or a group of snow cards. This schematic has gone through several iterations and reviews before being "frozen" in a graphic design.

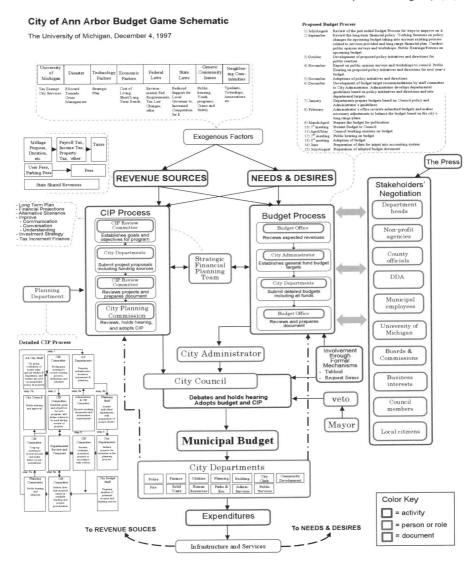

**FIGURE A-1 CITY BUDGET SCHEMATIC**

The following hints will help the designer build a schematic with a logical organizational structure and an appropriate visual appearance:

- Identify relationships among the elements of the problem and its environment, such as interactions, hierarchical structure, linkages, physical layout, influences, feedback, etc.

- Identify flows between the elements of the problem and its environment, such as decisions flows, resource flow, flow of activities, information flow, time, inputs/outputs, etc.

- Identify processes taking place within the problem environment such as project planning cycles, budget periods, research activities, design sequences, production process, development life cycles, analysis, planning, research, problem solving, sales, manufacturing, decision making, marketing, design, evaluation, etc.

The graphic artist preparing the schematic should:

- Emphasize the major groups of elements so that the structure is easy to recognize;
- Make the logic of a schematic visible by emphasizing major flow processes;
- Use as few different graphic elements as possible;
- Use the same sizes and styles for elements of the same significance;
- Elements of the same process or flow should employ the same technique;
- Avoid overcrowding of elements;
- Text should be written in fonts (type, size, style) that are easy to read;
- Select line types and widths that consistently reflect the desired emphasis;
- Avoid too many different styles and widths of lines;
- Avoid cross-over lines as much as possible; and
- Use shading of boxes only if the emphasis cannot be achieved otherwise.

**Step 13.** Concept Report
The concept report will define all the elements constituting the exercise. If proper care is taken in the development of this document, construction can be a highly organized and efficient process employing standard project management practice. If construction is undertaken *without* a complete and approved report, at least marginal chaos is to be expected. The larger the game, the more intricate the project management scheme must be. There should be a clear hierarchy with proper procedures for resolving differences of opinion. A routine passing of decisions before a technical review group is good policy, and the preparation of internal reports for working purposes is useful. The administrative structure should be established at the earliest point, with responsibility for personnel, budget, general administration, and subject content resolved as early as possible.

Personnel selection may prove difficult because there are few people with extensive experience in gaming/simulation. Therefore, consideration should be given to subcontracting the various tasks. Especially for the resolution of difficult problems, such as those dealing with basic theory or the definition of the schematic, consideration should be given to hiring a consultant.

Budget may be a major consideration. Attention should be given to the date of availability of funds, the duration over which the funds are available, possibilities of extension if delays are encountered, and possibilities of additional funding if problems are encountered. Even in relatively small projects, it is an excellent idea to have a simple budget accounting system that lists all possible expenditures. A listing of initial allocations as approved by the funding agency, monthly expenditures, encumbrances, and balance remaining may prove useful. The size and nature of the project will govern the extent of the system, but some techniques may help to avoid a crisis of exhausted funds before the project is completed.

There will seldom be enough money to build a game with quite the luxury desired. For this reason, it is important to establish a resource allocation system at the outset and to make periodic checks to see that the scheme is not being violated. The basic scheme is to have a schedule of specific tasks (reflecting the 21 steps) assigned both in terms of dollars and personnel. Some type of time scheduling system will also be required. Even with careful budgeting, scheduling of tasks, estimation of resources, and frequent checking, misallocation may occur. This may require a decision to modify the original design.

### TYPICAL OUTLINE FOR A CONCEPT REPORT
Introduction
Preliminaries
    Letter of Transmittal
    Title Page
    Client Name & Address
    Name of this Project
    Acknowledgments (List of participating staff, consultants)
    The Design Team
    Table of Contents
    List of Figures
Project Management and Administration
    Contract or Agreement
    Outline of Work to be Done (deliverables)
    Work Schedule Staffing, etc.
    Client - Designer Interaction
    Responsible Agent for Client
Legal Statement, (as may be required to establish ownership, rights, etc.).
Concept Report Review Process
Client Sign-off Procedures
Body of the Report
    Define the Problem (provides the substantive focus and context for the exercise)
    Schematic (model of the "real world")
    Specifications for Game Design

Goals and Objectives
Summarization of Gaming Elements from the SC/GE matrix
Repertoire of Gaming Techniques
Game Construction Process
Building the Game
Testing the Game
Using the Game
Game Sequence
Pre-Game Activities (prior to arrival of participants)
Game Activities (participants are present)
Post-Game Activities (after the participants have left)
Steps of Play
Player Materials
Graphics
Debriefing
Evaluation Procedures
Expected Results/White Paper
Executive Summary (3 to 5 pages capturing the essence of the problem, the solution presented, and the expected results. This is an opportunity to give a lively description of how the game might finally appear to the client as it is being played)

Design Considerations
- Are client expectations clearly spelled out?
- Is the game design to be approved by the client prior to construction?
- What are the primary constraints that must be observed as the design process proceeds (geographic, social, time horizon, time scale, the presentation of power or finances)?
- Is the order of processing of various models, components or decisions to be pre-specified?
- How are methods of interaction among participants, provision of feedback, etc. to be developed?
- What is the level of abstraction desired?
- Is a specific professional jargon to be used?
- Will evidence of productivity be demanded? At what stage?
- What is the desired level of complexity of the completed exercise?
- Are both major goals and specific objectives stated?
- How will the underlying systems model be represented?
- Does the game present a lucid metaphor?
- What time scale is to be employed?
- How will stylistic considerations (e.g. reflective, mutual problem-solving style) be resolved?
- What level of abstraction is desired?
- What stakeholders are to be represented?

- What will be the role structure for the exercise?
- Will participants be required to play roles other than their own real-life roles?
- What constraints are to be imposed on materials used by the game (staff, computer requirements for the accounting system, space, room layout, set-up, etc.)?
- Does the game design appear frivolous or silly?
- Is the design visual, dynamic, and interactive?
- Do simplicity and quality govern the design of the product?

And last, but certainly not least:

- How will the inquiry and debate during the exercise (the collective insights) be documented for later use?

**Step 14.** Build, Test, and Modify the Prototype
The objective here is to build and refine the prototype. Most games cannot be claimed as valid until the prototype has been run many times under test conditions (ten is a good rule of thumb). In games of any complexity, there are numerous components (roles, models, simulations, paraphernalia, accounting systems, etc.) that must be separately designed and constructed.

## TIPS ON BUILDING THE MODELS
The construction of models for the policy exercise includes developing the accounting system and appropriate simulations and heuristics. There must be a balance in detail, character and content among all of the many components as they are finally presented to the player. As a general rule, the simulation to be employed should be as simple as possible and still convey the required level of detail. There is a risk that a simulation too harshly restricted becomes compromised, and that its decreased authenticity fails to convey an accurate result. Decisions pertaining to the level of detail should be made in the context of the communication objectives. Overall balance must have a greater integrity than that of a particular simulation.

Models take three forms in a gaming/simulation: accounting systems, simulations, and heuristics. Accounting systems are the representation, at an acceptable level of detail, of some real-world throughput or transformation process, for use in the context of the game. As such, accounting systems are neither predictive nor speculative; rather, they are abstractions of processes that are well understood in the real world and that have been defined with sufficient clarity to permit their judicious abstraction for gaming purposes, e.g. a specific mechanical production process in industry.

Simulations, on the other hand, are theoretical speculations about the character of some complex process. Their logic is predicated on a series of evaluations of empirical data so that the output of a simulation should be scientifically defensible, e.g. an econometric model of a national economy. Because they are intended to predict, they are very useful in gaming/simulations that are oriented toward the resolution of "what if" questions.

Heuristics, the third type of model, are a substitute for simulation. They are frequently used in gaming as temporary measures in lieu of valid simulations. The function of the heuristic is to accept input and produce output comparable to that expected of a simulation. They are not predictive, but rather a simple abstraction of some complex process, e.g. a simple input/output matrix as an approximation of the production functions that underlie a complex manufacturing process. A major advantage of using a heuristic model is that it permits the preliminary inclusion of a phenomenon in the game and it allows replacement of the chosen heuristic with a more accurate simulation at a later date. Using this type of model requires that the participants confront the variables employed in the heuristic and that they factor these considerations into their thinking and discussions.

### DEFINE THE EXPLICIT INPUTS TO AND OUTPUTS FROM THE ACCOUNTING SYSTEM

The objective is to build an accounting system that continuously illustrates relationships among the roles and between them and other game components (e.g. models). Before construction of each game component, it is necessary to explicitly define what input will be processed and what output the component will generate. When developing the accounting system, two problems are encountered: a consistent level of detail (each of the components should provide information at more or less the same level) must be maintained; and the overall level of complexity resulting from these linkages must be prevented from becoming overwhelming.

It is possible to have very complex linkages within the computer, but the human brain can only deal with a limited set. The objective is to select those components and linkages that serve the communication need at hand. The test, then, is whether the inclusion of a particular linkage offers essential information to the participants; consideration must be given to time constraints during play and the limits of human comprehension.

### CALIBRATION OF THE COMPONENTS

The calibrating of components involves two stages, rough and fine-tuning. The initial stage requires that each individual component should be processed a number of times to establish that, within general margins of acceptability, it is functioning as expected. After the various components are linked together, the entire system must be tested and modified until the results are within levels of specification. The second stage, fine-tuning, requires more finesse because of the need to establish balance among components. At this stage, the game is a potpourri of elements, and it will not be easy to pinpoint components that require adjustment. The temptation to manipulate the final product must be resisted; to yield may result in a basic error in the logic, construction, data collection and/or manipulations of the accounting system. A word of warning – in a game supported by a computer, there is a tendency for errors to appear as a result of misinterpretations of the designer's intent by the computer programmer.

## DATA COLLECTION AND LOADING

Certain policy games require a large amount of data. The classical chicken and egg problem appears under a new guise here. Without data, we would have no means to clarify in operational terms the general concepts of the system to be simulated. However, the acquisition of data without a previously established conceptual structure can result in data acquired for its own sake. So, the data question has to be held off until this point in the game design process to ensure that the designer has thought through the reasons for building a game, its objectives, and its character. The design process helps to define and keep in balance the data needed for the game; the team will have become quite familiar with data sources pertinent to this game.

It is important to establish an acquisition plan for the collection of data. The plan should include definition of the data items, identification of sources, establishing rules for determining accuracy, developing guidelines for sampling procedures, etc. A storage (or loading) plan should include the definition and documentation of the storage formats. Failure to identify a bona fide use in the processing of the game will reveal data that is unnecessary. A final step, after the data has been collected, manipulated, and converted to the appropriate mechanical form, is the loading into the assembled components (e.g. tables, matrices, color codes, computerized algorithms, etc.).

## DESIGNING CYCLES AND STEPS: TIMING CONSIDERATIONS

Careful thought must be given to the time required to run the game. The game duration must be stipulated within the audience constraints. The duration of a run is the amount of elapsed time from the onset of the game to the completion of the debriefing. The pace of the game is closely associated with the level of abstraction and the amount of information presented to the player. The pace will probably not be known until the rule of ten (see below) is applied. If early trial runs of a game show that it is violating the criteria described in the concept report, review must be undertaken to ascertain if the original criteria or the game should be changed.

## STAGING THE GAME

How is the game to be staged? The designer must anticipate all pre-game, game, and post-game activities as they should take place to achieve a successful gaming experience. Are particular room arrangements or player configurations to be specified? Are warm-up exercises to be employed? Is the style to be free or more controlled? Are particular learning principles to be emphasized? How many cycles of play, minimum/maximum? Are the cycles to become sequentially more complex? How will the level of complexity be stipulated? Games are best perceived as environments for self-instruction; are players to have complete freedom of movement within the game, or will this be constrained by the designer? Are the players to be permitted to invent their own policies? Under what conditions may they alter game procedures?

## ELEMENTS CONTRIBUTING TO GAMINESS

What constitutes a good game? There is an elusive character that we might call "gaminess" that provides some indication of the players' enthusiasm and willingness to participate. However, "gaminess" is no accident. For those who are not blessed with an instinctual response, there are some clues that can be relied on during the thoughtful creation and construction of a game. "Gaminess" in the final analysis will depend on the skill of the designer. Some considerations, however, may be specified by the client which limit or direct this somewhat elusive characteristic. What degree of player involvement is desired? Should the emphasis be largely emotional or should the game be more intellectual? Ideally, periods of intense involvement will be interspersed with more detached or analytic sessions.

## PLAYER MOTIVATION

There is no doubt that, if you were to present a typical participant group with the fact that they were to be the principals on stage in a Broadway play without prior training or scripts, you would probably drive most of them away in a panic. Yet this is what the players confront in a game. The careful staging of the game permits this to be achieved with only a short period of anxiety. In any game, the first trial cycle inevitably introduces a strong sense of discomfort as the players encounter a complex, foreign environment in which they must commit to decisions publicly. The designer can employ a variety of techniques to increase excitement and to maintain player interest. The exercise should motivate the participants to make the best of it and challenge them to identify with the game. Players go through three stages of perception of the game environment:

Stage 1: The player is put off by the complexity
Stage 2: The player enters into a stage where he/she is in control
Stage 3: The player develops sophistication about the model: it supports him/her in contributing to the strategic "multilogue".

The designer must consider cooperation, competition, and cross pressuring. Cooperative situations require that the players engage in discussion to solve a mutual problem. In competitive situations (for example in business games), one player's gains may be another's losses; as a result, the participants' behavior varies significantly from cooperative games. Cross pressuring puts the player in a situation in which an action may produce both positive and negative results. The judicious use of a combination of cooperation, competition, and cross pressuring can be employed to quickly involve players and keep them motivated.

### ITERATIVE CYCLES

Games are iterative, meaning that cycle follows cycle and that the happenings within a given cycle repeat and reinforce those which have preceded it. The success of games in conveying gestalt is largely derived from their iterative nature. Earlier we spoke of a learning spiral and the need to establish an initial level of reference that permits a logical sense of closure. From this initial point, additional information can be assimilated through additional cycles of play. In a game, the frame of reference that establishes a complete cycle and returns it to its closure are the game phases or steps of play.

The first cycle is typically a bit more involved than the following cycles because the participants must be oriented to their environment. The exercise progresses through several cycles; each cycle consists of a sequence through the steps of play (activities which guide player action each cycle). The steps of play are different for each exercise, but these represent a typical cycle:

Phase 1 – Getting Organized
      Step 1. Read manuals; scenario update; events
      Step 2. Group meetings; discussion of policies
Phase 2 – Taking Action
      Step 3. Set your objectives for this year cycle; vote on policy
      Step 4. Interaction with other teams; negotiate deals
      Step 5. Complete all decision forms
Phase 3 – Evaluate your situation
      Step 6. Accounting system
      Step 7. Results
      Step 8. Critique

To ensure simplicity, the player decision form should be distinct from data entry forms for the accounting system. To simplify the game, any aspect (procedure, accounting activity rule, paraphernalia, or mechanical, etc.) that can be eliminated without injury to the game, should be.

### THE RULE-OF-TEN TEST RUNS

The game is transformed from a prototype to a final product using an iterative process; this entails testing the materials using the "rule of ten." Experience demonstrates that repeated runs of the evolving prototype are essential. These runs are only effective if the ground rules are followed. It is a mistake to develop any aspect of the game (content, structure and/or process) in too great detail early on, as this can lead to wasted effort or worse – a distorted product that does not meet the specifications that were established at the outset. The design team cycles the prototype through ten test runs, each progressively more rigorous. Late in this process, several of the game runs are specifically directed towards the client. These runs are used both to test with the client the relevance of the "metaphor" being developed as well as to evaluate the product against the specifications. The test runs present a thoughtful opportunity to review the entire game sequence from the introduction through the debriefing. This ensures that a balance evolves between content, process, and technical concerns. When the game runs smoothly, you are ready to proceed.

To be successful, the sequence of each test run must be as follows:

1. Develop a complete but rudimentary prototype
2. Conduct a rule-of-ten run
3. Evaluate the results
4. Gain consensus, in writing, on all problems identified
5. Agree on a solution to each problem
6. Modify the prototype to reflect the required changes
7. Continue to loop through the rule-of-ten runs (go back to step one).

During the rule-of-ten runs, it is advisable to introduce sophisticated players for the last three runs, and to facilitate the game very carefully. This means paying close attention to participant reactions particularly during the end-of-cycle critiques and the final debriefing. The design team should pursue in depth any reservations that participants have about the balance, level of detail, relevance, vernacular employed, models, the ability to maintain player interest, speed of play, or any other area of comment. There is probably no better test of the validity of a particular game than its acceptance by a sophisticated audience who are already known to be reasonably familiar with the problem presented by the game. Each rule-of-ten run serves a unique purpose as shown below:

1. Talk Through          (establish a verbal description of the exercise).
2. Crawl Through         (develop initial draft materials representing a cycle)
3. Trial of Sequence     (one steps of play sequence, with a "safe" audience)
4. Trial of Paraphernalia (two steps of play sequences with a "safe" audience)
5. Initial Rehearsal     (three cycles with a "safe" audience)
6. Second Rehearsal      (three cycles, with a trial audience)
7. Third Rehearsal       (three cycles, with the appropriate number of players)
8. Fourth Rehearsal      (three cycles, with the appropriate participants)
9. Full Dress Rehearsal  (three cycles, with the appropriate participants)
10. Formal Use by the Client (professional use with the appropriate participants)

Benefits of the Rule of Ten

A careful rule-of-ten run will yield five positive results:

1. A review of timing considerations. Problems here often require modifications to technique, process, and/or content; early runs are particularly valuable in this respect.

2. Improve learning and gain team consensus on the game "gestalt" as a representation of the macro-problem or overview. It is essential that agreement be reached as to how the final game will come together as a balance of content, process, and technical concerns.

3. Testing the transferability and relevance of the model. Is the game design effective and efficient in getting concepts across and will it serve as the optimal vehicle to create the intended strategic inquiry and debate?

4. Review of process concerns. Will the facilitator be required to have more skill and/or technical knowledge than defined by the game specifications?

5. Review of paraphernalia. Do the materials effectively support the game's strategic functions? Are they too costly, awkward, or poorly integrated?

### CONSTRUCTION ACTIVITIES WITH TEST PLAYERS PRESENT

The completed game must be put to the test with actual participants. This might prove to cause a dilemma for the client. One reason for using a game process is, of course, the desire to adopt a participatory process. However, in practice, management often finds it difficult to agree on who should be involved at what stage, and for what purpose. "Putting all the cards on the table" even before the management team (as final users of the game) have experienced the game itself, is not easy. The concept report should contain a specific plan for the involvement of informants and test players in the stages to come.

The client's responsibilities for test group participation should be spelled out in the concept report. In early runs, the players will probably be those who are assigned to help design it or those who have some authorized stake in the game. These participants will fit into a category of "sympathetic players" (those who understand that it is a test vehicle and will be willing to continue play even though difficulties are encountered). During the testing of the game with players, care should be taken to observe player response to roles and, in particular, the response to the game-specific language that the players must learn. Early runs may reveal unnecessary detail or a vernacular that is inappropriate. Listen to the players and pay particular attention to their complaints about the materials. After all, you are attempting to construct a language that will improve their ability to deal with a complex problem.

There are three ground rules for conducting a rule-of-ten run:

1. Always complete the entire game sequence, no matter how ragged the process or incomplete the materials may be;
2. Always review the results to identify problems; and,
3. Always initiate appropriate action to make agreed changes prior to the next test run.

## DESIGNING THE FACILITATOR MANUAL

The final product to be created is a facilitator's manual. It is "the treasury of the game" containing all the tools, tips, tricks and secrets that have been developed during construction and testing to make each game run a success. It ensures consistency of facilitation by different people if used on a variety of occasions. The objective here is to ensure practical use by the client when the product is completed. The manual needs to clarify all the questions concerning the conditions governing the use of the game (desired facilitator skill, physical environment, nature and availability of participants, practical storage of game materials, etc.).

This notebook includes all materials that exist in any other manual (e.g. the player's manual); in addition, it must contain notes to the facilitator to guide the run of the game. The facilitator's manual and pre-game handout must contain appropriate role and/or perspective descriptions. These are mostly prescriptions that instruct the players about required behavior; who a particular actor is in a structural sense; and the formal position, interests, status, objectives, etc. that characterize the role. It is important that a chart be provided to the facilitator that shows player distribution by role assignment; the facilitator should keep this close at hand. This matrix indicates how participants are to be allocated to roles based on differing numbers of participants (it is not always possible to guarantee that everyone will show up).

## PRE-GAME CHECKLIST
- Are facilities adequate?
- Are materials easily transportable?
- Information loading required?
- Schedule established at the outset?
- Adequate financial resources and staff available?
- Generic equipment (tables, chairs, blackboards, overheads, etc.)?
- Overhead projectors or video equipment required?
- Special lighting required?
- Room set-up?
- Colored tablecloths or signs to identify role locations?
- A checklist for room set-up?
- A schedule of events with timing?

## GAME CHECKLIST

- How much set-up time is required?
- Large wall with a tack board surface?
- Computer software?
- Consumable items?
- Safe environment for learning?
- Avoid distractions?
- Manuals, forms, etc. (as required)?
- Materials (a list of paraphernalia)?
- Points to be covered during the introduction to the game?
- Rules players must observe?
- Number of participants?
- Explicit decisions processed through the accounting system?
- Items to be covered during the critique of each cycle?

## POST-GAME CHECKLIST

- Final debriefing?
- Coordinate the game with some larger objective?
- How much clean-up time will be required?
- A list of items to be covered during the debriefing at game end?

### Step 15. Technical Evaluation

The selection of an appropriate testing procedure is important; this should be done in accordance with the original goals, objectives, and specifications. Three issues need to be addressed:

Validity – Does the game accurately reflect the "real world"? Is it at the proper level of abstraction? Is the subject matter (content) authentic?

Reliability – Are the results of the runs comparable and consistent? Can the client repeatedly use it as intended? Can they depend on the materials, the computer, and the time control mechanisms? Is the product of each run comparable with other runs?

Utility – Does it achieve the client's objectives? Does it compare favorably in time and cost with any available alternative methods? Can the results be measured?

Because games are hard to evaluate, criteria must be defined at the outset. It is important to determine at what stages the exercise will be evaluated, who will do the evaluation, what the measures of performance are to be, and what procedures will be used for resolving disputes (see Chapter 6). Some of the questions that need to be addressed include identifying the evaluation methods to be employed, resolving if participants' responses are to be recorded for later evaluation, and deciding how results are to be documented. The objective is to ensure that the final product meets the original specifications.

Quite often, subject matter experts, whose prime concern lies with the content of a problem, may evaluate the final exercise. They may be unfamiliar with gaming as a disciplined activity and, as a consequence, their evaluation may focus on the specifics conveyed rather than the systemic considerations of the problem.

Evaluations with post-game questionnaires tend to measure facts retained by the participant. However, games are designed to help discuss and understand complexity. Because the game is a gestalt mode of communication, the final exercise should be evaluated against appropriate alternative methods.

Development of an exercise goes through several stages, each of which could be subject to evaluation. If a review of the game is scheduled at various stages, the needed information has to be captured by the game design team. Each of these evaluations can and will increase the overall accuracy and validity of the model relative to the real world system. The opportunities for review and evaluation include:

- The research method proposed for exploring the problem;
- An evaluation of the design as presented in the concept report;
- An evaluation of the database and data presentation techniques;
- A review of the models selected;
- An analysis of the computer simulation employed;
- A review of the procedure for data calculation;
- The technical evaluation (Step 15); and
- The final "white paper" (Step 21).

Player response to the exercise needs a great deal of attention. What is the reaction of a sophisticated player to the game vis-à-vis the real world counterpart that it presumes to represent? Do any players finish their activities well in advance of other players? Are several players attempting to obtain the same information simultaneously, and competing with one another unnecessarily for documents? Is the process of conversion from a player's written form to a calculation form simple, straightforward and error-free? Are problems of timing worked out so that the players are given appropriate amounts of time to preview material, to review past cycle output, to discuss with one another inter-team and intra-team the decisions they will face in the cycle? Is there adequate time for the cycle critiques and the final debriefing? At the completion of the exercise, are the players dissatisfied and, if so, what is the cause? Are the players motivated to pursue the problem beyond the game experience?

Once the game is in use, relay of feedback to the designer from players is extremely important. Game designers are well advised to prepare a simple one-page pre-addressed form that would permit the participant to make comments about any aspect of the game that might strike their fancy. Another simple expedient for relaying feedback from players is special meetings within the fraternity of game designers at the national and international conventions. Those interested in a particular game can discuss different aspects of the use of the game.

## Step 16. Graphic Design and Printing

The objective to be achieved through the design of the graphics is both to develop a professional presentation and to secure the ergonomic effectiveness of the game materials. The specifications should address the responsibility for developing the final materials (design team, client as an in-house activity, or subcontractor). The character of the graphic presentation needs to be defined (can the materials be unique or must they conform to the client's motif)? The list below suggests some graphic aids that have proven useful in past situations:

- A steps-of-play wall chart
- All of the linkages implied by:
    o Model to role
    o Role to component
    o Component to model
    o From one model to all other models
    o From a given role to all other roles
    o From a particular component to all data sources
- Computer output format
- Cycle phasing
- Data file layouts
- Diagram of accounting system
- List of game components
- Major subroutines
- Man-machine relationships
- Maps, photos and pictures as appropriate
- Player activity flow chart
- Player decision forms
- Player support forms
- Room layout
- Run sequence
- Static and dynamic functional interaction diagrams
- Team matrix
- Typical accounting sequence

Remember: the players will not be allowed much time to familiarize themselves with the gaming materials. Make sure that the artistic quality of the final materials really supports the players' tasks. The product should look attractive, but utility is the first criterion.

**Step 18. Facilitating the Exercise, an Instruction to Future Facilitators**

### THE IMPORTANCE OF FACILITATION

The facilitator assumes a considerable responsibility in undertaking a run of the game. If this person "does their homework" and follows the procedures described in the materials, the exercise should go smoothly and predictably. It is very important to keep the participants' progress governed by the steps of play during the first two cycles (Cycle 1, which is effectively a review of "history," and Cycle 2, which is essentially a device to train the participants in the procedures required of them). In later cycles, as the participants become familiar with their roles, it is only necessary to require conformance to the steps of play as you enter each of the four phases of play and/or to regain control if the group becomes disoriented. As you begin, there are some facts known only to you as facilitator (e.g. the dynamics of the accounting system). These should remain "secret"; it is the task of the participants to explore their environment. However, the facilitator can reassure participants and give them hints as may be appropriate.

Facilitator(s) must become thoroughly familiar with game materials to use the exercise effectively. They should have a clear objective for each run; be fully informed about the mechanics of the game; and have appropriate experience in trial runs. The game has to be executed professionally with good possibilities for observation and rapid feedback of results. The facilitator must watch the clock, call time as required, and force the play to progress as planned. Games used for strategic implementation may have to be run repeatedly; many different facilitators may be involved and "train the trainer" sessions may need to be organized.

### TECHNIQUES FOR A SMOOTH-RUNNING GAME

The level of complexity of a given game will be a function of the nature of the macro-problem being addressed. Other things being equal, simplicity in all aspects of gaming is to be desired, so also in the way the facilitator acts out his or her role. Remember that you are asking a group of strangers to "learn a new language." The more involved the session becomes, the more resistance you might encounter in achieving this goal.

The inevitable result of facilitator errors is anger and frustration on the part of players. Such errors can cause the players to lose confidence in the game. Automatic accounting checks should have been designed to catch errors before they come to the attention of the players. As a consequence, the facilitator should be able to recognize at a glance whether responses from the accounting system are within the expected range. If not, the facilitator should make doubly sure they are the result of decisions that were intended by the players. If a player commits a gross error (unwittingly leaving a decimal out), the facilitator should automatically correct this. Whenever possible, be parsimonious in the accounting procedure. Techniques of rounding, truncating, and approximating are appropriate if they do not alter the significance of the result.

## SUSPENSION OF DISBELIEF

It is important for the facilitator to bear in mind the concept of the "suspension of disbelief." This requires that the participants "forget" that they are playing a game. They need to feel safe as they explore new alternatives and protected from any distraction that breaks their concentration on the game. It is only in this "cocoon" that they can gain the true advantage of the experience. Once this has been achieved, it is possible for players to become so fully "into" the experience that their participation results in a highly condensed version of real-world events that would require months or years to achieve on the job.

The suspension of disbelief is essential for player involvement. As the participants gather, they will be somewhat apprehensive; this will increase as they realize the pressures they will face (within half an hour, they will become "actors" who must suspend disbelief and enter into the scenario with conviction). Verisimilitude, that is, the creation of the appearance of reality through abstraction, is necessary for the suspension of disbelief. Curiously enough, relatively simple circumstances will often lead the players to accept a game as a substitute for reality.

## DEVICES FOR HEIGHTENING THE DRAMA OF THE GAME

Artificiality induced "drama" must never override the client's objectives. An enthusiastic group of participants is not sufficient evidence of the success of a game; on the other hand, enthusiasm is necessary for success. In order to increase player enthusiasm, surprise and chance may be introduced sparingly in order to model chance occurrences in the real world.

The period between the time the player has made a decision and the time that the response from that decision has been processed and returned to the player is usually quite suspenseful. This can be used to increase player involvement. Considerable suspense will build during the period when questions must be resolved on an interteam basis; the final announcement of a resolution will often result in a spontaneous and marked hubbub. Experienced game facilitators will recognize that communication following a period of suspense is frequently the time at which the exchange of information is at its peak fulfilling the communication intent of the game. The facilitator should not interfere during this period.

Paralleling this development is the need to maximize the opportunities for players to use their own initiative, both in terms of problem definition and the development of alternative solutions. This implies an increased freedom in the game as the cycle progresses so that imaginative player response will be encouraged (e.g. queries for specific information, new efforts at inter-role linkages for problem solving, and player improvisation of problem-solving techniques not programmed into the game).

## ROOM ARRANGEMENT

The participants should be organized in a comfortable and socially conducive arrangement. This is the environment the players will experience intensively for the duration of the game. Distractions must be minimized; tables and chairs must be so arranged as to focus on a central display of visuals. The room should be checked in advance, making sure that it satisfies all game requirements. The facilitator should try to mentally rearrange the furniture to ensure that there is enough space for both the roles and the graphics. Ensure that the room will be available, set up all materials beforehand, and double check everything; *make provisions to assure that the room will be locked and protected during the night.*

A warning from personal experience: Be sure no janitorial staff "clean" the room during the night – this can be a disaster if they throw away wall charts, rearrange furniture, etc.

It is important to bear in mind at all times that the purpose of this exercise is to prompt discussion of new alternatives. Whenever possible, when responding to participants, refer to the large wall schematic to discuss possible solutions. This will help the participants focus on the "real world" rather than the game.

## CONTROLLING PLAYER INVOLVEMENT

Once players are involved, if the authenticity and relevance of the game is clear, the process of learning and debate takes place automatically and the game facilitator's role is reduced to that of administrator. Many game facilitators find it difficult to accept this loss of importance, since they feel more comfortable in a teaching and leading role. In a good game, of their own volition, players will explore the system presented. They will seek to find answers to questions that they themselves have generated. This means that the facilitator's role is relatively limited. The main function is to follow the steps of play and deal with the resolution of technical and mechanical difficulties that inevitably occur.

There is a direct and positive relationship between the success of a game in conveying information and the degree of player involvement achieved. Player involvement can be deliberately manipulated by the rule of three (described below), cooperation/competition, ego threat/ego boost, information loading characteristics, level of abstraction, requirement of commitment, visibility of feedback mechanisms, relevance of substantive content, and staging (dramatics, phases, and timing).

The exercise is intended to be a freewheeling exchange of ideas drawn from carefully defined perspectives (the roles) in a carefully structured environment. To be successful, the facilitator must make a continuing trade-off between the "structure" of the exercise which serves as the control mechanism and the "freewheeling" open-ended, innovative, any-directional multi-party conversations which spring up among the participants as they go about their tasks. To achieve this, the facilitator should have a general sense of the timing of each phase of the exercise but be relaxed enough to permit the participants freedom of action, thought and conversation between the major steps of play.

### RULE OF THREE

Many players have no previous gaming experience and therefore feel ill at ease. One way to overcome this discomfort is to require the players to commit themselves right from the inception of the game; the rule of three can speed this process. The rule of three argues that, in any given decision-making role, the highest quality of play will occur if three people are assigned to play the role as though they were one. (Five and seven people together are conceivable, but are increasingly unwieldy). When three people are assigned to make a joint decision, there is an inherent imbalance that quickly builds the quality of the ensuing discussion. The quality of decisions that result is significantly higher than that achieved by one player making the same decision.

### PRE-GAME ACTIVITIES (PRIOR TO ARRIVAL OF PARTICIPANTS)

To prepare the participants for the exercise, it is often necessary to distribute materials beforehand. Preparations for the game run should be finished several days in advance; if unexpected circumstances arise, there will be ample time to deal with them. The sequence and timing of the distribution of these materials is situation specific but the materials might well include:

- A letter of invitation with the particulars of the logistics, an explanation of the purpose of the exercise, a description of what is expected of the participant, a description of the activities that will be associated with the game experience, and a phone number of a contact. A follow-up by phone is valuable to ensure an accurate head count; it serves as an opportunity to emphasize the need to attend once they commit.

- A careful assignment of participants to appropriate roles.

- A substantive notebook, which presents in summary form the basic materials with which the participant is expected to be familiar.

- Selected readings that will establish the proper frame of reference for the activities pursued by the game.

- A workbook which requires the participant to make explicit Cycle 1 decisions before arriving at the game run (this serves to familiarize them with both procedure and content.).

### POLICY GAME ACTIVITIES (PARTICIPANTS ARE PRESENT)

As the session begins, a series of formalities is conducted. These might well include introductions, a restatement of the purpose of the meeting, etc. The facilitator must provide the participants with a general overview of the exercise, introduce the participants to the game, and explain the game procedures. (Do not assume that participants have read and/or remember the materials that were provided). Introduce the ground rules for the day (e.g. no formal coffee breaks, have coffee in place; describe the sequence of happenings and the time schedule for lunch, dinner, etc.). The introduction needs to be very brief; it should be "scripted" (use a pre-printed wall chart with a few basic ideas to guide the facilitator). A video could easily be employed here to standardize the presentation and make it easier for inexperienced facilitators. Be sure to cover these two points:

- The game has been developed as a tool for facilitating a productive dialogue.
- The objective is to create a non-threatening environment wherein the various parties may exchange viewpoints and explore new alternatives for resolving a problem.

It is important for you, as facilitator, to keep this communication objective clearly in front of the group as the game is played out. The exercise is a "model of a model"! Just as an architect might use a three-dimensional model of a structure to obtain group consensus on various design aspects of the building, you as facilitator should use this "model" to draw a parallel between the game environment and the "real world".

Introduce everyone very briefly and indicate the role they will be playing. Establish the context for the game (Why are they here? What is the real-world problem being explored? Indicate that the debriefing will reconsider these two questions). Refer to the large wall schematic – be sure the participants understand that the game is an abstraction, but nevertheless based on a very detailed perception of reality (as illustrated by the schematic).

The best way to familiarize the participants with the structure of the exercise is to "walk" them through the first sequence. They actually make decisions and follow all procedures. After the first cycle, the participants are familiar with the process and a more flexible posture can be assumed with regard to the execution of the steps.

Whenever possible during the day, refer disputes between players back to the participants. Just say: "It is your problem. How do you want to solve it?" Remember that they are the "experts" and you are facilitating improved communication. *In general, a good facilitator will be seen and not heard.*

The exercise may be terminated in a number of ways. Typically, there can be only a set number of cycles to play because of design and time constraints. The exercise should be structured to end with ample time for a final debriefing session. This is held both to permit the players to vent their feelings and to highlight the message that was to be conveyed by the game. The game is a simple model of reality – the debriefing needs to help the participants make the transition from the "false" world of the game to the "real world" of their professional concerns. Because of this, all issues from the group should be rephrased in terms of real world concerns rather than in terms of the happenings of the day. Leave the game behind! The conclusion of the debriefing session is the proper time to inject evaluation devices for measuring the effectiveness of the exercise. Were clients' objectives achieved? Did the exercise achieve the stated purpose? Were there any unexpected outcomes?

### Post-Game Activities (After the participants have left)
A specific follow-up plan for the exercise should be developed. It is often necessary to provide the participants with materials that summarize the happenings of the game. This may include preparing a white paper that summarizes the agreements and/or disagreements that became apparent. Follow-up meetings with selected participants may be useful in reaching agreement on a policy document. These "notes" can also be circulated to confirm impressions derived during the exercise. They can serve as a further commitment of the participant to the process by reinforcing the "message" from the experience. It may also be useful to play the game for additional groups as a way of explaining the overall situation and/or as a way of explaining new policies that are being considered. Be sure to send a letter of thanks for their time and effort; follow up with a brief evaluation questionnaire if appropriate.

### Typical Introduction to the Game
Prepare a detailed checklist of all materials and preparatory activities. Be sure that all necessary computer printouts required for the game have been printed and distributed as required. All materials for each of the roles should be of the same color. Since the color is one of the major identifications of the role, the folders which contain materials given to each of the roles should have the appropriate color present on the outside of the folder.

The walk-through of Cycle 1 should be done in a very tightly controlled and deliberate step-by-step manner, making sure that all participants are listening and following the flow of forms presented by the facilitator. To begin, briefly introduce the layout of the room, the different roles present and the main responsibilities of each. *Walk them through this first cycle as quickly as possible.* Describe only the things that players must know – do not comment on things that are specific to the internal working of each role. The beginning and ending of each step should be clearly announced and reinforced.

The participants' ability to deal with the mechanics of the game during the walk-through (Cycle 1) will be greatly improved if each role has an "assistant" assigned to them. These assistants need to be trained in advance. Their primary function will be to make sure that participants become comfortable (as quickly as possible) with all the mechanics and processes associated with their roles, as well as gain a sense of overview of total game activities.

If the participants are to benefit from the exercise, it is essential that they understand and complete their duties under each of the steps of play. They may find these activities a bit confusing during the first cycle of play; however, they soon overcome the mechanics. Players need to ensure that their actions are purposeful towards the meeting of the client's goals.

### FACILITATOR CHECKLIST FOR THE INTRODUCTION
- Introduce the staff.
- Have participants stand and briefly introduce themselves to the group. This breaks the ice and gets the day started, participants become familiar with each other (and, it kills time while you are waiting for stragglers to arrive.)
- Be sure that participants have been assigned roles and are seated at the proper location. This is also a good time to introduce the color scheme, indicating that their tablecloth and role materials match.
- Introduce the participants to the concept of the game as an architectural scale model.
- Explain that it will seem to be chaotic, but this is misleading because the underlying process and structure give order to their activities.
- The objectives are to improve communication among the group and to explore alternatives.
- The problem has many solutions – to "win," you must work together as a team to find one solution.
- Rules must be followed for orderly process (for example, time constraints must be met).
- Policies are under the control of the participants.
- Emphasize that decisions of the game facilitator are always final, that data provided by the facilitator cannot be challenged.

- Point out the central features in the room arrangement: charts, the location of various roles, etc.
- Coffee and break arrangements (stay in the room until the end of the exercise).

## GUIDE FOR END-OF-CYCLE CRITIQUE

The last activity in each cycle is the critique. This is a facilitator-controlled discussion to review the previous cycle and launch the next cycle. Note that this discussion is "within the game", i.e. it deals with the simulation and not the real world. A critique is a systematic discussion to reveal the significance of play; it serves several purposes. It signals the participants that a cycle has concluded and that they will soon get another opportunity to prove their competence and/or explore a new set of ideas. It gives the participants an opportunity to "vent," to clarify, and to explain or defend their behavior. And, finally, the facilitator has an opportunity to interact with the participants to ensure that they are comfortable with the evolution of the exercise. Issues relevant to the debriefing should be acknowledged by placing them on a flip chart but *discussion should be delayed until the debriefing*. During the critique, players may request clarification on any procedural matters that may be unclear. The group, under the guidance of the facilitator, will discuss the results of the accounting system. The facilitator will decide any unresolved matters.

## GUIDE FOR FINAL DEBRIEFING DISCUSSION

The debriefing is not to be confused with the critique. The critique follows each cycle, is very brief, and deals only with the mechanics and particulars of the game. The debriefing has a very different purpose: to help the participants make the transition from the artificial world of the game to the real world of their professional concerns. For this reason, all issues raised during the exercise should be rephrased in terms of real world concerns rather than in terms of the happenings of the day. The large schematic of the problem environment should be used during the debriefing as much as possible to shift the focus away from the mechanics of the game. It is important to bear in mind at all times that the purpose of this exercise is to prompt discussion of new perceptions, alternatives and/or issues. The debriefing has two distinct phases:

Review the performance of the game. – It is essential for participants to have a chance to "come down" from the excitement of the game. Participants need the opportunity to congratulate themselves on a job well done, to explain their failures, to describe what they would have done if they had had more time, etc. Be sure that every participant has an opportunity to speak at least briefly (for example, ask a direct question of anyone who seems reticent). While this first debriefing phase is essential and must be conducted with care, it is not the main point of the exercise, which is to consider the policy matter at hand.
Review the real world issues brought to the surface by the game. – At this point,

the facilitator must deliberately shift the discussion from the game to real-world concerns. Participants will resist, wanting to remain in "Utopia". However, if the facilitator continuously restates matters in the context of the real problem, and requires participants to do the same, there will be a ready transformation of the discussion to the actual policy matter at hand. This is where the true payoff of the exercise begins. Be sure to plan a collective inquiry so that considerable time is available for this purpose. Remember that the game is "a model of reality." As such, it should serve as the underpinning of the discussion. Ideas can be exchanged much more quickly and effectively if participants use the "jargon" established during the play of the game. Be sure to capture the primary ideas, agreements, and disagreements on a blackboard or wall pad.

# Glossary

**accounting system**
as gaming element: the process in which player decisions are recorded and captured, and subsequently processed in some way to ensure accountability of the roles; the results are then reported back to the player to engender discussion

**analogy/metaphor**
as gaming element: the simile employed in a game, a "model of a model" that the participants will recognize and endorse

**basic referent system**
as gaming element: one or more frames of reference that underlie and give order to the policy exercise; these reflect the discipline or set of ideas that influenced basic decisions about the design of the exercise

(multi-party) **collaboration**
"a process through which parties who see different aspects of a problem can constructively explore their differences and search for solutions that go beyond their own limited vision of what is possible" (Gray, 1989, p. 5)

**commitment to action**
the voluntary and emotional element in decision making, i.e. the positive willingness to implement a selected path of action; it shows itself whenever the selected alternative requires an irrevocable allocation of time, energy, talent, and/or other resources

**communication**
transmission of any message from a source/sender to a receiver via a medium

**communication mode**
composed of three components: language, pattern of interaction among the respondents, and the communication technologies employed

**communication technology**
a tool for encoding, transmitting, and decoding a message

**complexity**
"composed of interconnected parts" ... "characterized by a very complicated or involved arrangement of parts..." ... "so complicated or intricate as to be hard to understand or deal with" (Webster, 1989)

**concept report**
a document containing the design agreements that will govern the policy exercise; it consolidates ideas into a workable blueprint and requires sign-off by the client

**cone of abstraction**
a means to show the interrelatedness of different actors' mental models; depending on actors' positions and experience, their mental models are located on different levels of abstraction on the cone

**consensus vs. conflict**
**conflict** is a perceived difference in interests and a perception that different aspirations cannot be achieved simultaneously
**consensus** is the absence of such a perception; it is the mutual feeling that all concerns have been addressed and that all parties have been heard and understood

**creativity**
"the process of generating unique products by transformation of existing products. These products must be unique only to the creator and must meet the criteria of purpose established by the creator" (Welsh, 1980; quoted in Isaksen, 1988, p. 258)

**debriefing**
as step of play: systematic facilitator-controlled discussion at the conclusion of the exercise to evaluate the initial objectives

**decision making**
the concept of decision making has to do with selection and commitment: "if a purpose or plan is selected as the best, but the decision maker does not feel committed to it, for all practical purposes no decision has been made" Noorderhaven (1995, pp. 7-8)

**decisions**
as gaming elements: the variety of selection or allocation actions required of roles during each cycle

**design sequence (of a gaming/simulation)**
the systematic process of design which falls into five broad phases containing a total of 21 specific steps

**events**
as gaming elements: incidents presented to specific players at the beginning of

each cycle of play to (re)focus the attention of the player on a particular aspect of the substantive problem being gamed; they are used to update the scenario as the game progresses and can be of three types: programmed, triggered, and random

## format

as gaming element: the physical configuration (the documents, visuals and arti-facts) of the game as well as the various processes that the participants encounter in the game

## future's language (see also multilogue)

a hybrid communication mode for multilogue; it allows many different communi-cation forms in any combination which best enhance the transmission of some complex reality; it is transient in format to permit the restructuring or more careful articulation of the problem as viewed by those participating in the dialogue; it is also dynamic, i.e. it responds during use to changing perceptions of the problem

## gaming-simulation (in this book, also game)

an operating model of a real-life system in which actors in roles recreate, at least partially, the behavior of the system. The words "at least partially" refer to the fact that a game can contain many other elements that play a part in simulating the system, such as maps, game pieces (e.g. poker chips) and computer software

## gaming elements

the building blocks used in the construction of a policy exercise (or game); they fall into three categories: content, structure and process
- **content**: scenario and events, theme or analogy/metaphor and the participants and their decisions
- **structure**: format and basic referent, policies, rules, scoring, steps of play, model, data, and accounting system
- **process**: facilitation and the three primary phases of a game, game artifacts (visuals and paraphernalia), and the evaluation of results (documentation, etc.)

## ill-structured policy problem: (Mitroff and Sagasti, 1973)

many decision makers are involved, there is conflict on values and objectives, and the number of alternative strategies or actions considered potentially rele-vant is unlimited. In addition, the possible outcome of these alternatives is unknown and there is little insight into the occurrence probability of certain out-comes. The distinctions are a matter of degree: a problem can be more or less ill-structured
(see also macro-problem)

## image

as gaming element: the primary impression to be conveyed by the game

**indicators**
as gaming elements: specific outputs of the accounting system (graphs, charts, etc.) that are presented to the players as feedback of the results of play

**knowledge household**
the system of arguments, claims, interests and values on which policy options are based; also referred to as: cognitive map, mental map, theory of practice, policy theory and mental model

**macro-problem**
a policy problem characterized by the following:
- "neither their full scope nor details are understood"
- "connections exist among the various factors"
- "useful to focus on them collectively"
- "defined by a focus rather than a boundary"
- "flexibility and adaptiveness are essential for dealing with macro-problems"
- "require a heuristic approach"
- "tend to have unintended consequences, side effects, unexpected spin-offs"

(Cartwright, 1987, p. 95)

**mental model** (see also **knowledge household**)
"networks of facts and concepts that mimic reality and from which executives derive their opinions of strategic issues, options, courses of action and likely outcomes" (Morecroft, 1988, pp. 12-13)

**model** (used in two ways in this book)
a. in a methodological sense: "Any person using a system 'A' that is neither directly nor indirectly interacting with a system 'B,' in order to obtain information about system 'B,' is using 'A' as a model for 'B.'" (Apostel, 1960, p. 160)
b. as gaming element: the quantitative system that will mimic (part of) the client's environment that is presented through the game

**multilogue**
the simultaneous dialogue in a game of multiple actors in pursuit of a greater understanding of the topic at hand; the situation-specific "future's language" that a game creates is not only transmitted via written or spoken words. A good game consists of many different symbols that support communication among the players: many kinds of cards, game pieces, and other paraphernalia can be used

**network management** (see also **policy network**)
changing the interdependencies, autonomy and diversity in a network and altering the substantive and temporal whimsicality (capriciousness) in order to create governing options for a governing actor

**paraphernalia**
as gaming elements: the various artifacts required by the facilitator to assemble
and play the game

**participation/involvement**
the productive and empathic engagement of relevant stakeholders in all or some
phases of a policy process

**participatory policy analysis**
"an applied social science discipline that uses multiple methods of inquiry, argument and process facilitation to assist a pluriform set of stakeholders in a policy
network to explore and exchange in a direct interaction with each other their different mental maps regarding values, definitions, causes and solutions of problems and to develop and test as effective as needed a shared and robust policy theory on an issue. The ultimate goal is to improve the problem-solving capacity of
the individual stakeholders and the policy network as a whole" (Geurts & Mayer,
1996, p. 17)

**play**
a voluntary, superfluous, activity (that one enters out of free will), involving stepping out of real life into a temporary sphere of activity, being limited in terms of
time and place, having fixed rules and following an orderly process, promoting
the formation of new and different social groupings, being itself the goal, and
being accompanied by a sense of tension and joy and the awareness that the
activity is different from normal life (Huizinga, 1955)

**policy** or **policy program**
a series of planned decisions regarding a policy problem intended to be binding
for actors in a policy network

**policies**
as gaming element: participant-imposed constraints controlling play, i.e. players
are permitted to alter, amend or enrich these procedures within the basic gaming structure

**policy analysis**
"an applied social science discipline which uses multiple methods of inquiry and
argument to produce and transform policy relevant information that may be utilized in political settings to resolve policy problems" (Dunn, 1981, p. 35)

**policy exercise** or **policy game**
a gaming/simulation that is explicitly created to assist policy makers with a specific issue of strategic management

**policy network**
the key defining elements are:
- actors in networks are (parts of) organizations, not individuals
- actors pursue different strategies based on different interests and power resources
- networks produce policy programs
- no single actor can control the formulation and implementation of the resulting program
- the distribution of power, the ownership of strategic information and sources of knowledge and the formal and informal rules of the network are decisive for the outcome

**policy theory**
see **knowledge household**

**problems vs. policy problems** (Dunn, 1981)
**problem**: an undesired state of affairs or expected undesirable future development
**policy problem**: assumes that one can or should do something about the undesired state of affairs or prevent and/or react against the unattractive development. So, behind a policy problem there is the assumption that it can be influenced

**problem structuring**
"activities of representatives of various organizations which are directed at influencing the definition of an issue" (Roelofs, 2000, p. 173)

**role**
as gaming element: a hypothetical set of interests, knowledge and responsibilities that are attributed to a given participant (or team). There are three types of roles: gamed (real players making decisions), simulated (theoretical players), and pseudo (present but not making decisions in the game)

**rule of three**
individual decision-makers (roles) should be used sparingly. Whenever possible, three roles should form a team with a single perspective; this group must work together to make a single decision

**rules**
as gaming elements: specific facilitator-imposed constraints that govern play; players must obey the rules, as these cannot be changed by the participants

**scenario** is used in two ways in this book:
a. (as gaming element): the storyline (history, present, and future) that all partic-

ipants are given as the game begins

b. (as futuring technique): a set of stories that hypothesize alternative futures that a social system might face in the coming years

## schematic

tool for game design: a visual presentation of the internal and external characteristics of the macro problem; it is a graphic on a wall-size chart which contains an overview of all of the potentially significant considerations

## scoring

as gaming element: a system of penalties and rewards reflecting the results of decisions taken by the players

## simulation

a conscious endeavor to reproduce the central characteristics of a system in order to understand, experiment with and/or predict the behavior of that system (Duke, 1980)

## steps of play and cycles

a policy exercise progresses through several "cycles"; each cycle consists of a sequence through the steps of play; steps of play are the sequence of activities that players must follow during each cycle of play

## strategic management

all those activities in an organization purposefully aimed at developing and successfully realizing a strategy; the activities are usually ordered under three headings: pre-decision strategic analysis, decision making (choice), and implementation

## strategic trajectory

planned set of interconnected decisions on how to organize the activities relevant for the successful participatory development and realization of one particular strategy; this will usually involve many design decisions, e.g., timing, number of participants, subject matter, tools, forum format

## strategy or strategic policy

in this book: a policy program for a macro policy problem, the implementation of which will have far-reaching consequences for the organization(s) involved

## systems component/gaming element matrix

process to transform the system (as represented in the schematic) from a model of the problem to a model of the game; it uses a large matrix on a wall with columns reflecting the systems components and rows reflecting the game elements

**theme**
as gaming element: the subject matter or substantive focus to be addressed by the game

**uncertainty vs. risk**
uncertainty refers to lack of knowledge, while risk adds an element of valuation to uncertainty; risk is a function of uncertainty and the degree to which the uncertain events are desirable or undesirable.

**visuals**
as gaming elements: the graphics, artwork, schematic, wall charts, tables, player activity flow chart, etc. that assist participants in gaining insight during the exercise

**wicked problem**
see **macro-problem**

# Bibliography

Ackoff, R.L. (1974). *Redesigning the future: a systems approach to societal problems.* New York: John Wiley.

Ajzen, I. (1991). The theory of planned behavior. *Organizational Behavior and Human Decision Processes*, 50: 179-211.

Allison, G.T. (1971). The essence of decision: explaining the Cuban missile crisis. Boston: Little, Brown and Comp.

Apostel, L. (1960). Towards the formal study of models in the non formal sciences. *Synthese*, 12: 125-161.

Aretin, W. von (1830). *Strategonon, Versuch die Kriegsführung durch ein Spiel darzustellen.* Ansbach: Dollfusz (in German).

Argyris, C.H. & Schon, D.A. (1978). *Organizational learning: a theory of action perspective.* Reading, MA: Addison-Wesley.

Armstrong, R.H.R. & Hobson, M. (1973). ALEA Local Government gaming simulation exercise. In: *Systems Behavior*, Birmingham (UK): The Open University.

Axelrod, R. (1976). *The structure of decision, the cognitive maps of political elites.* Princeton, NJ: Princeton University Press.

Beach, L.R. (1997). *The psychology of decision-making; people in organizations.* Thousand Oaks, CA: Sage.

Becker, H.S. (1983). Scenarios: a tool of growing importance to policy analysts in government and industry. *Technological forecasting and social change*, 23: 96.

Boer, P.C. & J. Soeters (1998). Gaming/simulation in the Dutch Armed Forces. In: Geurts, J.L.A., F. Joldersma & A. Roelofs (eds.) *Gaming-simulation for policy development and organizational change.* Tilburg (the Netherlands): Tilburg University Press, 159-165.

Bongers, F.J. (2000). *Participatory policy analysis and group support systems.* PhD thesis, Tilburg University (the Netherlands).

Boons, F. (1992). Environmental policy in Europe: mechanisms of internationalization. In: J.J.J. van Dijck & A.A.L.G. Wentink (eds.) *Transnational business in Europe: economic and social perspectives.* Tilburg (the Netherlands): Tilburg University Press, 323-339.

Bovens, M.& P. 't Hart (1996). *Understanding policy fiascoes.* New Brunswick & London: Transaction Publishers.

Brewer, G.D. (1986). Methods for synthesis: policy exercises. In: W.C. Clark & R.E. Munn (eds.) *Sustainable development in the biosphere.* Cambridge: Cambridge University Press, ch.17.

Brewer, G.D. & M. Shubik (1979). *The war game, a critique of military problem solving.* Cambridge, MA: Harvard University Press.

Brews, P.J. & M.R. Hunt (1999). Learning to plan and planning to learn: Resolving the planning school/learning school debate. *Strategic Management Journal*, 20 (10): 889-913.

Bruin, J.A. & E.F. ten Heuvelhof (1995). *Netwerkmanagement, strategiëen, instrumenten en normen*. Utrecht: Lemma (in Dutch)

de Caluwé, L.I.A. (1997). *Veranderen moet je leren*. PhD Thesis, Tilburg University. The Hague: Delwel Publishers (in Dutch).

de Caluwé, L.I.A. & J.L.A. Geurts (1999). The use and effectiveness of gaming-simulation for strategic culture change, in: D. Saunders & J. Severn (eds.) *Simulations and Games for Strategy and Policy Planning*. London: Kogan Page.

Campbell, J. (1982). *Grammatical man: information, entropy, language and life*. New York: Simon & Schuster.

Caplan, N.S. (1983). Knowledge conversion and utilization. In: B. Hozner, K.D. Knorr & H. Strasser (eds.), *Realizing social science knowledge*. Vienna: Physica-Verlag.

Cartwright, T.J. (1987). The lost art of planning. *Long Range Planning*, 20 (2): 92-99.

Casimir, R.J. (1995). *Gaming in information system development*. PhD thesis: Tilburg University (the Netherlands).

Checkland, P. (1981). *Systems thinking, systems practice*. Chichester (UK): Wiley.

Christopher, E.M. & L.E. Smith (1987). *Leadership training through gaming; power, people and problem solving*. London: Kogan Page.

Cooperrider, D.L., F.J. Barret and S. Srivastva (1995). Social construction and appreciative inquiry: a journey in organizational theory. In: D.M Hosking, P.H. Dachler & K.J. Gergen (eds.) *Management and organization: relational alternatives to individualism*. Aldershot: Averbury, 157-200.

Coutu, D. L. (2003). Sense and Reliability, a conversation with celebrated psychologist Karl E. Weick. *Harvard Business Review*, (April) 84-90.

Crookall, D. and K. Arai (eds.) (1992). *Global interdependence, simulation and gaming perspectives*. New York: Springer Verlag.

Crookall, D. and K. Arai (eds.) (1995). *Simulation and gaming across disciplines and cultures*. Thousand Oaks, CA: Sage.

Crosby, N., J. Kelley & P. Shaefer (1986). Citizen panels: a new approach to citizen participation. *Public Administration Review*, 46: 170-179.

Cyert, R.M. & J.G. March (1963). *A behavioral theory of the firm*. Englewood Cliffs, NJ: Prentice Hall.

DeBono, E. (1971). *Lateral thinking for managers*. New York: McGraw Hill AMA.

DeLeon, P. (1988). *Advice and consent; the development of the policy sciences*. New York: Russell Sage Foundation.

DeLeon, P. (1990). Participatory policy analysis: prescriptions and precautions. *Asian Journal of Public Administration*, 12: 29-54.

DeLeon, P. (1992). The democratization of the policy sciences. *Public Administration Review*, 52 (2): 125-129.

Dewey, J. (1910). *How we think*. Boston: Heath.

Dörner, D. (1996). *The logic of failure*. New York: Metropolitan Books.

Dror, Y. (1967.) Policy analysts: a new professional role in government service. *Public Administration Review*, 27 (3): 198.

Drucker, P. F. (1987). *Frontiers of management*. New York: Perennial Library.

Dryzek, J. (1982). Policy analysis as a hermeneutic activity. *Policy Sciences*, 14: 309-329.

Duke, R.D. (1966). *M.E.T.R.O.—A Gaming Solution*. Lansing, MI: Tri-County Regional Planning Commission.

Duke, R.D. (1974). *Gaming, the future's language*. Beverly Hills/London: Sage.

Duke, R.D. (1980). A paradigm for game design. *Simulation and Games*, 11: 364-377.

Duke, R.D. (1981). Development of the Conrail Game. In: I. Stahl (ed.) *Operational gaming, an international approach*. Oxford/New York: Pergamon Press: 245-252.

Duke, R.D. (1987). *Paradigms and perspectives of gaming/simulation*, paper presented at Simultec Geneva, Switzerland, 10 September 1987.

Duke, R.D. (1998). The gaming discipline as perceived by the policy and organization sciences. In: J.L.A. Geurts, F. Joldersma & E. Roelofs (eds.). *Gaming-simulation for policy development and organizational change*. Tilburg (the Netherlands): Tilburg University Press: 21-28.

Dunn, W.D. (1981). *Public policy analysis*. Englewood Cliffs, NJ: Prentice Hall (2nd edition: 1994).

Durning, D. (1993). Participatory policy analysis in a social service agency: a case study. *Journal of Policy Analysis and Management*, 12 (2): 297-322.

Eden, C. & F. Ackermann (1992). The analysis of cause maps. *Journal of Management Studies*, 29: 311-24.

Eden, C. & F. Ackermann (1998). *Making strategy: the journey of strategic management*. London: Sage.

Eden, C. & J. Radford (eds.) (1990). *Tackling strategic problems*. London: Sage.

Eden, C. , S. Jones, & D. Sims (1983). *Messing about in problems*. Oxford & New York: Pergamon Press.

Elgood, C. (1984). *Handbook of management games*. Worcester (UK): Gower.

Ellington, H., J. Addinall & F. Percival (1982). *A handbook of game design*. London: Kogan Page.

Forrester, J.W. (1968). *Principles of systems*. Cambridge, MA: MIT Press.

Freeman, R.S. (1984). *Strategic management; a stakeholder approach*. Markfield, MA: Pitman.

Gagnon, J. (1987). Mary M. Birhstein: the mother of Soviet simulation gaming. *Simulation & Games*, 18 (1): 3-12.

Geurts, J.L.A. & J.A.M. Vennix (eds.) (1989). *Verkenningen in beleidsanalyse*. Zeist (the Netherlands): Kerckebosch (in Dutch).

Geurts, J.L.A. & Vennix, J.A.M. (1989). De participatieve modelcyclus. In: J.L.A. Geurts & J.A.M. Vennix (eds.) *Verkenningen in beleidsanalyse*. Zeist (the Netherlands): Kerckebosch (in Dutch).

Geurts, J.L.A.& I.S. Mayer (1996). *Methods for participatory policy analysis, towards a conceptual model for research and development.* Tilburg University (the Netherlands): WORC paper.

Geurts, J.L.A., F. Joldersma & A. Roelofs (eds.) (1998). *Gaming-simulation for policy development and organizational change.* Tilburg (the Netherlands): Tilburg University Press.

Geurts, J.L.A., L.I. A. de Caluwé & A. Stoppelenburg (2000). *Changing organizations with gaming/simulation.* The Hague: Elsevier.

Geurts, J.L.A. & F. Joldersma (2001). Methodology for participatory policy analysis. *European Journal of Operational Research,* 128 (2): 300-310.

de Geus, A. (1988). Planning as learning. *Harvard Business Review,* March-April: 70-74.

Gordon, S. I. (1985). *Computer models in environmental planning.* New York: Van Nostrand Reinhold.

Gray, B. (1989). *Collaborating: finding common ground for multiparty problems.* San Francisco: Jossey-Bass.

Greenblat, C.S. & R.D. Duke (eds.) (1975). *Gaming-simulation, rationale, design, and applications.* New York: Halsted Press/Wiley & Sons.

Greenblat, C.S. & R.D. Duke (1981). *Principles and practices of gaming-simulation.* Beverly Hills/London: Sage.

Guetzkow, H. (1963). *Simulation in international relations: developments for research and teaching.* Englewood Cliffs, NJ: Prentice Hall.

Gyzicki, J. & A. Gorny (1979). *Glück im Spiel zu allen Zeiten.* Zürich: Stauffacher (in German).

Habermas, J. (1981). *Theorie des Kommunikativen Handelns.* Frankfurt am Main: Surkamp (in German).

Halal, William E. (1984). Strategic management: the state of the art and beyond. *Technological forecasting and social change,* 25: 239-261.

Hanken, A.F.G. & H.A. Reuver (1976). *Inleiding tot de systeemleer.* Leiden (the Netherlands): Stenfert Kroese (2nd edition) (in Dutch).

Hart, S.L. (1992). An integrative framework for strategy-making processes. *Academy of Management Review,* 17 (2): 327-351.

Hart, S.L. & C. Banbury (1994). How strategy making processes can make a difference. *Strategic Management Journal,* 15: 251-269.

Hawkesworth, M. (1987). *Theoretical issues in policy analysis.* Albany, NY: State University of New York Press.

Heclo, H. (1972). Review article: Policy analysis. *British Journal of Politics,* 2 (2): 87.

Heclo, H. (1978). Issue networks and the executive establishment. In: A. King (ed.) *The new America political system.* Washington, DC: American Enterprise Institute.

Heyden, K. van der (1996). *Scenarios, the art of strategic conversation.* Chichester (UK): John Wiley & Sons.

Heyne, G.A.W.M. (2000). *Participeren met beleid.* PhD thesis. Tilburg University (the Netherlands) (in Dutch).

Hickson, D.J. et al. (1986). *Top decisions: strategic decision-making in organizations.* San Francisco/London: Jossey-Bass.

Hirokawa, R.Y. & M. S. Poole (eds.) (1996). *Communication and group decision-making.* Thousand Oaks, CA: Sage (2nd edition).

Hirokawa, R.Y., L. Erbert & A. Hurst (1996). Communication and group decision-making effectiveness. In: R.Y. Hirokawa & M. S. Poole (eds.) *Communication and group decision-making.* Thousand Oaks, CA: Sage: 269-300.

Hoogerwerf, A. (ed.) (1992). *Het ontwerpen van beleid.* Alphen aan den Rijn (the Netherlands): Samson (in Dutch).

Hopkirk, P. (1990). *The great game; the struggle for empire in Central Asia.* London: Murray Ltd., New York: Kodansha.

Horn, R. & A. Cleaves (1980). *The guide to simulation games for education and training.* Beverly Hills: Sage (4th edition).

Huizinga, J. (1955). *Homo ludens; a study of the play-element in culture.* Boston: Beacon Press.

Isaksen, S.G. & D.J. Treffinger (1986). *Creative problem solving, the basic course.* Buffalo, NY: Bearly Ltd.

Isaksen, S.G. (1988). Concepts of creativity. In: P. Colemont, P. Gorholt, T. Rickards & H. Smeekes (eds.) *Creativity and innovation: towards a European network.* Dordrecht (the Netherlands), Boston & London: Kluwer Academic Publishers: 257-262.

Janis, I.L. (1982). *Groupthink: psychological studies of foreign policy studies and fiascoes.* Boston: Houghton Mifflin.

Jarboe, S. (1996). Procedures for enhancing group decision-making. In: R.Y. Hirokawa & M.S. Poole (eds.) *Communication and group decision-making.* Thousand Oaks, CA: Sage: 345-383.

Johnson, G. & K. Scholes (1997). *Exploring corporate strategy.* London: Prentice Hall (4th edition).

Joldersma, F. & J.L.A. Geurts (1998). Simulation/gaming for policy development and organizational change. *Simulation & Gaming,* 29 (4): 391-99.

Joldersma, F. (2000). Policy learning through simulation/gaming. In: D. Saunders & N. Smalley (eds.) *Simulations and Games for transition and change,* London: Sage: 77-85.

Kelly, M. & S. Maynard-Moody (1993). Policy analysis in the post-positivist era: engaging stakeholders in evaluating the economic development districts program. *Public Administration Review,* 53 (2): 135-142.

Keys, B. & J. Wolfe (1990). The role of management games and simulations in education and research. *Journal of Management,* 16 (2): 307-36.

Kingdon, J.W. (1984). *Agendas, alternatives and public policies.* Boston: Little Brown.

Klabbers, J.H.G., J.L.A. Geurts & P. van der Heijden (1977). *Report on the Conference Global Interactions Gaming/Simulation.* Nijmegen University (the Netherlands): Social Systems Research Group Report.

Klabbers, J.H.G. (1993). Gaming concerning the management of change. In: F. Percival, S. Lodge & D. Saunders (eds.) *Developing transferable skills in education and training.* London: Kogan Page: 130-137.

Klabbers, J.H.G. (1996). Problem framing through gaming, learning to manage complexity, uncertainty and value adjustment. *Simulation & Gaming,* 27 (1): 74-91.

Kolb, D.A. (1984). *Experiential learning.* Englewood Cliffs, NJ: Prentice Hall.

Kolb, D.A., I.M. Rubbin & J.S. Osland (1991). *Organizational behavior, an experiential approach.* Englewood Cliffs, NJ: Prentice Hall.

Kreitner, R. & A. Kinicki (1995). *Organizational behavior.* Chicago: R.D. Irwin Inc. (3rd edition).

Lane, D.C. (1995). On a resurgence of management simulations and games, *Journal of the Operational Research Society,* 46: 604-625.

Lindblom, C.E. & D. Cohen (1979). *Usable knowledge: social science and problem solving.* New Haven, CT: Yale University Press.

Lindblom, C.E. & E.J. Woodhouse (1968). *The policy making process.* Englewood Cliffs: Prentice Hall (3rd edition, 1993).

Maani, K.E. & R.Y. Cavana (2000). *Systems thinking and modeling, understanding change and complexity.* Auckland (New Zealand): Pearson.

Majone, G. (1989). *Evidence, argument and persuasion in the policy process.* New Haven, CT: Yale University Press.

Marsh, J.G. & J.P. Olson (1976). *Ambiguity and choice in organizations.* Bergen (Norway): Universitetsforlaget.

Mason, R.O. & I.I. Mitroff (1981). *Challenging strategic planning assumptions; theory, cases and techniques.* New York: John Wiley and Sons.

Massie, R.K. (1991). *Peter the Great, his life and his world.* New York: Wings Book.

Mayer, I.S. (1997). *Debating technologies: a methodological contribution to the design and evaluation of participatory policy analysis.* PhD thesis. Tilburg (the Netherlands): Tilburg University Press.

Mayer, I.S. & W. Veeneman (eds.) (2002). *Games in a world of infrastructures, simulation-games for research, learning and intervention.* Delft (the Netherlands): Eburon.

McCall, M.W. jr. & R.E. Kaplan (1990). *Whatever it takes, the realities of managerial decision-making.* Englewood Cliffs, NJ: Prentice Hall.

Meadows, D.L. et. al. (1974). *Dynamics of growth in a finite world.* Cambridge, MA: Wright Allen Press.

Meadows, D.L. (1989). Gaming to implement system dynamics models. In: P.M. Milling & E.O.K Zahn (eds.) *Computer based management of complex systems.* Berlin: Springer Verlag: 635-640.

Meckel, J. (1873). *Studien über das Kriegsspiel.* Berlin: Ernst Siegfried Mittler und Sohn (in German).

Meer, F.B.L. van der (1983). *Organisatie als spel: sociale simulatie als methode in onderzoek naar organiseren.* PhD thesis. Enschede (the Netherlands): Technical University Twente (in Dutch).

Meier, R. L. (1962). *A communications theory of urban growth.* Cambridge, MA: Harvard University Press.

Meier, R. L. & R.D. Duke (1966). Gaming simulation for urban planning. *Journal of the American Institute of Planners,* XXXII, (1): 12.

Meinsma, R., C. Termeer & G.J.de Vreede (1998) The impact of animated simulation on communication processes. In: J. Geurts, F. Joldersma & A. Roelofs (eds.) *Gaming-simulation for policy development and organizational change.* Tilburg (the Netherlands), Tilburg University Press: 113-20.

Merton, R. K. (1957). *Social theory and social structure.* Glencoe, IL: The Free Press.

Michael, D.N. (1973). *On learning to plan and planning to learn.* San Francisco: Jossey-Bass.

Mintzberg, H. (1987). Crafting strategy. *Harvard Business Review.* July/August: 66-75.

Mintzberg, H. (1994). *The rise and fall of strategic planning.* Englewood Cliffs, NJ: Prentice Hall.

Mitroff, I.I. & F. Sagasti (1973). Epistemology as General Systems Theory: an approach to the design of complex decision-making experiments. *Philosophy of the Social Sciences,* 3: 117-134.

Moore, O.K. & A.R. Anderson (1975). Some principles for the design of clarifying educational environments. In: C.S. Greenblat & R.D. Duke (eds.) *Gaming-simulation, rationale, design and applications.* New York: Halsted Press/Wiley & Sons: 47-71.

Morecroft, J.D.W. (1988). Systems Dynamics and microworlds for policymakers. *European Journal for Operational Research,* 35: 301-320.

Morecroft, J.D.W. & J.D. Sterman (eds.) (1994). *Modeling for learning organizations.* Portland, OR: Productivity Press.

Neuman, J. von & O. Morgenstern (1944). *Theory of games and economic behavior.* Princeton, NJ: Princeton University Press.

Noorderhaven, N.G. (1995). *Strategic decision making.* Worthingham (UK): Addison-Wesley.

Nutt, P.C., (2002). *Why decisions fail, avoiding the blunders and traps that lead to debacles.* San Francisco: Berrett-Koelhler.

Osvalt, I. (ed.)., (1993). Special issue: Military simulation/gaming, parts 1 and 2. *Simulation & Gaming,* 24 (2 and 3).

Ottenheijm, P.M. (1996). *What's the problem?* MA thesis. Policy and Organization Sciences. Tilburg University (the Netherlands).

Percival, F., S. Lodge & D. Saunders (eds.) (1993). *Developing transferable skills in education and training.* London: Kogan Page.

Peters, V., G. Vissers & G. Heijne (1996). The validity of games. In: F. Watts & A. Garcia Carbonell (eds.) *Simulation Now! learning through experience: the challenge of change.* València (Spain): Diputació de València: 21-34.

Pettifer, D., T. Coke & A. Gasson (2003). Creating a culture of disciplined empowerment. *European Business Forum,* 14 (Summer): 80-81.

Poole, S., M. Holems & G. DeSantis (1991). Conflict management in a computer supported meeting environment. *Management Science,* 37-3 (August): 926-953.

Pruitt, D.G. & P.J. Carnevale (1993). *Negotiation in social conflict.* Pacific Grove, CA: Brooks/Cole.

Raser, J.R. (1969). *Simulation and society, an exploration of scientific gaming.* Boston: Allyn and Bacon.

Rhyne, R. F. (1975). Communicating holistic insights. In: C. S. Greenblat & R. D. Duke (eds.) *Gaming-simulation, rationale, design and applications.* New York: Halsted Press/Wiley & Sons: 15-28.

Rip, A. (1991). Risicocontroverses en verwevenheden van wetenschap en politiek. *Kennis en Methode,* 63-80 (in Dutch).

Rittel, H. & M. M. Webber (1972). *Dilemmas in a general theory of planning.* Berkeley, CA: University of California: Working paper No. 194 (November).

Roelofs, A.M.E. (1998). The use of a game for quasi-experimentation. In J. Geurts, F. Joldersma & A. Roelofs (eds.) *Gaming-simulation for policy development and organizational change,* Tilburg (the Netherlands): Tilburg University Press: 361-67.

Roelofs, A.M.E. (2000). *Structuring policy issues, testing a mapping technique with gaming-simulation.* PhD thesis, Tilburg University (the Netherlands).

Rosenhead, J. (ed.) (1989). *Rational analysis for a problematic world; problem structuring methods for complexity, uncertainty and conflict.* Chichester (UK): John Wiley & Sons.

Ross, J. & B.M. Staw (1993). Organizational escalation and exit: lessons from the Shoreham Nuclear Power Plant. *Academy of Management Journal,* August: 701-32.

Rouwette, E., E. Fokkema, H. van Kuppevelt & V. Peters (1998). Measuring MARCO POLIS management game's influence on market orientation. *Simulation & Gaming,* 29 (4): 420-431.

Saint, S. & J. R. Lawson (1994). *Rules for reaching consensus, a modern approach to decision.* Amsterdam/San Diego: Pfeiffer & Co.

Saunders, D. & J. Severn (eds.) (1999). *Simulations and games for strategy and policy planning.* London: Kogan Page.

Saunders, D. & N. Smalley (eds.) (2000). *Simulations and games for transition and change.* London: Sage.

Savage, G.T. et al. (1991). Strategies for assessing and managing organizational stakeholders. *Academy of Management Executive,* 5 (2): 61-75.

Schon, D.A. (1986). Toward a new epistemology of practice. In: B. Checkoway (ed.) *Strategic perspectives on planning practice.* Lexington, MA.: Lexington Books: 231-239.

Schon, D.A. & M. Rein (1994). *Reforming: toward the resolution of intractable policy controversies.* New York: Basic Books.

Schruijer, S. (ed.) (1999). *Multi-organizational partnerships and cooperative strategy.* Tilburg (the Netherlands): Dutch University Press.

Schumpeter, J.A. (1934). *The theory of economic development.* London: Oxford University Press.

Schwartz, P. (1991). *The art of the long view*. New York: Doubleday/Currency.

Senge, P.M. (1990). *The fifth discipline: the art and practice of the learning organization*. New York: Doubleday/Currency.

Shaw, M.E. (1981). *Group dynamics: the psychology of small group behavior*. New York: Mc Graw-Hill (3rd edition).

Shubik, M. (1975). *Games for society, business and war*. New York and Amsterdam: Elsevier.

Shubik, M. (1975). *The uses and methods of gaming*. New York and Amsterdam: Elsevier.

Simon, H.A. (1969). *The sciences of the artificial*. Cambridge, MA & London: MIT press.

Simon, H. A. (1987). Two heads are better than one: the collaboration between AI and OR. *Interfaces*, 17 (July/August): 8-15.

Staw, B.M. & J. Ross (1990). Behavior in escalation situations: antecedents, prototypes and solutions. *Organizational Dynamics*, Spring: 419-26.

Sterman, J.D. (1988). Modeling managerial behavior. Proceedings of the 1988 *International Systems Dynamic Conference*. La Jolla, CA: 334-365.

Sun Tzu (1963). *The art of war*. London: Oxford University Press.

Susskind, L. & J. Cruikshank (1987). *Breaking the impasse; consensual approaches to resolving public disputes*. New York: Basic Books.

Thomas, C. J. & J. Deemer (1957). The role of operational gaming in operations research. *Operations Research*, 5 (February): 1-27.

Toffler, A. (1970). *Future shock*. New York: Random House.

Toth, Ferenc L. (1988). Policy exercises, objectives and design elements. *Simulation and Games*, 19 (3): 235-255.

Toth, F. L. (1988). Policy exercises, procedures and implementation. *Simulation and Games*, 19 (3): 256-276.

Tsuchiya, Sh. & T. Tsuchiya (2000). A review of policy exercise interactive learning environments. *Simulation & Gaming*, 31 (4): 509-527.

Underwood, S. & R.D. Duke (1994). *Concept report: policy exercise for the International Joint Commission*. Ann Arbor, MI: College of Architecture and Urban Planning, University of Michigan.

Vansina, L.S., T. Tailleu & S. Schruijer (1998). Managing multiparty issues: learning from experience. In: R.W. Woodman & W.A. Pasmore (eds.) *Research in organizational change and development*. Vol. 11. Greenwich, CN: JAI-Press: 159-181.

Vennix, J.A.M. & Geurts, J.L.A. (1987). Communicating insights from complex simulation models, a gaming approach. *Simulation and Games*, 18 (3): 321-343.

Vennix, J.A.M. (1990). *Mental models and computer models; design and evaluation of a computer-based learning environment for policy making*. PhD thesis, University of Nijmegen (the Netherlands).

Vennix, J.A.M. (1996). *Group modeling*. Chichester (UK): John Wiley & Sons.

Vennix, J.A.M. (1998). *Kennis geven en kennis nemen, de rol van participatief onderzoek in organisaties*. Nijmegen: Lauman & Friso (in Dutch).

Verburgh, L. (1994). *Participative modeling applied to the health care insurance industry.* PhD thesis. University of Nijmegen (the Netherlands).

Vissers, G.A.N. (1994). *The production of strategy.* PhD thesis. Delft (the Netherlands): Eburon.

Vissers, G.A.N., V. Peters, G. Heyne & J. Geurts (1998). Validity of games/simulations: a constructivistic view. In J. Geurts, F. Joldersma & A. Roelofs (eds.) *Gaming-simulation for policy development and organizational change,* Tilburg (the Netherlands): Tilburg University Press: 353-59.

Vroom, V.H. & P.W. Yetton (1973). *Leadership and decision-making.* Pittsburgh, PA: University of Pittsburgh Press.

Vroom, V.H. & A.G. Jago (1988). *The new leadership: managing participation in organizations.* Englewood Cliffs, NJ: Prentice Hall.

Warfield, J. N. (1976). *Societal systems - planning, policy and complexity.* New York: John Wiley & Sons.

Watt, K.F. (1977). Why won't anyone believe us? *Simulation,* 23 (1): 1-3.

Watts, F. & A. Garcia Carbonell (eds.) (1996). *Simulation Now! learning through experience: the challenge of change.* València (Spain): Diputació de València.

Watzlawick, P., J.H. Beavin & D.D. Jackson (1967). *Pragmatics of human communication.* New York: W.W. Norton.

Webster's (1989). *Ninth New Collegiate Dictionary.* Springfield, MA: Merriam-Webster.

Weggeman, M. (1995). *Collectieve ambitie ontwikkeling.* PhD thesis. Tilburg (the Netherlands): Tilburg University Press (in Dutch).

Weick, K.E. (1990). The vulnerable system: an analysis of the Tenerife air disaster. *Journal of Management,* 16 (3). Reprinted in: K.E. Weick (2001). *Making sense of the organization.* London: Blackwell: 125-147.

Weick, K.E. (1993). The collapse of sense making in organizations: the Mann Gulch disaster. *Administrative Science Quarterly,* 38 (4). Reprinted in: K.E. Weick (2001). *Making sense of the organization,* London: Blackwell: 101-124.

Weick, K.E. (2001). *Making sense of the organization.* London: Blackwell.

Weick, K.E & K. M. Sutcliffe (2001). *Managing the unexpected, assuring high performance in an age of complexity.* San Francisco: Jossey Bass.

Weiss, C. H. & M. Bucavalas (1980). *Social science research and decision making.* New York: Columbia University Press.

Weiss, C.H. (ed.) (1992) *Organizations for policy analysis; helping government think.* Newbury Park, CA: Sage.

Whyte, L. G. (1994). Policy analysis as discourse. *Journal of Policy Analysis and Management,* 13 (3): 506-525.

Wildavski, A. (1979). *Speaking truth to power: the art and craft of policy analysis.* Boston: Little, Brown.

Wolfe, J. (1993). A history of business teaching games in English-speaking and post-socialist countries: the origination of a management education and development technology. *Simulation & Gaming,* 24 (4): 446-63.

# Index

# About the authors

Richard D. Duke and Jac L.A. Geurts are academics of long standing; both have also been professionally engaged as consultants and practitioners in the areas addressed in this book. They are leading members of the International Simulation and Gaming Association, ISAGA and have both served as presidents of the organization. They have taught invited professional seminars on policy gaming in many different countries in Europe, America and Asia. They have published extensively over their careers. This book is the logical fruition of two lifetimes of research, practice and teaching.

**Richard D. Duke** is Professor Emeritus of the University of Michigan's College of Architecture and Urban Planning and former Chairman of the Certificate in Gaming/ Simulation of the Rackham Graduate School of the University of Michigan.

**Jac L.A. Geurts** is Professor Policy Science at the Department of Organizational Studies of Tilburg University in the Netherlands and he teaches strategic management at the TIAS Business School of this University.